THE AESOP'S FABLE PARADIGM

Encounters: Explorations in Folklore and Ethnomusicology
Ray Cashman and Michael Dylan Foster, *editor*

THE AESOP'S FABLE PARADIGM

An Unlikely Intersection of Folklore and Science

Edited by
K. BRANDON BARKER and DANIEL J. POVINELLI

INDIANA UNIVERSITY PRESS

This book is a publication of

Indiana University Press
Office of Scholarly Publishing
Herman B Wells Library 350
1320 East 10th Street
Bloomington, Indiana 47405 USA

iupress.org

© 2021 by The Trustees of Indiana University

All rights reserved

No part of this book may be reproduced or utilized in any form or by any means, electronic or mechanical, including photocopying and recording, or by any information storage and retrieval system, without permission in writing from the publisher. The paper used in this publication meets the minimum requirements of the American National Standard for Information Sciences—Permanence of Paper for Printed Library Materials, ANSI Z39.48-1992.

Manufactured in the United States of America

First printing 2021

Cataloging information is available from the Library of Congress.

ISBN 978-0-253-05922-2 (paperback)
ISBN 978-0-253-05923-9 (ebook)

CONTENTS

Preface vii

Introduction: The Perplexities of Water /
    Daniel J. Povinelli and K. Brandon Barker 1

1. The Animal Question as Folklore in Science /
    K. Brandon Barker 12
2. The Early Tradition of the Crow and the Pitcher /
    William Hansen 23
3. Going Meta: Retelling the Scientific Retelling of
    Aesop's the Crow and the Pitcher / *Laura Hennefield and
    Hyesung G. Hwang with Daniel J. Povinelli* 38
4. Anthropomorphomania and the Rise of the Animal Mind:
    A Conversation / *K. Brandon Barker and
    Daniel J. Povinelli* 60
5. Fabling Gestures in Expository Science /
    Gregory Schrempp 76

Conclusion: Old Ideas and the Science of Animal Folklore /
    K. Brandon Barker and Daniel J. Povinelli 95

Appendix: Doctor Fomomindo's Preliminary Notes for a
    Future Index of Anthropomorphized Animal Behaviors /
    Daniel J. Povinelli and K. Brandon Barker, with special
    assistance from Marisa Wieneke and Kristina Downs 105

Index 239

PREFACE

If life is like a carriage ride, and Death—personified and pretty—rides along, what about the horses? We know. There are always distractions along the way, so many things to see. The schoolyard charms. The fields of grain delight. The chilling breeze distracts. But it is the horses' heads, after all, that keep the poet pointed toward eternity. And because they are captive to the joyride, the horses—blinders in place—are likewise destined for a journey with no end. This book runs parallel as it explores the way that scientific storytellers (quite poetical themselves) drive animals on a never-ending journey—or more correctly, a *quest*—toward a goal that the animals cannot achieve. That goal? Nothing less than eternity.

A gently updated version of a special issue of *Journal of Folklore Research* originally published in 2019, this book concerns a recent (and ongoing) stage of the quest. In the Aesop's fable paradigm, scientists have wrangled "The Crow and the Pitcher" into a (thus far) unending series of scientific experiments to test crows for "insightful" understanding of the physical properties of water displacement. In the fable, a thirsty crow drops stones into a partially filled pitcher of water to raise the level and take a drink. In the experimental paradigm, a test tube replaces the pitcher, and a tasty worm, lazily floating, replaces the sip of water. As striking as this juncture is, as much as its initial vista amazes, we shall not stay long. Boredom (or in this case, skepticism) arises, and new routines (read: scientific variants) are on the horizon. Since 2019, the quest has continued. And like any other stagecoach line, new animals have joined the team.

In a recent study with parrots, one group of scientists deployed a trick test tube in which the waters could never rise, no matter how many pebbles were dropped inside. The scientists decided the parrots did not evince true causal understanding of water displacement—even though in other cases, when the parrots were not tricked by the experimenters, the parrots were able to raise the water level and retrieve the food reward. The whole thing was enough for the authors to clip the term *paradigm* and announce that higher-order, insightful understanding of water displacement "is not required for solving Aesop's Fable" (Schwing et al. 2019, 447). Scientists may find it striking that parrots have joined the team. Folklorists may find it striking that fables are now meant to be solved. Riddles, sure; jokes, maybe—but fables?

In another recent study, elephants (what took so long?) joined the procession. Twelve zoo-housed elephants were tested in the floating-object task—a related, previously used paradigm in which orangutans learned how to spit water into a tube to retrieve a floating peanut. Only one of the twelve elephants tested "solved" the task, but surely that is not the point. As the authors remark, "The cognitive abilities underpinning [elephants'] ability to solve the floating water task remain unclear" (Barrett and Benson-Amram 2020, 310). Take notice. If the Aesop's fable paradigm teaches us nothing about animals' minds anyway, then both folklorists and scientists can skip the results and proceed directly to Doctor Fomomindo's ever-expanding Folk Motif-Index of Animal Cognition (FOMANCOG) in the back of this book; search for entries such as elephant funeral rituals (A2b.3.), the drunken elephants (D2a.1.), or elephants making fly-swatters from sticks (B1f.); and see that elephants are far too central a fixture in fables and folklore to have been left out for this long.

Folklorists will be happy to know that we have returned to the origin story of these paradigms. Like Athena born from Zeus's skull, the Aesop's fable paradigm grew out of the earliest floating-object studies of the aforementioned spitting orangutans. Much dust was kicked up over the fact that those orangutans had not actually *dropped stones* to retrieve their food rewards, so they could not rightfully lay claim to "solving" the fable of "The Crow and the Pitcher." But separation is invariably followed by return, and orangutans have now rejoined the team. (Are we going in circles?) This time, one orangutan solved the floating-object task by spontaneously spitting into a completely dry vessel holding a peanut (DeLong and Burnett 2020, 338). That it be dry was essential. Water, sparkling before spitting begins, might inadvertently prime the pump of orangutan expectorate. Alas, spontaneity being what it is, scientists must move on down the line: "The mechanism underlying [the orangutan's] success remains unclear." This variant did show that "latency to spit water into the tube decreased exponentially across sessions" (327).

No, questing minds cannot linger in the past, so humanoid robots have been tested too. Futurologists will be pleased to know that—programmed with the underlying causal principles—at least one robot has solved Aesop's fable (Bhat and Mohan 2020). To be clear, the robot did not conjure generalizable "displacement" physics, so the quest must continue into the futurist's future—good news for anyone who was getting bored, or ethically concerned, with the animal routines. Folklorists might smile on learning that this particular robot did not perform any new morals for the fable. Alas, there can be no doubt that robot morals are just around the next bend.

Parrots, elephants, orangutans, and robots remind us, at the outset, that the Aesop's fable paradigm presents nothing more than a single stop, and stops are frequent. Recently, for example, having arrived at a house of magic, scientists argued—exactly as the FOMANCOG predicted (see section J. Animals and Magic [Sleight-of-Hand])—that scientists should bring the stage magician's techniques into the laboratory in order to "prompt the comparison of behavioral reactions among diverse species, in which magic effects might exploit similar perceptive blind spots and cognitive roadblocks" (Garcia-Pelegrin et al. 2020, 1424). Just like the never-ending handkerchief pulled from some magician's sleeve, the poet (Eureka!) eventually sees the trick for what it is; meanwhile, the horses' heads pull on toward eternity.

For our part, we have not traveled alone. Thank you to Ray Cashman, who worked with us as editor of the *Journal of Folklore Research*, for countless assists on matters large and small. Thank you to Gary Dunham at Indiana University Press for supporting our project and for his recommendations about our volume's title. Thank you to Solimar Otero, who took over as editor of *JFR* as our project went from special issue to a book. Thank you, especially, to each of the contributors—William Hansen, Laura Hennefield, Hyesung G. Hwang, and Gregory Schrempp—who took leaps of faith as they brought their expertise from disparate academic fields. In particular, we thank Kristina Downs and Marisa Wieneke for their tireless efforts and important contributions. We also thank colleagues and friends who assisted us in a number of ways with a variety of related projects. These include Susan Fitzpatrick at the James S. McDonnell Foundation and Claiborne Rice at the University of Louisiana. At Indiana University, we list with gracious appreciation Henry Glassie and Pravina Shukla, Nik Toth and Kathy Toth, Peter Todd, and Rob Goldstone.

To our equine friends (and all our other animal friends in the FOMANCOG), we hope you find a comfortable station; as Dickinson would say, "Hope is the thing with feathers."

Indiana University
Bloomington

Amherst
Massachusetts

References

Barrett, Lisa P., and Sarah Benson-Amram. 2020. "Can Asian Elephants Use Water as a Tool in the Floating Object Task?" *Animal Behavior and Cognition* 7 (3): 310–26.

Bhat, Ajaz A., and Vishwanathan Mohan. 2020. "Causal Learning by a Robot with Semantic-Episodic Memory in an Aesop's Fable Experiment." *arXiv preprint arXiv: 2003.00274*.

DeLong, Caroline M., and Christina Burnett. 2020. "Bornean Orangutans (Pongo Pygmaeus Pygmaeus) Use Water as a Tool in the Floating Object Task." *Animal Behavior and Cognition* 7(3): 327–42.

Garcia-Pelegrin, Elias, Alexandra K. Schnell, Clive Wilkins, and Nicola S. Clayton. 2020. "An Unexpected Audience." *Science* 369 (6510): 1424–26.

Schwing, R., F. Weiss, A. Tichy, and G. Gajdon. 2019. "Testing the Causal Understanding of Water Displacement by Kea (Nestor Notabilis)." *Behaviour* 156 (5–8): 447–78.

THE AESOP'S FABLE PARADIGM

DANIEL J. POVINELLI AND K. BRANDON BARKER

INTRODUCTION
The Perplexities of Water

For 350 miles, the Missouri River ambles eastward across the face of the Show-Me State until suddenly, just before the Illinois border, it veers wildly and throws a nasty uppercut into the throat of the Mississippi. This wayward hook knocks the Mississippi on its heels and leaves behind an ugly kink—a big bend in a big river. A couple of miles downstream, the city of St. Louis looks on, unfazed as the Big River gets down to business—its inexorable, snakelike sinuosity slithering south to New Orleans. Water, as the proverb goes, finds the lowest level. (Unless, of course, the Scientist pours the water into a test tube and the Crow starts dropping pebbles into it ... but more about that shortly.)

In an interview with the *Chicago Tribune*, Mark Twain once quipped that "the river below St. Louis ... is the least interesting part. One can sit on the pilot-house for a few hours and watch the low shores, the ungainly trees and the democratic buzzards, and then one might as well go to bed. One has seen everything there is to see" ([1886] 2006, 89–90). But above or below St. Louis—across two-thousand-plus miles and two million years—one thing about the Big River seems permanent: its bent on maintaining its twisted ways. Twain called the Mississippi "the crookedest river in the world" (a pun no doubt about its physical course and the gamblers and rabble-rousers he lived among during the four years he worked as a pilot on the riverboats): "In one part of its journey it uses up one thousand three hundred miles to cover the same ground that the crow would fly over in six hundred and seventy-five" ([1883] 1996, 21). (That's pretty smart of the Crow, to outwit the Water. But again, more on that later.)

Twain knew the waters of the Mississippi—he understood their character and moods. In *Life on the Mississippi*'s well-known and often anthologized ninth chapter, "Continued Perplexities," Twain recalls how a slant of reflected light at sunset foretold good winds the next day, how a ripple of the water's surface bespoke the untimely end of some luckless future steamboat, and how a floating log was a sign that the river was rising. "The face of the water," he writes, "became a wonderful book—a book that was a dead language to the uneducated passenger, but which told its mind to me without reserve, delivering its most cherished secrets as clearly as if it uttered them with a voice. And it was not a book to be read once and thrown aside, for it had a new story to tell every day" ([1883] 1996, 118). The young Twain who animates *Life on the Mississippi* is captive to both the surficial and the deep. He cannot resist the language the river speaks or the songs it sings.

Twain's knowledge of (and attraction to) the vagaries of water feels sufficiently anthropomorphic to justify turning to him to introduce this book—an exploration of a peculiar intersection of science and folklore in the context of the water-marked fable "The Crow and the Pitcher." For more than a decade, comparative psychologists have been hard at work, testing dozens of crows (and even a few raccoons) on dozens of variants of a peculiar experimental paradigm: training animals to drop stones into test tubes partially filled with water to retrieve a bit of food floating on the surface. This was not some happenstance collision of science and fable. The authors of the original 2009 report—Christopher Bird and Nathan Emery—explicitly invoked "The Crow and the Pitcher" as the frame that motivated their experiment (1410). In the years that have passed, the experimental "genre" has matured, becoming its own kind of bona fide tradition: the Aesop's fable paradigm, an experimental procedure to determine if crows and other creatures can grasp the causal connections between sinking stones and rising waters.

We think that if we had issued a posthumous invitation to Twain to serve as special guest editor for this volume, he would have seriously considered it. Our plinking about in water metaphors notwithstanding, we cannot imagine the quintessential American storyteller—and charter member of the American Folklore Society—passing up the opportunity to comment on a scientific story about a crow who knows how to use stones to disturb still waters. Twain was, after all, deeply attracted to science and technology. He was an inventor and a lifelong friend of Nikola Tesla. The year before he died, Twain was delighted when Thomas Edison recorded him using state-of-the-art motion picture equipment. But ever the skeptic, Twain was keen enough to see the absurdities of science as well. He once quipped, "Scientists have odious manners, except when you prop up their theory; then you can borrow money of them" (1917, 223). (From an insider's perspective, one of us can attest to the obsequious turn so often taken in a scientist's mind under conditions of elevated flattery of a pet theory.) It is easy to imagine watching Twain's legendary eyebrows rise as he learns of psychologists attempting to "validate" an Aesopian fable of a thirsty crow who patiently drops stones in a vase to slurp up water—a fable indexed under motifs such as "animal understands water movements" and "animal exhibits patience." As a riverboat pilot, Twain knew better than most that navigating even the stillest of waters is tricky—he knew it is all about taking one's time with the little things, not hurrying. (He even wrote his own animal fable in 1909—complete with a moral punch strikingly pertinent to many of the ideas explored in this volume; see conclusion.)

Twain's waters hold a still deeper connection to our folkloristic inquiry into the Aesop's fable paradigm of comparative psychology. That is, Twain's reflections on the perplexities of the river offer more than a set of fluvial observations about the character of the Mississippi between New Orleans and St. Louis. They constitute a memoir, one told by an older Twain struggling to capture his distinctly different experiences of the river during two epochs in his life: the waters of his youth, bestirred by the excitement of the unknown, and the stiller waters of middle age, long after he had abandoned the riverboats and headed west—the mystery of the Mississippi dispelled—absorbed into the schema of all-things-familiar:

> Now when I had mastered the language of this water and had come to know every trifling feature that bordered the great river as familiarly as I knew the letters of the alphabet, I had made a valuable acquisition. But I had lost something, too. I had lost something which could never be restored to me while I lived. All the grace, the beauty, the poetry had gone out of the majestic river. . . . All the value any feature of it had for me now was the amount of usefulness it could furnish toward compassing the safe piloting of a steamboat. ([1883] 1996, 119)

Here, we have the makings of this volume's first moral: "Once demystified, a thing can never be mystified again."

Not unlike the Mississippi River, each chapter in this book can be viewed in more than one way. Mutable and doppelgangerous, each essay grapples with different and difficult-to-maintain points of view on the ways humans project themselves onto animals. In his orienting essay, K. Brandon Barker explores the tension between two scientists who choose to join forces with a fable: one, a transactional affair wherein humans use animals to reflect human wisdom, and the other, an (equally transactional) affair wherein humans use animals to make points about animal wisdom. William Hansen, through his original historical research, reveals two points of view on the narrative of "The Crow and the Pitcher" (and others like it): its origin as a simple observation about a clever bird, and its later transformation into a decontextualized narrative adorned with the power of the moral. There are also competing ways of seeing *what the crows themselves* are doing in the scientific experiments, as detailed in Laura Hennefield and Hyesung G. Hywang's essay: one set of views that envisions crows experiencing their own personal eureka moments concerning the connection between object volume and water displacement, and a second set that sees them laboring under a less enchanting (but still undeniably intelligent) stockpile of trial-and-error learning. Barker and Povinelli's conversation picks up on this latter duality in several ways, one of which traces the diffuse worry among comparative psychologists that an objective description of animals might somehow leave them less interesting than our human stories would have it—possibly opening a floodgate of Twain-like regrets that might wash away our sense of mystery and connection to the natural world. Finally, Gregory Schrempp closes the essays by addressing the nuanced intermingling of folkloric and scientific thinking in the "fabling gestures" that complicate popular science, hinting that there are at least two views of how fables such as "The Crow and the Pitcher" can influence human cultural practice: one restricted to human activities outside science, and another that admits fables as permeating most human activities (including those of humans who pride themselves as being more "objective").

Perplexities being what they are, we confess that there is another, less compelling reason to start with Twain, one that feels better to us—closer to the origin story of the story-behind-the-story of this interdisciplinary encounter with an Aesopian fable—one that has more to do with our very subjective points of view. Our meta-story also begins along the Mississippi, in St. Louis, where two friends, a young folklorist and a former monkey mind scientist, discover that their professional worlds have collided in ways neither could have predicted.

It was a Thursday, and the young Folklorist had just arrived in St. Louis with his wife and six-month-old baby. They were there for the weekend, visiting their friend, the former Monkey Mind Scientist. Years earlier, the three of them had become friends when they had all lived in Lafayette, Louisiana, a town just a couple hours west of New Orleans. The Scientist was on sabbatical at Washington University in St. Louis for a couple of years, dipping his toes back in the turbulent waters of animal cognition. He had rented a small loft apartment in the Central West End, near the Gateway Arch and the river. The Folklorist was living in Bloomington, Indiana, just beginning his first academic post. Now, the usual human activities associated with *couple-with-baby-visiting-single-friend* were occurring. The Folklorist was hauling suitcases and baby bags up from the car, and his wife and the Scientist were shifting furniture around under the giant arched window of the apartment, creating a makeshift bedroom. Amid all of this, baby Zoa woke up, crying for milk. As her mother hurried to fill a bottle, Uncle Monkey Scientist picked her up and began singing a tune. . . .

Zoa, Zoa, Zoa,
On the floor, floor, floor,
Screaming more, more, more,
She's swinging her pink boa...
But little does she know-ah—
A boa constrictor—
Is coming—to get her!

Everyone was settling in for a relaxing weekend....

"By the way," the Folklorist said a few hours later as he gently deposited Zoa on a blanket to change her diaper, "if it's okay, we need to do a little shopping sometime this weekend. We're looking for a new crib and some other stuff. It'll only take an hour or so."

"Perfect," the former Scientist said. "How about tomorrow afternoon? I have to give a little talk for a group over at the medical school anyhow."

"Perfect," the Folklorist repeated, distractedly unfastening Zoa's diaper. "What's the talk about, anyhow?"

"Just some work I've been doing with a few of the graduate students in the seminar I'm teaching. Reanalyzing a bunch of published data."

"Nice... chimp stuff?"

"Actually, no."

"Ah, child stuff?"

"Crow stuff."

"Whew, Zoa! That's some stinky stuff!" the Folklorist exclaimed, pulling away the diaper and slipping on a fresh one—only to suddenly catch himself and look up at the Scientist. "Wait, did you say... crows?"

"Yeah, did I ever tell you about this? The year I was closing down my chimp center, some colleagues of mine published a study about an Aesop's fable about a crow who needs to drop stones into a jar to get a drink of water. I took it as a sign from God that I was getting out at the right moment."

The Folklorist looked up.

"The Crow and the Pitcher?"

"Yeah—it's an Aesop's fable."

"I know it's an Aesop's fable—I'm a folklorist!"

"Oh, sorry... of course. Anyhow, I was like, great, my fellow comparative psychologists are now teaching crows to drop stones into a test tube of water to get a floating worm—brilliant."

"That's crazy!"

"I know. I thought we were over rats pressing levers. But as I was preparing to teach my seminar, I discovered it's become a cottage industry in the field—I think something like three dozen experiments have been published about it."

"No, I mean that's crazy that animal cognition scientists are using the frame of a fable to design experiments!"

"Oh, right... exactly. I was like, oh boy, here we go. Let's see, how many Aesop's fables are there...?"

"You're missing my point—"

"I could just imagine the next ten years of studies! For a moment I even thought about tracking down the collection of Aesop's fables we had in my house as a kid and designing one myself."

"Listen to me: fables are stories humans tell to express a lesson that is applicable, you know, to the lives of people—human people. They don't actually have anything to do with animals, much less animal cognition!"

"Huh. I never thought about it quite like that."

"What time's your talk?"

"You're welcome to come, but it's just an informal lunchtime work-in-progress kind of thing."

"Uh—I'm coming."

The talk (and the weekend) came and went. But the Folklorist and the Scientist parted company forever altered. In the back of the Scientist's mind was one of the first conversations he'd had with the Folklorist, years earlier, in Louisiana. The Folklorist had been a graduate student at the time, and they had met playing Ultimate Frisbee—a game enjoyed by hundreds of thousands of people worldwide that revolves around chasing a flying plastic disc.[1] One afternoon on the sidelines, the Folklorist and the Scientist struck up a conversation about animal cognition. The Scientist now recalled how quickly he had demurred from the experimental work, wanting to avoid the endless technical conversations about the methodological details of experiment 1, experiment 2, experiment 3 . . . and on and on up into the hundreds.

"The experimental stuff is interesting, but frankly, for a long time I've been far more interested in the sociology of the field."

"The sociology?"

"Yeah, why comparative psychologists who try to study higher-order intelligence in animals keep doing what they're doing, even though it's pretty obvious it reveals more about the ways we think than the ways animals think. I'm really interested in the sociology that keeps all that going."

"I think you mean the folklore."

"Folklore? No, I mean the sociology."

"Pretty sure you mean the folklore."

The Folklorist's words were finally starting to make sense. To be fair, the Scientist really had been interested in human social relationships and institutions within science that he believed perpetuated certain unproductive practices. But as he looked out his arched window into the St. Louis sky, he thought about the titles he had been using for his latest academic projects: a recent book chapter, "Through a Floppy Tool Darkly: Toward a Conceptual Overthrow of Animal Alchemy" (Povinelli and Penn 2011); a rough-and-ready dog-and-pony-show talk, "How the Chimpanzee Got Its Theory of Mind without Even Trying," that he had been giving for the past year (Povinelli 2015); a tongue-in-cheek appendix, "Some Folk Psychological Challenges to the Objective Study of Ape Intelligence," that he had snuck into his latest book (2012); and even the terse teaser "Anthropomorphomania!" for an upcoming talk at New York University (2015). He looked up a quick definition for folklore: a body of popular myths and beliefs relating to a particular culture, subculture, or group of people and their transmission from one generation to the next. There was more, of course, but the Folklorist had been right. He *was* interested in folklore—*scientific folklore*.

The Folklorist's mind was racing too. Sure, folklorists have long doubted the possibility of absolute objectivity, but he always thought of science as operating under a different set of rules. What would come next? Would scientists use "The Tortoise and the Hare" to design an experiment to test for higher-order notions of athletic strategy? Would ants be tested against grasshoppers for economic aptitude? And fables were only the tip of the anthropomorphic iceberg! What of the hedgehogs and wolves in Märchen? Or mythological serpents? Or elephant jokes? And then there was the ethical problem—the agnostic stance to which he had been committed for so long. On the one hand, he was comfortable problematizing the kind of scientistic thinking that always wants clear, positivist answers to murky, humanistic questions. On the other hand, even humanists have to draw the line somewhere.

And so it was only a matter of time, after their respective minds had settled, that the weekly phone calls began—at first an hour at a time, then several. Initially, they centered on the crow and the pitcher project, but quickly their view expanded into the timeless performance space where humans tell stories about animals, a giant rotunda that corralled science, popular science, pseudoscience, popular culture, ancient mythology, urban legend, children's play, pets, poetry, political agendas, art, and even the musings of the casual naturalist walking through the park. To be sure, there were plenty of similar precedents in other fields, but this felt different.[2] For the Scientist, it was a better way of exploring what he saw as the powerful engines that drive the wheel-spinning machinations of his former field. For the Folklorist, it was a more honest way to think about how the "relativistic" thinking in folkloristics interacts with the more "objective" truths sought by science. Numerous research projects flooded their minds—some scholarly, others performative—all with a common aim: ringing a new interdisciplinary bell that could connect known folklore about animals to the underlying and less obvious *scientific folklore* embedded in the scientific study of animals: a study of *cognitive folklore*.

This volume presents the fruition of one of those projects. It began as a panel at the 127th annual meeting of the American Folklore Society (held jointly with the International Society for Folk Narrative Research) in Miami in October 2016, consisting of presentations by Barker, Hansen, Povinelli, and Schrempp. Their contributions to this book represent slightly reworked versions of those talks. To those presentations, we add the essay of Hennefield and Hwang, whose interests in the intersection of developmental and comparative psychology prepared them for a deeper examination not only of this scientific retelling of "The Crow and the Pitcher" but also of the role that storytelling in general has played in their own scientific subdisciplines (and even their early careers).

A closing word about a shadow contributor to this volume, Doctor Fomomindo.[3] For the past several years, we have been touring a coauthored "traveling theatrical lecture" featuring this retired comparative psychologist (a fictionalized persona of the Scientist) and an only slightly more fictionalized talking inner ego of a chimpanzee, Mojo. We have also turned to this duo in our published fiction and more traditional theatrical work.[4] Across these performance spaces, the genders of the Doctor and the Ape have been fluid in the sense that for each project we have chosen genders and enlisted performers that have seemed best suited to perform the intellectual and dramatic work we have intended. But one thing about Doctor Fomomindo remains fixed: here is a character who—though steeped in the objective enterprise of the science of animal cognition—is sober enough to realize how quickly human storytelling intrudes. In the context of this work, his sporadic appearance serves as an overt nod to the broader blending of genres contained herein (historical exegesis, folkloristic theory, cross-disciplinary interviews, scientific data, comparative literary analysis, and even wonderfully playful drawings). It is our hope that this admixture of academic traditions can nudge new ways of thinking about a very old set of problems.

To wit, the appendix, "Doctor Fomomindo's Preliminary Notes for a Future Index of Anthropomorphized Animal Behaviors," adds one more monkey wrench into the folkloristic toolkit: an examination of our not-too-mythical former monkey mind doctor grappling with the complexities of folkloristic motif and tale-type indexes as a possible methodological solution to his lifelong attempt to capture the genuinely paradoxical ways in which scientists—people, really—anthropomorphize animals. We intend Doctor Fomomindo's effort to serve as a map to guide us not just through the choppy waters of the laboratory crows who turned into the Crow but also through the wilderness of cats, dogs, dolphins, bonobos, elephants, ants, seals, ferrets, alligators, fish, scrub jays, and who knows what other animals that peer out through the thicket of Fomomindo's preliminary index. Moreover, Doctor Fomomindo's valiant and ever-expanding catalog sheds much-needed light on the growing interface between folklore and science, and beyond (see Schrempp's essay and our conclusion herein). To be as direct as a blow from John Henry's hammer, this volume, complete with Doctor Fomomindo's never-ending index, constitutes a rough-and-ready starting point for our proposed future subdiscipline of *cognitive folkloristics*.

For the supposedly objective science of animal minds (and the scientists who we hope will read this book), our genre-blending exercise serves one more purpose: to help future generations of comparative psychologists get a more focused perspective on the scientific folklore embedded in the practice of their field. After all, these young scientists are (or soon will be) members of a species that demands interminglement with other animals in ways no other animals do. If the science of animal cognition is as steeped in mythos as the essays in this volume suggest, then comparative psychologists might well heed Franz Kafka's admonition that sometimes getting what one wants requires a deliberate leap in the opposite direction. Doctor Fomomindo might thus help us turn the mirrors of our minds just enough to see that many of the extant genres of research into animal cognition (not just the Aesop's fable paradigm) are the (re)enactment of prescientific beliefs about both humans and animals. Though never at the expense of the facts of the experimental record, the fictional Doctor Fomomindo wants to raise the problem of anthropomorphism to the top of the beaker. And he has no problem exploring the problem through mixed genres. He claims the science of animal cognition has been a mixed genre from the get-go. Not just in the trivial (if still surprising) way that the Aesop's fable paradigm has blended fable and science but in the more pervasive sense that the entire enterprise of comparative cognition begins with—began with—the problem of anthropomorphism (see chapters 3 and 4 of Darwin [1871] 1969). As the century-and-a-half history of the field attests, the latest proliferation of experimental apparatus and method may stand little chance against the older (dare we say, primordial) human drive to tell stories. Overcoming that part of the human animal's cognition will not be easy—the Borgesian efforts of our good Doctor Fomomindo's appendix notwithstanding.

University of Louisiana
Lafayette

Indiana University
Bloomington

Notes

1. For a complete description of the higher-order, role-based rules of this particular human game, see "2020–2021 Official Rules of Ultimate" (usaultimate.org/rules).

2. Far too many people have thought about the human-animal relationship for us to attempt to properly characterize here. But we do have some idiosyncratic reasons for suggesting Babcock-Abrahams (1975), Lévi-Strauss (1963), Gillespie and Mechling (1987), and DeMello (2012). Perhaps our personal favorite is Lester's (1976) *Animals, Animals, Animals*—a Peabody and four-time Emmy Award–winning educational television series that aired on the ABC network in the United States from 1976–1981. Every episode was hosted by the actor Hal Linden, who each week raced through a historical, cultural, and scientific examination of a different group of animals. The lyrics of the show's theme song say it all:

> (Verse 1)
> There are animals in history, in fables and in books
> Animals that climb in trees and fish that swim in brooks
> Man is just an animal who's managed to survive
> A bear can sleep all winter and come out of it alive
> You can lead a horse to water, you can even milk a cow
> a tiger's just a great big cat . . . a lady pig's a sow
> (Chorus)
> Oh animals (animals) animals (animals) animals here and there
> Animals, animals, animals, animals, animals everywhere!
> (Verse 2)
> There are animals in games we play and in mythology
> Animals we keep as pets, the whole ecology
> A whale is just a mammal that spouts water in the air
> A worm can turn and disappear and then he isn't there!
> (Repeat Chorus)

3. FOrmer MOnkey MINd DOctor. Although Doctor Fomomindo spent his career mainly investigating chimpanzees (and therefore he ought to rightly be named Fo*chi*mindo), he has intentionally adopted and incorporated the technically incorrect vernacular *monkey* into his name as a way of hinting at the academic realignment of his postexperimental primate activities.

4. See Povinelli and Barker (2016) and (2018). Earlier versions of *Confessions of a Former Monkey Mind Doctor* were produced in Göttingen, Germany, in 2016 and Tartu, Estonia, in 2017. Most recently, the show was performed at the Acadiana Center for the Arts in Lafayette, Louisiana, October 4–5, 2019.

References Cited

Babcock-Abrahams, Barbara. 1975. "Why Frogs Are Good to Think and Dirt Is Good to Reflect On." *Soundings* 58 (2): 167–81.

Bird, Christopher David, and Nathan John Emery. 2009. "Rooks Use Stones to Raise the Water Level to Reach a Floating Worm." *Current Biology* 19 (16): 1410–14.
Cooper, Lester. 1976. *Animals, Animals, Animals*. ABC.
Darwin, Charles. (1871) 1969. *The Origin of Species and the Descent of Man*. New York: Modern Library.
DeMello, Margo. 2012. *Animals and Society: An Introduction to Human-Animal Studies*. New York: Columbia University Press.
Gillespie, Angus K., and Jay Mechling, eds. 1987. *American Wildlife in Symbol and Story*. Knoxville: University of Tennessee Press.
Lévi-Strauss, Claude. 1963. *Totemism*. Translated by Rodney Needham. Boston: Beacon.
Povinelli, Daniel J. 2012. "Appendix I. Some Folk Psychological Challenges to the Objective Study of Ape Intelligence." In *World without Weight: Perspectives on an Alien Mind*, by Daniel J. Povinelli, 343–44. Oxford: Oxford University Press.
———. 2015. "Anthropomorphomania!" Invited Lecture. Center for the Study of Human Evolution. New York University. December 10. New York, NY.
———. 2015. "How the Chimpanzee Got Its Theory of Mind without Even Trying." Invited Mind-Brain Lecture, Berlin School of Mind and Brain. July 9. Berlin, Germany.
Povinelli, Daniel J., and K. Brandon Barker. 2016. "Searching for Ratzinger." *Turnip Truck(s)* 2 (2) *Animals*: 94–128.
———. 2018. *Confessions of a Former Monkey Mind Doctor*. Written by Daniel J. Povinelli and K. Brandon Barker. Directed by Paul C. Daily. Ivy Tech Waldron Arts Center and Indiana University, Bloomington, IN. November 28–29, 2018.
Povinelli, Daniel J., and Derek Penn. 2011. "Through a Floppy Tool Darkly: Toward a Conceptual Overthrow of Animal Alchemy." In *Tool Use and Causal Cognition*, edited by Teresa McCormack, Christoph Hoerl, and Stephen Butterfill, 69–104. Oxford: Oxford University Press.
Twain, Mark. (1883) 1996. *Life on the Mississippi*. New York: Oxford University Press.
———. (1886) 2006. "Amusing the Children." In *Mark Twain: The Complete Interviews*, edited by Gary Scharnhorst, 89–90. Tuscaloosa: University of Alabama Press.
———. 1917. *What Is Man? and Other Essays*. New York: Harper and Brothers.
USA Ultimate. 2021. "2020–2021 Official Rules of Ultimate." Accessed June 5, 2021. https://usaultimate.org/rules/.

DANIEL J. POVINELLI is Professor of Biology at the University of Louisiana at Lafayette. His primary interests center on the characterizations of the higher-order cognitive functions in great apes and humans. He is author of *Folk Physics for Apes: The Chimpanzee's Theory of How the World Works* (2000) and *World without Weight: Perspectives on an Alien Mind* (2011). (povinelli@louisiana.edu)

K. BRANDON BARKER is Assistant Professor of Folklore in the Department of Folklore and Ethnomusicology at Indiana University. He teaches and publishes on topics at the intersections of embodied, cognitive processes and folkloric traditions. He is coauthor of *Folk Illusions: Children, Folklore, and Sciences of Perception* (2019) with Claiborne Rice. (barkerbr@indiana.edu)

K. BRANDON BARKER

THE ANIMAL QUESTION AS FOLKLORE IN SCIENCE

Abstract: Looking to answer ancient questions about the similarities and differences between humans and nonhuman animals, animal cognition scientists have deployed a traditional Aesopian fable, the Crow and the Pitcher, as narrative frame and structural precedent for experimental investigation. Herein, I consider the theoretical implications of this peculiar intersection between folklore and science in the contexts of Alan Dundes's notion of folk ideas (1971) and folkloristic genre theory. Ultimately, I gauge whether the so-called Aesop's Fable Paradigm is simply a folkloric cameo in science or a more complicated case of genuine scientific folklore.

In a 2009 issue of *Current Biology*, scientists Christopher David Bird and Nathan John Emery published a compelling study on birds' problem-solving behaviors: "Rooks use Stones to Raise the Water Level to Reach a Floating Worm." Therein, Bird and Emery detail their findings that captive rooks, which have been trained to drop stones via a cleverly designed collapsible platform task, will—when faced with the problem of an out-of-reach worm floating on the surface of the water in a partially filled tube—displace the water by placing stones in the tube. Raising the water level in this manner, the rooks successfully obtain the worm. The scientists frame their work in the context of a well-known Aesopian fable, the Crow and the Pitcher:

> The results of these experiments provide the first empirical evidence that a species of corvid is capable of the remarkable problem-solving ability described more than two-thousand years ago by Aesop.
>
> What was once thought to be a fictional account of the solution by a bird appears to have been based on a cognitive reality. (2009, 1411)[1]

Inasmuch as the Aesop's Fable experiment demands attention from both sides of the humanist/scientist divide, it also represents the conglomerate of ancient, pervasive questions we humans ask ourselves about the inherent similarities and differences between people and nonhuman animals.

Oversimplifying, I will refer to this amorphous, unwieldly set in the singular as the animal question.

Animals surround us. Animal studies continue to sweep across the face of humanistic and so-called posthumanistic scholarship; contemporary debates concerning ethical treatment of nonhuman animals rage on in both scholarly and legal environments.[2] Animal presence in popular culture is nearly too pervasive to summarize. Alongside Animal Planet and cute dog memes, I could not help but notice that in 2017 (the year after our 2016 American Folklore Society panel on the Aesop's Fable Paradigm that gave rise to this book), *Time* magazine, *National Geographic*, and *Scientific American* all published special issues on animals—respectively, *The Animal Mind: How They Think. How They Feel. How to Understand Them*; *Inside Animal Minds: What They Think, Feel, and Know*; and *Secret Lives of Animals: Strange True Tales from the Wild Kingdom*.[3] Whether we are children being told a traditional animal tale, or children watching videos of anthropomorphized cartoon animals; whether we are scientists comparing cognition between children and chimpanzees, or philosophers pondering the mental states of physical and subjective self-awareness in species ranging from elephants to ants; whether we are biological anthropologists doing fieldwork in some remote forest, or animal rights activists fighting for more humane treatment of domesticated livestock; whether we are folklorists hoping to understand the complexities of human representations of animals in totemic material culture and traditional narratives, or even if we are simply dog owners trying to house train our family pet, it seems we cannot stop ourselves from asking the animal question.

More germane to our topic, Bird and Emery's Aesop's Fable experiment joins the litany of animal questions asked in the scientific investigation of animal cognition. Folklorists and humanists looking for an accessible entry into the history of animal science in psychology will find a short, but culturally insightful, discussion in Graham Richards's chapter on the "Psychological Uses of Animals" in his *Putting Psychology in Its Place* ([1995] 2010). Therein, Richards identifies ways that animals are used by psychologists:

1. To trace the evolutionary roots of human behavior.
2. As "behavioral units" for studying something called "behavior."
3. As sources of insight into behavioral dynamics, especially social dynamics.
4. To trace the borderline of what is distinctively human. (234)

Scientists have in recent years published more than thirty variants of the original Aesop's Fable experiment, featuring different animal species as well as human children. Taken together, they constitute, for the scientists, an experimental paradigm.[4] The Aesop's Fable Paradigm fits easily into Richards's second category as it studies problem solving behavior in the contexts of causal regularities, into the first category as it studies the breadth of similar problem solving abilities across a range of distantly related species, and into the fourth as it compares the performance of crows and other animals with the performance of human children.[5]

The Aesop's Fable Paradigm's source of inspiration, however, seems to also fit the experiments into Richards's category 3—though probably not in any way that the scientists intend. That is, while the Aesop's Fable Paradigm does not explicitly test the crows' social behaviors, the paradigm may yet tell us something about the social dynamics of people.[6] Richards observes that the entire topic can be viewed "as an expression of the intrinsic psychological significance of animals for humans" ([1995] 2010, 240). He adds, "The fact that modern Psychology is still involved in this game, at however a sophisticated level, further testifies to the inseparability of Psychology [the discipline] and psychology [i.e., the psychology of psychologists]" (240). And here, another—more folkloristic—question emerges: As a presentation of human psychology, can we consider the Aesop's Fable experiments as scientific culture reflecting a more genuine kind of folklore?

We can safely say that, broadly considered, scientific paradigms have been conceptualized as at least partially constituted by the socioculturally maintained ideas of scientists since, at least, the work of Thomas Kuhn, and the Aesop's Fable Paradigm is clearly folklore in science in at least one sense—as the transposition of a traditional narrative.[7] But is the Aesop's Fable Paradigm folklore in science in another sense—as the distilled presentation of communal answers to the animal question, answers such as animals are similar to humans, animals solve problems in human-like ways, animals behave in ways that seem analogous to humans because their inner-workings are similar to humans' inner-workings, animals are like children, animals *and* children are just simplified adult humans? I argue that it can be, and if we desire a folkloristic name for these communally maintained, scientific answers to the animal question, Alan Dundes's *folk ideas* could serve.

For Dundes, folk ideas are "traditional notions that a group of people have about the nature of man, of the world, and of man's life in the world" (1971, 95). On one hand, any serious answer to any iteration of the animal question is likely to overlap with the parts of Dundes's definition that deal with nature and human life in the world. On the other hand, it remains unclear whether we should think of the scientists' answers as traditional folklore. We would dangerously stretch the reach of folkloristic thinking, for example, by categorizing experimental investigations in science as a genre of folklore (consider the issues of anonymity, communal ownership, variation, etc.). But it is important to keep in mind, here, that Dundes was not thinking in terms of a genre: "Folk ideas would not constitute a genre of folklore but rather would be expressed in a great variety of many genres" (1971, 95). As a matter of fact, Dundes frames his entire premise of folk ideas with a critique of genre-theory: "Despite the practical necessity of defining and refining genre categories, the fact remains that the folklorist's habit of thinking of his field almost exclusively in terms of traditional genres tends to be a limiting one" (94). Perhaps, we can thread the needle. Since the scientists *have* co-opted a fable for their experimentation, I suggest we use genre-theory as a folkloristic point of view from which we can search for cryptic expressions of folk ideas in the Aesop's Fable Paradigm.

The Crow and the Pitcher is an animal tale, a fable; how has this fable become science? It is an arresting question because we must face a certain amount of surprise before setting out for sober answers. We are—of course—surprised and impressed that Bird and Emery's clever crows are capable of, at least, some form of goal-directed problem solving that allows them to obtain the floating worm. But, if we are being honest, folklorists are also surprised because we have learned that the behavior of an animal character in a well-known fable has been actualized in scientific experimentation. Discomfort follows surprise as we realize that the fable has suddenly been ripped from its ancient discursive function as a fantastic rhetorical device that, William Hansen teaches us, was meant to "exemplify a proposition metaphorically" *and* from its traditional literary function as a piece of short fiction meant to express an "explicit moral" (1998, 259–61). Variability and context shifts are not newly recognized phenomena, but a fable being forced into dialog with the scientific arbitration of veridical reality raises other issues for genre theory.

Consider the problems that arise when we invert our truth evaluation by describing the Crow and the Pitcher as a mere fictional, and ultimately flippant, account of a bird solving a problem. So much analysis tells us that literal interpretations—based upon veridical truth values—miss implied truths and cultural commentary embedded within the semantics of traditional narratives—not to mention the sociocultural contexts of any given telling. The Crow and the Pitcher is cataloged in the *Motif-Index* as an example of Wisdom Gained from Experience (J101), and modern literary variants of the fable often express a moral concerning the nature of problem-solving, such as *Where force fails, patience will often succeed*; or *With a little planning, you can gain what at first seems impossible*; or a frequently attributed version of the moral, which Bird and Emery cite in their conclusion, *Necessity is the mother of invention*:

> Aesop used his fable to ascribe the moral that "necessity is the mother of invention." Our evidence suggests that in this case, it is cognitive generalization that may provide the toolbox from which the solution could be drawn. (2009, 1412)[8]

In this case, the reflexivity embedded in the moral seems to engulf both the narrative plot of the fable *and* the breakthrough that made the fable scientifically relevant, for the "invented" experimental design "has proven useful for testing whether tool-using and non-tool-using birds understand the causal properties of objects, as well as comparing their understanding with that of human children" (Emery 2016, 132).[9] Suddenly, the Aesop's Fable Paradigm's professed topics of birds' causal understanding of water displacement become fully intertwined with folk ideas about the mind, such as parents mentally invent their offspring, or mental problems are solved in ways analogous to physical problems, or both mental and physical problems are solved with tools.

That we are dealing with folk ideas about the mind is important precisely because the correlative "findings" associated with the Aesop's Fable Paradigm claim discovery of a staggering set of mental abilities in the birds, such as insight and a complex understanding of the physics of water displacement. Some authors go so far as to compare the crows' understanding of causal relationships in the physics of water displacement to five-, six-, and even seven-year-old children. If comparisons to seven-year-old children raise the stakes in these experiments, they also prompt another serious question for folklorists. In the contexts of contemporary print traditions, in which Aesop's Fables most frequently appear in children's literature, the folk—we presume—immediately recognize that the anthropomorphized actions of animal characters in a fable say more about the world of humans than they do about the real-world animals the characters represent. Take, as a bit of evidence, a seven-year-old's impromptu recitation of "The Tortoise and the Hare" published by the scientifically well-versed folklorist Brian Sutton-Smith in *The Folk Stories of Children* (1981):

> Once upon a time there was an ox and a tortoise. And they were fighting over to see who was the fastest. So they decided to have a race. So the rabbit ran as fast as he could when he saw the tortoise. So the ox laid down and took a nap. And when he woke up he saw the tortoise three miles away from him. And then he ran as fast as he could. Before he could reach the finish line the tortoise won. And he saw the tortoise taking home diamonds and diamonds and diamonds. And he was so mad that he went to the manager and the ox said, "I demand this money!" But the mayor said, "But Ox, the tortoise won so he gets the money."

But the rabbit ran as far as he could and nobody ever saw him again. And that was the end of the rabbit. And the tortoise stayed rich and rich. The end. (121)

The fables humans tell are not *actually* about animals' physical speediness or mental capabilities for insight. They *actually* concern human ideas about perseverance, mindset, or in the case of the seven-year-old's story above—the monetary success that accompanies sustained effort. Why would these core elements of the fable—as humans perform these elements—be overlooked in a truly comparative science?

To be fair, scientists working in the Aesop's Fable Paradigm must constrain their investigations in order to test for birds' and children's understanding of the regularities among causal relationships in the physical world. Because children are still developing and only recently linguistic and because crows are always nonlinguistic and a completely different species, it is not easy finding workable comparative scenarios. Lead psychologist Sarah Jelbert from the University of Auckland and her coauthors communicate these complications in the introduction to their 2014 study, "Using the Aesop's Fable Paradigm to Investigate Causal Understanding of Water Displacement by New Caledonian Crows":

> As adult humans we are capable of recognizing that objects in the world behave in predictable ways. For example, we know that two objects cannot occupy the same space, round objects will roll down hills, and heavy objects sink in water. Many of these expectations are present very early in life, whilst others emerge and evolve over the course of development. It is easy to imagine that an ability to attend to causal regularities in the world, and to understand the forces underlying them, would have adaptive significance for many animal species. Whether animals do attend to causal regularities has been studied using various methodologies in different species. However, finding comparative tasks to assess how causal information is processed by different species can be difficult. Existing tasks are often tied to specific ecologically relevant behaviors such as tool use, involve face-to-face interactions with humans, or are too cognitively challenging to be attempted by more than a select few animals. (2014, 1)

The authors go on to praise the Aesop's Fable tasks as "a more informative paradigm for testing causal understanding across a wide range of species" (1). Adding, "The strength of [the paradigm] is [its] ability to examine the reaction of animals to novel problems that are not related to the animal's habitual or customary tool use behaviors" (2). So again, why or how has a fable risen to the position of *bona fide* scientific paradigm? One possibility, the one expressed in these scientists' passages, is that the narrative actions of the fable actually provide a strong scientific hypothesis for realizable behavior in the real-world version of the fable's featured animals that—even more importantly—is not already found in the real-world animal's natural behavior.

Before we begin the process of creating a new motif category—*animal behavior demonstrating possible scientific breakthrough*—let us rest on old ideas and consider another possibility: The Aesop's Fable Paradigm's roots in folklore—not the experimental design hidden in its narrative—have fueled its rise to scientific fame. To address this possibility, we can conduct our own thought experiment of sorts by considering competing possible explanations for the experimental data. After publishing the study mentioned in the previous paragraph, Sarah Jelbert with Alex Taylor and Russel Gray reconsidered possible explanations for the Aesop's Fable Paradigm one year later in a review article for *Communicative and Integrative Biology*. Early in that review, the authors introduced the paradigm as possible evidence for insight:

> In the classic fable, Aesop's clever crow insightfully recognized that stones would displace water and raise the water level in the pitcher. To examine whether corvids could indeed find such ingenious solutions to problems, Bird and Emery provided rooks with a pile of stones and a tube of water containing a floating worm; examining whether they would spontaneously drop stones into the tube to bring the worm within reach. In line with the fable, and seemingly insightfully, the rooks picked up the stones and dropped them into the tube, some of them on the very first trial. (2015, 1)

The doubly-adverbial phrase, *seemingly insightfully*, jumps out. It is an important expression of the Aesop's Fable tasks' typically intended outcome—to demonstrate higher-order, human-like insight in corvids.

Now, let us introduce ourselves to a possible alternative explanation that Jelbert and her colleagues note "could account for the birds' performance on all tasks": *the perceptual-motor feedback hypothesis*:

> [*Perceptual-Motor Feedback* involves] repeating actions which bring the reward incrementally closer, coupled with the crows' goal-oriented behavior. Unlike an account which relies on insight or mental scenario building (imagining to some degree the effect that stones will have on the water level of the tube, before acting) the perceptual-motor feedback hypothesis proposes that a bird first recognizes the effect that dropping a stone has on the position of the reward after each stone has been dropped, then repeats those actions which bring the reward closer. In this case, birds do not need to understand any aspect of water displacement. (2015, 4)

In the context of these competing explanations, we must ask, "Why don't more of these studies lead with the perceptual-motor feedback hypothesis as a sufficient explanation of the involved behaviors?" Nothing in the perceptual-motor feedback hypothesis excludes the obvious fact that crows—endowed with their unique set of mental tools—are powerful problem solvers. The hypothesis does not downplay the crows' intelligence, and the scientists, here, admit that first-order feedback *does* provide a viable alternative explanation for the crows' behavior. Returning to our thought experiment, it is important to note that we do not need to accept the perceptual-motor feedback hypothesis as objective truth. In fact, we could imagine an infinite amount of equally plausible (but never completely confirmable) hypothetical explanations for the crows' abilities. Given this infinite set of possible scientific explanations, we need only ask ourselves if it is important that one interpretation of the data—the one that aligns the mental processes governing the crows' behavior with the mental processes governing humans' behavior—also aligns with the morals of the fable? My answer is yes. As Gregory Schrempp puts it, "traditional gestures and genres . . . have always radiated power and appeal" (2014, 1).[10]

Ultimately, the animal question persists precisely because the problems it foregrounds are difficult to solve. The rise of the Aesop's Fable Paradigm simultaneously raises the possibility that scientific work on animal cognition is exceedingly difficult to parse because of the weight attached to animals (both real and symbolic) in human culture. Folklorists who read headlines about crows being smarter than seven-year-old children should seriously consider the science, in scientific *and* folkloristic terms, before mistaking sweeping comparisons of mental processes across species for (objective) truth. It remains entirely possible that scientific focus on insight or on some other human-like causal understanding of water displacement in the Aesop's Fable Paradigm has more to do with the traditional content of the morals and the lessons implied by the narrative structure of the fable than it does with the actions of the real-world crows. By framing their studies with the contents of a fable, scientists imply that any rook or crow that can solve the problem of raising and receiving the worm must understand—on some level—that the state of being in need is best approached as an opportunity to think creatively, that we must invent fresh solutions in order to persevere, that we should think outside of the box, that we can employ mind over matter, that an entire host of complementary folkloric ideas are applicable to the experimental situation.

Indiana University
Bloomington

Notes

1. In a preceding section, Bird and Emery recognize that a previous study by Mendes, Hanus, and Call, "Raising the Level: Orangutans Use Water as a Tool" (2007), involved orangutans spitting

mouthfuls of water into a plastic tube in order to raise the water level and retrieve a floating peanut. While Mendes et al. do mention the Crow and the Pitcher in the text of their publication, they do so only passingly. Their title, for example, does not mention the fable. Commenting on the relative quality of the evidence for tool use, Bird and Emery note that the orangutan experiments were "not directly analogous to Aesop's fable—in Aesop's fable, the water was not transported to the pitcher but was already present. Thus, the water in Aesop's context does not fit the standard definitions of a tool; rather, the stones are used as tools acting as displacing agents on a medium that can be manipulated by these agents" (2009, 1412). They make no mention in this section of the incongruity that is the absence of a food reward floating atop the water's surface in the typical Aesop's version of the fable.

2. In an instructive 2009 *PMLA* article, Cary Wolfe, deftly captured the essence of animal studies when he likened summarizing the bourgeoning field to "herding cats" (2009, 564). Therein, Wolfe lists off a range of cultural arenas that commonly feature discourse on animals, including Western literature, art, and culture; "non-Western literature and culture, written and oral"; philosophy (continental and analytic); legal debates concerning animal rights (and personhood); television shows; and "last but certainly not least," food (564–65). Wolfe is not gesturing toward this complex web of animal discourse in service of simplistic demonstrations, he is, in fact, worried as the article's title suggests that the entire enterprise may be "Human, All too Human."

3. *Time*'s special issue was actually an updated reissue from 2014 edited by Jeff Kluger. *Scientific American*'s special issue was released in the spring of 2017, and *National Geographic*'s was released in the summer of 2017.

4. For folklorists unfamiliar with experimental studies, here is a good, textbook definition of *experimental paradigm*:

> An experimental paradigm is a model of research that is copied by many researchers who all tend to use the same variables, start from the same assumptions, and use similar special procedures. Those using the same paradigm tend to frame their questions similarly. Examples of experimental paradigms in psychology are rats (or pigeons) in a Skinner box pressing a lever (or pecking a key) for food or water that is usually contingent on some aspect of the response, human subjects using paired nonsense syllables (or word pairs, or picture word pairs, etc.), rats being run through mazes, and ablation techniques to localize brain functions. (Levine and Parkinson 1994, 352)

5. Of these four uses, Richards identifies one common assumption: "Namely, that animal behavior is somehow simpler than ours, though how precisely this simplicity is conceptualized varies, and sometimes the aim is to show that it is less simple than hitherto assumed" ([1995] 2010, 234). Breaking down such apparent binaries remains an obstacle for scientists working with animals.

6. Of course, in other experimental paradigms, such as the seed-caching Theory of Mind studies, scientists have explicitly studied the social behavior of crows and other corvids. See, for example, Dally et al. (2009).

7. I thank Jay Mechling for his insightful suggestions on the intermingling of science and scientific culture. For an excellent folkloristic consideration of the topic as it relates to Kuhn's work, of the strong program in the sociology of science, and of scientists' folkloric play, see Mechling's "Homo Ludens Subsp. *Scientificus*" (1984). Especially pertinent are Mechling's thoughts on the artificiality of the distinction between "the context of discovery and the context of justification in science" (265).

Using Franz Boas and Alan Dundes as case studies, folklorist Rosemary Zumwalt (2013) has recently reimagined Kuhn's notion of a "disciplinary matrix" in close proximity to folklore while examining the roles that charismatic leaders play in the development and progress of academic disciplines.

8. Generally, neither this nor any other moral appears in the associated published studies of the Aesop's Fable tasks.

9. This commentary on the Aesop's Fable task appears in Nathan Emery's book, *Bird Brain: An Exploration of Avian Intelligence* (2016). The book, which purposefully straddles the line between science and popular science, allows for a plethora of playfully anthropomorphic references, such as "Geese Ganging Up," "Machiavellian Maneuverings," "Do Birds Believe in Magic?" Interestingly, the book's primary antagonist is, in fact, the folk idea associated with the term, *birdbrains*: "It is time we stopped using the derogatory term 'birdbrain.' Studies of birds have exposed intimate details of their complex social and emotional lives" (182).

10. In his introduction to *Science, Bread, and Circuses* (2014), Schrempp reminds his readers that folkloric/popular influencers on science and scientific worldviews are neither new nor emergent. They are, instead, old and pervasive.

References Cited

Bird, Christopher David, and Nathan John Emery. 2009. "Rooks Use Stones to Raise the Water Level to Reach a Floating Worm." *Current Biology* 19 (16): 1410–14.

Dally, Joanna M., Nathan J. Emery, and Nicola S. Clayton. 2010. "Avian Theory of Mind and Counter Espionage by Food-Caching Western Scrub-jays (*Aphelocoma californica*)." *European Journal of Developmental Psychology* 7 (1): 17–37.

Editors of *National Geographic*. 2017. "Inside Animal Minds, What They Think, Feel, and Know." *National Geographic*. August 4, 2017.

Editors of *Scientific American*. 2017. "Secret Lives of Animals: Strange True Tales from the Wild Kingdom." *Scientific American* 26 (2), March 2017.

Emery, Nathan. 2016. *Bird Brain: An Exploration of Avian Intelligence*. Princeton: Princeton University Press.

Hansen, William. 1998. *Anthology of Ancient Greek Popular Literature*. Bloomington: Indiana University Press.

Jelbert, Sarah A., Alex H. Taylor, Lucy G. Cheke, Nicola S. Clayton, and Russell D. Gray. 2014. "Using the Aesop's Fable Paradigm to Investigate Causal Understanding of Water Displacement by New Caledonian Crows." *PLoS ONE* 9 (3): e92895.

Jelbert, Sarah A., Alex H. Taylor, and Russell D. Gray. 2015. "Investigating Animal Cognition with the Aesop's Fable Paradigm: Current Understanding and Future Directions." *Communicative and Integrative Biology* 8 (4): e1035846.

Kluger, Jeff, ed. 2017. "Animal Minds: How They Think. How They Feel. How to Understand Them." *Time*. September 8, 2017.

Kuhn, Thomas S. 1962. *The Structure of Scientific Revolutions*. Chicago: The University of Chicago Press.

Levine, Gustav, and Stanley Parkinson. 1994. *Experimental Methods in Psychology*. New York: Psychology Press.

Mechling, Jay. 1984. "Homo Ludens Subsp. *Scientificus*." *Play & Culture* 4 (3): 258–71.

Mendes, Natacha, Daniel Hanus, and Josep Call. 2007. "Raising the Level: Orangutans use Water as a Tool." *Biology Letters* 3 (5): 453–55.

Richards, Graham. [1995] 2010. *Putting Psychology in Its Place: Critical Historical Perspectives*. 3rd ed. New York: Routledge.

Schrempp, Gregory. 2014. *Science, Bread, and Circuses: Folkloristic Essays on Science for the Masses*. Logan: Utah State University Press.

Sutton-Smith, Brian. 1981. *The Folkstories of Children*. Philadelphia: University of Pennsylvania Press.

Wolfe, Cary. 2009. "Human, All Too Human: 'Animal Studies' and the Humanities." *PMLA* 124 (2): 564–75.

Zumwalt, Rosemary Lévy. 2013. "The Shaping of Intellectual Identity and Discipline through Charismatic Leaders: Franz Boas and Alan Dundes." *Western Folklore* 72 (2): 131–79.

K. BRANDON BARKER is Assistant Professor of Folklore in the Department of Folklore and Ethnomusicology at Indiana University. He teaches and publishes on topics at the intersections of embodied, cognitive processes and folkloric traditions. He is coauthor of the book *Folk Illusions: Children, Folklore, and Sciences of Perception* (2019) with Claiborne Rice. (barkerbr@indiana.edu).

WILLIAM HANSEN

THE EARLY TRADITION OF THE CROW AND THE PITCHER

Abstract: For all the familiarity of the Aesopic fable of the Crow and the Pitcher, at least in Anglophone lands, no scholarly study of it has ever been made. A survey of the ancient texts reveals some surprising results. First, the early narrators relate the bird's actions mostly as an actual occurrence rather than as a folktale. Second, only toward the end of antiquity did some unknown author convert the narrative of the crow into a fable and invent a moral for it. How did it become a fable? The present essay illustrates how ancient makers of fable books went about their work, collecting and retelling traditional fables but also remaking narratives of other kinds into fables. Once the narrative of the Crow and the Pitcher was recast as a fable, it became a staple of written fable collections and has frequently been given visual treatment by illustrators.

The tale of the Crow and the Pitcher, as we may call the story, is one of the dozen or so Aesopic fables that are likely to be familiar to everyone who is acquainted with any fables at all, at least in Anglophone countries.[1] As such, it must rank as one of the world's best-known stories. But no study of the tale exists; for all its familiarity we do not know much about its history or forms or meanings or uses, or even what makes it a fable at all.[2]

The Ancient Texts

The ancient evidence for the Crow and the Pitcher consists of six short texts dating from around the first century BC to the fourth century AD, a period stretching from Hellenistic times to late antiquity. I consider these texts one by one.

1. Bianor, Palatine Anthology 9.272 (probably First Century BC)

Our earliest attestation of the tale is an epigram composed by the Greek poet Bianor that appears in the *Palatine Anthology (Gow and Page 1968, 1:190, 2:203)*. It goes as follows:

> When Phoebus's servant [a raven], parched with thirst,
>> Saw atop a woman's grave-marker a small pitcher with rainwater,
> It croaked around the pitcher's lip but could not reach its depths with its beak.
>> So you, Phoebus [Apollo], inspired your bird with a timely trick:
> The bird, raising the elusive drink by means of a pebble and
>> Shaking the water with the stone, reached it with its greedy lip.[3]

The narrative has no real situational context, since the poem is a stand-alone composition, independent of circumstance other than being one epigram among many in an anthology of epigrams. But it does have a character and a setting: a thirsty raven and a cemetery. The cemetery implies that the site lies outside the boundaries of a town, where in antiquity tombs and graves were customarily situated. Within the cemetery, there is a sepulchral monument with a pitcher containing some rainwater.[4] A thirsty raven notices the partially filled pitcher but cannot reach its contents, whereupon the bird's divine patron, Apollo, gives it the idea of raising the level of the water by means of a stone.[5] Only one stone is mentioned, and the bird seems not so much to force the water up as to shake it with the stone, but in any case the thirsty raven employs the stone as a tool and manages to get a drink.

Bianor's tale is not a fable. That is, it is not a tale told to make a point metaphorically that might be applied to a human situation. It is just a story of a clever bird.

2. *Pliny,* Natural History *10:125 (First Century AD)*

Perhaps a century after Bianor the Roman author Pliny includes a narration of the raven and the water vessel in his encyclopedic work, *Natural History*. Book 10 is devoted to the physiology and behavior of birds. The passage that concerns us is one of a series of anecdote-like legends about remarkable crows and ravens. Pliny mentions a particular raven that lived during the time of the emperor Tiberius, learned to talk, and flew daily to meet the emperor and greet him. He goes on to mention a particular crow belonging to a Roman knight that could utter whole sentences. Next comes a report about a Greek who trained ravens to hunt with him. Then we get the author's account of the cleverness of a thirsty raven:

> Some persons have thought it worth recording that a raven was seen during a drought piling up stones in an urn on a grave-marker, an urn in which some rainwater remained that the bird was unable to reach. Afraid to go down into the urn, the bird piled up stones in this manner and so raised the water high enough for itself to drink. (1983, 372)

Pliny is reminded of the thirsty raven in the context of reports of ravens and crows that exhibited uncommon intelligence, meaning birds manifesting talents that are usually thought of as being human traits—the ability to speak, to utter greetings, and so on. The thirsty raven is a bird that, it appears, can reason logically, figuring out the principle of displacement.

The setting of Pliny's narration is much the same as Bianor's: a cemetery with a sepulchral monument featuring a vessel with rainwater in it. The action is likewise about the same: a thirsty raven employs a stone or stones to raise the level of the water so that it can drink. For Pliny the behavior of the raven is noteworthy as an instance of uncommon avian intelligence, and Bianor must believe the same, since he attributes the bird's idea to divine inspiration.

As in the foregoing text, the narrative is not a fable. It offers no lesson or moral, and invites no application. Pliny relates it as a legend, a narrative that, true or not, makes a claim to historicity.

3. Plutarch, Which are More Intelligent, Land Animals or Sea Animals? 10 (Moralia 967a) (First–Second Century AD)

Plutarch's dialogue on the relative intelligence of terrestrial and marine creatures takes the form of a friendly discussion among several men (1957, 364–66). One of the participants, arguing for the mental superiority of land animals, mentions by way of example that spiders not only construct admirable webs—strong, viscous, and almost invisible—but also employ considerable skill in closing in on their victims. These abilities, he says, are confirmed by our own observation.

> Otherwise [i.e., if we ourselves had not observed spiders in action], it [their clever behavior] would seem to be a mere fiction, as I myself used to deem the report about Libyan ravens, that when they want a drink, they drop stones into a vessel, filling it and raising the water until it is within their reach. But later, aboard a ship, I witnessed a dog dropping pebbles into a half-empty jar of olive oil when the sailors were not around, and I was amazed that it perceived and understood that lighter substances are forced upwards when heavier ones settle to the bottom.

Unlike the foregoing narrations by Bianor and Pliny that focus upon a moment in the life of an individual bird, Plutarch's narration about the ingenious ravens of Libya is a report of a recurrent event involving an unspecified number of birds.

Once again, however, the narration is not a fable. Indeed, strictly speaking it is not even a tale since it reports a recurrent event. Rather, it is an ethological observation about the behavior of African ravens.

4. Aelian, On the Characteristics of Animals 2:48 (Second–Third Century AD)

Aelian's work, *On the Characteristics of Animals*, is comprised of stories about and observations on different kinds of animals. Concerning the ravens of Libya he has this to say:

> When through fear of thirst humans draw water, fill vessels, and place them on rooftops so that the air may keep the water fresh, Libyan ravens help themselves to a drink by bending over and inserting their beaks as far down as they will go. When the water gets too low, they gather pebbles in their mouth and claws and drop them into the earthenware vessels. The pebbles are borne down by their weight and sink, while owing to the pressure the water rises. So by a most ingenious contrivance the ravens get their drink. They know by some mysterious instinct that one space will not contain two bodies. (1958, 146–48)

As in the foregoing report, Aelian's narrative is a general observation about the behavior of Libyan ravens. He provides more details about the site of the activity, which is not a stone urn in a cemetery but pots of water on rooftops.

Once again the narrative is not a fable. Rather, as in the case of the previous texts, the narrator's purpose is to illustrate, for its own interest, a surprising indication of animal intelligence—surprising in that the raven's ability to reason and solve a problem seems to human observers to be much like human reasoning.

5. Pseudo-Dositheus, Hermeneumata 43, no. 8 (Perry 1952, no. 390)[6] (Early Third Century AD)

The *Hermeneumata*, or *Interpretations*, by an unknown author (or authors) conventionally called Pseudo-Dositheus, is a bilingual schoolbook written in Greek and Latin. It contains *inter alia* a small collection of fables that the composer has likely taken entirely from earlier written works.[7] The eighth fable goes as follows:

> A thirsty crow went to a water jug and tried to turn it over. Since the jug stoutly held its ground, the bird could not knock it down. But by means of shrewdness the crow succeeded in what it wanted. It dropped pebbles into the jug, and the large quantity of these caused the water to overflow from bottom to top. In this manner the crow put an end to its thirst.
>
> So intelligence trumps force.

Here for the first time in surviving literature the narrative of the bird and the water vessel is recounted as a fable, meaning that it is a short narrative that has been structured so as to make a point that can be applied metaphorically to human situations. A possible application is appended at the end of the narration in the form of an epimythium ("after-tale"), or moral, which here is, "intelligence trumps force." Such epimythia came to be a conventional feature of fables in the written tradition, as opposed to fables in live oral discourse. In order to support this moral, the author (or his source) introduces into the narrative an explicit contrast between physical and mental activity: the bird is not strong enough to knock over the water jug but succeeds in getting at the contents by means of cleverness. As usual in literary fables, the moral generalizes the situation in the manner of practical wisdom.

The bird is also called a crow here for the first time. Ravens and crows belong to the same family of birds, of course, both being corvids. Since they look much alike, Greeks and Romans sometimes confused them, as people do today, so that it is of no real significance that in our texts the protagonist varies between being a raven and a crow.[8]

The setting of Pseudo-Dositheus's fable is neither a cemetery somewhere in Greece nor a rooftop somewhere in Africa, but simply an unspecified locale where a half-empty container of water might be found. This vagueness suits the narrative well because ideally a fable should not possess too much inherent interest as a narrative, lest it undercut its supporting role.

6. Avianus, Fables 27 (Perry 1952, no. 390a) (Fourth Century AD)

The last treatment of the Crow and the Pitcher by an ancient author is a poem in Latin elegiac couplets that appears in a fable book composed by a certain Avianus.

> A thirsty crow had spied a huge urn
> > Containing a little water at the bottom.
> Long did the crow strive to spill this water onto the level plain,
> > To banish thereby its excessive thirst.
> But when no valiant effort could provide a way,
> > It lost its temper and with fresh cunning applied all its crafty devices.
> It threw pebbles in, and the low level of water rose naturally
> > And so furnished an easy way of drinking.
> This tale shows the superiority of foresight over stout efforts,
> > Since the crow accomplished thereby the task it had undertaken.
> (1887, 30 and 100–2)

Avianus's versified tale is much like the foregoing prose narration by Pseudo-Dositheus. It is a fable focusing upon a single moment in the career of a single bird in an unspecified setting, and its epimythium agrees with that put forth in the preceding text: wit is superior to force.

Figure 2.1. The Crow and the Pitcher. Wood engraving by Thomas Bewick, from Bewick 1784.

The Forms of the Narrative

The evidence shows that the Crow and the Pitcher developed several distinct forms from the time of its first appearance to late antiquity. The texts sort themselves readily into three sets of narratives.

The two earliest texts, those by Bianor and Pliny, are accounts of a single raven on a single occasion. They are set in a cemetery in which a grave marker features a half-empty vessel of rainwater. Unable to reach the water as it is, the raven drops one or more pebbles into the vessel, raising the level of the liquid. The interest of the narrative lies in the cleverness of an individual raven.

The second set, the texts of Plutarch and Aelian, are ethological accounts of the behavior of Libyan ravens. The setting is Africa, one of the texts locating the action specifically at pots of water stored on rooftops. When ravens are unable to reach the water, they drop pebbles into the vessels and so raise the level of the liquid. The interest of the narrative lies in the cleverness of Libyan ravens as a species.

Finally, the most recent pair, those of Pseudo-Dositheus and Avianus, recount a fable of a single crow on a single occasion in an undefined setting. After the crow is unable to overturn a half-empty jug of water, it drops pebbles into the vessel and so raises the height of the water. Epimythia explain the point of the story as being the superiority of reason to force. The authors regard their narratives as fables. Pseudo-Dositheus announces, "Now I will write some Aesopic fables" (Goetz 1892, 39), and Avianus expressly declares in his prologue that he is bringing his reader a selection of Aesopic fables.

The narrative of the Crow and the Pitcher was presumably transmitted both orally and in writing in antiquity, as it is today, when the tale exists mostly as a book fable but is encountered occasionally as an oral story.[9] Whereas Bianor possibly had his story directly from oral tradition, Pliny, Plutarch, and Aelian drew much upon other written compilations for their material, and so probably did so here, compilers being voracious consumers of other compilations. The latest pair, Pseudo-Dositheus and Avianus, are known to have drawn mostly or wholly upon written sources.

From Legend to Fable

How did a narrative that was told sometimes as a simple legend or tale, as in the initial pair of stories, and sometimes as an ethological observation, as in the second pair, become transformed in the end into an Aesopic fable, as we find it in the third pair of narratives and as we know it today?

The likely answer is to be found in the way that ancient fabulists went about their work. Compilers of fable books, in their eagerness to fill out their collections and provide entertaining material for their readers, incorporated into their collections not only fables in the strict sense—tales such as that of the Tortoise and the Hare, the Town Mouse and the Country Mouse, and the Belly and the Members—but also narratives drawn from other genres such as novellas, comic tales, and animal lore.[10]

For example, Phaedrus includes in his fable book the internationally known novella of the chaste matron. A loving wife who had lost her husband followed his corpse to his tomb, refusing to be parted from him. Meanwhile, some soldiers were stationed nearby to guard the bodies of several crucified men in order that the victims' relatives not remove the bodies for burial. One of the soldiers encountered the beautiful widow, conceived a passion for her, and in time seduced her. While the lovers passed their nights together in the tomb, the body of one of the crucified men was stolen away. The soldier feared punishment for his neglect of duty, but the widow turned over to him the body of her late husband to be fastened on the cross as a replacement. In this way, Phaedrus concludes, shamefulness laid siege to good fame.[11] Although the ribald novella of the faithful widow is a fine and amusing tale, it is too long and complex to do duty as a proper fable in a real discursive context. Moreover, it scarcely lends itself to illustrating a moral, and the best Phaedrus can do is to conclude with a comment about shamefulness laying siege to good repute.

A second example is furnished by a tale appearing in another ancient fable book, the so-called *Collectio Augustana*, composed by an unknown author (or authors). An ailing man was asked by his physician how he was doing, and he said he was sweating a lot. The doctor said that was good. When on a subsequent occasion the doctor asked him how he was doing and he said he was shivering, the doctor said this too was good. On a third occasion the doctor asked the same question, heard the man's complaint, and gave the same assessment. When a member of the household subsequently came into the sick man's room and inquired how he was doing, he said, "I'm dying of good symptoms" (Perry 1952, no.170). This comic tale, which mocks incompetent and unhelpful doctors, certainly did not begin life as a fable, and it is not easy to imagine how one might employ it as one. Still, the unknown fabulist manages to come up with this epimythium: "Many people are congratulated by their friends for the very things that they themselves find unpleasant."

A third case is provided by a strange tradition about the behavior of beavers. According to a fable recounted by Phaedrus, when a beaver perceives that it cannot escape the dogs that are after it, it bites off its own testicles and casts them aside, knowing that it is being pursued on their account. In his epimythium the author offers this application: "If people were willing to give up all their belongings, they would live safely, for no one would attack a naked body."[12] In fact, many ancient authors declare that when beavers see they are being hunted, they save their lives by biting off their own testicles.[13] This bizarre idea was obviously an item of widespread popular belief. Beavers were indeed hunted anciently for a substance called castoreum that was extracted from their inguinal glands and used for various medical purposes. Although the lore about beavers is not a tale, only a general observation (and, as it happens, a false one), it certainly makes a striking narrative, and the fabulist Phaedrus added it to his book. The narrative of the beaver became a fable, as it were, by virtue of being included in a book of fables.

As the ancient texts reveal, the narrative of the Crow and the Pitcher is precisely this sort of story. The evidence shows that it began life, not as a fable, but as a simple yet interesting tale about a clever bird as well as an ethological report about a clever species of bird. It had no obvious moral, or point, other than that some birds are more intelligent (in a human sense) than most people think. It appears that someone, presumably a fabulist, encountered the corvid narrative, probably in the form of a brief story like that known to Bianor and Pliny, appreciated its potential as an instructive tale, gently restructured it in order to support a moral lesson about force and wit, and included it in his book of fables. The crow was now doubly clever. It not only succeeded in getting water from the bottom of a vessel but also discovered a general truth, that reason is more effective than force. The existence of such a fable prior to Pseudo-Dositheus and Avianus is implied by the similarity of their narratives, which suggests that their tales go back to a common source. This tale may have been part of the *Mythiamboi Aisopeioi*, or *Aesopic Fables in Iambic Verse*, composed by the fabulist Babrius (ca. second century AD), for Pseudo-Dositheus and Avianus are known to have borrowed from his work, which survives only in part.[14]

Once Avianus versified the tale for his collection of Aesopic fables, its credentials as an Aesopic narrative were established, for Avianus was popular reading in the Middle Ages and his fables were frequently paraphrased by others (Schwarzbaum 1979, xxx; Holzberg 2002, 71). In our own day the folklorist and fable scholar Joseph Jacobs (1854–1916) drew upon Avianus for his own retelling of the Crow and the Pitcher in his book, *The Fables of Aesop* (1894), which has been very influential in English-speaking lands.[15]

THE ADVANTAGES OF BEING A FABLE

Being a fable has its benefits. In the present case, the corvid narrative, once a mere account of a curiosity of nature, becomes something more active, a tale with an edifying lesson for human beings. The bird, which had been a mere object of narrative gaze, as it were, now serves as a model.

Just what do we humans learn from this wise bird? For the fabulists Pseudo-Dositheus and Avianus, as we have seen, its lesson is that reason is more effective than force. Is this the invariant message of the tale? No, it is not, as a sampling of later references to the fable readily reveals.

In his *Motif-Index of Folk-Literature* Stith Thompson classifies Motif J101 "Crow drops pebbles into water jug so as to be able to drink" as a subset of J100 "Wisdom (knowledge) taught by necessity." Simply put, then, for Thompson the bird solves the problem because it has to, and the essence of the tale is that, as the proverb has it, necessity is the mother of invention. But children's author Pamela Turner, in her book about the clever crows of New Caledonia, gives the moral rather as "Think, think, and you'll get a drink" (2016, 48), whereby, like Thompson, she sets aside the opposition of force and reasoning that figures in the ancient fable texts. In his well-known book of Aesopic fables, folklorist Joseph Jacobs offers still a different epimythium: "Little by little does the trick." That is, small steps lead to big results, an edifying lesson but not one put forth in Jacobs's source, Avianus. Jacobs's epimythium answers instead to his own retelling, in which he describes pebble by patient pebble the process by means of which the crow manages to raise the level of the water.

Figure 2.2. The Crow and the Pitcher. Ink drawing by Richard Heighway, from Jacobs 1894.

So the fable's message is variable. Like other raconteurs, these narrators have manifestly allowed themselves to interpret the tale as they wish, and have even adjusted the narrative to fit the message they wished to convey (Hansen 1982). Indeed, the setting, the number of birds, the role of physical versus mental effort, the virtue of patience, the epimythium, and so on—all these vary in different versions of the narrative. What is persistent across the tradition, pre-fable and fable alike, is only a basic kernel of action: a thirsty corvid ingeniously adds pebbles to a partially empty vessel, thereby raising the level of the water, and gets a drink. The bird is always clever, but the lesson we carry away depends upon the narrator from whom we chance to get the story.

A second benefit that accrues to the Crow and the Pitcher from its change of genre is its being more frequently retold by writers and illustrated by artists, so that it enjoys far more exposure than it would otherwise have had. From antiquity onward, fables have made popular reading, and fable compilations are many. If the corvid narrative had remained a simple legend, as in Pliny, or a brief ethological report, as in Plutarch, the chances are slim that most of us, including modern biologists who study avian intelligence, would be acquainted with it.

The ancient fable was primarily a narrative genre employed by adults in discourse with other adults, orally or in writing. Many ancient authors pepper their dialogues, essays, speeches, letters, poems, and the like with the occasional Aesopic tale in order to emphasize or clarify a point and also to add a light touch. The great written collections of fables—the anonymous compilations in Greek prose such as the *Collectio Augustana*, the fable book by Phaedrus in Latin verse, the fable book by Babrius in Greek verse, and the fable book by Avianus in Latin verse—were created with adult readers in mind. At the same time ancient textbooks such as the *Hermeneumata* of Pseudo-Dositheus show how fables were also used in schools to teach writing, composition, foreign languages, and rhetoric, and so also had young readers. Today the situation is approximately the reverse. Fables have ceased to be a living narrative genre for adults, and nowadays most fables are written down (or produced for other media such as television) for consumption by children. It is likely that readers of this essay, like its author, first encountered the Crow and the Pitcher as a children's tale. Happily for its career, it is well adapted for this role, since like the Tortoise and the Hare (don't be a sluggard), the Boy Who Cried "Wolf!" (don't lie), and other such moral tales, the Crow and the Pitcher conveys a message (or messages) that adults regard as edifying for children. Unsurprisingly, the Crow and the Pitcher ranks among the most frequently anthologized folktales in children's readers (Ranke et al. 2015 volume 8, 934).

The earliest fable books were designed as sourcebooks for speakers and writers. Accordingly, the authors of these books related their tales succinctly in unadorned prose. They nurtured no literary ambitions beyond that of producing a useful handbook. The fables gathered together in the anonymous *Collectio Augustana* and in Pseudo-Dositheus's *Hermeneumata* are examples of this kind of work. Presently another kind of fable book arose, one that was intended by its author to be not so much a practical sourcebook as a collection of entertaining and instructive tales. The authors of this kind of book nurtured literary aspirations. They presented the individual fables as poems and elaborated them in the interest of making the stories pleasurable reading

Figure 2.3. The Crow and the Pitcher. Illustration by Keith Ward, from Diemer 1955.

for their own sake. Examples are the fable books composed by Phaedrus, Babrius, and Avianus. The two ways of telling a fable are illustrated here by the texts of the Crow and the Pitcher composed respectively by Pseudo-Dositheus and by Avianus. The former is told in plain, terse prose, whereas the latter is recounted in leisurely verse. It takes Avianus ten lines to narrate the tale that Bianor manages to do in six.

Down the line we see an heir of Avianus's treatment in the prolix narration of the Crow and the Pitcher by the fable scholar Joseph Jacobs (1894).[16]

> A Crow, half-dead with thirst, came upon a Pitcher which had once been full of water; but when the Crow put its beak into the mouth of the Pitcher he found that only very little water was left in it, and that he could not reach far enough down to get at it. He tried, and he tried, but at last had to give up in despair. Then a thought came to him, and he took a pebble and dropped in into the Pitcher. Then he took another pebble and dropped it into the Pitcher. Then he took another pebble and dropped that into the Pitcher. Then he took another pebble and dropped that into the Pitcher. Then he took another pebble and dropped that into the Pitcher. Then he took another pebble and dropped that into the Pitcher. At last, at last, he saw the water mount up near him; and after casting in a few more pebbles he was able to quench his thirst and save his life.
>
> Little by little does the trick.

Jacobs makes the tale into a sort of short-short story to be savored in the telling, and styles it in a manner that, one supposes, is meant to appeal to younger readers. The five-fold repetition of "Then he took another pebble" sets up the eventual epimythium, "Little by little does the trick."

I conclude with a brief consideration of the fable in book illustration. There is an unbroken tradition of fable illustration in print from the fifteenth century down to the present day. Indeed, as John McKendry observes, "The fables of Aesop are the only text that has been illustrated so often, so diversely, and so continuously that the history of the printed illustrated book can be shown by them alone" (1964, 5). As a consequence, countless readers have not only encountered the tale of the crow in print but also seen the resourceful bird in pictures, since modern representations are plentiful; in contrast, there exist no pre-fable illustrations of the tale at all. The three illustrations reproduced in the present article date respectively to the eighteenth, nineteenth, and twentieth centuries. The two earlier books (Bewick 1784; Jacobs 1894) are semi-learned compilations of Aesopic fables intended for a readership of adults as well as younger persons, while the most recent volume (Diemer 1955) is a schoolbook designed for the use of young children.

To sum up, the familiar narrative of the thirsty crow and the water vessel is traceable back to ancient Greece and Rome, where it is attested initially as a legend about a clever raven in a cemetery, next as an ethological observation about ravens active on African rooftops, and eventually as an Aesopic fable about a crow in an indefinite setting. In this last instance, an unknown author—perhaps Babrius—reworked the narrative by adapting it to the then-popular genre of the literary fable. Notably, the fabulist introduced into the action an opposition between brains and brawn, which set up an edifying epimythium about the superiority of reason over force, and, crucially for the later career of the story, the author expressly identified the narrative generically as a fable by publishing it in a compilation of Aesopic fables. This new identity gained for the tale, now seen as bearing a kind of practical wisdom, exposure to a larger and more varied audience than it would otherwise have had, such that over the years the tale of the clever bird has frequently been retold in fable books and other venues, including scientific literature, and has been a favorite of illustrators.

Indiana University
Bloomington

Notes

1. The fable title, "The Crow and the Pitcher," comes from Jacobs (1894, 129).

2. The bibliography of fable literature compiled by Pack Carnes (1985) lists no investigation of it, and the recently completed, fifteen-volume encyclopedia of the folktale, *Enzyklopädie des Märchens: Handwörterbuch zur historischen und vergleichenden Erzählforschung* (Ranke et al. 2015), devotes no entry to it. Brief scholarly comments on the fable can be found in Holbek (1965, 2:192 no. 173), Schwarzbaum (1979, 443–44), and Adrados (2003, 3:469–70).

3. This and all subsequent translations are my own.

4. Kurtz and Boardman (1971, 127–29) discuss stone and clay vases in association with ancient Greek grave markers.

5. For the close relationship of Apollo and ravens see, for example, Kallimachos (*Hymn to Apollo* vv. 65–68; see Callimachus 1955, 54–5) and Arnott (2007, 111).

6. Fables in Ben E. Perry's *Aesopica: A Series of Texts Relating to Aesop or Ascribed to Him or Closely Connected with the Literary Tradition that Bears His Name* (1952) are cited as "Perry + number."

7. On this work see Adrados (2000, 2:221–35) and Holzberg (2002, 30–31 and passim).

8. Arnott 2007, 109, 113.

9. See ATU 232D* *A Crow Drops Pebbles into a Water Jug*.

10. Perry 1965, xxii–xxix. For a brief introduction to the ancient fable see Hansen (1998, 259–64) and, more extensively, Perry (1965, xi–cii) and Holzberg (2002).

11. Phaedrus *Appendix* 15 (Perry 1952, no. 543). On the tale and the tale-type see Hansen (2002, 266–79) and ATU 1510 *The Matron of Ephesus*.

12. Phaedrus *Appendix* 30 (Perry 1952, no. 118).

13. For example, Pliny *Natural History* 8.47.109 and Aelian *On the Characteristics of Animals* 6.34.

14. A prominent editor of Babrius, Otto Crusius, held this opinion and, in the belief that the *Hermeneumata* text represents a retelling in Greek prose of Babrius's lost fable in Greek verse, includes the tale of the crow and the water jug in his critical edition of Babrius (1897, 181–82, no. 200). However, the most recent editors of Babrius's text, Maria Luzzatto and Antonius La Penna (1986, xviii–xix), treat the Babrian derivation as uncertain. For the present investigation it is sufficient to observe that an unknown person retold the narrative of the thirsty corvid as an Aesopic fable by the beginning of the third century AD, when it is first attested in surviving literature as a fable.

15. Jacobs 1894, 128–30. In his note (LV) to the text he gives as his source the twenty-seventh fable of Avianus.

16. See the preceding note.

References Cited

Adrados, Francisco Rodríguez. 1999–2003. *History of the Graeco-Latin Fable*. Translated by Leslie A. Ray. 3 vols. Boston: Brill.

Aelian. 1958. *On the Characteristics of Animals*. Translated by A. F. Scholfield. Vol. 1. Cambridge: Harvard University Press.

Arnott, W. Geoffrey. 2007. *Birds in the Ancient World from A to Z*. New York: Routledge.

Avianus. 1887. *The Fables of Avianus*. Edited with Prolegomena, Critical Apparatus, Commentary, Excursus, and Index by Robinson Ellis. Oxford: Clarendon Press.

Bewick, Thomas. 1784. *Select Fables of Aesop and Others*. Newcastle: T. Saint.

Callimachus. 1955. *Hymns and Epigrams; Lycophron, with an English Translation by A. W. Mair; Aratus, with an English Translation by G. R. Mair*. Revised. Cambridge: Harvard University Press.

Carnes, Pack. 1985. *Fable Scholarship: An Annotated Bibliography*. New York: Garland Publishing.

Crusius, Otto, ed. 1897. *Babrii Fabulae Aesopeae*. Editio Minor. Leipzig: Teubner.

Diemer, George W., ed. 1955. *The How and Why Program: Story Unit*. Kansas City: T. G. Nichols.

Goetz, Georgius, ed. 1892. *Hermeneumata Pseudodositheana*. Corpus Glossariorum Latinorum, vol. 3. Leipzig: Teubner.

Gow, A. S. F., and D. L. Page, eds. 1968. *The Greek Anthology: The Garland of Philip*. 2 vols. Cambridge: Cambridge University Press.

Hansen, William. 1982. "The Applied Message in Storytelling." In *Folklorica: Festschrift for Felix J. Oinas*, edited by Egle Victoria Žygas and Peter Voorheis, 99–109. Indiana

University Uralic and Altaic Series, 141. Bloomington: Research Institute for Inner Asian Studies.
———, ed. 1998. *Anthology of Ancient Greek Popular Literature*. Bloomington: Indiana University Press.
———. 2002. *Ariadne's Thread: A Guide to International Tales Found in Classical Literature*. Ithaca and London: Cornell University Press.
Holbek, Bengt, ed. 1962. *Æsops Levned og Fabler*. 2 vols. Copenhagen: J.H. Schultz Forlag.
Holzberg, Niklas. 2002. *The Ancient Fable: An Introduction*. Translated by Christine Jackson-Holzberg. Bloomington: Indiana University Press.
Jacobs, Joseph. 1894. *The Fables of Aesop: Selected, Told Anew, and Their History Traced; Done into Pictures by Richard Heighway*. New York: MacMillan.
Kurtz, Donna C., and John Boardman. 1971. *Greek Burial Customs*. London: Thames and Hudson.
Luzzatto, Maria Jagoda, and Antonius La Penna, eds. 1986. *Babrii Mythiambi Aesopei*. Leipzig: B. G. Teubner.
McKendry, John J. 1964. *Aesop: Five Centuries of Illustrated Fables*. New York: Metropolitan Museum of Art.
Perry, Ben E. 1952. *Aesopica: A Series of Texts Relating to Aesop or Ascribed to Him or Closely Connected with the Literary Tradition that Bears His Name*. Urbana: University of Illinois Press.
———. 1965. *Babrius and Phaedrus*. Cambridge: Harvard University Press; London: William Heinemann.
Pliny. 1983. *Natural History*. With an English Translation in Ten Volumes by H. Rackham. Vol. 3. 2nd ed. Cambridge: Harvard University Press.
Plutarch. 1957. *Moralia*. With an English Translation by Harold Cherniss and William Helmbold. Vol. 12. Cambridge: Harvard University Press.
Ranke, Kurt, et al., eds. 1977–2015. *Enzyklopädie des Märchens: Handwörterbuch zur historischen und vergleichenden Erzählforschung*. 15 vols. Berlin and New York: Walter de Gruyter.
Schwarzbaum, Haim. 1979. *The Mishlé Shu'alim (Fox Fables) of Rabbi Berechiah Ha-Nakdan: A Study in Comparative Folklore and Fable Lore*. Kiron: Institute for Jewish and Arab Folklore Research.
Thompson, Stith. 1955–58. *A Motif-Index of Folk-Literature: A Classification of Narrative Elements in Folktales, Ballads, Myths, Fables, Mediaeval Romances, Exempla, Fabliaux, Jest-Books and Local Legends*. Rev. ed. 6 vols. Bloomington: Indiana University Press.
Turner, Pamela S. 2016. *Crow Smarts: Inside the Brain of the World's Brightest Bird*. Boston: Houghton Mifflin Harcourt.
Uther, Hans-Jörg. 2004. *The Types of the International Folktales: A Classification and Bibliography*. FFC 284–86. Helsinki: Academia Scientiarum Fennica.

WILLIAM HANSEN is Professor Emeritus of Classical Studies and Folklore at Indiana University, Bloomington. His books include *Ariadne's Thread: A Guide to International Tales Found in Classical Literature* (Cornell 2002) and *The Book of Greek and Roman Folktales, Legends, and Myths* (Princeton 2017). (hansen@indiana.edu).

LAURA HENNEFIELD AND HYESUNG G. HWANG
WITH DANIEL J. POVINELLI

GOING META
*Retelling the Scientific Retelling of
Aesop's the Crow and the Pitcher*

Abstract: The Crow and the Pitcher, a classic Aesop's fable, has surprisingly (re)captured the interest of comparative cognition scientists in the past decade. These researchers examine whether corvids (e.g., rooks, crows, and jays) can complete a laboratory analog of the fable by training the corvids to drop stones and other similar objects into tubes of water to retrieve floating worms. This Aesop's Fable Paradigm is argued to be an experimental method that can prove corvids have the ability to engage in complex causal reasoning—implying that they understand something fairly rich about the ideas of volume and water displacement. However, critiques—including our own meta-analysis—suggest that corvids' behaviors in this paradigm could be explained by trial-and-error learning combined with an instinctive, initial preference for functional objects rather than complex causal reasoning. With this line of research as the case example, we explore historical and sociocultural factors in the field of psychology that incentivizes scientific research that tells a "good story."

As we sit down to write, we are both postdoctoral research fellows in psychology. More colloquially, we are "postdocs"—members of that swelling army of young PhDs competing for a seemingly shrinking number of tenure-track faculty positions in the sciences. Specifically, we are both developmental psychologists who are building our careers studying the social and cognitive abilities of infants, toddlers, and preschool-aged children.

In this essay, we are not writing about children *per se*. Instead, we want to provide some insight into our experience with a puzzling development in the closely allied field of animal cognition: the widely celebrated experimental research with crows based on the classic Aesop's fable of the Crow and the Pitcher, in which a thirsty bird uses pebbles to raise the level of water in a vase to get a drink. Let us say at the outset that our experience with these studies does not, as one might expect, concern the nature of children's psychology in the contexts of narrative, or of fables. We are not going to consider questions of human development and narrative comprehension; we are not going to discuss children's understanding of water displacement. Rather, this is our (unexpected) retelling of the scientific retelling of an ancient fictional story.

AN EXPERIMENTAL PARADIGM BASED ON A FABLE

For more than one hundred years, psychologists who study the cognitive abilities of human children have been intrigued by cognitive studies involving animals.[1] Even undergraduate students of developmental science cannot escape reading about such research involving chimpanzees or dolphins or birds. Early and often, developmental psychologists are reminded that the animal-cognition literature is replete with discoveries of cognitive capabilities once thought to be solely present in humans [*Editors' Note:* See Appendix, "Doctor Fomomindo's Preliminary Notes for a Future Index of Anthropomorphized Animal Behaviors."]

As young students (and technically as outsiders to the animal science disciplines), we had always thought that the various claims about animal cognition seemed rather muddled and tricky to interpret. On the surface, the studies seemed to show that other animals are very similar to humans. We learned that tool use and tool making—once considered uniquely human—has been observed in the behavior of many animal species in the wild. This list includes chimpanzees, capuchin monkeys, gorillas, dolphins, sea otters, woodpecker finches, and yes, even some species of crows.[2] But, it was never clear to us whether or not the ethological evidence of tool use proves that when chimpanzees or crows, for example, use sticks to probe for insects or larvae, they understand what they are doing in the ways that human children—not to mention human adults—do. And although we were confident that nonhuman animals communicate (clearly, they do), we were not completely convinced that the waggle-dance of bees has anything to do with the human language's abstract properties, such as recursion or complex hierarchical syntax. Then there were the claims of empathy in rats and numerical reasoning in monkeys, the abilities of orangutans to play games, self-awareness in elephants, and even autobiographical narratives in chimpanzees [*Editors' Note* : see Appendix]. It all seemed simultaneously convincing ("There are so many studies and everyone else seems to be buying into it!") and unconvincing ("There are so many gaps in the experimental logic; how can we look past them?").

Later, when we were both graduate students at Washington University in St. Louis during the Fall of 2014, an expert in animal cognition, Daniel

Figure 3.1. Dropping stones into the water-filled tube on the left raises the level of the water and brings the worm closer to the crow; dropping stones into the sand-filled tube on the right does not. Cartoon by Gavin Rackoff.

Povinelli, showed up in our department as a visiting professor. We decided to take a class with him to learn more about the field of animal cognition—straight from the horse's mouth, as they say. The surface structure of the course was familiar enough. Each week, we had to read a gathering of empirical research papers on a particular topic, and we needed to be prepared to discuss and to critique the papers in seminar. Other aspects were less familiar. For one, we were encouraged to perform our own literature searches and to bring to class the best and most compelling research in support of each given topic that we could find. For another, in every class someone was in charge of commenting on how the popular press had reported on the studies we were covering that week. We quickly began to detect certain patterns. Not surprisingly, what we read in the popular press (and in some textbook summaries) did not always match up very well with the details in the actual papers and studies themselves. More interestingly, the press seems to be *inexhaustibly* interested in studies about smart—especially "human-level" smart—animals.

The research directly inspired by the ancient fable of the Crow and the Pitcher immediately raised our suspicions. In these studies, researchers had taught some crows to drop stones into test tubes of water in order to raise the water level high enough to retrieve a floating worm.[3] Some of the crows became so adept that they even learned to avoid dropping stones in test tubes filled with sand (see Figure 1).[4] The researchers claimed that these results show that crows are capable of "complex cognition"—implying that the crows understood something fairly rich about the ideas of volume and water displacement.[5] And it was not just one study. To our surprise, we discovered that over a period of about eight years, five peer-reviewed research articles containing over thirty-two experiments had been inspired by the fable! Each paper focused on a small number of birds and a growing list of slight variants of the task. Time and time again, the researchers concluded that the fable-inspired tasks were somehow special—uniquely suited to reveal the higher-order mental abilities of animals.[6] One research group even claimed that their work showed that crows understand the physics behind the test even better than seven-year-old children.

We were puzzled. How could such a uniquely productive experimental design have been buried in an ancient folkloric narrative? How could crows be outsmarting seven-year-olds? Upon closer reading of the original research, our suspicion and puzzlement quickly turned to doubt: No matter how intelligent crows are, we began to find reasons to think that this fable-induced test was not a good way of measuring it. How could training birds to drop stones into a test tube (using an Aesopian fable as inspiration) necessarily show complex cognition? What, exactly, do we mean by "complex cognition" in this case? Surprisingly, none of the researchers seemed to tackle these issues head-on. Moreover, when we saw how popular these studies had become in the science news media, we found ourselves asking, "Why does no one else seem to be skeptical?"

Committed to acting as our own skeptics, several aspects of the experimental designs struck us right away. First, the birds that participated in the original study, rooks (part of the crow family), do not naturally use tools. In addition, in the initial "pre-test" phase (before they had to decide whether to drop stones in a test tube filled with water versus one filled with sand), the birds were taught to drop stones into a single, water-filled test tube. In other words, the birds did not encounter the pile of stones an experimenter conspicuously set next to the test tube and spontaneously start dropping them into the test tube. Instead, the crows had to be cajoled to do so: the experimenters had to balance a stone on the lip of the test tube, whereupon the birds would accidentally knock it into the tube and fortuitously see the worm rise a little. Only then did the birds start manipulating stones on their own. This pretraining was a necessary precedent for each of the dozens of variants of the same basic paradigm—having crows drop objects of all sorts into tubes while attempting to systematically vary key aspects of the objects, such as heavier vs. lighter or sinking vs. floating. But again, the amount of training required for the birds to perform even the most basic variant of the task (just dropping stones in a single tube filled with water) made us pause—if crows need extensive training to perform the stone dropping action, how could any subsequent learning "prove" higher-order cognition?

In fact, everything about the test appeared to scream "associative (trial-and-error) learning." Each time a crow drops a stone in the water-filled tube, the worm rises and gets a little closer to the surface where the waiting bird can snatch it. All that the experiments could demonstrate was that the birds could learn to keep repeating the same action over and over until they got their reward.

So, even at first glance, it seemed to us that the birds could just be learning to drop stones the same way a rat might learn to press a blue lever several times instead of a red one—analogous, for example, to a hungry rat placed in one of B. F. Skinner's classic "Skinner boxes." The rat initially wanders around, exploring the box until it bumps into a lever, which releases a food reward. But after several instances of this accidental behavior, every time the rat is subsequently placed in the box, it heads straight toward the lever and paws at it until the food is released. From there, the rat can learn any contingency the experimenter decides to impose on the situation (e.g., that the lever will only release food after it is pressed three times, or that pressing a blue lever releases food, but pressing a red lever does not). In fact, the predictable ways in which reward and punishment shape this kind of learning is so well established—it dominated American experimental animal psychology for half a century or more—that any assertion of a "new" type of learning or reasoning needs to first account for the roles of these already well-known processes. With these basic learning principles in mind, we became increasingly dubious of what the Aesop's fable-inspired studies could tell us about higher-order cognition. The crows' behavior in these tasks did not seem to be capturing anything like human insight: We were not hearing Archimedes shout "Eureka!" as he leapt from his bathtub and raced naked through the streets of Syracuse. What about these studies would make researchers jump to the conclusion that crows understand that the volume of one set of objects (the stones) "displaces" a comparable (or even any) volume of water?

A second component of these experiments that struck us even more was that most of the time the data from the main tests (for example, the choice between a water-filled versus a sand-filled tube) was judged as an all-or-nothing, either/or set of possibilities, and a given bird either "passed" or "failed" each trial. That is, after a crow had dropped all of the stones, it either succeeded in getting the worm or it did not. Thus, depending on the final outcome of twenty trials, the original researchers concluded that a crow had either "understood" the test or had "not understood" the test. But even when later researchers discussed the results in terms of learning, they focused on how many trials it took the birds to become regularly "successful" in getting the worm. But to us, an obvious fact about each trial was being swept under the rug. After all, each trial consisted of many individual stone drops. And just like the rat pressing levers, each individual stone drop was a learning opportunity: the worm either rises a little (water tube) or it does not (sand tube).

Thus, it was the treatment of the data in the Aesop's fable-inspired experiments that became central to our decision to investigate the data in these experiments using a more fine-grained approach. By analyzing the data at the level of each trial (or group of twenty trials) and not at the level of each stone drop, the researchers are essentially masking valuable information provided by each discrete data point (i.e., each stone drop). It was curious though. Every article did visually depict the data for the individual stone drops. For example, Figure 2 depicts sample data from a bird named Oliver. The way to understand this table is to see that in this experiment Oliver was given five stones per trial for twenty total trials—twenty different opportunities to try to use a pile of stones to get a worm when presented with the water-filled versus sand-filled tubes. Each trial began when the bird dropped the first stone into a tube, and each trial ended when the bird either 1) was able to retrieve the food from the water-filled tube, 2) exhausted all available objects, or 3) gave up and stopped dropping stones. Reading Figure 2 horizontally, however, you can see that each trial consisted of multiple, discrete acts of stone dropping. Sometimes Oliver dropped the stones into the water-filled tube and sometimes into the sand-filled tube (dark-gray squares for the former and light-gray squares for the latter). In fact, if you have the patience to count them up, you can see that although Oliver was given only twenty trials, he was given one hundred opportunities to learn about the different consequences of dropping stones in the two tubes (he seemed to catch on after about fifty and only dropped seventy-three stones across the twenty trials). Analyses of the results by trial, instead of by individual stone-drop, obscure important clues about how crows initially approached the task and if or how their behavior changed as the task progressed.

The Aesop's fable-inspired researchers claimed that crows demonstrated "complex cognition" in the water versus sand task because crows "rapidly"

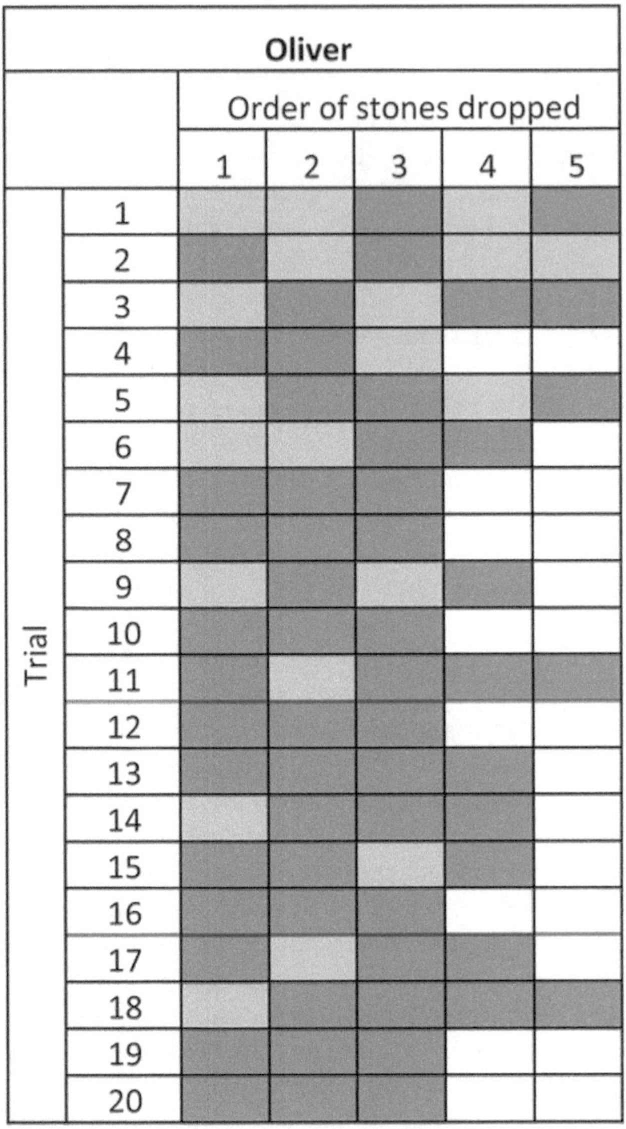

		Oliver				
		Order of stones dropped				
		1	2	3	4	5
Trial	1					
	2					
	3					
	4					
	5					
	6					
	7					
	8					
	9					
	10					
	11					
	12					
	13					
	14					
	15					
	16					
	17					
	18					
	19					
	20					

Figure 3.2. An example of how the data was depicted in the published articles. Light gray squares indicate that Oliver dropped a stone into the sand tube; dark gray squares indicate his choice of the water tube. The white squares indicate he did not use the remaining stones. Researchers provided this stone-drop level of data for each bird in each task but did not use it in their analysis. This bird (Oliver), for example, would likely have been described as "successful" despite the fact that he exclusively dropped stones into the incorrect (sand) tube on the first trial and his behavior was essentially random across the first twenty individual stone drops!

learned to drop the stones into the water tube. To that end we realized that at least three specific questions could be addressed by a meta-analysis:

1. Did the crows show any preference for the water tube (over the sand tube) at the very beginning of the tests?
2. How quickly did the crows learn to select the water tube over the sand tube (i.e., what exactly does "rapidly" mean)?
3. What was the source of the bird's learning?

The third question was especially intriguing to us: Did the birds learn anything when they dropped stones into the sand-filled test tubes, or did the learning only occur when they dropped stones in the water-filled tubes? The question made us realize that it would be possible to reanalyze the data from each test (e.g., the water vs. sand task) on a drop-by-drop basis within each article and then to combine the data from across multiple articles in the form of a meta-analysis—an analysis in which all the birds could be included to increase the power of the analyses. Because many of the research reports conducted multiple variants of the Aesop's fable task, we were also able to analyze how well the birds transferred what they learned in earlier tasks to later tasks. Below we discuss this further.

The Work of the Meta-Analysis

The first Aesop's fable-inspired study was published in a journal called *Current Biology*—a prominent and well-respected, peer-reviewed journal with a reasonably high impact factor.[7] The majority of the subsequent replications and variants of the paradigm, conducted by researchers across several well-established laboratories, were published in journals with lower impact factors, journals that were nonetheless well-respected and peer-reviewed (e.g., *Animal Cognition* and *PLoS ONE*). In other words, these studies were quite prominent, not something dredged up from some dark repository of questionable repute.

The first concrete step in any meta-analysis is to define the criteria for what articles to include in the larger data pool. We settled on three criteria that a given article had to meet in order to be included in our analyses:

1. The research had to be published in a peer-reviewed journal.
2. The subjects (birds) in the studies had to belong to the same taxonomic group (the Corvidae family, see note 3).
3. At least some birds in the articles had to take part in at least the original water vs. sand test, plus at least one other variant.[8]

We then launched a broad search of the literature, which included combing databases with multiple variants of our search terms (e.g., corvid or crow;

Aesop fable; water displacement) and consulting review articles and other articles that cited the original *Current Biology* paper. After searching through nearly one hundred abstracts, and examining several dozen papers in detail, five articles made our final cut. Two additional peer-reviewed articles were considered but ultimately rejected from inclusion—one because subjects were western scrub jays and thus not members of Corvidae and one because the subjects were grackles—who *are* members of Corvidae—but only one grackle took part in the key water vs. sand task and that grackle refused to continue past the second trial.[9]

In the end, we were able to compile the data from twenty-eight birds from five separate peer-reviewed research articles: nineteen New Caledonian crows, five Eurasian jays, and four rooks. Of particular importance to our project was the fact that the majority of these birds (22 out of 28) participated in the original water vs. sand task. This enabled us to combine the data from these birds to investigate patterns of learning using a statistical technique called "multilevel modeling." Multilevel modeling essentially estimates or "models" underlying patterns in a dataset, and thus requires a larger amount of data than was available in any individual article.[10] In addition, across all of these articles, the subjects took part in over a dozen variations of the task.[11]

On a more practical note, each of the articles depicted the results from each bird (the "raw" data) in grids similar to that depicted in Figure 2, with one grid representing each bird's performance on a particular task. Each row represented one trial, and each column represented which object or tube the birds chose. This format allowed us to compile the data from across the studies to enter into our meta-analysis, but to do so, we had to enlist several undergraduate students to transpose the data for each choice, for every bird, and for every task variant into a giant excel spreadsheet organized by task. And we had them do this twice! To give some perspective, for the water vs. sand task we entered 1,528 data points. Across ten of the key task variants, we entered and kept track of 6,724 choices. After the data had been entered, one of us had to cross-check each data point to be sure it had been entered correctly.[12] By way of comparison, because they ignored the individual stone drops and only analyzed the results of each trial, the combined group of original researchers (spread out across the five separate publications), only had to keep track of 408 data points across the variants we analyzed. Having summarized the data in this way, we could "model" the data to get some answers to our three main questions (see above), as well as several others.

The easiest way to think about our statistical approach is to realize that on each trial the bird is confronted with either one pile of objects and two test tubes (sand vs. water), or one water test tube and two kinds of objects (floating vs. sinking blocks). Either way, the bird has two options. If the birds were just picking test tubes (or objects) at random, they should pick each one about 50 percent of the time. We can thus ask: When the birds initially began each task, was their performance random? If so, how many choices did it take for their performance to improve? Were some tasks learned faster than others? When they made a "good" choice, was their next choice more likely to also be a "good" choice? What about "bad" choices—did they learn anything from those? And finally, did they get any better as they encountered new variants of the task, or did they have to learn each one from scratch?

We have since completed and published our meta-analysis (see Hennefield, Hwang, et al. 2018).[13] In Figure 3, we have graphically depicted the choices that the crows made in three of the most important variants of the Aesop's Fable Paradigm. Each thin line represents one bird and relates their preference for one option over another as a function of increasing number of individual stone drops. The thick lines represent the overall relationship. Thus, it is possible to see how each bird's behavior changed (or did not change) as they progressed through each task.

Two things are immediately striking about these results. The first is that for the water vs. sand and float vs. sink tasks, the birds' choices started out near the 50 percent mark (statistically their choices did not initially differ from chance). As the task progressed, however, nearly all birds began to choose the "good" choice with increased regularity. This pattern is exactly what we would expect to see if the birds are learning how to more quickly retrieve the worm as they gain experience with the God's-eye, immutable facts about what happens when a stone is dropped into a test tube of water with a worm floating on top (the worm moves closer) versus when a stone is dropped into a test tube filled with sand (the worm remains just as far away).

The second aspect of Figure 3 worth noting is that in the solid vs. hollow task, the birds' choices were essentially at ceiling throughout the entire task. That is, they started out by initially choosing the solid "good" option and kept choosing that option as time went on. This result is compatible with several hypotheses. First, the birds' may have begun the task with an understanding of volume and water displacement. Second, the birds may have learned something general from their prior testing (to pick up and drop objects that require *this much effort*). Or third, as some of the authors themselves argue, the birds either have an *a priori* preference for the solid objects, dislike the feel of the hollow objects in their beaks, or any number of possible alternative reasons. We should note that although there may have been some exceptions (see fig. 3.3), our modeling revealed that the birds did not, in general,

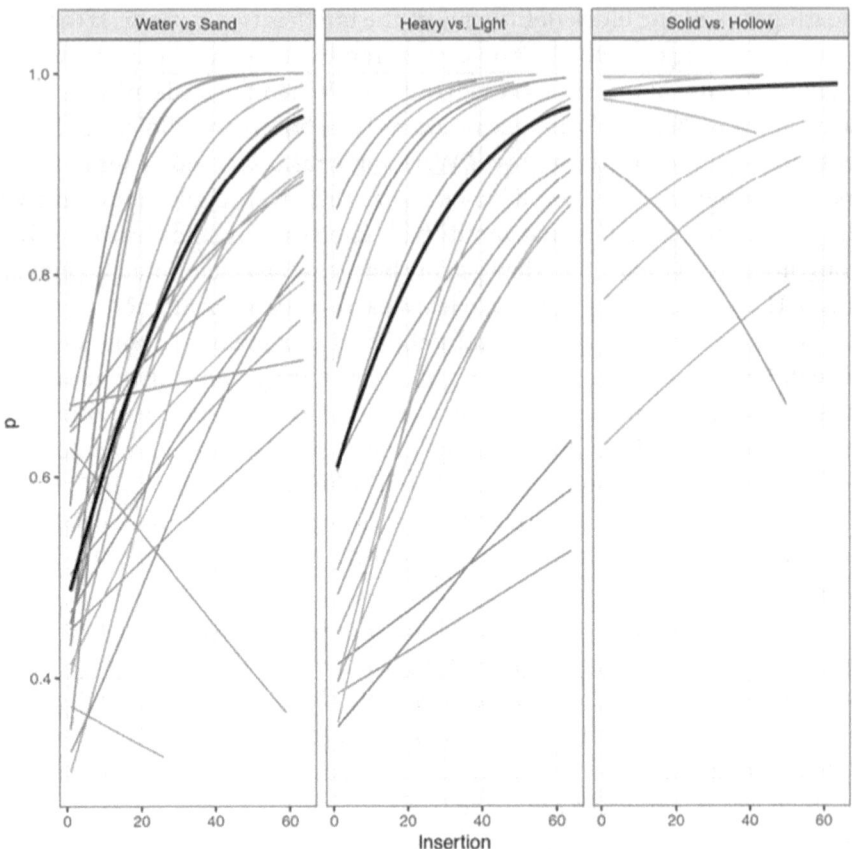

Figure 3.3. This figure depicts the choices each crow made in three key variants of the Aesop's fable tasks. Each thin gray line represents one bird and depicts their preference for one option over another as a function of increasing number of individual stone drops. The thick dark line represents the overall relationship. For example, in the water vs. sand task crows' initial choices tend begin near chance (the 0.5 mark on the y axis) and the upwardly sloped lines indicate the crows that increasingly chose to drop stones into the water tube as the task progressed.

transfer information learned in one task to the many subsequent tasks they were given. That is, the birds did not perform better on later as opposed to earlier tasks. This suggests to us that the birds did not "frame" these tasks as, for example, any good folklorist would: variants of the same underlying motif, such as water displacement. (Just to give a flavor for the diversity of those variants, here are some of their names: large vs. small stones, air vs. water, sinking objects vs. floating objects, baited test tube vs. unbaited test tube, hollow object vs. solid object, narrow test tube vs. wide unequal test tube, etc.) The complete list of tasks that we analyzed can be found in our published report (Hennefield, Hwang, et al. 2018).

We have saved our most important finding for last: our models revealed a curious fact about the source of the bird's learning, hidden in the flurry of stone drops across the many trials they were given on each task—a fact that is difficult to reconcile with the idea that the birds either started with or learned something about water displacement. Specifically, in the tasks where they performed better across time (the water vs. sand and float vs. sink tasks), the source of their learning was restricted to their successful stone drops! This is rather remarkable. Let us use the water vs. sand task to illustrate. When a bird made a good choice (i.e., dropped a stone in the water) their very next choice was about 5 percent more likely to be a good choice as well. This small but steady bias (presumably the result of the worm moving closer to their beaks), incrementally led them to home in on the correct choice from the beginning. Startlingly, however, when the birds dropped stones into the sand tube (the bad choice), they were just as likely to repeat that bad choice on the next stone drop. In other words, they learned nothing from dropping stones into the sand tube. Our modeling revealed the same pattern in the float vs. sink task.

Our primary conclusion from our meta-analysis is that these studies simply do not tell us anything new or interesting about animal cognition. Our results are highly consistent with a model suggesting the birds were learning through trial and error, not higher-order ideas like "volume" or "mass" or "displacement." In sum, we find no evidence of these birds having their Archimedes-like "Eureka!" moments.

In a strange bonus of sorts, after we had completed our work and submitted it for publication, we discovered that one other team had suspected a similar explanation of the Aesop's Fable Paradigm and conducted their own meta-analysis.[14] Although they raised several of the issues that we have discussed, they still chose to base their analyses on the trial-level data as reported in the original articles, rather than the drop-by-drop data. Equally puzzling to us, they did not challenge the ability of the paradigm to provide new insight into crow cognition.

How Crows Helped Us Become More "Compleat" Academics

At first, our investigation of the Aesop's Fable Paradigm was just an interesting intellectual exercise that closely mirrored the challenges we were facing as young experimental psychologists designing and conducting our own studies with children. Animals have a lot in common with children. Animals do not use language and young preschoolers' grasp of language is limited, so the problem of developing experimental tasks that can assess their respective cognitive abilities is similar.

Because we are not comparative psychologists, it felt somehow easier to be objective as we started digging into the research literature on animal cognition. We had nothing directly at stake in the questions, and we did not really know who the "key players" were in that field. It is an inescapable fact that seeing a "famous" psychologist's name before reading an article definitely colors one's assessments of the work. Here, there was a lot less pressure and background noise as we began to assess the premise, methods, and interpretations of the Aesop's Fable Paradigm. We could deploy our passion in understanding the experiments, ranging from seemingly minor details of methods (e.g., how many training trials did the crows need before they could even do the test trials?), to deeper conceptual questions (e.g., does dropping stones into a tube to retrieve a worm indicate that crows have an idea of water displacement?), without worrying about how it might affect our careers.

We entered experimental psychology with a strong passion for and trust in experiments. We thought, "Experimental research is the real key to science. Experiments provide us with the means to objectively test hypotheses via systematic manipulation of variables, and to make subsequent causal claims about objective truths. Experimentation is the tool to getting us closer to the real truth." We have come to realize that experiments are not always objective. The experimenters—the scientists themselves—have subjective biases that influence how they set up experiments and how they interpret the results and then present the findings to the public. Experimenter bias runs on a continuum from biases as benign as only looking for evidence that supports one's theory and not evidence that disproves it to as malicious as altering the data itself. Simply put, subjectivity is an inescapable issue in all experimental fields.

Then, too, there was the pall of the replication crisis that was hanging over psychology.[15] Just as we were starting graduate school, a distributed effort of scientists around the globe had discovered that a sizeable collection of very famous psychological findings were not replicable. Despite the fact that these findings were in textbooks and widely heralded in both the scientific and popular media, the results seemed to be illusions—statistical and sociological artifacts. The replication crisis has been attributed to numerous factors, but one of those factors felt all-too-real to us: the pressure to present nice, tidy findings and to ignore null findings (i.e., when experiments do not show a statistically significant difference between two conditions). Our increasing awareness of the threat to experimental psychology from nonreplicable or exaggerated research claims also played some role in our decision to dive into the meta-analysis of the Aesop's fable-inspired research.

Let us be absolutely clear: we are not seeking to lead a crusade against crow intelligence. We have nothing against the idea of crows having a concept of water displacement. We even admit that earlier in our careers we would have reacted to any refutation of the Aesop studies with boredom and distaste. Let's face it: there is nothing flashy and exciting about a couple of graduate students trying to undermine research that produces headlines such as "The Rook and the Test Tube: Fable Made Fact" (*Science Magazine*), "Much to Crow About" (*The Economist*), "Clever Crows Prove Aesop's Fable is More than Fiction" (*Wired*), "Crows Understand Water Displacement Better Than Your Kid" (*Smithsonian*), "Aesop's Fable? This One Turns Out to Be True" (*The Independent*), and "The Moral: Aesop Knew Something About Crows" (*The New York Times*).

Throughout our career as graduate students, we had heard that it was difficult to publish experiments that do not show directionality in their findings ("under condition Q, outcome X is far more likely than outcome Y"). Even if the design is well done, we were told, no journal wants to hear a story that is not exciting or definitive. We had been told over and over that we had to be able to tell a good story about our research in order to get noticed. We even took a career development seminar taught by a prominent psychologist and based on his coauthored book, *The Compleat Academic*. In hindsight, one of the quotes on the back jacket of that book seems especially revealing: "You may think science is somehow the opposite of storytelling, but this is not the case. Good science tells a story."[16] From this vantage point, it made perfect sense to us why the Aesop's Fable Paradigm had become so popular. It was a tidy story with a catchy interpretation.

Digging deeper into the Aesop's fable, though, also made us recognize the tendency in the study of both developmental and animal/comparative cognition to approach cognitive questions by putting forth a theory (which is a great first step) but not trying to actively disprove it. This is a fundamental philosophical problem in trying to establish the viability of an idea. Whereas you cannot hope to find all of the necessary evidence to prove a theory, you only need one contrary piece of evidence to disprove it. This is the classic, "All swans are white" idea.[17]

On the one hand, you can spend your time and money trying to gather all the swans in the world (or as experimental psychologists have come to tackle this problem, trying to get a representative sample of all the swans in the world). On the other hand, you can design your approach and your resources to do everything possible to find that one black swan. Of course, it is difficult to come up with a disprovable, falsifiable theory and to present that theory in ways that can be actively tested. In the search for mental continuity between

Figure 3.4. Tidy stories drive scientific conversation ... so we are told. Cartoon by Gavin Rackoff.

humans and animals, it is a much more common practice to gather evidence *supporting* a theory rather than it is to work toward disproving it. We have come to wonder if this has something to do with the practical impact of finding that "black swan"—the fear that you will not have a good story to tell, that you will fail to produce the kinds of novel and exciting research that will allow your work (and with it your scientific career) to rise to the top.

In our minds, the Aesop's Fable Paradigm came to exemplify this problem. The inherent goal in these studies, it seems, is to find evidence that proves crows have complex cognition rather than to find evidence that disproves this statement. The fact that these articles got picked up by the popular press and widely disseminated also contributed to our decision to devote our time to reanalyzing and writing up the findings in our meta-analysis—not that we had any expectations that our work would receive any popular acclaim. Even our initial inspection of the data (see, for example, our discussion of Figure 2 above) strongly suggested that our results might be quite deflationary. That is, we did not feel that our meta-analysis would make a good story. Nonetheless, we felt compelled to proceed.

We were taught early on how difficult it is to be objective in one's own research—that there is a psychological bias to give more weight to evidence that fits one's current framework than to evidence that contradicts it. Psychologists should know these biases exist—these tendencies that distort our thinking—but knowing this does not mean we are not susceptible to the biases just the same. It is a bit like St. Louis's iconic Gateway Arch. The Arch looks much taller than wide, but actually its height and width at the base are exactly the same. It is an optical illusion that is hard to unsee—even when you know the measurements (630 feet in both directions, as a matter of fact). We thought that, as outsiders, tackling a meta-analysis of the Aesop's fable tasks would be an opportunity to provide a different perspective on the broad theoretical and methodological assumptions employed in the Aesop's Fable Paradigm. This perspective, we fully recognize, is much easier to proffer when one is less familiar with the players and the conventions of a given field.

How Many Stone Drops Does It Take to Be Human?

Data is the gold standard of scientific research. For scientists, new data has the potential to provide new knowledge about the world. Small sample sizes and the painstaking work that goes into collecting each data point is something that connects researchers studying cognitive development in animals and humans. Trying to elicit a meaningful response from a two-year-old child in a word-learning paradigm ("Which one is the *blicket*?"), or to elicit a valid verbal response from a four-year-old in an event-expectation task ("Do you think the kite will or will not get stuck in the tree?") is no small feat. It cannot be any easier to figure out how to ask a crow if it understands why dropping a stone in a waterfilled test tube makes the floating worm get closer.

The theoretical and methodological shortcomings encountered in the Aesop's fable-inspired studies are not unique to the paradigm. Instead, they exemplify many of the pitfalls that appear with surprising regularity in comparative and animal cognition. As we diligently sifted through recent research in comparative cognition in that seminar back in 2014, time and time again we found researchers presenting clever experimental designs purporting to demonstrate some new cognitive ability—complete with a bevy of sometimes very odd (i.e., irrelevant) control conditions. The researchers would proceed to employ a rich interpretation of the behaviors that went far beyond those warranted by the experiment. The fact that there were so many poorly designed studies and lapses in critical thinking was disheartening—so much so, that we began to keep a running list of "Fundamental Obstacles in a Valid Science of Comparative Cognition" that detailed some of the same pitfalls we encountered repeatedly in our readings.

When we first read the Aesop's fable experiment, we were just starting to learn about the rules of the game of publishing and surviving in academia. In the years that have passed since then, we worked on our meta-analysis while working hard to finish our own doctoral research with preschoolers and to secure grant funding for our postdoctoral experiences. We have had a lot of time to think about how individual researchers (including ourselves) struggle to shape this game. And now, as we both start to establish new lines of developmental research and navigate our increasing scientific independence, we see how this project has sharpened our focus on things that have concerned us all along: How do we manage the need for objectivity in our science with the need to be a complete academic—to tell a good story about our research, to raise money to run our labs? How do we make our work stand out from the background? Why do some findings rise to the top? Faced with these challenges, will we have the courage to see limitations in our own research? We hope our work on the Aesop's Fable Paradigm constitutes a first step in the right direction.

That being said, we also see a larger, cautionary tale unfolding—namely, the dangers of humans' folk narratives becoming embedded into scientific storytelling. Aesop's fable is the most obvious example, but the fact that an alternative explanation for the results of such a widely heralded set of studies has been largely overlooked, leads us to wonder just how much of science is being driven by the need to tell good stories. We wonder whether or not the story used to frame the findings is more culturally important in codifying findings into the scientific canon than the quality of the methods used to obtain those findings. We wonder whether turning to folktales and fables for inspiration is a reasonable way to advance science. And finally, we still wonder exactly how the fable-turned-science has risen to the top.

No fable ends without its moral, and as with many fables, the moral of our meta-fable is variable. Variants might include: Crows are as smart as lever-pressing rats. Twenty-eight crows as smart as lever-pressing rats do not a good story make. Even if a chimpanzee sitting at a typewriter might eventually hack out a line of Shakespeare, crows will never drop enough stones to produce *The Tempest*.

Washington University
St. Louis

University of Chicago
Chicago

University of Louisiana
Lafayette

Acknowledgments

It is an important tradition among scientists to acknowledge any applicable funding sources that support our research and our writing. Laura Hennefield's work was supported by NIH training grants T32 MH100019 and F32 HD093273.

Notes

1. This interest has come from both directions. From the standpoint of those studying animals, consider the closing paragraph of Wolfgang Köhler's 1917 landmark monograph regarding chimpanzee intelligence:

> One would like to have a standard for the achievements of intelligence described here by comparing with our experiments the performances of human beings (sick and well) and, above all, human children of different ages. As the results in this book have special reference to a particular method of testing and the special test-material of optically-given situations, the psychological facts established in human beings (especially children), under the same conditions, would have to be used. But such comparisons cannot be instituted, as, very much to the disadvantage of psychology, not even the most necessary facts of this sort have been ascertained. Preliminary experiments—some have been mentioned—have given me the impression that we are inclined to over-estimate the capabilities of children of all ages up to maturity, and even adults, who have had no special technical training in this type of performance. We are in a region of *terra incognita*.... As experiments of this kind can be performed at the very tenderest age, and are certainly as scientifically valuable as the intelligence tests usually employed, it does not matter so much if they do not become immediately practicable for school and other uses. M. Wertheimer has been expressing this view for some years in his lectures; in this place, "where the lack of human standards makes itself so much felt, I should like to emphasize particularly the importance and—if the anthropoids do not deceive us—the fruitfulness of further work in this direction." ([1917] 1925, 268)

From the perspective of the child psychologist, there is no better early report than Lightner Witmer's report of his investigations of a chimpanzee named Peter, who Witmer was able to examine in his Boston clinic after seeing him perform in a traveling Vaudeville show. Although initially skeptical, Witmer opens his report with great optimism:

> Since that day I have seen Peter in five public performances, have tested him at my Psychological Clinic at the University of Pennsylvania, and privately on three occasions. I now believe that in a very real sense the animal is himself giving the stage performance. He knows what he is doing, he delights in it, he varies it from time to time, he understands the succession of tricks which are being called for, he is guided by word of mouth without any signal open or concealed, and the function of his trainer is exercised mainly to steady and control. (1909, 182)

But Witmer ends his report on a decidedly ambiguous note:

> Peter's activity is not the result of mere animal spirits; he is mentally alert and possessed of unusual power of concentration, not merely for an animal but for a child of his own age.... [However] even though we may grant a fair prospect in the direction of intellectual development, we must assume from our present knowledge of men and apes that Peter is and will remain morally imbecile. It would be a nightmare flight of the imagination to suppose that an ape could acquire a will determined consciously by moral motives. [His owners] claim that no one really knows how intelligent Peter is and they appear to believe that Peter excels the human being in quickness of action, thought and comprehension. If they are right, Peter should become the ward of science and be subjected to proper educational influences. He has been trained, he is partly educated, but no effort has yet been made to give him what an education really stands for. I venture to predict that within a few years chimpanzees will be taken early in life and subjected for purposes of scientific investigation to a course of procedure more closely resembling that which is accorded the human child. (1909, 203–5)

2. For a short review of tool use in animals, including a pointed discussion of the current controversies surrounding tool use in comparative cognition and citations to original research, we recommend Amanda Seed and Richard Byrne's "Animal Tool-Use" (2010).

3. The studies actually involve a variety of birds from the Corvidae, a taxonomic family that includes rooks, jays, and crows. For simplicity sake, throughout this article we colloquially refer to them all as "crows."

4. Throughout this essay, we use the term "sand" as a general term to cover this variant of the task. In some cases sand was used, in other cases sawdust or wood chips were used.

5. In their original *Current Biology* article, Bird and Emery suggest that the rapid learning and efficient solutions demonstrated by rooks provide evidence that rooks solve "complex physical problems via causal and analogical reasoning" (2009, 1410). A subsequent article by Taylor and colleagues seemed to temper this claim by suggesting that the "crows' performances were not based on associative learning alone" (2011, 1). More recently, Jelbert and colleagues stated in their abstract that "results indicate that New Caledonian crows possess a sophisticated, but incomplete, understanding of the causal properties of displacement, rivaling that of 5–7 year old children" (2014, 1).

6. Specific formulations of the special nature of the tests—that is, what sets them apart from nearly a century's worth of preceding studies on animal learning—are difficult to work out from the articles. However, several of the researchers do briefly touch on this topic. Taylor et al. suggest the paradigm measures whether subjects "can process causal information" (2011, 1). Likewise, Jelbert et al. state that the paradigm can be used to investigate whether the subjects understand "causal regularities" (2014, 2). Unfortunately such descriptions are of limited use because phrases such as "process causal information" and "understanding causal regularities" do not define the underlying processes in question, nor do they elucidate why this test is more suited to measure these abilities than the hundreds (if not thousands) of others that comparative psychologists have devised over the past century.

7. Possibly less important in humanities and social-science disciplines, an impact factor is a score assigned to academic peer-reviewed journals that reflects the number of citations, relative to number of articles, for recent articles published in that journal. Impact factor is often used as an indicator of the relative quality and importance of a journal within a given field. In science, publishing "early and often" in journals with high impact factors is considered a measure of career success, with impact factors often considered in hiring and promotion decisions.

8. Most of the studies included in our meta-analysis followed the rough steps of the first Aesop fable experiment published by Bird and Emery (2009). All subjects first underwent a training procedure in which they learned to drop stones into a tube to retrieve a food reward (either a worm or piece of meat). Then, in a majority of the articles, subjects participated in the sand vs. water task, followed by several other task variants.

9. Our decision to restrict inclusion to the members of the Corvidae family— and thus exclude Logan, Harvey, Schlinger, and Rensel's (2015) study with four western scrub jays (not members of Corvidae)—was twofold. First, using the established taxonomic grouping of the biological "family" as our cut-off has face validity—that is, on the surface it seems like a reasonable decision. Second, the western scrub jays were not considered "successful" in the tasks by the authors of the study. Two jays did not learn to drop stones into a tube during the training phase. Of the remaining two jays that "passed" the training, one did not complete the water vs. sand task (possibly because his preference for the sand tube resulted in few rewards and decreasing motivation to continue to drop stones) and the other completed the task but did not exhibit a preference for the water tube. This second point is important because our goal was to try and achieve maximum "buy in" from both reviewers and other researchers. Not only do we want our decisions to *appear* objective, but when faced with decisions that others might find questionable, we aimed to be as conservative as possible in our choices. In other words, if we included the jays, it is quite possible that we would have gotten pushback because the birds are not members of Corvidae. After all, including two birds in our analyses who never showed a preference for the water tube could strengthen our conclusions about the role of learning in these tasks (i.e., the jays simply did not learn), but do not serve to advance a story of "complex cognition" throughout the order of Passeriformes (of which corvids and jays both belong).

10. There were two features of the data in the Aesop's fable tasks that governed our choice of analyses. First, although it is possible to count and add and combine data within and across these tasks, each individual data point is *binary*. For example, in the sand versus water test, the subjects either chose the sand tube (which we can assign a score of 0) or the water tube (score of 1). In the other variants, involving choices between two objects (such as light versus heavy), we could also use this binary coding: object A or object B. Binary data is discrete and thus different from measures that are continuous (consider, variables such as income, age, or the amount of time it takes someone to complete a task. Second, the data points are *not independent*. That is, the same subjects repeatedly performed each behavior and each bird contributed multiple data points to each task (up to one-hundred stone drops per task for some birds). Independence is an assumption that must be met in order to use conventional statistical analyses such as t-tests and ANOVAs. Properties of data—in this case binary and not independent—constrain the analyses that are appropriate to use to test the data. These particular constraints led us to multilevel modeling. Multilevel modeling is typically used when the data is "nested" at more than one level; for example, stone drops were nested within subjects, and subjects were nested within articles. Although we were each familiar with this statistical technique, neither of us were experts, so we recruited the assistance of our colleague, Sara Weston, who has expertise in this area. Sara worked closely with us to build code that produced the models, to help us select which models to include in the meta-analysis, and to create the figures for our manuscript that best captured our key findings.

11. In much the same way that we developed the inclusion criteria to select the five articles that we used in the meta-analysis we also developed inclusion criteria to determine which tasks within each article to include in the analyses. We used a fairly minimal inclusion criteria here to retain as much data as possible—namely that the task had to involve water (displacement) and a binary choice. These criteria yielded a total of ten tasks across the five articles. Only a handful of tasks were excluded, and these excluded tasks each appeared only once across the articles and did not clearly relate to the broad topic of water displacement (e.g., one involved the use of an arbitrary reward; another was a tube-search task).

12. We had our undergraduate students double-enter the data from the original grids in the published Aesop's fable articles. Each data point was entered twice (by two different students), both blind to the hypotheses of the study, and then the data points were checked for consistency. We found agreement to be extremely high (Cohen's Kappa = 0.985; the score for perfect consistency would be 1), and the few discrepancies were resolved by one of us.

13. Hennefield and Hwang contributed equally to this manuscript.

14. Although it was a bit disheartening to discover they had published a meta-analysis on the same topic as the one we had been working on for several years, we feel a sort of camaraderie with Ghirlanda and Lind (2017) through our mutual skepticism of the claims put forth by the Aesop's fable researchers. In fact, we had not known about their meta-analysis until it was brought to our attention by a journal editor upon the submission of an initial version of our manuscript. It is true, our meta-analysis was a side-project, and perhaps if we had spent more time earlier on with it we could have been the first to publish. It was also mildly frustrating that after carefully preparing our original manuscript (again, not knowing that Ghirlanda and Lind were simultaneously thinking about similar ideas) we had to subsequently revamp large portions of the introduction and discussion to account for their findings and more clearly elucidate what sets our work apart from theirs. However, it is likely that this revision has served both to clarify and strengthen our arguments, and is just one the many types of stumbling blocks that we have learned to handle in our budding careers.

15. For an applicable discussion of the replicability crisis, see Pashler and Harris (2012). They identify three arguments of central importance to the replicability crisis: 1) the prevalence of false-positive findings in the scientific literature, 2) the costs and benefits of direct replications versus conceptual replications, and 3) the notion that the scientific process is self-correcting and erroneous findings will eventually get weeded out. For a discussion of the intersection between replication and falsification, we suggest Earp and Trafimow (2015).

16. Quote by Robert J. Sternberg, Professor of Human Development at Cornell University, on the back cover of *The Compleat Academic: A Career Guide* (2004).

17. Karl Popper (1935) famously argued against the classical approach toward science that seeks to prove theories or hypotheses (such as "all swans are white"). He argued that it is logically impossible to prove a hypothesis from individual cases: "no matter how many instances of white swans we may have observed, this does not justify the conclusion that all swans are white." ([1935] 2002, 4). However, if we can find that one single swan that is not white, deductive logic allows the conclusion that the hypothesis of "all swans are white" is false. Popper argued that the goal of science should therefore be attempts at falsifying hypotheses and emphasized the importance of reproducibility of experiments and observation. Ultimately, he argued for considering reproducibility necessary for observations to be admitted as sound evidence in science.

REFERENCES CITED

Bird, Christopher D., and Nathan J. Emery. 2009. "Rooks use Stones to Raise the Water Level to Reach a Floating Worm." *Current Biology* 19 (16): 1410–14.

Earp, Brian D., and David Trafimow. 2015. "Replication, Falsification, and the Crisis of Confidence in Social Psychology." *Frontiers in Psychology* 6: article 621.

Ghirlanda, Stefano, and Johan Lind. 2017. "'Aesop's Fable' Experiments Demonstrate Trial-and-Error Learning in Birds, but no Causal Understanding." *Animal Behaviour* 123: 239–47.

Hennefield, Laura, Hyesung G. Hwang, Sara J. Weston, and Daniel J. Povinelli. 2018. "Meta-Analytic Techniques Reveal That Corvid Causal Reasoning in the Aesop's Fable Paradigm Is Driven by Trial-and-Error Learning." *Animal Cognition*. 21 (6): 735–48. doi.org/10.1007/s10071-018-1206-y.

Jelbert, Sarah A., Alex H. Taylor, Lucy G. Cheke, Nicola S. Clayton, and Russell D. Gray. 2014. "Using the Aesop's Fable Paradigm to Investigate Causal Understanding of Water Displacement by New Caledonian Crows." *PLoS ONE* 9 (3): e92895.

Köhler, Wolfgang. [1917] 1925. *The Mentality of Apes*. Translated by Ella Winter. New York: Harcourt.

Logan, Corina J., Brigit D. Harvey, Barney A. Schlinger, and Michelle Rensel. 2015. "Western Scrub-Jays Do Not Appear to Attend to Functionality in Aesop's Fable Experiments." *PeerJ* 4: e1707.

Pashler, Harold, and Christine R. Harris. 2012. "Is the Replicability Crisis Overblown? Three Arguments Examined." *Perspectives on Psychological Science* 7 (6): 531–36.

Popper, Karl. 2002. *The Logic of Scientific Discovery*. 2nd ed. New York: Routledge.

Taylor, Alex H., Douglas M. Elliffe, Gavin R. Hunt, Nathan J. Emery, Nicola S. Clayton, and Russell D. Gray. 2011. "New Caledonian Crows Learn the Functional Properties of Novel Tool Types." *PLoS ONE* 6 (12): e26887.

Seed, Amanda, and Richard Byrne. 2010. "Animal Tool-Use." *Current Biology* 20 (23): R1032–R1039.

Witmer, Lightner. 1909. "A Monkey with a Mind." *The Psychological Clinic* 3 (7): 179205.

LAURA HENNEFIELD is a postdoctoral scholar in the Department of Psychological and Brain Sciences and the Department of Psychiatry at Washington University in St Louis. Her current research focuses on the development of optimism in preschoolers, including how optimism affects how children learn from and about the world around them, neural correlates of optimism, and how a lack of optimism may contribute to psychopathology in early childhood. (lhennefield@wustl.edu).

HYESUNG GRACE HWANG is a postdoctoral fellow in the Department of Psychology at University of Chicago. Her research investigates the development of social discrimination and exclusion by examining how infants and children learn to categorize and view people based on race and language, the impact of racial and linguistic diversity on development, and the neural mechanism behind the preference for one's own social group. (hyesung@uchicago.edu)

DANIEL J. POVINELLI is Professor of Biology at the University of Louisiana at Lafayette. His primary interests center on the characterizations of the higher-order cognitive functions in great apes and humans. He is the author of *Folk Physics for Apes: The Chimpanzee's Theory of How theWorld Works* (2000) and *World without Weight: Perspectives on an Alien Mind* (2011). (povinelli@louisiana.edu)

K. BRANDON BARKER AND DANIEL J. POVINELLI

ANTHROPOMORPHOMANIA AND THE RISE OF THE ANIMAL MIND
A Conversation

Abstract: The conversation that follows concerns patterns of thinking. Comparative psychologist Daniel Povinelli, in conversation with folklorist Brandon Barker, argues that certain anthropomorphizing notions have impeded scientists' attempts to answer these questions: How are animals and humans the same? How are animals and humans different? This conversation supplements other considerations of the Aesop's Fable Paradigm in this special issue by articulating the perspective of an insider to both the science and the culture of comparative psychology, animal cognition, and their related disciplines.

Anthropomorphism in the Science of Animal Minds

Daniel J. "Danny" Povinelli became infatuated with chimpanzees very early. As a high school student searching for some far-reaching mystery to ponder while researching in the library for his role on the debate team, he came across the psychologist Gordon G. Gallup Jr.'s now famous mirror self-recognition (MSR) studies with chimpanzees. Gallup's MSR studies, Povinelli learned, involved the presentation of a chimpanzee's self-image in a mirror after rouge or a sticker had been surreptitiously placed on the animal's face.[1] The central claim of those studies was that chimpanzees who could use mirrors to investigate their own bodies must have some form of self-awareness—not unlike humans. The search for self-awareness in mirror-gazing chimps constituted Povinelli's first encounter with the search for the boundaries of human distinctiveness in nonhuman animals. As a matter of fact, Gallup's work affected young Povinelli so deeply that he led a charge to liberate all captive chimpanzees, recruiting his high-school debate teammates into a grassroots organization of Povinelli's own making: The Liberate the Chimps Society—LTCS!

In some ways, the LTCS was much more than a teenage infatuation. Povinelli has, after all, spent more than three decades experimentally investigating chimpanzees and human children. But he has come to think about the mirrors in Gallup's MSR studies quite differently. Back then, at the genesis of the LTCS, he did not see that those mirrors—Gallup's investigatory implement of choice—were really just another reflection of the scientific search for humanness in nonhuman animals. They constituted yet another example of a cadre of projective questions in the science of animal minds: Do animals have language? Do they use tools? Do they possess a theory of mind? Do they dance? Make war? Love? Do animals tell jokes? Play games? Trick each other? Suffer grief? Know beauty? Get religion? The list goes on and on. Folklorists will recognize the historicity of these questions and their inherent search for humanness in animal "others" as an intellectual survival of sorts, an outgrowth of nineteenth-century theories of biological evolution. Povinelli referred to this history in the abstract for his presentation, which was a part of our original panel concerning the Aesop's Fable experiments, at the American Folklore Society's Annual Conference in Miami, Florida (2016):

> Since Darwin's publication of *The Descent of Man* (1871), the assumption of mental continuity between humans and other species has deeply infected the study of animal cognition. Any ability present in humans is asserted to exist, at least to some extent, in other species. Insistence on mental continuity has limited scientists' experimental methods and muddled the interpretations of data that emerge from them.

The mention of survivals and of evolutionary theories might also call forth, for folklorists, historical reminders of our own pitfalls, represented by such pejorative terms as *anthropocentrism* or *adultocentrism*— both constituting methodological and philosophical problems of projection. That being said, the assumption of mental continuity across species skews more than our understanding of other animals; the assumption lessens our awareness of that which makes humans uniquely human.

Povinelli and his coresearchers argue that only humans reason via higher-order, theory-like relational abstractions such as space, time, intentions, ghosts, god, and weight. The latter abstraction, weight (as it exists as a part of human psychology), can be easily brought to mind. Our higher-order theories of weight affect our behavior. For example, we understand that the felt perception of a heavy object (compared to the felt perception of a lighter object) is deeply connected to the heavier object's relative usefulness for holding down a stack of papers, for throwing through an abandoned window, for hurling at an unwanted intruder, or for smashing open a thick walnut shell. Humans instinctually abstract from these disparate perceptual scenarios a theory of how weight functions in the world. While chimps and some other nonhuman animals can and do behave in goal-directed ways that afford them "success" in some of these scenarios (e.g., successfully lifting heavy objects or successfully cracking nuts), animals are not successful in these tasks because they wield a higher-order concept of weight. Instead, the animal's achieve their goals via mental processes operating at the level of first-order, perceptual variables, without the necessity for, or dependency upon, higher- order theories. Animals—even impressively intelligent animals like chimpanzees, elephants, dogs, and crows—do not, necessarily, act the way they act and do the things they do for the same reasons as humans. Thus, crows can fly, but they will never build skyscrapers. Yes, they excel at vocally mimicking sounds from their environment (including human words), but they do not carry on conversations. They can be trained to drop stones into a beaker of water in order to retrieve a food reward, but they will never create and share fables.[2]

The difficult task facing animal studies, Povinelli argues, is not convincing ourselves that we can find evidence of humanness in them. Doing that, it turns out, is easy. Anthropomorphism, like ethnocentrism or adultocentrism, comes easily. The difficult task is finding the will to look more critically into apparent similarities and more honestly at observable differences. In lieu of mirrors in MSR protocols, Povinelli now focuses on metaphorical mirrors: the animals we turn into mirrors when, for example, our experiments reflect folk narratives.

A Conversation with Daniel J. Povinelli and K. Brandon Barker

KBB: It is striking—an Aesop's Fable being used as a prompt for experimental design. You have said that these kinds of frames say more about the current culture of scientists working on animal cognition than they do about the animals. What do you mean when you say that?

DJP: Oh, for sure. So various birds including corvids will pick up walnuts and other nuts and drop them to crack them open as they are flying around. Or the birds will pick up stones and drop them on mollusks' shells to try to crack them open. And that's pretty impressive, right? Now, without the frame of an Aesop's Fable, did anybody suggest that when a bird drops a stone from that high, and it hits a mollusk shell and cracks it open, that the birds have any theory of the connection between force and the acceleration of mass?

The answer is no. But when the endpoint of their training involves stone-dropping behavior that supposedly actualizes a well-known folk narrative, suddenly the behavior is evidence of a human-like, higher-order understanding of the physics of water displacement.

KBB: Here is the description of the end-point training effect as you described it in *World without Weight*:

End-point training effect: The similarity between human and ape behavior produced as the result of training can be so emotionally striking that it overwhelms the skepticism that might otherwise be generated by the knowledge that it took dozens, hundreds, or even thousands of trials to achieve it. (2012, 343)[3]

Can you say more about this effect?

DJP: My awareness of the end-point training effect as an overarching challenge to objectively studying animal cognition started quite early in my career, although the significance of it only grew very gradually in my mind. But the fact that it was going to be a big challenge? I remember it distinctly dawning on me, even though it didn't strongly influence my work yet.

I was in graduate school, and a couple of my fellow graduate students—one in archaeology and another in sociocultural anthropology—decided the students needed to publish a journal, *The Yale Graduate Journal of Anthropology* . . . or something like that. And this is around 1986, 1987. So they went around soliciting papers from us, and I said, "Yeah sure, I've got a little something I've worked on for one of my graduate classes." It was a forward-looking prospectus of the kind of research I wanted to do—that is, comparing apes who recognize themselves in mirrors and are maybe self-aware (you know, Gallup's mirror theory), to monkeys who don't recognize themselves in mirrors, and who, according to Gallup's theory, are not self-aware. So my article was outlining the experiments that I was going to do for my dissertation, a broad overview of the different kinds of experiments. I gave a copy of this article to a senior graduate student, Todd Preuss, who was working with monkeys, becoming a neuroscientist. Todd said, "You know, this is really great, Danny. This is really great. I can't believe you're going to be doing all this work, this is great." And then he said, "But, you know, I think you better loosen up a little bit on the criteria you've got down here where you seem to be suggesting that if the animals solve this test correctly on the first, on trial one, that means they have these higher-order abilities (theory of mind, self-awareness, et cetera). But if they don't pass on trial one, then the animals don't have these higher-order abilities. I think you better make some room for . . . I mean, trial one is pretty demanding."

And I thought well, "What are we going to do? Use trial two or three or ten?" And I mean, I was driven. I wasn't in graduate school to become a professor. I just wanted to do these experiments. I just wanted to work with chimps and do all this creative experimental stuff. I thought, I can't be spending all this time sorting this out. Trial one would be the most important data point. Anything after that could just be trial and error learning. Rats pressing levers. But the question Todd raised became a pebble in my shoe, and that little pebble in my shoe, as time went on, started cutting both ways. The first one was the way Todd meant it. That, well, you know, it might take even a really smart chimp three or four trials to catch on. And doesn't mean that they don't understand higher-order theory of mind or empathy the way you or I do. But, it cut the other way too. I realized that, even if the subject solves the tasks on trial one, I could never really rule out some alternative theories about what the apes or monkeys or children had already learned—before being in my tests—about the ways people and other animals interact and behave, things they had already learned that they could be using to solve my little task. In other words, they had already had lots of trial ones! Slowly I began to realize what was going on in these experiments wasn't going to be, by itself, diagnostic of the higher-order abilities I was after.

To illustrate the problem, I remember a few years after opening my own chimpanzee laboratory, I put together a videotape of my apes doing a bunch of amazing things and then used the video when I gave academic and public talks. The tape showed trial after trial of the chimps solving amazing tool-using problems. So, a chimp would come in, it would be a hook stick versus a straight stick, for example, and they'd pick up the hook stick and use it to hook something in a precise way when only the hook stick would work. Or, there would be a little hole, and they'd pick up the stick that would fit through the hole and not the one with all of the little prongs on it that couldn't fit through. Or, somebody would show the chimp a floppy tool, and then a rigid tool. The chimp would correctly pick the rigid tool immediately without fooling around with the other one, et cetera, et cetera, trial after trial after trial. But then I would tell the audience, "I don't like to show videos at my talks because, depending on how you edit them, you can tell any story you want." And then I'd show, in reverse order, the chimps going through the same tests, but now all the early trials, over and over, the same tests, over and over and over again, with the chimps picking all the wrong answers, appearing to be fumbling about blindly.

The whole point of this video was, sure, if you get the chimps to a point of competence, they behave just like you or I would. And if I were to test you and then ask you why you're doing it, you'd come up with some explanation, which may or may not be true. Your explanation may or may not be related to the causal factors that determine whether or not you pick up the short stick or the long stick, but you definitely have a theory about it, so you report that theory, that story. And of course we humans do have those kind of theories, or those kind of broad, higher-order explanatory frameworks that we can leverage when we get into a sticky wicket. But if I take an ape, and I train it to some endpoint, and then I just show you that, well, what do you make of the history that brought him or her to that point? Do you think it's relevant somehow? If you do, you might be dismissive and say, "Oh, the apes just *learned* that." But, the argument is powerful both ways. What do you mean they just learned it? Humans learned it, too. Are you saying just because they learned it, they don't understand it? And, conversely, what about the fact that it might take them five trials, ten trials . . . or fifty to have learned it? Let's just pick a number. Say, a dozen trials doing the kookiest things, even though they're fully competent adult chimpanzees, and even though they have a lot of experience with other, similar situations. Does that not mitigate against the idea that the chimps are wielding some higher-order, explanatory ability? See? It cuts both ways.

So that little pebble that Todd put in my shoe when I was in graduate school thirty years ago, has only grown bigger. It's become a fundamental organizing challenge to understanding animal minds that I still don't think we know how to solve. What is our theory that tells us if the animals do it in three trials, they have access to human-like higher-order cognitive frameworks, but if it takes twenty trials, well then, no, they don't? Do we have some kind of cognitive theory that can really tell us that, in the abstract? I don't see one. I think it's a fundamental problem pressing against the heart of comparative psychology. Every time the discipline turns a little bit, I think that thorn punctures its heart and drains the blood out of the whole organism of comparative psychology. It's an Achilles heel for 99.9 percent of these kinds of studies in comparative psychology.

Take a crow, for example, and give it a straight wire. The crow has to stick the wire inside a tube to fish out a little basket with a handle that has been put in the bottom of a test tube, a little glass tube. They've got to stick that wire down there and hook the mini Easter basket to get their eggs, which in this case are mealworms. Well okay, the crow sticks the wire in there, fiddles around, steps on the wire, bends it, and then eventually after, I don't know, thirty seconds, a minute, two minutes (it varies), the crow has bent the wire and hooked the Easter basket, and they get the mealworms. Well, okay, how often do animals bend things— especially birds twisting pretty detailed nests? It's one of the things they do the most with an object like that. And when they stick the wire in the test tube, it bends a little bit, and the Easter basket moves a little bit. So, they pull it out and bend it a little bit more and it moves a little bit more. Then they hook it, and they get it. Was that one trial? How do we divide up the behavior? Is that one trial? And even if somebody wants to call it one trial, how do we divide up the behavior as arbitrarily defined as one trial by the comparative psychologist? What are all the infinitesimally small steps that led up to that successful action—the endpoint of the animal being able to do it—and come in the next time and be able to do it a little faster and a little sooner, and after that even more faster and sooner?

This goes straight back to Wolfgang Köhler's ideas about "insight." What he called insight was the phase-like transition from one behavioral form to another. He was looking at a situation in which the ape is blindly fumbling around with the wooden crates. Then, the ape goes sit; then suddenly comes back over, stacks the crates (or whatever the task requires) perfectly. Köhler was looking for insight, big transitions, phase transitions. That is when Köhler would go, "Aha, that's evidence of insight!" See, even in the early parts of the twentieth century, Köhler knew that to call it insight—which was a very technical term in his mind—wasn't to say that chimps have the kind of higher-order relational kind of mind humans have—that they have an understanding of space or gravity or time at a higher-order level. What Köhler was saying was that whatever perceptual representations the chimps have in their head, they're reorganized to fit together in a smooth function, and then the ape is then able to go do it, go stitch together little units of action it already has in its behavioral tool-kit and execute the new composite behavior smoothly. But he knew the endpoint positive evidence, the "insightful behavioral transitions," could not tell us whether the chimps had a theory of gravity, a theory of mind, or some other theory like that.[4]

KBB: So in the past, stone-dropping-type behaviors in crows had not been interpreted as evidence of higher-order cognition. If the endpoint-training effect is one reason, are there others?

DJP: Definitely! One other reason, I think, is that the crows in the experiments are constrained in a human-like, controlled environment. I mean, a glass tube, a water vessel—what could say *science* more than a standing test tube with liquid in it? And by the way, I'm not criticizing. The scientists constrained the ways the animals could learn. That's what we do. Their apparatus, the test tube with the water in it, and the glass box with the flapping platform that they used to initially train the crows, it all made sense. Incrementally, it all makes perfect sense. But when you put an animal in that context—that human-like context when you have a stone and a test tube—there's really only three things that can happen: 1) nothing, the crow can just hop around, or 2) the crow can drop the stone outside the test tube, or 3) the crow can drop the stone inside the test tube.

And I want to explain to you, at a very personal level, why I reacted so strongly to these studies. I'm sure I would have reacted pretty strongly to any study of an Aesop's Fable in animal cognition, but this particular study really got to me, and for the following reason. I had spent five years—actually over ten at that point—working on very similar ape physics problems.[5] Call us obtuse, call us pedantic—you know, maybe some positive epitaphs too . . . patient? But we kept doing systematic variations on every experiment in order to pit some plausible alternatives against each other. We were rigorously testing for higher-order abilities, but we didn't do experiments that said, "Oh look, we gave them a blue stick and they used that to fish in a banana. So now let's see how smart they are; let's give them a yellow stick and see if they can still do it." I don't know what theory would tell you the chimp, or some other animal, would not solve it with the yellow stick. What possible theory would that be? I don't understand that. The chimps thought that yellowness was contacting the banana? Color? No, it's the extended form, it's the perceptual projection of the length of the stick on the retina. That's why they pick the long one and not the short one. That's why they learn to do that. And so, when you change the color of the long stick . . . well, that was never relevant to their initial learning anyhow. We—very purposefully—didn't do things like that.

And, okay, so what did we conclude? What are the bedrock principles that govern the chimps' behaviors? Those principles are certainly not about unobservable, higher-order theories about how the world works. They're first-order, perceptual principles. Especially *physical contact* between objects. Chimps and other animals are very sensitive to perceptual contact between objects. Contact seemed to be their bedrock principle—making one thing, a stick, contact another things, an out-of-reach apple. Now, they learn more than that—relationships among perceptual forms more than that. For example, they might learn "Oh, actually, place the tool *behind* the banana, and then make contact." But, even these instances are silent with respect to whether or not the chimps have any idea of *force* or related theoretical phenomena. The bedrock principle is contact. That is what the chimpanzee starts with. This is a primitive operator in their perceptual-action system. It's about contact. When they are trying to get an object, they're trying to get one implement to make contact with another, just like they would with their hand. If they can do that, they are going to ignore a lot of other perceptual information they might otherwise attend to. Contact is so primitive and so bedrock that it sucks the animals in, causing them to make all kinds of mistakes early on that seem ridiculous from a human perspective.

Here's an example that we first looked at in *Folk Physics*. We presented the chimps with two towels stretching away from them and gave the chimps the option to pull one or the other towel in order to retrieve an apple. In one scenario, an apple was resting on top of one of the towels and another apple was resting on the floor close to the second towel, but not touching it. In this situation, the chimps had no problem grabbing and pulling the correct towel to retrieve the apple. But when we changed the scenario just slightly, and had the apple resting on the floor but *touching* the second towel, the chimps pulled the second towel just as frequently as the first towel. They didn't intuitively grasp the obvious connection between the apple's weight and why pulling the first towel is the only way to retrieve the apple.

So, what do we have in these Aesop's Fable studies? We have a crow, who sticks his beak inside a test tube, but the worm is too far away to make contact with it. But if the crow has a stick, it picks up the stick and spears it down in the tube, right? Why? Because they can make contact. And eventually, the crow pulls the worm up. Oh, but now the crow doesn't have a stick, it has a rock. So, what happens when they drop the stone into the tube? Oh, and by the way, the crows have to be taught to drop the stone inside the tube. Well, the stone can make contact with the worm, because the worm's *inside* the tube, not outside of the tube. And when the crows do that, the worm jiggles or comes closer to them.

When I explain this, some people say, "Oh, the worm doesn't move that much closer to them." But think about it like this. I have a chimp and a string and a rope, and the rope is tied to a banana over there, out of reach. Then, I tie another string over here that is not tied to the banana. If the chimp pulls on the connected string a little bit, the banana wiggles. If they pull on the unconnected string, it doesn't wiggle. What do you think the chimps are going to do? Surely chimps are smart enough to keep track of which of their actions make the banana wiggle! I mean, really, what animals couldn't keep track of that? Then some people say, "Okay fine, but the crows don't try to push the stone through the bottom of the glass tube. They actually drop it at the top—furthest away from the worm." Wait, who thinks birds are so dumb that they don't realize that they can't make contact through the glass? I mean, you're seriously saying that the fact that the crows learn that a rock won't pass through glass somehow implies the alternative that they understand the physics of mass and water displacement? I honestly thought we were past that kind of faulty reasoning.

The crow is trying to drop the stone to hit the worm. And when they do, the worm moves closer to them. Or they get the worm to wiggle. And then they repeat the behavior with another stone. How is that any different than the chimp with the string and the banana? But if you ask this question, supporters of scientists running Aesop-Fable-like experiments say, "Hah, you're just a skeptic." Or you're told, "Hey, we're just being neutral. We just want to show what the crows can do."

KBB: This seems to be closely aligned with another cultural pattern you named in *World without Weight*:

Scrub-jay imperative: Any [task which purportedly demonstrates a] cognitive-like phenomenon in one species (read: scrub jays), is an immediate threat to the cognitive integrity of other species (read: apes) until [the ability] is demonstrated in them—regardless of whether [the task] makes any ecological sense whatsoever to other species. (2012, 344)

Does competition between the animals (and consequently between the scientists studying the animals) drive any of this?

DJP: Long before the Aesop's Fable studies, I had been very sensitive to the dynamic with chimps versus orangutans and gorillas, and maybe monkeys a little bit. I knew there were reactions to a perceived chimpocentrism. Somebody would say, "That, what you trained your chimp to do, that's nothing, I can get my orangutan to do that too." Or, "Don't leave out the gorillas." Or even, "Don't leave out my monkeys!" But, once the scrub jays became a thing—at first because of claims these birds had autobiographical-like memories or that they could reason about when another bird was trying to deceive them—a curious thing happened to me. At first, I thought, "Okay, perfect. Now, we can at least start to think more critically about what kinds of behaviors could ever really provide evidence of higher-order cognitive abilities. I mean, if we just want to understand chimps the way we understand leopards, or ants, or gazelles, that's one thing, right? But, if we're aiming toward some understanding of their cognitive economy that we are then trying to really distinguish from human cognitive economies, that's a totally different enterprise. So I was thinking, "Great, as soon as people learn that the crows and scrub jays can do exactly what the chimps are doing, and maybe even doing it faster or more accurately, maybe we can finally make some progress." I thought we would start to recognize, "Okay, so these kinds of experiments don't have anything to do with the evidence of higher-order thinking that we are after." Or, at least, I thought we could begin to try to specify how the scrub jay's reasoning relates to the higher-order processes we are trying to understand in humans. But that's not what happened at all. Instead, people said, "Our crows do something nobody's ever shown in chimps, or they do it faster, or whatever, so we have better evidence with the crows than you do with your chimps." Totally ignoring the fact that the evidence with the chimps wasn't diagnostic of higher-order reasoning in the first place. No, see all of those studies are operating on the basis of intuitive folk theories that we humans have come up with to explain our own behavior. In other words, those tests aren't diagnostic for *human* higher-order abilities any more than they are for the chimps or crows.

KBB: So, we are still trying to understand how higher-order mental processes like theories about weight, water displacement, of theory of mind affect human behavior?

DJP: So, yes exactly... precisely. Let me just elaborate a little bit on it. I'm not denying that we have—to use an analogy—I'm not denying that we have keys that can solve puzzles involving opening up locked boxes or figuring out our own and others' inner psychology. I'm not denying that some of our keys are of that type. We have some keys that represent people's wicket safes, so to speak—keys allow us to open the boxes of our own and other people's minds. Hence, those keys affect our behavior. We can figure out, "Oh, I get it. Brandon *believes* this. Now wait, why's he doing that? Oh, he must *feel* this way." And somehow those keys are causally related to things that we actually *do*. I'm not denying that. What I am denying is that our folk theories are a good way to know which of all the different types of keys—our human higher-order representational keys, as well as the perceptually-based keys that we share in common with animals—we are using in any given situation. It's as if we're blind, fumbling around with all these keys and then... boom, the box unlocks. Then we say, well, how did I do that? And when we search into the contents of our consciousness for an answer, the only keys we can really see—or at least the sexiest ones—are in the language economy. These are the higher-order keys and boxes, such as the components of our explanatory narrative: "Oh, I did that because I *thought* he was *feeling* such-and-such." Now, look, I'm not saying we didn't use a key like that in that example. But, I'm saying we're pretty much blind unless it's really effortful, from the ground up, problem solving. When Einstein sits down and starts postulating four-dimensional space-time, he's wielding—with a lot of time and with great effort—some of these higher-order keys. When couples are having a discussion, you know, about whether they love each other or not, they get tangled up in all that. They're explicitly wielding these keys. But in that case, how does the lovers' higher-order key wielding connect to what they actually do? How does it fit into the causal steps—the smooth, or even erratic, shape of their behavior? That's what I'm saying is pretty opaque.

And this is very difficult to communicate. On the one hand, to deny that we know exactly the causal effects of those keys on our everyday behavior, or even in some test, is not to deny that they actually do have a causal effect on our behavior. It is to say, "Look, it's really, really complicated even for humans. You think having a crow drop a stone in a tube to get a worm is going to answer the same question for a crow?"

KBB: Let me see if I can rephrase what you're saying. If a human were to do something that seems like the human is doing it because the human has a theory of time or gravity or some other theory, that may or may not be true? There are gaps in the scientific understanding of human and animal cognition on both sides affecting comparative psychology?

DJP: You know, narratives... a couple decades ago, I started writing a paper called "On Naturalizing Narrative." I started playing around with an idea a little bit that lots of people have thought through really carefully.[6] The questions I had in mind were these: What are explanations for? And, how do explanations fit into storytelling? And in particular, how do things like theory of mind and references to mental states fit together in the mental worlds that narratives create? We started doing some experiments comparing chimps and children in situations where humans would naturally search for explanations about why an unexpected phenomenon occurred. And I remember when it dawned on me: An ape could never tell a story, out loud or even in its head.

KBB: When?

DJP: Well, it was in the late nineties when I was writing up all the results from our first big set of tool-using studies, the folk physics studies, and I put a little vignette, a little thought experiment, at the end of the book. And I was like, you know even something as simple as the story about "Why did the chicken cross the road?" The little kid will come up with a million explanations for why. They may or may not understand the joke related to it, but they can come up with a narrative-like answer: "Oh, because his mom was lonely and she had to go over there." Or, "Her daughter chicken was over there, her little chicken was over there, she needed to go be near her." Any explanation under the sun. And then it occurred to me that, wait, what if chimps do not have these higher-order abilities, these explanatory frameworks, at all? Their answer to why did the chicken cross the road, would be, "Yes."

In other words, chimps keep track of—form memories of—all sorts of perceived regularities. They can predict them; they can see them and hear them, notice them. The regularities of experience are vital to them in the sense that they have important consequences for what is going to happen. They can even be curious and do things that gather information about those regularities. And so do we, we notice all those same things. Well, not exactly the same things—what any species notices and keeps track of perceptually is going to be different, say the difference between what a tick or bee or a monkey of human keeps track of. So for both of us—chimps and humans—those sorts of things, the relationships among all these first-level perceptual representations we form in our heads, are crucially important in driving our behavior. But if we set aside chimps for a minute, there is this other way that humans think, which is tangled up with language somehow, that allows us to do all this other stuff, like telling jokes and creating fables. And, most of the time that is where our minds are, so to speak—in this higher-order explanatory narrative space—so we give explanations and we give them in a narrative form most of the time. But that does not mean that most of the time we really directly see ourselves wielding specific keys and turning specifics locks.

KBB: What was it about being at the end of *Folk Physics* which was so much about tool use, that brought on this question about narrative?

DJP: It really went more like this. At my labs, we started doing all this work on theory of mind, just as a global flare of interest had started on the subject. The more I did that work, however, the more I became convinced that my childhood exuberance about the chimps' mind was not very well grounded in the evidence. And the more I worked with chimps, the more their behavior seemed to be saying, "We have no idea what the hell you're asking us right here." And, in my mind that got tangled up with the problem of the endpoint training effect. Because it took them so long to learn something I thought they would understand instantly—I made the false assumption they couldn't possibly understand it the way I understood it if they had to learn it.

Okay, so as the kind of evidence like that mounted, it began to put a lot of pressure on the folk theories that scientists were using, and most importantly, me. The folk theory I had was, "Oh, well I know how I would do, I know what I would do in that situation, and I know *why* I would do it. And, so if the chimps don't do it, that's because they don't understand it the way I do." But then I started realizing that there was a problem for all of us working in the field. Well, for everyone, really. How do I know why I'm doing what I'm doing—you know . . . the key problem? I'm still talking about the theory of mind research right now. I started wondering about where we could find the causal imprint of the human ability to represent other minds in our behavior, in our free-flowing behavior. I was not trying to think about an experiment. At this point, I was just thinking about everyday interactions. I said, "Well, obviously, we talk about mental states. We talk about unobservable mental phenomenon. So, you know, we *do* represent these things." But still, what about the imprint on our nonverbal behavior?

And I started thinking, "Well maybe, it has to do with building up narrative, stories about other people." You know, so we trade back and forth our impressions of people's dispositions—their mental dispositions. And that's tied up to those people's behavioral dispositions. And, we go offline from social interactions and start building up a linguistic representation of others in terms of mental states— beliefs and desires and emotions—all these things. And that allows us to make shortcuts to determine others' behaviors. I published this—a little tiny little summary of this idea—in a book chapter, called "When Self Met Other." But that book chapter—you know, like all these book chapters in science, I wrote it in 1995, and it wasn't published until 1998, or so.[7] That was in the heyday when we were doing all these tool studies. When I went back to finally look at the proofs of this, when it came out, I read that paragraph, and I realized what we were finding with the tools was analogous with what we were finding in the theory of mind studies. You know, animals just couldn't generalize from one context to another unless it's a perceptual generalization.

I realized at that time that this whole thing might be best captured in terms of a broader framework that was outside of theory of mind. So it occurred to me that the apes—and crows and bees, whoever—have a rich *what*-system. They're actively exploring; their minds and brains are churning away trying to figure out what is around them. They're building up perceptual representations of what *has* happened, and then that's related to what *will* happen, and so in the end that's what motivates their actions. It's a *what*-system. And, it has to be that way—even for humans—sounds, sights, colors, shapes, other organisms, their actions, fruits falling from trees, green fruits taste bitter. All the senses, the sense of touch, all the ways we can go about perceptually representing things that then correlate with what happens next. Hearing a loud lion definitely is predictive of seeing a lion show up. That is a hallmark of a rich *what*-system.

But humans, in addition to having the same kind of *what*-system that chimps have because of our evolutionary similarities—we also evolved a *why*-system that's tied up with natural language, somehow. It was coincident, I speculated, with the evolution of natural language. Now, that was not a very meaningful speculation because I had no thought or specific claim—I didn't side with any of the theories about language, you know, theory of mind or any of these other things. I just noted that, well, what makes humans really different is language. And it probably is no coincidence that it's in language that we talk about these higher-order things—whether it's tools or whether it's mental states. And see that story about the chicken crossing the road and asking the child? Of course, the answer to that question can be about more than mental states. But I began to suspect that even the framework, even the form of having an explanation... a chimp might not have that. Even if they tried to substitute perceptual content into the framework, they do not have a *because*. Things do not happen *because of* another thing. This kind of thing happens, and then this kind of thing happens. This is more likely than that. And we're like that, too. But because we have language, we have this other format, and one of the effects of that are higher-order concepts and these explanatory formats.

Apes wouldn't even have an explanatory format. They form symbolic representations of perceptual content, and they can arrange those things with some degree of flexibility, but there would be no complex, higher-order syntax. There is a weak compositionality about their mental economy. But there's no linguistic framing. All of the things that make language possible, for example, explicitly keeping track of what philosophers call *types* versus *tokens*... For chimps, there's no type *because*, there's no type *why* that they can track in their mental economy. Of course for that matter, there's no *type* mental state, gravity, ghost, and so on and so on.

KBB: Fables that humans tell—at least in their contemporary iterations—are often attached to a moral. It seems interesting and somewhat paradoxical, then, to associate an animal's behavior with a narrative that expresses a moral, which would be understood as a quintessential part of people's *why* and *because* ways of thinking. I mean, necessity is the mother of invention because necessity makes "people" think harder about difficult situations, or it makes people persevere when obvious, old answers do not solve a problem. Either way, this feels like a *because/why* scenario. Why map that onto animal behavior?

DJP: I have lived through this trend, where we think that science should create a sensation of interest or wonder in the general public who are looking at it—a sensation that is about more than just the content of the science. So in this case, the idea, it seems, was to try to explicitly find some cultural frames and stories to package some scientific research into. Then, come up with headlines that say my crows that are smarter than your five-, your seven- year-old child. Come on, because of this Aesop's Fables thing? The enterprise is weirdly inverted: "We're going to give the same test that we invented from an Aesop's Fable to five-year-old children. And look, the fable's actually truer about crows than it is about children!" Brandon, as you've pointed out a million times to me, the fable was never about the cognitive ability of crows dropping stones and a pebble to get the level of the water to rise up. It was never about the cognitive ability of anybody—humans or crows.

So when I first saw that, I was just like, "Okay, it's over." I was already getting out of the field at the time, but I was, like, "Now we're doing Aesop's Fables? Okay, it's over. They're just going through the fables one by one." I was apoplectic because I knew that there was no way to engage intellectually with these arguments. I started calling it *anthropomorphomania*. How can you rationally engage with a mania? When I read the Aesop's Fable experiments, I said, "It's rats pressing levers. That's all this is. It's rats pressing levers and learning that they get a pellet—a Noyes trademark food pellet." I thought, "How did we go this far backwards?" We've returned to rats-pressing-levers-to-get-a-pellet, but now we're wrapping them in the cultural frame of a fable. Just when I thought there was a chance we'd start really exploring the *animal* complexities of the minds of different animals, and stop with the obsessive search for human higher-order abilities—just when I thought we had realized how difficult experimentally addressing those questions about higher-order mental abilities is even in humans—we're back to lever-pressing rats?

Indiana University
Bloomington

University of Louisiana
Lafayette

Notes

1. Gallup (1970) exposed four chimpanzees to their mirror images and reported the emergence of behaviors that included exaggerated facial movements while looking at their image and using their hands and fingers to explore and manipulate otherwise visually inaccessible parts of their bodies (e.g., their noses, eyes, teeth, and anogenital areas). To confirm their apparent ability to recognize the correspondence between their own body and the image in the mirror, Gallup drugged the subjects using one mg/kg phencyclidine hydrochloride (brand name Sernylan, also known as

PCP or angel dust). He then marked their left upper eyebrow and right upper ear, using a bright red, tactile free, odorless dye (Rhodamine B). These regions of the face, along with the specific marking substance, were explicitly chosen so that upon recovery from the PCP the subjects would have no tactile, olfactory, or visual cues that they had been marked. Five to eight hours later, the subjects were observed for thirty minutes. During this thirty-minute control period, the number of times the subjects touched the marked regions of their face was recorded by a human observer. Immediately following this period, the mirror was reintroduced, the subjects were again observed for thirty minutes, and all mark-directed touches were recorded. Gallup reported a substantial increase in touches to the marked regions in the test period compared to the control period.

2. For more complete introductions to Povinelli's core arguments—including accessible explanations of the ways that humans reason vis-à-vis the ways chimpanzees reason—we recommend two articles, "Behind the Ape's Appearance: Escaping Anthropomorphism in the Study of Other Minds" (Povinelli 2004) and "Through a Floppy Tool Darkly: Toward a Conceptual Overthrow of Animal Alchemy" (Povinelli and Penn 2011).

Those interested in Povinelli's technical and experimental work should seek out his books, *Folk Physics for Apes: The Chimpanzee's Theory of How the World Works* (2000) and *World Without Weight: Perspectives on an Alien Mind* (2012). Of course, strong scientific arguments are based upon copious amounts of empirical, experimental data, and the task of considering a large amount of data at once is made easier by the fact that both of these books buck the scientific trend of publishing every experiment as a one-off journal article by gathering many experiments (twenty-seven in *Folk Physics* and thirty-two in *World without Weight*) into a single manuscript in order to make a cohesive and sustained argument.

3. This description of the End-point Training Effect was first published as a "Folk Psychological Challenge to the Objective Study of Ape Intelligence" in Povinelli (2012, 343).

4. See Köhler (1927). For a more complete discussion of Köhler's work on insight, see Povinelli 2000, 75–84.

5. See *Folk Physics for Apes* (2000) and *World without Weight* (2012), also mentioned in the previous note.

6. Consider local character anecdotes for folkloric evidence supporting the notion that people's stories about other people affect our understanding of other people's behavior (e.g., Mullen 1988, 113–29; Cashman 2008, 125–37.)

7. See Povinelli and Prince (1998).

References Cited

Cashman, Ray. 2008. *Storytelling on the Northern Irish Border: Characters and Community.* Bloomington: Indiana University Press.
Gallup, Gordon G. 1970. "Chimpanzees: Self-Recognition." *Science* 167 (3914): 86–87.
Köhler, Wolfgang. 1927. *The Mentality of Apes*, 2nd ed. New York: Vintage Books.
Mullen, Patrick B. 1988. *I Heard the Old Fisherman Say: Folklore of the Texas Gulf Coast.* Logan: Utah State University Press.
Povinelli, Daniel J. 2000. *Folk Physics for Apes: The Chimpanzees Theory of How the World Works.* Oxford: Oxford University Press.
———. 2004. "Behind the Ape's Appearance: Escaping Anthropomorphism in the Study of Other Minds." *Daedalus* 133 (1): 29–41.
———. 2012. *World without Weight: Perspectives on an Alien Mind.* Oxford: Oxford University Press.
Povinelli, Daniel J., and Derek Penn. 2011. "Through a Floppy Tool Darkly: Toward a Conceptual Overthrow of Animal Alchemy." In *Tool Use and Causal Cognition*, edited by Teresa McCormack, Christoph Hoerl, and Stephen Butterfill, 69–104. Oxford: Oxford University Press.

Povinelli, Daniel J., and Christopher Prince. 1998. "When Self Met Other." In *Self-Awareness: Its Nature and Development*, edited by Michel Ferrari and Robert J. Sternberg, 37–107. New York: Guilford Press.

K. BRANDON BARKER is Assistant Professor of Folklore in the Department of Folklore and Ethnomusicology, Indiana University. He teaches and publishes on topics at the intersections of embodied, cognitive processes and folkloric tradition. He is coauthor of the book, *Folk Illusions: Children, Folklore, and Sciences of Perception* (2019) with Claiborne Rice. (barkerbr@indiana.edu).

DANIEL J. POVINELLI is Professor of Biology at the University of Louisiana at Lafayette. His primary interests center on the characterizations of the higher-order cognitive functions in great apes and humans. He is the author of *Folk Physics for Apes: The Chimpanzee's Theory of How the World Works* (2000) and *World without Weight: Perspectives on an Alien Mind* (2011). (povinelli@louisiana.edu).

GREGORY SCHREMPP

FABLING GESTURES IN EXPOSITORY SCIENCE

Abstract: Ranging from pre-Socratic philosophers to contemporary popular science writers, I analyze seven instances in which fable-like scenarios have been utilized in the exposition and/or promotion of philosophy and/or science. I examine the motives and strategies that propel such novel uses of fabling gestures and also explore the ironies and pitfalls that the genre poses when invoked in scientific discourse. For example, one pervasive assumption of the fable genre is that the animal characters are *really humans*; might this genre conceit subtly introduce a bias when a fable-like scenario of animal behavior, such as a crow confronting a pitcher, is examined by animal cognition specialists attempting to understand the relationship of human and nonhuman animal intelligence?

In the last few decades I have been exploring the ways in which expositors of science, especially popular science writers, tap into folkloric forms in order to make science appealing and humanly compelling. Although the fable genre appears not to be a favorite of such expositors, along the way I have encountered a smattering—seven to be precise—of what I will call fabling gestures, by which I mean either allusions to established fables or new verbal creations with some fable-like quality, adduced around a particular scientific theory. Following Michael Dylan Foster and Jeffrey A. Tolbert who coined the term the "folkloresque" we might refer to such contrived fables as the "fablesque"; or alternatively, in Dorson-style neologism, a fake fable would be a "fakle."

The fable qualities I will emphasize are three. First, there is a terse story or scenario deployed in order to deliver a specific moral. Second, the protagonists are generic and nameless—as in the folktale, perhaps indexing fictionality—so that we have a prince rather than Prince Charles, and a hare rather than Thumper. Individual identifiers would take the formulation in the direction of legend or exemplum. Third, as implied in the example just cited, the nameless protagonist is often a nonhuman animal, the mention of the animal or animals—as in the Lion and the Mouse—often being enough to call to mind the moral.

Not all fables involve nonhuman animal characters. Given our focus on the Crow and the Pitcher, however, I will emphasize the five fabling gestures that involve nonhuman animals, from the seven total I have found; the remaining two I will mention in passing at the end. Two of the five involving animal characters are from the pre-Socratic era, the era of ancient science, and three are from the twentieth century. For convenience, I will concede to a bit of anthropocentric ambiguity embedded in our language; that is, hereafter in this essay "animal" will mean "nonhuman animal."

My first fabling gesture is, as far as I can determine, the first articulation of what we now understand as anthropomorphism as an epistemological problem, namely, a fragment from the pre-Socratic philosopher Xenophanes, who said:

> The Ethiopians say that their gods are snub-nosed and black, the Thracians that theirs have light blue eyes and red hair. But if cattle and horses or lions had hands, or were able to draw with their hands and do the works that men can do, horses would draw the forms of the gods like horses, and cattle like cattle, and they would make their bodies such as they each had themselves. (Kirk, Raven, and Schofield 1983, 169)

One of the human characteristics Xenophanes projects onto the animals is none other than our need to project our image onto other beings, in this case the gods. It may be that some theologies anthropomorphize divinity itself in a similar way, by projecting onto divine beings a need to project their image, most obviously in creation stories in which gods create us in *their* image—but perhaps also in more abstruse ways, such as one divine being emanating into further divine beings.

Xenophanes's gesture is not a fable but a blueprint for a fable; inspired by Xenophanes, I offer a fakle of the cow, the horse, and the lion:

> One day a cow, a horse, and a lion were discoursing on the nature of the gods. Unable to agree, they decided that each would draw a picture, and the most pleasing image would be promulgated as religious doctrine, with the runners-up consigned to heresy. When it came time to decide, it became apparent that each had produced a theologized selfie: For the first, a nurturant countenance emerging above a cosmic firmament that resembled an udder:

For the second, a fleet spirit with lithe legs galloping across the heavens, drawing the sun along:

For the third, a kingly face with mane unfolding as the Aurora Borealis:

They argued all afternoon, gesticulating wildly, each claiming to offer the most pleasing image. When evening came, unable to agree on a winner, they parted in mutual scorn—and later their descendants fought a religious war.

The moral is: We each construct the cosmos in our own image.

If one wants a single text to point to as the foundation of Western academic critical thought, the fragment from Xenophanes would be a contender. Xenophanes's challenging of what amounts to mythological portrayals of the gods is surely one of the formulations that distinguished philosopher of science Carl Popper had in mind in his famous claim, now circulating as an adage, that "science must begin with myths," that is with the challenging of myths. To make a two and a half-millennia-long story short, the tendency of humans to project their own image onto the cosmos, rather than seeing it and themselves objectively, has, ever since Xenophanes, held a revered place in the catalog of defects of human reason—a defect that philosophy first, and now science, claim to remedy.

My second fabling gesture is actually a fabling-cum-epicizing gesture, because it draws in both fable and epic characters. Set in the pre-Socratic era, about a century after Aesop is thought to have lived, this complex creation comes to us from the most illustrious student of Parmenides, Zeno of Elea, who is said to have produced a book of paradoxes of which only a few remain. One of the best-known variations is the so-called Achilles, in which fleet-footed Achilles is trying to overtake a tortoise (generally taken to be the one who, in the fable, achieves an upset victory over a hare).

> Achilles ... cannot possibly overtake the tortoise he is pursuing. For the overtaker must ... first come to the point from which the pursued started. But during [that] time the pursued advanced a certain distance. ... And so, during every period of time in which the pursuer is covering the distance which the pursued ... has already advanced, the pursued advances a yet further distance. And so by taking distances decreasing in a given proportion *ad infinitum* because of the infinite divisibility of magnitudes, we arrive at the conclusion that not only will Hector never be overtaken by Achilles, but not even the tortoise. (Lee 1967, 51)

The place of Zeno in the development of science is at least as ancestrally significant as that of Xenophanes, for Zeno is often cited as adumbrating the central problems of change and motion, and even the methods of differentiation and integration, now addressed in the mathematical field of calculus, one of the cornerstones of modern astronomy and other sciences. Ironically, in disclaiming the possibility of motion Zeno gives us a glimmer of how to approach and represent it mathematically. Even now there is debate about whether calculus really solves the Zeno problem or merely gives us an effective way to manage it. But in Zeno's mathematical paradox, does anything remain of the original tortoise-and-hare moral? Just possibly so, because the triumph of the slow and arduous over the fast and nimble does correspond to the image that early philosophers had of their new method of inquiry.

For my third fabling gesture, we jump to the late twentieth century and one of the most influential popular science writers of all time, the late Stephen Jay Gould, and to the self-proclaimed favorite of his books, *Full House*.[1] The point of this book is specifically to combat our anthropocentric proclivities by undercutting the notion that biological evolution is progressive—that is, that it is somehow driven to produce increasingly "higher" species, with particular reference to ourselves. Like Xenophanes, Gould indulges in anthropomorphism ultimately to expose the defects of doing so. One of Gould's strategies involves an encomium on bacteria that extols their amazing characteristics, which include the ability to live in ecozones far more extreme than those humans can inhabit, allowing bacteria to achieve a collective mass that dwarfs ours, on earth and perhaps elsewhere in the cosmos.

Like numerous traditional fables—such as the Lion and the Mouse—Gould thus sets up a comparison of two sets of contrastive qualities epitomized in two very different, and different-sized, species, leading to a boast. Gould says, "any truly dominant bacterium would laugh with scorn at this apotheosis"—meaning human self-apotheosis as reflected in our imagining of our special place in the kingdom of life. But Gould's scenario of the bacterium and the man never makes it beyond a proto-fable, perhaps because, vis-à-vis the traditional conventions of the fable genre, it is riddled with problems. It should be the large one, the human, who, paralleling the lion's attitude toward the mouse, laughs with scorn at the puny bacterium, and then gets its comeuppance when the little one strikes back through septicemia or some other malady. So far, so good.

But wait! In Gould's larger argument, the bacterium is not laughing at the man from the standpoint of a single bacterium, but rather as a representative of the total mass of bacteria and its stable place in evolutionary process, arrayed against the evolutionarily late and comparatively tiny biomass thus far constituted by *Homo sapiens*. The only criterion that Gould in biological mode is able to muster for assessing the comparative merits of different species is their overall success or biodominance as measured in collective mass; and from this perspective it is rightly the bacterium who, as the giant, laughs with scorn. But then, according to the formula, it would be puny little us who would get the last laugh. And at the end of his tribute to bacteria, Gould does partially concede: "I do realize that bacteria can't laugh (or cogitate)—and that philosophical claims for our greater importance can be based on the consequences of this difference between them and us. But do remember that we can't live on basalt and water six miles under the earth's surface" (1997, 198)—yeah, like we'd actually want to!

A would-be fable showdown of pride and comeuppance thus blows up in Gould's face, and the best he can salvage is a draw: they are an admirable species, but in a different way so are we. In defense of humans I have to add one more thing. Inspired by a comment that Aristotle made about the advantage the philosophically minded hold over the unphilosophically minded, I suggest that if a bacterium and a human had an argument about who is better, the human would certainly win, because if, as Gould says, bacteria cannot cogitate, it follows that they will not be able to formulate a convincing argument. But given that fable protagonists, whether human or not, generally cogitate, is there a false rigor here in calling out Gould for his cogitating bacteria? No, because as his own comment makes clear, Gould *really is* comparing bacteria to humans with respect to the merits of these two species, not, as per the usual fable pattern, comparing humans with other humans via stand-ins drawn from other species. The interspecies contest that inspires the would-be fable also sinks it, because of the literal intent.

Gould's misadventure can alert us to a sort of trap that fables or fable-like scenarios set for interspecies comparative cognitive scientists. Specifically, Gould's abrupt termination of his fable might be seen as prompted by a sudden burst of realism, or, more narrowly, merely as a pullback from one constitutive conceit of the fable genre, a conceit through which Gould may have been drawn into the genre in the first place, namely, that *within fables animals are really humans*. Even the more brutish takes on the world attributed to animal protagonists in fables are dramatized precisely so that humans may recognize themselves in them. This genre conceit could hardly be helpful to an investigator who strays into fable territory while attempting to avoid anthropocentric/anthropomorphic bias.

My fourth fabling gesture is Isaiah Berlin's classic 1953 essay "The Hedgehog and the Fox," for which Berlin derives the framing contrast from a classical Greek poet, Archilochus—Greekness of course making the image more fablesque. Berlin's essay, which focuses on novelist Leo Tolstoy, is well enough known that I am going to limit my comment to pointing out that Berlin, and Tolstoy, are also centrally concerned with science. Berlin's thesis is that Tolstoy was a fox—who knows many small things—attracted to the vision of the hedgehog—who knows one great thing. That is, Tolstoy's true gift lay in his ability to observe and present the myriad tiny details of individual lives; nevertheless, he was drawn, agonizingly, to the great unifying, monistic visions of eighteenth- and nineteenth-century thinkers such as Auguste Comte, E.B. Tylor, Herbert Spencer, and Karl Marx. It is important to note that what unifies the grand theorists whom Tolstoy admired was the vision of bringing human history under the methods and purview of the physical sciences—making it possible to discover in human life and culture regularities as certain as the laws that govern the planets and the tides, in E.B. Tylor's famous image. The polarity has since acquired many names, including, in the twentieth century, that of so-called nomothetic vs. idiographic inquiry.

In describing Tolstoy's attempts to cope with the dichotomy, Berlin also notes a quirk that brings us back to the tortoise and the hare. For like Herman Melville's *Moby Dick*, the narrative flow of Tolstoy's *War and Peace* is interrupted by analytical interludes, in which action is frozen and the author ruminates on what has been happening. Berlin emphasizes that in one of these interludes we have the Zeno thing. Specifically, we encounter Tolstoy (2001, 651–52) reflecting on the race between the tortoise and the hare, and then offering calculus as a metaphor for integrating the infinitesimals of individual wills and acts into the grand movement of history.

There is another, related invocation of the Hedgehog and the Fox, by Stephen Jay Gould once again, in his book *The Hedgehog, the Fox, and the Magister's Pox* (2003), which I group with Berlin's essay because of its close connection, both in substance and in inspiration. (Gould [2003, 3] refers to Berlin as "my personal intellectual hero, and a wonderful man who befriended me when I was a shy, beginning, absolute nobody.") Gould's book is about the need to integrate science and the humanities, for which he thinks the fox and hedgehog "proverb" provides a worthy metaphor—though interestingly he insists that neither science nor the humanities should be thought of as exclusively paired with either the fox or the hedgehog. Gould presents his thoughts on the interrelation over against the arguments of E.O. Wilson in *Consilience* (1998), which Gould sees as offering a "reductionist unification into a single hierarchy" (2003, 262), a point congruent with my own assessment of Wilson: that "consilience" in the end amounts to a hierarchical encompassment of the humanities by the sciences.

The issue of hierarchy in fables is complex and subtle. In the scenario just considered, for example, our sentiments, fed in part by other analogous fables, might incline us toward the hedgehog. The fox is quick like the hare, while the hedgehog is slow like the tortoise, and both the tortoise and hedgehog are ungainly—perhaps triggering sympathy for the apparent "underdog," and ultimately a favoring of the virtues of persistence over those of surface dexterity, or of the virtues of quality over quantity. One can add the proverb that "still waters run deep."

But consider one further fable:

> The story goes that a sow who had delivered a whole litter of piglets loudly accosted a lioness, "How many children do you breed?" asked the sow. "I breed only one," said the lioness, "but he is very well bred!" (Gibbs 2008, 99 [#195])

If we are drawn to the underdog, are we also drawn to the one over the many? Though Berlin himself may be dissatisfied with the hierarchy, his essay takes off from the claim that Tolstoy was drawn to the hedgehog over the fox. And whether or not Gould's complex commentary really succeeds in redressing the imbalance between science and the humanities that he sees in Wilson, it is notable that on the level of the fable he too subtly accords a higher position to the hedgehog than the fox by presenting the former as end and the latter as means: "all the fox's skills now finally congeal to realize the hedgehog's great vision" (2003, 6).[2] If, as Louis Dumont (1980) forcefully argues, hierarchy is fundamentally a relation of encompassment, it just may be that the large vision has an advantage over the small in compelling our attention. But then of course, in parallel with the fable world, big, lumbering, grand theories might be challenged by nimble little ones (see Noyes 2008 on "humble theory").

For my fifth fabling gesture, I cite a peculiar and frequently-noticed line from famed twentieth-century philosopher of language Ludwig Wittgenstein's work *Philosophical Investigations*: "If a lion could talk, we could not understand him" (1958, 223). This line occurs suddenly amidst a long and complex discourse about the incommensurability between and within human natural languages, a discourse that comes close to concluding that no human can understand another—a state of affairs that Wittgenstein's philosophical prose cannot but abet. Wittgenstein's *Philosophical Investigations* is not a work of science, but it is not far from science, especially given that analytical philosophy as a movement grew up under a widespread assumption that, displaced by science as the preeminent discipline, philosophy could still play a necessary role in clarifying language, thus making science possible and defining its limits.

Admittedly the lion line is meager, but we might still salvage a little fakle, to wit:

> A lion attempted to initiate a conversation with a man. Eventually, though, concluding that humans could not speak, he gave up and walked off.

But this is not quite enough; we need a little more punch. In reading through fables one encounters obvious structural types, such as the brains over brawn pattern, which includes the Lion and the Mouse, the Tortoise and the Hare, and, I will argue, the Crow and the Pitcher. At first glance this might seem a promising paradigm for our fakle, but on closer inspection the lion trying to speak to the man turns less on a contest between two than the frustration of one. Especially considering that some think of Wittgenstein as holding a cynical view toward his craft, we might consider, as an alternative, the pattern of the Fox and the Grapes, from which we might derive:

> A lion attempted to initiate a conversation with a man. Eventually, though, concluding that humans could not speak, he walked off muttering, I didn't want to talk to *him* anyway!

Or we could go for a more academic grab, and have the lion walk off muttering the moral that Wittgenstein himself gives us in the numinous closing of his *Tractatus*, a line that has taken on a proverbial life of its own: "Whereof one cannot speak, thereof one must be silent" (1960, 189).

Perhaps the uncomprehending lion of the *Philosophical Investigations* is intended, consciously or unconsciously, as a gesture of denial toward the fable world. For as in some origin myths, the fable world seems to presuppose an original cosmos-wide universal language: animals can converse with other animals and with humans. It is conceivable that Wittgenstein alludes to, or perhaps just reinvents, the myth/fable world as a symbol of the theory of language that he wishes to challenge. Rather than assuming a universalizable system of reference, we should approach languages as game-like systems deeply rooted in particular "forms of life," to invoke another Wittgensteinian phrase. Wittgenstein's fabling gesture is a fable-stopper.

There is yet another possibility, suggested by my colleague William Hansen, who notes an affinity of Wittgenstein's scenario to the fable of Aphrodite and the Weasel. In this fable, a weasel falls in love with a young man, and Aphrodite allows the weasel to change her appearance into that of a beautiful woman, so she and the young man could marry. But on the wedding day, a mouse runs by and the bride runs after it, terminating the wedding. "Nature had proved stronger than Love" (Gibbs 2008, 166 [#350]). Hansen's suggestion (personal communication) is:

> Here one could have a lion who yearns to talk with human beings. Compassionately, the god Hermes grants the lion the gift of human speech. The lion eagerly seeks out a human and initiates a conversation. The human hears the lion's words . . . but doesn't understand what he is trying to say. The lion concludes that communication between lions and humans is not meant to be.

This fakle seems quite parallel to the one I have suggested, but emphasizes an immutable quality of the world over the consternation of the protagonist who would challenge it. In sympathy with the weasel's relapse, and wearied by his failed endeavor, the lion might eat the man in lieu of talking with him, or perhaps as compensation for his effort.

At this point consider one more fable, and one more lion, in Aesop's "The Lion and the Man Disputing." This fable, which flies in the face of Wittgenstein's claim about the incommensurability of human- and lion-speech, provides a moral that parallels the one that I had devised from Xenophanes's comment, and in its own way makes a case for getting beyond anthropomorphic/anthropocentric visions and toward empirically-based science:

> A man and a lion were arguing about who was best, with each one seeking evidence in support of his claim. They came to a tombstone on which a man was shown in the act of strangling a lion, and the man offered this picture as evidence. The lion then replied, "It was a man who painted this; if a lion had painted it, you would instead see a lion strangling a man. But let's look at some real evidence instead." The lion then brought the man to the amphitheater and showed him, so he could see with his own eyes, just how a lion strangles a man. The lion then concluded, "A pretty picture is not proof: facts are the only real evidence."

As I noted in my comments on Xenophanes, recognition of anthropocentrism as an epistemological defect is generally an insight attributed to philosophy over against the prephilosophical view of the world. However, it is plainly evident that many folkloric fables—beating philosophy to the punch?—present various forms of species bias as epistemological defects; and in the fable just quoted we also hear a proposed remedy, namely, empirical observation. Like philosophers, fables zero in on potential flaws in the unexamined, centric ways in which we assess the world.[3] They often do this by projecting contrastive human perceptions or strategies onto animals whose different species characteristics figure in and thus dramatize the contrasts being drawn (the nimbleness of the fox, the deliberative persistence of the tortoise, the preoccupied, nerdy look of the hedgehog). They ask which is better, A or B: the strength of the lion or the incisiveness or the mouse, the speed of the hare or the persistence of the tortoise, the many local theories of the fox or the totalizing grand-theory of the hedgehog. In a few, like the Crow and the Pitcher, there is only one actor, but there are still two strategies: brute force first—since the crow is said to first exhaust itself by trying to tip the jar over—followed by a turn to cunning reason. The contest of lion and mouse is thus redistributed as a contest between a crow's lower and higher cognitive powers.

One other alternative sometimes posed in fable deserves mention, especially for the present project, specifically, the contrast between trying to accomplish a task as a whole vs. breaking it up into smaller tasks. In one Aesopian fable, that of the Old Man and His Sons (Gibbs 2008, 227–28 [#493]), a man demonstrates strength in numbers to his son by showing that sticks that can be broken individually cannot be broken as a bundle. Zeno's Achilles paradox works on the contrast too, as does modern calculus, by breaking motion into smaller parts. So does the fable version of the Crow and the Pitcher. Breaking a task up emerges as a sort of threshold, a breakthrough into analytical reason; indeed, the Greek term for "analyze" literally means to loosen or break-apart (*analyein*). Earlier it was noted that fables tend to be anonymous, and that attaching the breakthrough to specific, named human characters takes the fable in the direction of legend. Here it should be noted that there are numerous such "Newton's apple" legends recounted in the annals of science, and that one of these—specifically Archimedes's *eureka* moment—shares a peculiar affinity to the fable of the Crow and the Pitcher, since the legend and the fable both center around the discovery of the principle of the displacement of water. This fable/legend parallel begs for further consideration in the future.

But having noted that fables do often juxtapose a lower and a higher way of understanding in dealing with a situation, it is necessary to add a caution, specifically, that the breakthrough portrayed in fables is presented in a quite different way from a similar breakthrough that is often encountered in myth scholarship. Specifically, scholars of myth and philosophy sometimes speak of a passage from *mythos* to *logos*—recall Popper's comment above about science necessarily beginning with myths—sometimes in ways that, ironically, are given over to the richest mythologizing. We hear for example of the "Greek miracle"—a moment when a higher form of understanding arose and cast off the shackles of a lower one, leaving behind a hierarchical dichotomy between worldviews and their respective adherents (philosophers vs. the ordinary people who rely on myths).[4] Over against the Greek miracle, it must be noted that the breakthrough from ordinary to analytical reason portrayed in fables is presented in a nonexclusive, generous spirit. Anyone willing to consider these colorful examples will be able to grasp the difference—giving up one's previous worldview, or enrolling in Plato's academy, is not required! Like proverbs, fables are wisdom for everyone, presented in the vulgate.

I have argued elsewhere (e.g., Schrempp 2012) that popular science writers often present the development of science, the new *logos*, in ways that resemble the mythologizing of the birth of philosophy. Here I will add that if the fable is not one of the favored genres of popular science exposition, it could be because scientists might prefer the more radical, worldview-shaking version of breakthrough offered by the passage from *mythos* to *logos* or of cosmic shakeups such as the Copernican revolution, to the more embracive portrayal of the transition offered by fables. But also note that the less heroic rhetoric of the fable does not imply that the scientific topics subjected to fabling gestures are frivolous. Just consider the topics we have broached thus far: the problem of objectivity (Xenophanes), analyzing change and motion (Zeno), teleology in Darwinian evolutionism (Gould), the relation of science and the humanities, and the possibility of a natural science of human history (Berlin, Gould), and the limits of natural languages (Wittgenstein).

As noted above, my emphasis has been on the five fabling gestures I have encountered that include animal characters, since the topic of our discussion is animal intelligence. However, I will add some quick comments on the other two fabling gestures I have come upon, both of which are built around scenarios with only human characters, partly because they offer, by way of contrast, insight into what it is we want from animal characters.

The first of these two human-based fables is the biblical episode of David and Goliath, which forms the framing scenario for Malcolm Gladwell's recent book *David and Goliath: Underdogs, Misfits, and the Art of Battling Giants*, a work I have analyzed in more detail elsewhere (Schrempp 2016, 7–19). Gladwell approaches David and Goliath as a fable, that is, a scenario offering worldly, practical wisdom, summarized in a moral: "There is an important lesson... for battles with all kinds of giants. The powerful and the strong are not always what they seem" (2015, 15), which is of course also the lesson of the Lion and the Mouse among other traditional fables. While calling attention to David's fervent belief in divine providence, Gladwell finds the keys to David's success in nonreligious factors, such as the possibility that Goliath was impaired by a pituitary tumor (the source of his gigantism) and in a ballistic analysis of the surprising firepower of David's sling. The story becomes less about sacred history than about practical wisdom and strategy, which Gladwell juxtaposes to many other scenarios from the present-day worlds of sports, business, and politics. Even though concerned with human protagonists, the fablization of the story by Gladwell offers a possible insight into one (though certainly not the only) source of the attraction of animal characters for fable roles. Specifically, fables are about practical, not metaphysical, wisdom. As portrayed in fables, and no doubt based on everyday observations, animals are rather practical people, short on philosophy but long on astonishing maneuvers and life skills. Xenophanes's fabling gesture, considered earlier, might seem an exception, but his image of animals imagining the gods is presented in a contrary-to-fact tone intended only to satirize the religiosity of humans.

The final fabling gesture I will consider is the allusion to "The Emperor's New Clothes" (a tale probably best known from Hans Christian Andersen, but with a longer history of adaptations for varying morals) by Roger Penrose in his book on cognitive science, *The Emperor's New Mind*. Penrose's book opens with a fictional gathering that took place for the inauguration of an

"Ultronic" supercomputer, which among other things was to "take over all those awkward decisions of State" (1999, 1). When the activation switch was thrown and the audience was invited to ask a question, "all were afraid, seeming to sense a new and all-powerful consciousness" (1999, 2). But one young boy, alone unintimidated, volunteers. At this point, Penrose segues directly to his first chapter, entitled "Can a Computer Have Mind?" Nearly six hundred pages of technical arguments follow, and then, in drawing his work to a conclusion, Penrose says:

> Beneath all this technicality is the feeling that it is indeed "obvious" that the *conscious* mind cannot work like a computer, even though much of what is actually involved in mental activity might do so.
> This is the kind of obviousness that a child can see—though that child may, in later life, become browbeaten into believing that the obvious problems are "non-problems," to be argued into non-existence by careful reasoning and clever choices of definition. Children sometimes see things clearly that are indeed obscured in later life.... Children are not afraid to pose basic questions that may embarrass us, as adults, to ask. (1999, 580)

It seems that we humans have certain favored objects onto, or into, which we project selective images, direct or inverse, of ourselves. These include animals, celestial phenomena, tools with which we develop daily familiarity, human "others" (such as "exotic" peoples), humans with special physical/mental conditions such as autism, and human children. Nineteenth-century social evolutionism often treated these various "others" as analytically intersubstitutable (for example in the notorious equivalency of children and savages in Freud's *Totem and Taboo*). But clearly there are specific and distinct things that we want from each of these objects. For example, the history of ethnology suggests that what we want from exotic human "others" is either a nobler, more robust version of ourselves, or an image of their "savagery" as a foil for our own cosmopolitan civility (or some combination of these). From heavenly bodies we want familiar images, notably as inscribed in star constellations, that make us feel at home in the cosmos.

The "little animals" that are our children are other than us in a different way than the animals from other species; the former is us ontogenically incomplete, the latter are phylogenic paths parallel to ours and sharing some characteristics. In his appeal to an obviousness that has been obscured, Penrose has pinpointed one of the things we want from children: a purified image of ourselves, one in which we are unencumbered by socialization. This desire is like, but more radical than, the desire of nineteenth-century folklorists for the simple purity of the peasant, for the peasant is merely unencumbered by city ways, while the wise child is unencumbered by socialization in general. This object of desire is not less self-contradictory than that of talking animals (who sometimes draw pictures), because what we really want from the mind of a child, in this trope, is a fully-functioning adult mind that is free from the constricting effects of education and socialization, which of course is already an impossibility by the time a child is developed enough to ask a question. The issue of why we speculate about ourselves through such impossible, self-contradictory objects remains a vexing question.

The mind of a child is a trope with no fixed content, for one encounters it as well in support of a conclusion opposite to Penrose's, namely, that the innocent, appealing, childlike view of the world is one in which the poetry- and empathy-destroying binaries of animate and inanimate, person and thing, have not yet hardened. What reason has a child for assuming that an object of silicon and metal cannot have a mind? The innocence depicted in the prebinarized child's mind in such examples may overlap with the child-like qualities sought in religious invocations ("Except ye be converted, and become as little children, ye shall not enter into the kingdom of heaven" [Matthew 18:3]).

Animals may still be the most complex and multifaceted of our objects of projection and desire. One has only to look at the intellectual history of

theories of totemism for confirmation—a history in which the extravagance of so-called totemic institutions is equaled if not surpassed by the doubly-projective extravagance of European intellectuals speculating about how human others think about those other others—the animals. Investigation into the possibility of contemporary scientists anthropomorphizing animals offers yet another way in which to pursue an answer to the question of what humans want from animals. What we want ranges from food and sacrificial victims, to laborers for herding and plowing, to protectors and sources of affection, but in the present case we seem also to want something from their minds. The situation brings together in a heightened way methods that profess objectivity with objects that—through their nobility, skillfulness, cuteness, and other admirable and fearsome qualities—have often succeeded in evading our efforts at an objective stance.

PostScript: The Saga Continues

In briefest terms I would like to mention two developments that occurred since the AFS conference that gave rise to this volume, both of which suggest intriguing new directions.

First, just a few months after our AFS panel, and as though in response to it, a long-overdue English translation of André Jolles's *Simple Forms* (2017) appeared (with a Foreword by Fredric Jameson). Jolles's theory of "simple forms" had been rudimentarily known about by many folklorists trained in the mid-twentieth century through a terse and stimulating summary of it by Kurt Ranke entitled "Einfache Formen" that appeared in *Journal of the Folklore Institute* (precursor to *JFR*) in 1967. I expect Jolles's book to be a major resource for the topic of folklore and science, for two main reasons. First, more than any other major genre theorist, Jolles roots his concept of genre not in issues of style or form but in the mental/cognitive/emotional stance or disposition that constitutes a genre: what the genre assumes about the cosmos, its intellectual/emotional posture and orientation, what it wants to learn or teach about. Secondly, Jolles argues that the range of stances or "takes" on the world that constitute the simple forms—myth, legend, fairy tale, riddle, saying, and other folklore genres—remain at the base of "complex" forms such as literary novels or historical treatises produced by literate, cosmopolitan societies. In our contemporary intellectual environment, dichotomies of "simple" and "complex" of course trigger suspicions of social-evolutionism. However, given the historical context and spirit in which he wrote, I suggest that what Jolles means by "simple" is approximately what, writing in the same epoch, comparative sociologist Emile Durkheim means by "elementary" in his great and influential work *The Elementary Forms of Religious Life*: it means something basic and universal in human consciousness and in the human condition. If, for Durkheim, totemism is the elementary form of religion, then high Anglicanism is totemism in brocade robes. Jolles's claim that the various fundamental stances of folklore genres live on in cosmopolitan literary products is in essence what I am suggesting to be the case with folkloric forms in expository science. The ultimate question is whether folkloric forms go beyond strategies of exposition, and enter into the very process of scientific reasoning. At this point I will say, minimally, that I am not convinced that they do not.

Second, on June 7, 2018, "Weekend Edition" of National Public Radio offered an investigation of the capacities of bees, and interestingly that report involves and parallels some of the central themes we are considering in relation to the Crow and the Pitcher. The claims presented in the NPR report rest on evidence that bees can be trained to distinguish between cards with *fewer* vs. *more* symbols on them, and also between cards with *no* symbols vs. *some* symbols on them. Through the piece runs a kind of equivocation on what is going on in the bees' brains, in which the capacity to react differently becomes layered with various attributions of mathematical skills. The most striking similarity of this report to the Crow and Pitcher is that the scientific importance of the claims regarding animal intelligence in each case rests upon our anthropocentric history, specifically the belief that the achievement in question marks a watershed moment for humanity in the history of mathematics and science. Just as we have often heard the story of Archimedes's "eureka moment" with the principle of displacement, so have we also heard the story that zero appeared late in human history, and proved critical to the further development of mathematics and science—as though these fields were languishing around waiting for the concept to appear. If I were to argue that it is obvious to anyone what zero means, I can imagine scientists responding by restricting the meaning of zero: what is at issue is not some gross sense of absence or of nothing vis-à-vis something, but a highly technical, versatile, and mathematically-operationalized concept and symbol. This is definitely not the treatment the bees get in the NPR report, the commentators seeming to bend over backward to see in the bees' behaviors evidence of their admissibility into the zero-club, as though fueled by a desire to cheer the little guys on and find ourselves in them.

The appeal of the report is surely related to fact that quantitative reasoning is discovered specifically in bees, a species that we admire for its organization, industriousness, and productivity—concerns we hear about in the daily stock-market and economic reports, which are steeped in quantitative buzz. While this NPR report on bees does not quite qualify as a fabling gesture, the bee is a much-fabled creature, and, along with the ant and the grasshopper and others, reminds us that the insect realm too attracts human curiosity and the desire to draw lessons—about efficient economic behavior among other things. Thinking about the NPR piece triggered for me a memory of an eighth fabling gesture, one that I encountered decades before engaging in my research on folkloric forms in science. Specifically, Louis Dumont sought to elaborate his theories regarding hierarchy (which I mention above) through a historical study of economic ideologies; his initial work in this direction was *From Mandeville to Marx* (1977). Chapter 5 of this book is "Mandeville's *Fable of the Bees*: Economics and Morality." The fable in question is one offered in the early eighteenth century by physician and social theorist Bernard de Mandeville; Dumont summarizes:

> A hive, presented as a mirror of human society, lives in corruption and prosperity. Harboring some nostalgia for virtue, it prays to recover it. When the prayer is granted, an extraordinary transformation takes place: with vice gone, activity and prosperity disappear and are replaced by sloth, poverty, and boredom in a much reduced population. (1977, 63–64)

Dumont points to evidence suggesting the influence of Mandeville on Adam Smith's *The Wealth of Nations*; and from that point of view, although Dumont himself does not phrase it this way, one might conclude that modern economic theory originates with a fabling gesture about bees![5]

Indiana University
Bloomington

Acknowledgments

I am grateful to Bill Hansen, Brandon Barker, Daniel Povinelli, and Richard Handler, as well as to our enthusiastic conference audience members, for their many and diverse comments and contributions to this paper.

Notes

1. In an earlier discussion (Schrempp 2012, Chapter 3), I consider this fabling gesture in relation to Gould's other strategies of persuasion in *Full House* and his style of science popularizing generally.

2. See also the razzle-dazzle of hedgehog and fox, of hierarchy and symmetry, and of unity, duality, and plurality in the closing pages (2003, 259–60) of Gould's argument.

3. Interestingly, and perhaps presciently for gender studies, the fable just considered, the Lion and the Man Disputing, is alluded to as a metaphor of gender bias in the "Wife of Bath's Tale" in Chaucer's *Canterbury Tales*.

4. Particularly enlightening discussions of the idea of a transition from mythos to logos are found in J.P. Vernant (1982) and Bruce Lincoln (1999).

5. E.O. Wilson's *Anthill: A Novel* (2010) also might be approached as a fabling gesture—though one with enough complexities to require a separate treatment. The field of sociobiology, Wilson

its most visible proponent, integrates human and nonhuman behavior in the study of social organization; so we would seem to have another context in which scientific interests dovetail with the genre-conceit of fables that animal characters are really humans. The main human protagonist of *Anthill* concludes: "The foibles of ants ... are those of men, written in a simpler grammar" (2010, 169).

References Cited

Berlin, Isaiah. 1993. *The Hedgehog and the Fox: An Essay on Tolstoy's View of History*. Chicago: Ivan R. Dee, Inc.
Dumont, Louis. 1977. *From Mandeville to Marx: The Genesis and Triumph of Economic Ideology*. Chicago: University of Chicago Press.
———. 1980. *Homo Hierarchicus: The Caste System and its Implications*. Rev. ed. Chicago: University of Chicago Press.
Durkheim, Emile. 1995. *The Elementary Forms of Religious Life*. New York: The Free Press.
Freud, Sigmund. 1950. *Totem and Taboo*. New York: W.W. Norton & Company.
Gibbs, Laura, trans. 2008. *Aesop's Fables*. Oxford: Oxford University Press.
Gladwell, Malcolm. 2015. *David and Goliath: Underdogs, Misfits, and the Art of Battling Giants*. New York: Back Bay Books.
Gould, Stephen Jay. 1997. *Full House*. New York: Three Rivers Press.
———. 2003. *The Hedgehog, the Fox, and the Magister's Pox*. New York: Harmony Books.
Greenfieldboyce, Nell. 2018. "Math Bee: Honeybees Seem to Understand the Notion of Zero." *NPR*. June 7, 2018. Accessed September 20, 2018. https://www.npr.org/2018/06/07/617863467/math-bee-honeybees-seem-to-understand-the-notion-of-zero.
Jolles, André. 2017. *Simple Forms*. London: Verso.
Kirk, G.S., J.E. Raven, and M. Schofield. 1983. *The Presocratic Philosophers: A Critical History with a Selection of Texts*. 2nd ed. Cambridge: Cambridge University Press.
Lee, H.D.P., trans. 1967. *Zeno of Elea*. Amsterdam: Adolf M. Hakkert.
Lincoln, Bruce. 1999. *Theorizing Myth*. Chicago: University of Chicago Press.
Noyes, Dorothy. 2008. "Humble Theory." *Journal of Folklore Research* 45 (1): 37–43.
Penrose, Roger. 1999. *The Emperor's New Mind*. Oxford: Oxford University Press.
Ranke, Kurt. 1967. "Einfache Formen." *Journal of the Folklore Institute* 4 (1): 17–31.
Schrempp, Gregory. 2012. *The Ancient Mythology of Modern Science*. Montreal: McGill-Queen's University Press.
———. 2016. *The Science of Myths and Vice Versa*. Chicago: Prickly Paradigm Press.
Tolstoy, Leo. 2001. *War and Peace*. Hertfordshire: Wordsworth Editions Limited.
Vernant, Jean-Pierre. 1982. *The Origins of Greek Thought*. Ithaca: Cornell University Press.
Wilson, Edward O. 1998. *Consilience: The Unity of Knowledge*. New York: Alfred A. Knopf.
———. 2010. *Anthill: A Novel*. New York: W.W. Norton & Company.
Wittgenstein, Ludwig. 1958. *Philosophical Investigations*. Englewood Cliffs: Prentice Hall.
———. 1960. *Tractatus Logico-Philosophicus*. London: Routledge & Kegan Paul.

GREGORY SCHREMPP is Professor of Folklore at Indiana University Bloomington. His books include *Magical Arrows: the Maori, the Greeks, and the Folklore of the Universe* (1992); *The Ancient Mythology of Modern Science: A Mythologist Looks (Seriously) at Popular Science Writing* (2012); and *The Science of Myths and Vice Versa* (2016). (gschremp@indiana.edu).

K. BRANDON BARKER AND DANIEL J. POVINELLI

CONCLUSION
Old Ideas and the Science of Animal Folklore

Ideas about animals seem to float, like the Crow's food reward, atop a tide of cultural representations of animals. Recently, some folklorists have argued that—in both science and folklore—this appears to be a moment when the tides are coming in *toward* the idea that humans and animals are very much alike and *away* from the idea of human uniqueness, of recognizable borders between animals and humans.[1] That very well may be true, but even if we are living in a time when the tides are changing, we conclude this special issue where we began—reaching out from a flood of anthropomorphized behaviors, metaphors, and narratives in an attempt to snag the shirt sleeves of involved humanists and social scientists riding the waves. If we can grab your attention, we offer a warning: Be wary, look skeptically toward the recent trends in the scientific study of animal cognition that suggest it is time to welcome, with open arms, nonhuman animals into our comfortable anthropocentric analyses. As the science-minded folklorist Jay Mechling espouses, the border between human and nonhuman animals is "every bit as arbitrary and, hence, as cultural as those normally the focus of folklorists' attention" (1989, 312).[2] For our part, we remain dubious that this tide—this most recent redrawing of the borderline, this animal turn—has much, if anything, to do with animals.

Like the animals who appear in fables, contemporary experiments in the Aesop's Fable Paradigm only confirm, once again, humans' perennial interest in other animals. We have looked closely at one genre of traditional narrative, the fable. We have considered one story from within that genre, the Crow and the Pitcher. We have focused on scientific and folkloric representations of a single animal, the crow. We have done all this in order to zoom in on the problems that surround recent assertions that crows possess a higher-order cognitive ability to comprehend and to act in accordance with a theory-like understanding of water displacement. Even if many of our readers still believe that crows may understand the physics of water, we hope that our tempered interpretations of the Aesop's Fable experiments demonstrate how maddeningly puzzling work in animal cognition can be. For humanists and social scientists wanting to make claims in nonscientific disciplines that experimentation with animals and the science of animal behavior have proven the humanness of nonhuman animals, we suggest truly opening that can of worms by perusing the index in the Appendix. Then, consider seriously each and every one of the hundreds (or thousands) of studies that present critical ambiguities similar to those inherent in the Aesop's Fable Paradigm. Overwhelmed readers may soon find themselves asking, "What do we really want from animals?" After all, tides come in, and tides go out, time and time again...

> I will conclude by quoting a remark by the illustrious Humboldt. "The muleteers in S. America say, 'I will not give you the mule whose step is easiest, but *la mas racional*,—the one that reasons best;'" and as he adds, "this popular expression, dictated by long experience, combats the system of animated machines, better perhaps than all the arguments of speculative philosophy." Nevertheless some writers even yet deny that the higher animals possess a trace of reason; and they endeavor to explain away, by what appears to be mere verbiage, all such facts as those above given.
> —Charles Darwin (1871, 456)

> If we find a dog or a monkey exhibiting marked expressions of affection, sympathy, jealousy, rage, &c., few persons are skeptical enough to doubt that the complete analogy which these expressions afford with those which are manifested by man, sufficiently prove the existence of mental states analogous to those in man of which these expressions are the outward and visible signs.
> —Georges Romanes (1878, 8)

> It is an old belief that animals, and even plants, talk to each other, and that men can freely understand and answer them. But this belief, born of that primitive communism which makes the whole world kin, is gradually dispelled by a more exact observation of nature; and men, beginning to draw the line more sharply between themselves and the lower creatures, are fain to confess that they understand the beast language no longer.
> —James G. Frazer (1888, 81)

> The only indication of deliberate plan and effort that I have ever noted in Unk Wunk [the Porcupine] was in regard to teaching two young ones the simple art of swimming—which porcupines, by the way, rarely use, and for which there seems to be no necessity. I was drifting along the shore in my canoe when I noticed a mother porcupine and two little ones, a prickly pair indeed, on a log that reached out into the lake. She had brought them there to make her task of weaning them more easy by giving them a taste of lily buds. When they had gathered and eaten all the buds and stems that they could reach, she deliberately pushed both little ones into the water. When they attempted to scramble back she pushed them off again and dropped in beside them and led them to a log farther down the shore, where there were more lily pads.

The numerous hollow quills floated them high in the water, like so many corks, and they paddled off with less effort than any other young animals that I have ever seen in the water. But whether this were a swimming lesson or a rude direction to shift and browse for themselves is still a question.
—William J. Long (1902, 234)

If the writers who make such startling discoveries in the wilderness would really study even the denizens of a barnyard, they would be saved from at least some of their more salient mistakes. Their stories dwell much on the "teaching" of the young animals by their elders and betters. In one story, for instance, a wild duck is described as "teaching" her young how to swim and get their food. If this writer had strolled into the nearest barnyard containing a hen which had hatched out ducklings, a glance at the actions of those ducklings when the hen happened to lead them near a puddle would have enlightened him as to how much "teaching" they needed.
—President Theodore Roosevelt (1907, 430)

There are some chimps who, far more than others, constantly seem to try to ingratiate themselves with their superiors. Melissa, for one, particularly when she was young, used to hurry toward and lay her hand on the back or head of an adult male almost every time one passed anywhere near her. If he turned toward her, she often drew her lips back into a submissive grin as well. Presumably Melissa, like other chimps who constantly attempt to ingratiate themselves in this way, is simply ill at ease in the presence of a social superior, so that she constantly seeks reassurance through physical contact. If the dominant individual touches her in return, so much the better.

There are many human Melissas: the sort of people who when trying to be extra friendly reach out to touch the person concerned and smile very frequently and attentively. Usually they are, for some reason or other, people who are unsure of themselves and slightly ill at ease in social contexts.
—Jane Goodall (1971, 243)

Lastly, the old silverback came forward. In all my years of research I never met a silverback so dignified and commanding in respect. His silvering extended from the sides of his cheekbones, along neck and shoulders, enveloped his back and barrel, and continued down the sides of both thighs. Having little to go by in comparison, except for zoo gorillas, I estimated his age as approximately fifty years, possibly more. The nobility of his character compelled me to seek a name for him immediately. In Swahili, *Rafiki* means "friend." Because friendship implies mutual respect and trust, the regal silverback became known as Rafiki.
—Diane Fossey (1983, 139)

Language is obviously as different from other animals' communication systems as the elephant's trunk is different from other animals' nostrils. Nonhuman communication systems are based on one of three designs: a finite repertory of calls (one for warnings of predators, one for claims to territory, and so on), a continuous analog signal that registers the magnitude of some state (the livelier the dance of the bee, the richer the food source that it is telling its hivemates about), a series of random variations on a theme (a birdsong repeated with a new twist each time: Charlie Parker with feathers). As we have seen, human language has a very different design. The discrete combinatorial system called "grammar" makes human language infinite (there is no limit to the number of complex words or sentences in a language), digital (this infinity is achieved by rearranging discrete elements in particular orders and combinations, not by varying some signal along a continuum like the mercury in a thermometer), and compositional (each of the infinite combinations has a different meaning predictable from the meanings of its parts and the rules and principles arranging them).

Even the seat of human language in the brain is special.

—Steven Pinker (1994, 342)

When the lively, penetrating eyes lock with ours and challenge us to reveal who we are, we know right away that we are not looking at a "mere" animal, but a creature of considerable intellect with a secure sense of its place in the world. We are meeting a member of the same tailless, flat-chested, long-armed primate family to which we ourselves and only a handful of other species belong. We feel the age-old connection before we can even stop to think, as people are wont to do, how different we are.

Bonobos will not let us indulge in this thought for long: in everything they do, they resemble us. A complaining youngster will put his lips like an unhappy child or stretch out an open hand to beg for food. In the midst of sexual intercourse, a female may squeal with apparent pleasure. And at play, bonobos utter coarse laughs when their partners tickle their bellies or armpits. There is no escape, we are looking at an animal so akin to ourselves that the dividing line is seriously blurred.

—Frans de Waal (1998, 1)

It took me many years to realize that these stories offered a worthy glimpse into animal minds. I was cautious simply because stories don't prove anything. Like most people who take this issue seriously, I wanted to see hard evidence and verifiable studies, particularly since concepts of human uniqueness are at issue, and the stakes are very high. Unfortunately, I'm still waiting. Studies have been done—scores of them—but they, too, almost always, contain some maddening ambiguity, at least in the eyes of other scientists. . . .

Even the hardest of hard-nosed scientists, those sifting through impossibly large piles of data in cosmology and quantum mechanics, resort to metaphor and analogy when trying to explain or understand their data. . . . Ultimately, when we look at studies of animal behavior, we are looking for a familiar story that helps us understand what we are seeing. . . .

In any event, the sciences that study intelligence and consciousness still swirl with new studies and controversy. Many of the stories that will unfold

offer a perspective on this debate, and carry with them their own implications about the nature of intelligence. There is no agreement about the definition of this signal ability—there is even a longstanding debate about whether intelligence is one ability or an ensemble, of many. When you think about it, this is astonishing in itself, since the planet's greatest minds have been struggling to understand intelligence since antiquity. Still, there is plenty of lively thinking, as well as a flood of new evidence about what is going on in the brain when we and other species think, communicate, and dream.
—Eugene Linden (2002, 7–19)

Old ideas, drowned in the passage of time, do not stop rising to pertinence. Letting the water take us, we find ourselves thinking again on Mark Twain, who personified more things than the Mississippi River. Twain also had a knack for juxtaposing human and anthropomorphized animals in pertinent scenarios. In the first decade of the twentieth century—during the controversial times of the *nature fakers* referenced in the preceding quotes—Twain wrote a fable entitled, "A Fable," which he published in 1909, one year before his (actual) death. Twain's fable begins with an artist having made a small, beautiful painting, which the artist then hangs in such a way that he can see its reflection in a mirror. The artist says, "This doubles the distance and softens it, and it is twice as lovely as it was before" (1909, 59). By way of anthropomorphized word of mouth, the animals in the woods soon learn of the beautiful painting from the house cat whose position as a civilized, learned (enculturated?) pet brings him much admiration from the other animals. With great zeal and adjectival embellishment, the cat tells the other animals about the "wonderfully flat . . . oh so beautiful" painting. Impressed and encouraged, the animals also ask the cat to tell them about the mirror, which the cat describes as a "hole in the wall" that one looks into in order to see the "unimaginable beauty" of the painting (1909, 59).

Despite the cat's performance, the ass remains dubious: "When it took a whole basketful of sesquipedalian adjectives to whoop up a thing of beauty, it was time for suspicion" (61). (There's always one!) Predictably, the ass—challenged by the cat—ventures off to the house of the artist to see the painting for himself. When ass arrives, he—of course—naively stands between the mirror and the painting so that the only thing he sees in the mirror is, quite simply, an ass: "a handsome ass, and friendly, but just an ass" (61). Upon hearing the ass's report, other animals cannot resist making the trip and looking in the mirror-hole for themselves. The bear, Baloo, returns to say that both the cat and the ass have lied: "there was nothing in the hole but a bear" (62). And the process is repeated for the cow, the tiger, the lion, the leopard, the camel, and eventually even the elephant king Hathi, himself, who dismisses the lot: "Anybody but a near-sighted fool could see that there was nothing in the hole but an elephant." Foolish at its core, Twain's fable ends with this moral by the cat:

> You can find in a text whatever you bring, if you will stand between it and the mirror of your imagination. You may not see your ears, but they will be there. (62)

Twain clearly thought a great deal about the relationship between humans and animals, and it is interesting that his more ameliorative gestures were often saved for any animal but humans, whom he eventually deemed to be the lowest of all species.[3]

Twain wants to show us that there is beauty to behold if we could only get out of our own way. Literary critics have interpreted Twain's "A Fable" as a critique of the very enterprise of literary criticism or as a defense of writers—with at least one anthropomorphizing writer, Twain's friend Rudyard Kipling, being overtly referenced via Twain's names for the bear and the elephant. We have no corroborating evidence that Twain's fable refers directly to the problems of anthropomorphism in the study of animal cognition, but is applicability across a range of contexts not a key feature of the lessons fables teach us? Is Twain not telling us to be wary of projections, of mirrors, and specifically of mistaking our projections in the mirror for our own foregone conclusions? Can we see our ears? If not, can we at least feel them and recognize them as our own?

Folkloristic genre theory suggests that a conflict arises when "objective" animal-cognition science is framed with an Aesopian fable because such a frame makes it impossible not to interpret the animal subjects as always partially human. If the anthropomorphized animal characters in fables have nothing to do with the experimental designs in the Aesop's Fable Paradigm, then why were the chosen animal subjects crows—as opposed to rabbits, dogs, squirrels, or raccoons? (Actually, raccoons were recently subjected to the Aesop's Fable Paradigm; see the Appendix, H1a.2) If our genre-based argument is correct, it would go a long way toward explaining the apparent hesitancy, or even unwillingness, to accept other, less anthropomorphized explanations for the crows' behaviors. And if it turns out to be the case that our argument only relates to the Aesop's Fable Paradigm, we think, at least, we would be identifying an interesting and important historical interlude. But this is not a one-off historical moment. Claude Lévi-Strauss teaches us that animals-and-humans are good to think, and we wonder if animals (and humans) are impossible not to think.[4] These are questions of animal scientists: Do Bees understand math? Does Chimpanzee have religion? Does Seal dance? Does Dog play games? What about Orangutan's charades? Does Rat empathize with her cage mates? Does Raven, peeking through a tiny hole in a wall, think about the thoughts of the other ravens? These questions are ours: Do animals as thought magnets—as *intuition pumps* in Daniel Dennett's nomenclature—pull us closer to the actual contents of other animals' minds? What if the integrative tendencies of people's minds produce—in the case of a scientific understanding of animal others—a deluge of untruths?

We have reached a familiar endpoint, the point where one side's anxieties about anthropomorphism can be mistaken for a weak characterization of animals, and where the other side's anxieties about over-reaching human exceptionalism can be mistaken for anthropomorphism disguised as science. Whether or not we end here, the cycle will continue. But if we end here, we know that future progress will be difficult. So let us attempt to move this interdisciplinary discussion of science and folklore toward a less familiar (starting) point: For every specific domain of cognition—space, time, colors, food, sex, physics, and so forth—humans and animals must be radically the same and radically different.[5] As for similarity, even when comparing humans and birds, shared characteristics related to the presence of cognition, goal-directed behavior, and the ability to learn and to adapt cannot be denied. But folklorists, who work across such a wide range of traditionalized human contexts, must recognize the patterns of behavior that are not shared.

It is like the duck and goose decoys traditionally used to lure water fowl to the surface of some delta marsh. The bird, detecting a familiar shape in familiar contexts, acts accordingly—not having to wonder at all about whether the decoy is made of reed, Styrofoam, or wood. Humans, too, recognize and react to familiar contexts without the need for higher-order, abstract representations of that context. But only humans have created laws (necessary conservation laws) regulating hunting practices associated with the decoys. And after having ripped the hand-shaped models from their original purpose, only humans have reinterpreted the value of these wooden figurines within the contexts of art. Carved and painted to a point of high realism, the decoy presents the duck or goose just as it appears out in the world, with the only difference being that the decoy cum folk art has nothing to do with actual birds except as manifestations of human imagination and action—as art.

Are we saying that science, like art, can produce "birds" that have nothing to do with *birds*? Remember, animals can be treacherous to think.

> Wading—knee deep—through interdisciplinary waters, the Scientist and the Folklorist moved carefully. As they looked across the surface, every ripple promised some new monster. Holding a flickering torch, the Scientist looked down and whispered, "Here there be dragons." The Folklorist tried to sing away anxiety:

> Sing a song of sixpence,
> A pocket full of rye.
> Four and twenty blackbirds,
> Baked in a pie.

Having forgotten the end of the rhyme long ago, he trailed off into silence. There was only the sound of sloshing feet. Suddenly, the Scientist: "Four and twenty black birds! What an excellent idea!"

"Idea? That was only a nursery rhyme my mother sang to me as a child," the Folklorist said.

"Yes, I too know of that rhyme. But I mean the number of birds." Recently, the Scientist had haggled over a meta-analysis of experiments in the Aesop's Fable Paradigm. The meta-analysis showed that crows dropping stones were *at least* as likely to be learning from trial-and-error as from some conceptual understanding of water displacement. Even though the meta-analysis used all of the crows from the original experiments, some dissenters argued that the meta-analysis lacked a sufficient amount of data to be valid. The Scientist found himself asking, *how many birds does it take to prove a fable?* And, now, thanks to the Folklorist's song, he had his answer.

"Four and twenty. That is how many birds it takes to prove a fable," the Scientist winked. "Don't you see? The idea was right there in the rhyme."

The Folklorist agreed: *Four and twenty is a good number of birds.*

Indiana University
Bloomington

University of Louisiana
Lafayette

Notes

1. In her introduction to a special issue of *Journal of Folklore Research* on the intersection of animals and folklore, Sabina Magliocco outlines recent trends in scholarship of animals as the "animal turn":

> Moreover, recent research on animals has illustrated that many of the distinctions we have drawn to separate ourselves from them—language, culture, self-awareness—in order to justify their instrumentalization and commodification, may well be arbitrary and wrong. Today, some biologists and animal ethologists [...] increasingly write about animal languages, cultures, emotions, and even morality. The growing interest in this fluid boundary, and the ethical reflection it entails, are known as the "animal turn" in scholarship. (2018, 3)

Magliocco and the other authors of the special issue also foreground contemporary notions of "posthumanism," which grants personhood to nonhuman entities such as animals and cyborgs.

2. Inasmuch as the animal/human border is nothing more than an abstract line of demarcation that can only be "recognized" and "traced" by humans wielding our species-specific, cognitive capacities for creating spatial (and geometric) metaphors as we attempt to answer perennial questions—"what is human?" and "what is animal?"—we certainly agree.

3. In his philosophical essay, "The Lowest Animal" (1896), Twain reverses the (colloquially understood) direction of humans' evolutionary "ascension/descension," placing man at the bottom of all evolutionary processes. With a wink, Twain responds ethically to Darwin's theories. The essay details several "experiments" that demonstrate, for examples, the facts that anacondas do not kill for cruelty's sake (though man does), that man is avaricious (while animals are not), that only humans enslave (while "higher" animals do not), and that only "reasoning" humans kill in the name of religion.

4. Lévi-Strauss's famous adage comes from *Totemism* (1962). Here, is the passage as translated by Rodney Needham:

> The animals in totemism cease to be solely or principally creatures which are feared, admired, or envied: their perceptible reality permits the embodiment of ideas and relations conceived by speculative thought on the basis of empirical observations. We can understand, too, that natural species are chosen not because they are "good to eat" but because they are "good to think." (1962, 89)

By aligning totemism with processes of human minds, Lévi-Strauss deftly avoids overly simplified explanations according to bottom up processes ("a natural stimulus") or top-down processes (arbitrary pretext).

5. For a discussion of this radical approach to similarity and difference in comparative psychology, see Povinelli's *Folk Physics for Apes* (2000), especially Chapter 12, "Toward a Folk Physics for Chimpanzees."

References Cited

Darwin, Charles. (1871) 1969. *The Origin of Species and The Descent of Man*. New York: Modern Library.
de Waal, Frans, and Frans Lanting. 1997. *Bonobo: The Forgotten Ape*. Berkeley: California University Press.
Fossey, Diane. (1983) 2000. *Gorillas in the Mist*. Boston: Houghton Mifflin.
Frazer, James G. 1888. "The Language of Animals." *The Archaeological Review* 1 (2): 81–91.
Goodall, Jane. 1971. *In the Shadow of Man*. Boston: Houghton Mifflin.
Lévi-Strauss, Claude. 1963. *Totemism*. Translated by Rodney Needham. Boston: Beacon.
Linden, Eugene. 2002. *The Octopus and the Orangutan: New Tales of Animal Intrigue, Intelligence, and Ingenuity*. New York: Plume.
Long, William J. 1902. *School of the Woods: Some Life Studies of Animal Instincts and Animal Training*. Boston: Athenaeum Press.
Magliocco, Sabina. 2018. "Folklore and the Animal Turn." *Journal of Folklore Research* 55 (2): 1–7.
Mechling, Jay. 1989. "'Banana Cannon' and Other Folk Traditions between Human and Nonhuman Animals." *Western Folklore* 48 (4): 312–23.
Pinker, Steven. 1994. *The Language Instinct: How the Mind Creates Language*. New York: Harper Perennial.
Povinelli, Daniel J. 2000. *Folk Physics for Apes: The Chimpanzee's Theory of How the World Works*. Oxford: Oxford University Press.
Romanes, Georges. (1878) 1882. *Animal Intelligence*. London: Kegan Paul.
Roosevelt, Theodore. 1907. "Nature Fakers" *Everybody's Magazine* 17 (3): 427–30.
Twain, Mark. (1896) 1962. "The Lowest Animal." In *Letters from the Earth*, ed. Bernard DeVoto, 75–84. New York: Harper & Row.
Twain, Mark. (1909) 1992. "A Fable." In *Mark Twain: The Celebrated Jumping Frog and Other Stories*, by Mark Twain, 59–62. Pleasantville: Reader's Digest Association.

K. BRANDON BARKER is Assistant Professor of Folklore in the Department of Folklore and Ethnomusicology, Indiana University. He teaches and publishes on topics at the intersections of embodied, cognitive processes and folkloric tradition. He is coauthor of the book *Folk Illusions: Children, Folklore, and Sciences of Perception* (2019) with Claiborne Rice. (barkerbr@indiana.edu).

DANIEL J. POVINELLI is Professor of Biology at the University of Louisiana at Lafayette. His primary interests center on the characterizations of the higher-order cognitive functions in great apes and humans. He is the author of *Folk Physics for Apes: The Chimpanzee's Theory of How the World Works* (2000) and *World without Weight: Perspectives on an Alien Mind* (2011). (povinelli@louisiana.edu).

DANIEL J. POVINELLI and K. BRANDON BARKER,
with special assistance from MARISA WIENEKE
and KRISTINA DOWNS

APPENDIX
Doctor Fomomindo's Preliminary Notes for a Future Index of Anthropomorphized Animal Behaviors

Note from the Editors: To help our readers understand why we decided to include Doctor Fomomindo's admittedly unusual (and eternally unfinished) catalog (the FOMANCOG) as an appendix to this book, let us begin by asserting something we believe to be uncontroversial: humans like to tell stories about things they are interested in, and the more these stories relate to the human condition (imagined or otherwise), the more interested (most) humans will be.

When we first learned of the FOMANCOG's existence, we thought it would be little more than an interesting source of inspiration for future projects aimed at understanding parallels among the stories scientists tell about animals and those already well cataloged by folklorists. As we dusted off the binder that contained Doctor Fomomindo's notes, however, the full scope of his ambitions became apparent. We realized his would-be catalog had far greater import than we could have ever suspected.

The doctor's catalog and his introductory remarks speak for themselves. Nonetheless, we feel compelled to publicly acknowledge that our understanding of his project continues to evolve. This should not be surprising. It is, after all, a liminal project, straddling the emic/etic razor's edge on which Doctor Fomomindo has for so long danced. At this moment, we envision it as an attempt to lay bare the sources of cognitive folklore that motivate much of the scientific enterprise in which he spent decades as a participant. From this perspective, his efforts can be seen as reducing to the claim that because the scientists who study higher-order animal cognition are, themselves, fully enculturated humans, their methods, results, and conclusions can only be understood by mapping (aligning) their work to the folklore they know and have (sort of) forgotten.

A disclaimer: we do not (necessarily) endorse Fomomindo's methods or his mappings. Nor do we (as of yet) possess the requisite expertise to judge the merit of what we understand to be his claims. We are increasingly convinced, however, that his catalogic work could be the foundation for an important enterprise aimed at understanding the scope of motifs, tale types, aphorisms, parables, myths, and legends that encage the human animal cognition project. Doctor Fomomindo is acutely aware that his incomplete catalog, his partially filled pitcher, contains no more than a drop of water from the ocean of comparative psychology—a sea of empirical results that has been rising for a century and a half. Nonetheless, from the notes to his colleague, Doctor Folklomindo, that appear sporadically throughout the FOMANCOG, it is clear to us that it remains his unshakable belief that a structural juxtaposition of the questions, methodological quagmires, and theoretical controversies in animal cognition alongside known folklore might one day serve as a trail of bread crumbs leading us out of a very dark forest. (NB: We are aware that this appendix will be seen in a different light by those who have very recently begun to ponder the possibility of approaching the question of animal cognition through a folkloristic lens. Yet any intelligent and informed future discussions of "animal folklore" will necessitate that all interested parties become intimately familiar with [read: *read*] the science. If nothing else, Doctor Fomomindo's catalog could be a jumpstart in that direction.)

Finally, a note about format. Although we recognize the archaic tint of the old-school Courier font, Doctor Fomomindo's laboratory had a standard operating procedure prescribing differing fonts for protocols, data sheets, and result summaries. We therefore have elected to reproduce the index, with no apologies, precisely as we found it.

```
8709-01
94-TALES
Notebook 1
```

A Future Index of Anthropomorphized Animal Behaviors and Their Connection to Comparative Psychology

```
A dear colleague of mine, Doctor Folklomindo, recently introduced
me to several catalogs that folklorists use to both empirically
document and indexically categorize certain structural and the-
matic elements of the narrative body of work that Homo sapiens
have produced. As I studied these indices, I was both astonished
and puzzled. Good heavens, the endless hours of human labor that
must have been spent producing such exhaustive and detailed ref-
erence works! My perplexity soon gave way to excitement, however,
as I realized how these scholarly tomes could animate my ongoing
efforts to catalog the folk psychological challenges that confront
anyone who attempts to objectively study animal intelligence. In
a flash, I realized how naive and frail (nay, anemic!) my past
attempts had been. All along, folklorists had already devised sev-
eral rough-and-ready systems that I could co-opt to fulfill the
boldest dream of my career: to document how the uniquely human
mental faculty to ask (and answer) why-questions limits our pro-
gress in understanding animal minds.
    Yes, I still recall that morning, years ago, when, like the
mythologized box-stacking chimpanzees of my hero, Wolfgang Köhler,
I was struck with my own personal eureka moment—a divine revela-
tion that all my efforts to ground higher-order human concepts in
the animal mind were (to use an admittedly folksy turn of phrase)
a fool's quest. Oh, but not just my research . . . the entire sci-
entific edifice of animal cognition . . . a century-long exercise
in tail chasing. All of the ethereal, higher-order, analogical
constructs we imputed to animals—constructs such as space, time,
fairness, force, minds, weight, religion, culture, causes, fam-
ily, motherhood, maps, mortality, feelings, numbers, language (I
could go on)—were no more than human redescriptions of the myriad
```

first-order mental operations we already knew we shared in common with animals of every size, color, and stripe. But the unearthing of the operations of such ancient mental systems brought us no closer to answering if other species engage in higher-order redescriptions—if they share with us the analogical (metaphorical) wherewithal to conceive of gods, ghosts, or gravity. Rather, we were simply uncovering the fodder for our human redescriptions. To be sure, this was a noble effort in its own right. But like [character {A}] in [tale type {Q}], we thought we were pursuing [goal {X.14-2}] when we were really pursuing [goal {Y.1}], so we were destined to meet [tragic end {Z.15-5}]. Our "scientific" protocols were increasingly resembling the storyboards of movies or plays or even fables.

But behold! Thanks to my friend, the good Doctor Folklomindo, I now possess a new vocabulary to express myself: I can say with both rectitude and a high degree of confidence that motifs and tale types inundate the study of animal cognition! I challenged myself: Could a **FO**lk **M**otif-index of **AN**imal **COG**nition (a FOMANCOG, for short) be generated to rigorously catalog human stories and proverbs and fables and motifs and legends and myths and anecdotes and jokes and sayings and epics and folk songs that inform—nay, constitute—the very wellspring of the scientists' research efforts? Could every entry in said FOMANCOG become a focal point for a future folkloristic (I love this word!) investigation? And could such research be conducted under the umbrella of a yet-to-be-named subdiscipline dedicated to quantitative and theoretical investigations of the impact of folklore on the cognitive operations of humans studying animals under the auspices of science? I have now read more than a thousand animal folktales, and the FOMANCOG that follows is my initial attempt to hurry this future forward.

A confession: I must admit that after reading so many animal folktales, I became itchy to write one of my own, one that could sum up what Doctor Folklomindo and I believe offers an important moral for the field of animal cognition. Once again, I challenged myself: If my former colleagues were to gather on a mountaintop to write a cautionary fable that captured what *they* believed was the primary obstacle to the objective study of animal cognition, what would it be? After some deliberation, I wrote the following:

The Fox and the Ape
A fox who was gathering grapes happened upon an ape in a cage.
   The Fox proposed an arrangement: "You have been captured by hunters and left in this cage, and so you must be very hungry. I will leave my grapes here out of your reach and gather more. If you agree to scare away any thieves, I will split all the spoils when I return."

The Ape promptly agreed. But as soon as the Fox disappeared into the brush, the Ape reached out from his cage and snapped a branch off a nearby bush and used it to rake in the grapes.

When the Fox returned and saw the Ape had eaten her grapes, she exclaimed, "I do not know how you managed to steal my grapes, but it was my fault for assuming that I was so much smarter than you."

Moral: Only the fool underestimates the intelligence of others.

Although I may lack the objectivity to know for certain, I do believe this fable accurately summarizes the view currently dominant among leading comparative psychologists. Of some minor interest and by way of contrast: in consulting several bibliographic sources focused on African folktales—which I have discovered are underrepresented in the extant folkloristic indexes—I stumbled upon a Nigerian folktale entitled "The Tortoise and the Gourd of Wisdom." In it, the wise tortoise decides to gather all the wisdom in the world and put it inside a gourd and then hang it in a tree. After collecting the wisdom, he ties the gourd to his chest and attempts to climb the tree. Alas, despite several tries, the gourd gets between him and the tree, and he falls repeatedly. A man who is watching tells him it would be easier if he tied the gourd to his back. The tortoise does so and discovers the man was right. But herein lies a tortoisian paradox: If he had truly collected all the wisdom in the world, how can the man have known a new trick? Despondent, the tortoise cracks the gourd open and lets the wisdom spill out. He realizes it cannot contain all the earth's wisdom because man is wiser than the wisest of the animals (for the reference, see below: NFT/"The Tortoise and the Gourd of Wisdom").

In conclusion, though my work here surely remains *in progress*, I hope it will at least convince Doctor Folklomindo that we were right: there is significant overlap between the Psychologist's description of animal cognition and the characteristic representations of animals in the handful of folkloristic indexes and idiosyncratic bibliographic sources I have consulted. Folklomindo well warned me that any such index could prove to be a siren song of sorts, and as I now run my fingers down the punctate, ever-expanding (and in some places uncomfortably haphazard) categories in this preliminary FOMANCOG, his caution proves prescient. With this in mind, I conclude by emphasizing my hope that this work be viewed as a rapid gesture sketch, an outline of the problem that might stimulate additional unending research into timeless questions, including, most importantly, what do humans really want from animals? My working hypothesis is quite simple: to be just as human as we need them to be.

The (Preliminary) FOMANCOG

Sources:

ADLG — *A Dictionary of Latin and Greek Quotations, Proverbs, Maxims and Mottos.* Edited by Henry Thomas Riley. London: George Bell and Sons. 1909.

AFS^ — *African Folktales and Sculpture.* Selected by Paul Radin and Einore Marvel. New York: Bollingen Foundation, Series XXII Pantheon. 1952.

AGFT* — *Agikuyu Folk Tales.* Ngumbu Njururi. London: Oxford University Press. 1966.

ATU — *The Types of International Folktales: A Classification and Bibliography, Based on the System of Antti Aarne and Stith Thompson.* Hans-Jörg Uther. Folklore Fellows Communications, no. 284-286 (vol. 133-135). Helsinki: Suomalainen Tiedeakatemia, Academia Scientiarum Fennica. 2004.

BAF* — *The Book of African Fables.* Jan Knappert. Studies in Swahili Languages and Literature, Vol. 3. New York: Edwin Mellen. 2001.

CFT* — *Cajun Folktales.* J. J. Reneaux. Little Rock: August House. 1992.

CIP — *Curiosities in Proverbs; A Collection of Unusual Adages, Maxims, Aphorisms, Phrases and Other Popular Dicta from Many Lands.* Dwight Edwards Marvin. New York and London: G. P. Putnam's Sons. 1916.

FOB* — *Kalila and Dimna, or the Fables of Bidpai.* Translated by Wyndham Knatchbull. Oxford: W. Baxter for J. Parker. 1819.

FTC — *The Folktale Cat.* Edited by Frank de Caro. Little Rock: August House. 1992.

FTFL* — *Folk Tales from French Louisiana.* Corinne L. Saucier. Baton Rouge: Claitor's. 1972.

FTM* — *Folk-Tales of Mahakoshal.* Verrier Elwin. London: Oxford University Press. 1944.

GGS — General Google Search

IMF — *Index of Mexican Folktales.* Stanley L. Robe. Folklore Studies: 26. Berkeley: University of California Press. 1973.

JSS^ — *Jamaican Song and Story.* Edited by Walter Jekyll. New York: Dover. [1907] 1966.

MRT* — *A Treasury of Mississippi River Tales.* Edited by B. A. Botkin. New York: Bonanza. 1978.

NAAS* — *Native American Animal Stories.* Joseph Bruchac. Golden, CO: Fulcrum. 1992.

NCF* — *The Frank C. Brown Collection of North Carolina Folklore*, Vol. 1. Edited by Newman Ivy White. Durham, NC: Duke University Press. 1952.

NFT* — *Nigerian Folk Tales.* Told by Olawale Idewu and Omotayo Adu and recorded by Barbara K. and Warren S. Walker. New Brunswick, NJ: Rutgers University Press. 1961.

PER — Perry Index (NB: The modern summaries are from fablesofaesop.com, an online archive linking the Perry Index to short summaries connected to variants of the full text fables. Versions include Townsend, L'Estrange, Eliot/Jacobs, Jones, Crane Poetry Visual, JBR Collection [an 1874 collection], *Aesop for Children* [a 1919 collection with pictures by Milo Winter], *One Hundred Fables* [by J. Northcote], *Some of Aesop's Fables* [by A. and R. Caldecott], *Mille Fabulae et Una: 1001 Aesop's Fables in Latin*, *Fables de La Fontaine*, *Aesop in Rhyme* [by Jefferys Taylor], and *Fables of Aesop and Others* [by Samuel Croxall]).

TMI — *Motif-Index of Folk-Literature: A Classification of Narrative Elements in Folktales, Ballads, Myths, Fables, Mediaeval Romances, Exempla, Fabliaux, Jest-Books, and Local Legends.* Stith Thompson. Revised and enlarged edition. Bloomington and Indianapolis: Indiana University Press. 1955–1958.

RFT* — *Russian Folk Tales*. Edited by Albert B. Lord. Avon, CT: Heritage. 1970.

SAI — Source as Indicated

SFFS* — *Scottish Fairy and Folk Tales*. Edited by George [Brisbane] Douglas. New York: Arno. 1977.

SFLS* — *Storytellers: Folktales and Legends from the South*. Edited by John A. Burrison. Athens: University of Georgia Press. 1989. [Chapter numbers indicated in brackets.]

^Tales are identified by numerals that correspond to numbered tales inside the cited work.
*Tales are identified by titles provided in the source text.

A. Animals and Spirituality[1]

A1. Animals and Awe
   A1a. Apes awed by (and dance for) rain[2]

---

1. Using methods from both religious studies and anthropology of religion, James Harrod (2014) concludes that chimpanzees engage in religious behaviors: "A comprehensive review of primatology reports reveals that chimpanzees do perform ritualized patterns of behavior in response to birth, death, consortship, and elemental natural phenomena. A structuralist analysis of these patterns shows that chimpanzees deploy similar formulaic action schemas involving recombination of syntagmatic and paradigmatic behaviors across all four of these life-situations. In the course of these performances, chimpanzees decontextualize and convert everyday communicative signals to express non-ordinary emotions of wonder and awe. The patterning of chimpanzee ritual behaviors evidences all the components of a prototypical trans-species definition of religion" (8).

Note that he also suggests the possibility of extending this analysis to other species (cf. Bering 2001, "Theistic Percepts in Other Species: Can Chimpanzees Represent the Minds of Non-Natural Agents?" in *Journal of Cognition and Culture*).

2. Jane Goodall (1971) first described the now-famous chimpanzee "rain dance," which has often been linked to the possibility of a preternatural predilection among chimpanzees. Whiten et al. (2001) define the behavior as follows: "At the start of heavy rain, several adult males perform vigorous charging displays. Displays tend to return the males to their starting position, to be coordinated or in parallel,

(ADLG/"Then the prating of the crow, with loud note, invites the rain") (IMF/*82—In time of drought, animals direct litany to opossum to intervene and bring rains: "Saint opossum, ears of plush, hide of velvet, snout of amber, paws of silk!" Opossum is flattered.) (TMI/B192.2.—Rain-withholding deer killed: rain released. B791.—Elephants have power to bring rain. D2143.1.1.—D2143.1.13.—Rain produced by [various forms of] magic. F420.1.3.11.—Water-spirit as apelike creature.)

A1b. Apes awed by waterfall[3]

(TMI/F141.4.—Waterfall as otherworld barrier. B11.3.1.2.—Dragon's home beneath waterfall.)

A1c. Apes awed by the sea from a cliff[4]

(BAF/"The Elephant and the Hare"—Animal council awed by miraculous intervention of spiritual world on behalf of elephant.) (TMI/F808.—Extraordinary cliff, thin as a hair, sharp as a blade, slippery as an eel's tail, high as a mast.)

A1d. Apes awed by forest fire[5]

---

may include slow charges as well as rapid and may involve a variety of display patterns" (1492). After witnessing it for the first time, Goodall shares her reactions: "I continued to sit there, staring almost in disbelief at the white scars on the tree trunks and the discarded branches on the grass—all that remained, in the rain-lashed landscape, to prove that the wild 'rain dance' had taken place at all. I should have been even more amazed had I known I would only see such a display twice more in the next ten years. Often, it is true, male chimpanzees react to the start of heavy rain by performing a rain dance, but this is usually an individual affair" (1971, 53).

3. Goodall (1999) offers another classic anecdote in which she recounts chimpanzees stopping at a waterfall: "Is it not possible that the chimpanzees are responding to some feeling like awe? A feeling generated by the mystery of water; water that seems alive, always rushing past yet never going, always the same yet ever different. Was it perhaps similar feelings of awe that gave rise to the first animistic religions, the worship of the elements and the mysteries of nature over which there was no control? Only when our prehistoric ancestors developed language would it have been possible to discuss such internal feelings and create a shared religion" (18).

4. An overlooked but ought-to-be-classic incident of chimpanzee awe occurred during Wolfgang Köhler's landmark studies of chimpanzee intelligence detailed in his monograph, *The Mentality of Apes* ([1917] 1925). Köhler directed a well-known series of experiments (including the iconic box-stacking-to-get-the-banana-hanging-out-of-reach study) using seven captive chimpanzees. The studies took place on Tenerife in the Canary Islands during World War I. The apes lived in a compound not far from the bluffs overlooking the Atlantic Ocean. At one point, his apes escaped from their outdoor compound only to be found hours later, sitting quietly in a line on the rocks, staring out over the sea as the evening fell (see Ley 1990, 12).

5. Lin Edwards (2010) reports:

Unusual behaviors have been observed in wild chimpanzees in West Africa in the face of grass fires. The chimps did not

(FTM/"The Too-Helpful Monkey"—Frustrated monkey sets boy's house on fire.) (TMI/B251.8.—Animals observe sacred revelation.)

A2. Animals and Rituals

A2a. Chimpanzees worship at tree temples[6]

(BAF/"The Monkeys"—Monkeys were once great builders who were tempted by the devil. They constructed a tower to try to reach heaven and kill God with bows and arrows. (BAF/"The Goat Becomes a Pilgrim"—Goat heads to Mecca.) (IMF/72*E—Coyote becomes a priest and starts out for his new parish with rabbit as altar boy.) (TMI/B253.1.—Snakes have

---

panic or flee, and some made ritualistic displays that suggest they understand fire and do not fear it, and they may even be able to control it. . . . Dr. Pruetz saw the behavior, including "fire dancing" on two occasions in 2006, and said she was surprised at how well the chimps could predict the behavior of the fires, which was better than her own ability. She said in one case there was fire on three sides, and yet the chimps remained calm, even though the flames and smoke were clearly visible. Pruetz said she thought their calmness could represent a key stage in controlling fire since it is necessary to overcome the fear before control becomes a possibility.

6. A recent account in *Nature Scientific Reports* describes video records of chimpanzees throwing stones at trees (Kühl et al. 2016). This behavior has prompted the speculation that these trees are chimpanzee temples. Laura Kehoe, one of the authors of the report, notes: "Maybe we found the first evidence of chimpanzees creating a kind of shrine that could indicate sacred trees. Indigenous West African people have stone collections at 'sacred' trees and such man-made stone collections are commonly observed across the world and look eerily similar to what we have discovered here" (2016).

The possibility of chimpanzee religion caused the story to be covered in forty-five news outlets and elevated the impact of this article to the ninety-ninth percentile of all articles tracked by Almetrics (a rating system tracking the amount of online attention an article receives). Writing for the *Daily Mail*, Simon Barnes (2016) expounds:

Everything I have read and observed of humans and animals in the entire course of my life writing about our natural world has confirmed that we have so much more in common with our fellow creatures than we think. Whether we are talking about communication, intelligence, problem-solving, tool-making, awareness of self, the ability to experience grief, happiness, love and consciousness itself, Charles Darwin was—as usual—spot on when he said: "The difference in mind between man and the higher animals, great as it is, certainly is one of degree and not of kind." So why not add religion to the list?

Rowan Hooper (2016), at *New Scientist*, agrees: "Perhaps [the chimpanzees] are paying respect to it, in some way. I've also heard stories of chimps performing dances in front of waterfalls. Maybe chimps have some understanding of impressive natural phenomena such as rain storms, wild fires and waterfalls and are paying 'respect' to them. So I always hoped that we'd find evidence of a 'temple' in the forest."

mass. B253.2—Wolves have annual [church] feast. V111.3.1.—Birds indicate site where a church is to be built. J1447.—The favored swine. Dog reproaches sow that Venus will not allow those who have eaten swine to enter her temple. Sow says that it is because the goddess abhors those who kill swine. F171.5.—Animals in otherworld pass in and out of church and become humans.) (ATU/613—"The Two Travelers." Two travelers argue over whose religion is more powerful. The travelers call on people and animals to act as judges.)

A2b. Funeral rituals
    A2b.1. Magpie tries to bury friend[7]
        (TMI/B251.2.12.—Birds take part at saint's funeral.)
    A2b.2. Scrub jay funerals[8]
        (TMI/A2223.7.—Ravens show Adam how to bury dead. Z32.—The funeral procession of the hen. Animals one by one join the procession.)
    A2b.3. Elephant funeral rituals
        A2b.3.a. Paying respect to bones of the dead
            A2b.3.a.1. Elephant pays respect to relatives' bones[9]
                (ATU/68—"The Jackal Trapped in the Animal [Elephant] Hide." The elephant's children inspect their parent's carcass to discover a hyena inside.) (NAAS/"The Dogs Who Saved Their Master"—Dog makes hunter a promise to come back and gather his bones if he

---

7. Marc Bekoff (2009), professor emeritus of ecology and evolutionary biology at the University of Colorado, describes the burial rituals of magpies: "One approached the corpse, gently pecked at it, just as an elephant would nose the carcass of another elephant, and stepped back. Another magpie did the same thing. Next, one of the magpies flew off, brought back some grass and laid it by the corpse. Another magpie did the same. Then all four stood vigil for a few seconds and one by one flew off" (85).

Bekoff also notes, "We can't know what they were actually thinking or feeling, but reading their action there's no reason not to believe these birds were saying a magpie farewell to their friend" (84).

8. Iglesias, McElreath, and Patricelli 2012, "Western Scrub-Jay Funerals: Cacophonous Aggregations in Response to Dead Conspecifics," in *Animal Behaviour*.

9. Douglas-Hamilton and Douglas-Hamilton 1975, *Among the Elephants*; Moss 1988. *Elephant Memories: Thirteen Years in the Life of an Elephant Family*; Spinage 1994, *Elephants*; and Douglas-Hamilton, Bhalla, Wittemyer, and Vollrath 2006. "Behavioural Reactions of Elephants towards a Dying and Deceased Matriarch," in *Applied Animal Behaviour Science*. And for a pop cultural gem, see Scar to Simba in *The Lion King* (1994): "An elephant graveyard is no place for a young prince."

        gives his life fending off monster.) (PER/447—"The Lark Burying Her Father." A lark found no place to bury her father and so used her head. This is why the lark now has a crest.)
    A2b.3.a.2. Elephant does *not* pay respect to relatives' bones[10]

        (NAAS/"Salmon Boy"—Boy does not respect bodies of the dead salmon, so he is drowned. Salmon people teach salmon boy how to respect the bones of the salmon he eats. He comes back to life.)

A2c. Grieving over the dead[11]
  A2c.1. Mothers and babies
    A2c.1.a. Mothers who carry dead babies
      A2c.1.a.1. Orca whale mom sets world record for grief over dead baby[12]

        (TMI/A2275.4.1.—Green pigeon cheated out of its chick and is always mourning.)

---

  10. McComb, Baker, and Moss 2006, "African Elephants Show High Levels of Interest in the Skulls and Ivory of Their Own Species," in *Biology Letters*

  11. For an overview of animal grief by an anthropologist, see Barbara King's book *How Animals Grieve*, published by University of Chicago Press in 2013. Another cultural gem is *Elephant's Graveyard*, by George Brant (2010) (winner of the 2008 Keene Prize for Literature), which is billed as "the true tale of . . . the only known lynching of an elephant. Set in September of 1916, the play combines historical fact and legend, exploring the deep-seated American craving for spectacle, violence and revenge" (Samuel French 2019).

  12. Lori Cuthbert and Douglas Main (2018) reported on a major news story for *National Geographic*:

    An orca named J35 has finally dropped her dead calf, which she'd been pushing with her head for at least 17 days and 1,000 miles off the Pacific Northwest coast, in an unprecedented show of mourning that drew international attention. The sad spectacle was a prime example, and confirmation, of the complex emotional lives of these sophisticated cetaceans, experts say. Other orcas, and similar animals like dolphins, have been seen apparently mourning their dead, but this is by far the longest recorded example of such behavior. J35, nicknamed Tahlequah, is a 20-year-old member of the long-studied J Pod of Southern Resident Killer Whales. These orcas, along with their endangered extended family—K and L pods—inhabit a huge territory that includes waters off Seattle, Vancouver, and Victoria, British Columbia. Researchers worried that this "tour of grief" might seriously endanger the health of J35, but luckily, she appears to have made it through physically unharmed.

A2c.1.a.2. Primates (variants: chimps, gorillas, baboons, macaques][13]
(BAF/"The Hyena and the Jackal"—Ram and ewe say death prayers.)

A2c.1.a.3. Dolphin protects her dead infant[14]
(TMI/B256.3.1.—Deer furnish bier and bear saint's corpse to church.)

A2c.1.a.4. Giraffe cows react to dead baby[15]
(TMI/B301.6.2.—Faithful cow refuses to move for grief at master's death.)

A2c.1.b. Other reactions to dead babies

A2c.1.b.1. Chimp mom eats dead babies[16]
(FTM/"The Wagtail and the Mouse"—Babies (eggs) whisper that they want to eat mother when they are hatched.) (CIP/*English*—"The ape claspeth her young so long that at last she killeth them.")

A2c.2. Grief between different species

A2c.2.a. Koko the gorilla mourns Robin Williams's death[17]

---

13. Biro et al. 2010, "Chimpanzee Mothers at Bossou, Guinea Carry the Mummified Remains of Their Dead Infants," in *Current Biology*; Cronin et al. 2011, "Behavioral Response of a Chimpanzee Mother toward Her Dead Infant," in *American Journal of Primatology*; Warren and Williamson 2004, "Transport of Dead Infant Mountain Gorillas by Mothers and Unrelated Females," in *Zoo Biology*; Fashing et al. 2010, "Death among Geladas (*Theropithecus gelada*): A Broader Perspective on Mummified Infants and Primate Thanatology," in *American Journal of Primatology*; Sugiyama et al. 2009, "Carrying of Dead Infants by Japanese Macaque (*Macaca fuscata*) Mothers," in *Anthropological Science*.

14. Hubbs 1953, "Dolphin Protecting Dead Young," in *Journal of Mammalogy*.

15. Bercovitch 2013, "Giraffe Cow Reaction to the Death of Her Newborn Calf," in *African Journal of Ecology*.

16. Goodall 1977, "Infant Killing and Cannibalism in Free-Living Chimpanzees," in *Folia Primatologica*; Kooriyama 2009, "< Note> The Death of a Newborn Chimpanzee at Mahale: Reactions of Its Mother and Other Individuals to the Body," in *Pan Africa News*.

17. Before his death, Robin Williams visited Koko, a gorilla that had been hand raised by Dr. Francine Patterson since the early 1970s. After Williams's death, Patterson shared the news with Koko. An official press release of The Gorilla Foundation (2014) describes Koko's reaction:

> On Monday, Aug. 11, the day news broke of Williams' passing, Koko and Penny and Ron (Drs. Patterson and Cohn) were together when phone calls started coming in about the sad event. After the first call, Koko came to Dr. Patterson with an inquiring look on her face. Dr. Patterson explained that "we have lost a

(CFT/"M'su Carencro and Mangeur de Poulet"—Buzzard laments that his lot in life is to wait for other animals to die before he can eat.) (TMI/B301.7.—Faithful lapdog dies when mistress dies. A2275.1.—Animal cries a lament for person lost when animal was transformed.) (ATU/37—"Fox a Nursemaid [or Mourning-Woman] for Bear." Fox hired as mourning-woman by bear, eats corpse while mourning father prepares for funeral.)

A2c.3. Chimpanzee grief[18]
(AFS/23—Fox grieves for days over mother's death.) (BAF/"The Fly, or the Power of a Name"—Louse mourns death of husband.)

A2c.4. Pseudo-grief in piranhas[19]
(AFS/23—Wolf in grief after intentionally killing his mother.) (TMI/B301.6.1.—Cattle shed horns in grief.)

A2d. Reaction to sudden/tragic deaths

---

dear friend, Robin Williams." Koko was quiet and looked very thoughtful. . . . More phone calls about the news came in, and Koko overheard one from a former colleague who had worked with Williams while he filmed a public service announcement for The Gorilla Foundation (based on his visit with Koko) in 2003. The colleague's voice broke at the end of the conversation. About half an hour later, Koko signed to Penny: "CRY LIP" (LIP is Koko's sign for woman). At the end of the day, Koko became very somber, with her head bowed and her lip quivering.

For related episodes in elephants, see Douglas-Hamilton et al. 2006 and note 11.

18. Brown 1879, "Grief in the Chimpanzee," in *The American Naturalist*.

19. In a recent interview, Professor Frans de Waal of Emory University was asked about the widespread belief that animals mourn their dead. The interviewer recounted how, when one of his pet piranhas died, the other six behaved quite strangely. The interviewer then asked de Waal whether they were grieving for their companion. Frans de Waal replied, "I don't think so. Piranhas also take bites out of each other; I don't think they are very friendly with each other. In general, grieving is unlikely in fish—unless you have individually bonded fish which might be possible in some species." When asked why they were behaving so strangely, he stated, "Piranhas—like most fish—don't grieve. There is something called *Schreckstoff*—it is a substance that fish release when they are distressed. It is possible that your fish were just influenced by whatever happened to the other fish, in a more physiological way." Next, he was asked to explain the difference between that and "real" grieving. He replied: "Typical grieving happens with mothers and offspring in mammals. Usually, you find grieving with animals who have individual attachments, not just schooling or flying together, but having friends" (Osterath 2016).

        A2d.1. Chimpanzees witness death by fall from tree[20]
            (AFS/22—Porcupine witnesses tragic death of her husband. 28—Tortoise mourns his mother's tragic fall from tree.)
        A2d.2. Magpies gather after sudden death[21]
            (TMI/F1041.21.6.2.—Bird in great grief tears out feathers.) (BAF/"The Hyena and the Jackal"—Ram and ewe say death prayers.)
    A2e. Animals and odors of the dead
        A2e.1. Rats with a nose for the dead[22]
            (AFS/31—Hare disguises himself in the skin of murdered lion king and poses as king. King's wife becomes suspicious as death odor from her husband's skin grows stronger.)
        A2e.2. Sea lampreys avoid deathly odors[23]
            (BAF/"The Spider and the Jackal"—Jackal tells dog he can "smell a lot of dead rats here," and they leap out of the trap that the spider has tricked the rest of the animals into building around themselves.)

---

20. Teleki 1973, "Group Response to the Accidental Death of a Chimpanzee in Gombe National Park, Tanzania," in *Folia Primatologica*.

21. Miller and Brigham 1988, "'Ceremonial' Gathering of Black-Billed Magpies (*Pica pica*) after the Sudden Death of a Conspecific," in *The Murrelet*.

22. Carr, Landauer, and Sonsino (1981) state:
In a two-choice preference test, 48 adult male rats responded to the odors collected from pairs of adult males, one member of each pair having been lethally poisoned earlier and the other not poisoned. Sixteen subjects reliably preferred ($p < .02$) the odor from a nonpoisoned male over that from a poisoned male that had died 5 min before the odor-collection period was terminated, as did 16 subjects whose poisoned male had died 45 min before the odor-collection period was terminated. Sixteen subjects whose poisoned male was alive but moribund when the odor-collection period was terminated showed no reliable preference for either odor. Laboratory rats can discriminate between the odors from living vs freshly sacrificed conspecifics. The discrimination is not mediated by the odor of the poison used or by a stress odor induced by malaise. (67)

23. Wagner, Stroud, and Meckley (2011) state: "Here we confirm a long-standing anecdotal observation; the sea lamprey (*Petromyzon marinus*) actively avoids the odor emitted by decaying conspecifics. We extracted the semiochemical mixture produced by the putrefying carcasses of sea lampreys via Soxhlet extraction in ethanol and exposed groups of 10 migratory-phase lampreys to either the putrefaction extract (N = 8) or an ethanol control (N = 8) in a laboratory raceway. Sea lampreys rapidly avoided the putrefaction odor while exhibiting no response to the ethanol control" (1157).

A2e.3. Crabs find new homes by smelling out shells of the dead[24]

(FTM/"The Crab-Prince"—Crab pleads not to be killed repeatedly and is saved each time.) (JSS/XXIII.—Spider tricks crab into believing he is baptizing him, when really he is lowering him into a boiling pot. Crabs turns bright red. Spider eats crab for breakfast.)

B. Animals and Tool Use[25]

B1. Animals and Sticks[26]

B1a. Sticks for reaching (variants: great apes, lesser apes, monkeys of all sorts [including baboons], other mammals, birds, etc.)[27]

(TMI/A1446.—Acquisition of tools; A1446.0.1.—Culture hero steals tools for men.)

---

24. Small and Thacker (1994) state: "Crabs were attracted to dead conspecific odors up to 10 times more than to food odors. Crabs attracted to dead conspecifics displayed significantly more shell-acquisition behaviors: touching other crab's shells in an exploratory manner and switching shells if an empty shell was available" (169).

25. Charles Darwin described reports of tool use by chimpanzees and other primates in his 1871 classic, *The Descent of Man and Selection in Relation to Sex*:

> It has often been said that no animal uses any tool; but the chimpanzee in a state of nature cracks a native fruit, somewhat like a walnut, with a stone. Rengger easily taught an American monkey thus to break open hard palm-nuts, and afterwards of its own accord it used stones to open other kinds of nuts, as well as boxes. It thus also removed the soft rind of fruit that had a disagreeable flavour. Another monkey was taught to open the lid of a large box with a stick, and afterwards it used the stick as a lever to move heavy bodies; and I have myself seen a young orang put a stick into a crevice, slip his hand to the other end, and use it in the proper manner as a lever. (51)

Since Darwin, the study of tool use and manufacture in animals has exploded. For a somewhat dated (but stunningly expansive) catalog of animal tool behavior, see Beck's 1980 book *Animal Tool Behavior: The Use and Manufacture of Tools*. More recent historical overviews, summaries, and catalogs of animal tool use and manufacture are provided by the following: Bentley-Condit and Smith 2010, "Animal Tool Use: Current Definitions and an Updated Comprehensive Catalog," in *Behaviour*; Shumaker, Walkup, and Beck 2001, *Animal Tool Behavior: The Use and Manufacture of Tools by Animals*; and Seed and Byrne 2010, "Animal Tool-Use," in *Current Biology*.

26. Beck 1980.

27. As Benjamin B. Beck (1980) notes: "The use of an object as a rake to reach an otherwise unreachable incentive is a classic paradigm in laboratory studies of primate tool use" (47). I propose to create a separate catalog to keep track of all the ways in which humans have studied animals making and using stick and hooklike sticks.

B1b. Long vs. short sticks[28]
  (TMI/A2335.3.1.—Origin of anteater's proboscis, transformed digging stick.)
B1c. Rigid vs. floppy sticks[29]
  (TMI/A185.2.2.—God makes man's hand rigid so he can no longer torment captive.)
B1d. Rakes and hook sticks (variants: chimps, monkeys, New Caledonian crows, ravens, rodents)[30]
  (AFS/31—Animal villagers pursue hare to burrow and use a hooked stick to try to fish him out.) (BAF/"The Frog and the Lion"—Lion fetches hoe to get rabbit out of his hole. "The Animals at the Market Place"—Lioness goes fishing.) (MRT/"The Eel and the Catfish"—Eel is hooked by fisherman but saves his life by turning into a hook and seizing larger catfish for fisherman.) (TMI/A1457.1.—Origin of the fishhook. F531.3.12.1.—Giant threads an elephant on a fishhook.) (SFLS/"Rabbit and Fox at the Well"—Fox goes fishing and catches fish.)
B1e. Touching sticks vs. connected sticks[31]
  (TMI/A625.2.1.—Heaven and earth originally connected by navel strings.)
B1f. Elephants make flyswatters from sticks[32]
  (BAF/"Mbuli the Hartebeest and the Mosquito"—Mosquito torments hartebeest, who breaks her leg trying to swat him.)
B1g. Sticks for honey[33]
  (TMI/A2823.—Origin of churning stick.)
B1h. Miscellaneous stick tricks
  B1h.1. Metasticks
    B1h.1.a. Chimp puts short sticks together to make long stick[34]
      (AFS/31—Hare ties hoe to lizard's tail so he can help him till the fields.)
    B1h.1.b. Ever-expanding stick trick[35]

---

28. Beck 1980.
29. Beck 1980.
30. Kumazawa-Manita et al. 2013, "Tool Use Specific Adult Neurogenesis and Synaptogenesis in Rodent (*Octodon degus*) Hippocampus," in *PLOS One*.
31. Beck (1980), but specifically, see Povinelli 2001, *Folk Physics for Apes*; and Seed et al. 2012, "Chimpanzee 'Folk Physics': Bringing Failures into Focus," in *Philosophical Transactions of the Royal Society of London B: Biological Sciences*.
32. Hart et al. 2001, "Cognitive Behaviour in Asian Elephants: Use and Modification of Branches for Fly Switching," in *Animal Behaviour*.
33. Yamagiwa et al. 1988, "Evidence of Tool-Use by Chimpanzees (*Pan troglodytes schweinfurthii*) for Digging Out a Bee-Nest in the Kahuzi-Biega National Park, Zaire," in *Primates*.
34. Beck 1980.
35. Beck 1980. See also Yerkes 1916, "The Mental Life of Monkeys and Apes: A Study of Ideational Behavior," in *Behavior Monographs*.

(BAF/"The Jackal and the Lion"—Jackal hammers sticks into ground to trap lion.) (ATU/225A—"The Tortoise Lets Itself Be Carried by Birds." A tortoise is carried into the air by two herons who are holding onto a stick that the tortoise has in its mouth.)

B1h.2. Crow uses short stick to make/get long stick[36]
(BAF/"The Leopard and Squirrels"—Squirrels fetch twigs to make a pit trap. "The Elephant and the Hare"—Hare makes resin and glues horns on his head.)

B1h.3. Parrot avoids the floppy stick[37]
(AFS/31—Lion's subjects cut rigid staves to beat him to death.)

B1h.4. The probing stick (a.k.a. the fishing wand)[38]
(AFS/23—Wolf finds a stick and uses it to stir pot.)

B1h.5. Gorilla stick tricks
    B1h.5.a. Gorilla uses a wading stick[39]
(BAF/"Ingratitude, or the Hippopotamus, the Hare and the Hyena"—Hyena gets ride across river on back of hippopotamus. "The Tortoise and the Baboon"—Baboon forced to wade across river.)
    B1h.5.b. Gorillas use water-smacking stick[40]
(BAF/"The Drought"—Animals bring digging sticks to dig for water.)

B1h.6. Savanna chimpanzees use digging sticks[41]
(FTM/"The Ant and the Charcoal"—Crows request horn from deer to dig for clay to make pot.) (NAAS/"Octopus and Raven"—Octopus uses wooden stick to dig for clams.)

B1h.7. Monkey without prehensile tail learns to use tail as a stick[42]

Yerkes was impressed that his orangutans learned to connect up to five (human-made) sticks to make a pole to push a food reward from a long, tube-like tunnel he had built.

36. Beck 1980; Clayton 2007, "Animal Cognition: Crows Spontaneously Solve a Metatool Task," in *Current Biology*.

37. Lambert et al. 2017, "Function and Flexibility of Object Exploration in Kea and New Caledonian Crows," in *Royal Society Open Science*.

38. Beck 1980.

39. Beck 1980.

40. Brown, Dunlap, and Maple 1982, "Notes on Water-Contact by a Captive Male Lowland Gorilla," in *Zoo Biology*.

41. Hernandez-Aguilar, Moore, and Pickering 2007, "Savanna Chimpanzees Use Tools to Harvest the Underground Storage Organs of Plants," in *Proceedings of the National Academy of Sciences*.

42. Erwin 1974, "Laboratory-Reared Rhesus Monkeys Can Use Their Tails as Tools," in *Perceptual and Motor Skills*.

(ATU/2—"The Tail-Fisher." The bear [wolf] is persuaded to fish with his tail through a hole in the ice. His tail soon freezes. When he is attacked and tries to escape, he loses his tail.)

B2. Animals and Ladders

B2a. Apes use boxes as stepping stools to get banana[43]
(NFT/"Why the Tortoise's Shell Is Cracked and Cooked"—Dog prays for mother in heaven to lower a rope so he can climb up and eat with her.)

B2b. Time-traveling apes from Earth's past are insulted at being asked to stack boxes to get bananas[44]
(FTFL/"The Hungry Bear"—Bear makes disparaging remarks about nest of wrens. Mother wren is deeply insulted; she finds bear and demands he take back his insulting comments.) (FTC/"Why Leopard Meets His Enemy Face-to-Face [Benin]"—Kitten proposes to insult leopard until she goes away.)

B2c. Apes use pogo stick to get bananas[45]
(GGS/"What's striped and bouncy? A *tiger on a pogo stick.*"[46])

B2d. Mouse makes ladder[47]
(BAF/"The Survivor Marries"—Rat and mole climb silk rope ladder spun by spider.)

B2e. Chimps use each other as ladders[48]
(ATU/31—"The Fox Climbs from the Pit on the Wolf's Back." A fox falls into a well and entices a wolf to jump into the well so that they can climb on each other's backs to escape. The fox uses the wolf's back as a ladder but leaves the wolf stranded in the well.)
(See also H5b. Chimps escape from compound to freedom using [fallen] trees)

B3. Animals and Projectiles

B3a. Projectiles and Food

B3a.1. Crow drops the walnut on hard pavement[49] (variant: Japanese crow learns to use cars to crack nuts for him and observes traffic lights so as to not be killed)[50]

---

43. Beck 1980, but the classic reference is Köhler (1917) 1925.
44. *Escape from the Planet of the Apes*, 1971.
45. Köhler (1917) 1925.
46. Whitlock 2015.
47. Zimmerman 1952, "Werkzeug-Benutzung durch eine Zwergmaus," in *Zeitschrift für Tierpsychologie*.
48. Köhler (1917) 1925.
49. Cristol and Switzer 1999, "Avian Prey-Dropping Behavior. II. American Crows and Walnuts," in *Behavioral Ecology*.
50. Crows in Japan are reported to have not only learned how to drop hard-to-crack nuts onto pavement but also how to drop them in the middle of traffic intersections so that cars will run over the nuts and crack them. In addition, the birds are reported to have learned to

(TMI/J101.—Crow drops pebbles into water jug so as to be able to drink. B31.1.2.—Roc [legendary bird of prey] drops rock that is so large it destroys ship.)

B3a.2. Gulls drop shellfish on rocks[51]

(BAF/"The Lizard and the Chain of Events"—Monkey drops heavy fruit on elephant's head.) (TMI/K401.2.2.—Crow drops stolen necklace in snake's hole; snake is killed.)

B3a.3. Crows drop mollusks on hard rocks[52]

(TMI/A2211.11.—Tortoise dropped by eagle—hence, cracks in his shell.) (SAI—J. M. Synge's ethnography *Aran Islands* becomes ethology when he reports an anecdote of crows dropping shellfish on the rock to break them open. One crow, however, is dropping a golf ball "continually without any result" [Synge (1907) 1992, 126–27].)

B3a.4. Animals drop crushing projectiles

---

wait for the pedestrian crossing signs to flash WALK so that they can safely venture into the street to retrieve the crushed nuts. A YouTube video excerpt of a David Attenborough/BBC Wildlife film (2007) showing the behavior has received 1,699,380 views. Though I agree with Doctor Folklomindo that the textual presentations of online profiles are at least twice removed from genuine, human reports, I cannot help but attend to a sampling of the most recent viewer comments, which depict a range of anthropomorphism, skepticism, and ambivalence: "I once saw a crow fill out a 1040 IRS tax form, then drop it in a mailbox" (DEO); "Very impressive! Think if I was driving in Tokyo and saw a nut in the road id run over it on purpose just for the crow" (Shane Earley); "Just wait 'till they figure out how to push the button . . ." (HowlingWolf518); "There are humans i know who are not as clever as these crows" (Karl White); "We used to watch the crows in Washington State put chestnuts under our car tires. It seemed like they had mostly learned to put them in front of my car's tires, because I always pulled forward away from the curb, and under my roommate's tires, because he always backed out of the driveway. Really smart critters. Came out one morning to find around 8 chestnuts in front of each of my tires and a whole bunch of crows sitting in the tree next to our house watching me get into my car!" (Post Epoch); "Laugh now, but one day they'll be in charge" (Solitaria Nihilista); "TIL [Today I learned] crows use crosswalks better than humans do" (Alexander Kemble); "Nothing to be surprised about. The crow is Asian" (LilWayne MetalGod); "crows are good peoples" (Zeckza); "Dolphins have to step up cause crows are in the lead now" (inkilass). At the least, we can assume that the animals are not posting these comments. See also Grobecker 1978, "Crows Use Automobiles as Nutcrackers." in *Auk*; and Maple 1974, "Do Crows Use Automobiles as Nutcrackers?," in *Western Birds*.

51. Barash, Donovan, and Myrick 1975, "Clam Dropping Behavior of the Glaucous-Winged Gull (*Larus glaucescens*)," in *The Wilson Bulletin*; Oldham 1930, "On the Shell-Smashing Habit of Gulls," in *Ibis*.

52. Whiteley, Pritchard, and Slater 1990, "Strategies of Mussel Dropping by Carrion Crows *Corvus c. corone*," in *Bird Study*.

B3a.4.a. Egyptian vultures throw stones to crack ostrich eggs[53]
(TMI/2163.5.1.—Saint's prayer brings large flight of birds carrying stones in talons; these missiles dropped upon enemies cause terror.)

B3b. Animals using weighted tools

B3b.1. Monkeys use stones to crack nuts (variants: bearded capuchins, yellow-breasted capuchins)[54]
(AFS/29—Lioness uses massive stone to block entrance to her cave, which is controlled by saying "Stone, open" and "Stone, close.")

B3b.2. Chimps use rocks to crack nuts[55]
(AFS/23—Fox uses rock to break wolf's teeth.)

B3b.3. Chimps roll heavy balls down ramp to get food[56]
(BAF/"The Frog and the Lion"—Lion chases hare into a hole and puts a stone at entrance to trap him.)

B3b.4. Bird uses heavy stones to open trapdoor[57]
(BAF/"The Frog and the Lion"—Lion threatens to put heavy stones on frog to punish him.)

B3b.5. Sea otters use hammer stones[58]
(BAF/"The Jackal's Greed"—Jackal uses stone to open gazelle's skull.)

B3b.6. Kanzi the bonobo makes a stone tool[59]
(FTM/"The Monkey Son-in-Law"—Monkey requests an ax.)

B3b.7. Anvil-using banded mongooses[60]

---

53. Van Lawick-Goodall and van Lawick-Goodall 1966, "Use of Tools by the Egyptian Vulture, *Neophron percnopterus*," in *Nature*.

54. Visalberghi et al. 2007, "Characteristics of Hammer Stones and Anvils Used by Wild Bearded Capuchin Monkeys (*Cebus libidinosus*) to Crack Open Palm Nuts," in *American Journal of Physical Anthropology*; Anderson 1990, "Use of Objects as Hammers to Open Nuts by Capuchin Monkeys (*Cebus apella*)," in *Folia Primatologica*; and Canale et al. 2009, "First Record of Tool Use by Wild Populations of the Yellow-Breasted Capuchin Monkey (*Cebus xanthosternos*) and New Records for the Bearded Capuchin (*Cebus libidinosus*)," in *American Journal of Primatology*.

55. Boesch and Boesch 1984, "Mental Map in Wild Chimpanzees: An Analysis of Hammer Transports for Nut Cracking," in *Primates*.

56. Povinelli 2012, *World Without Weight: Perspectives on an Alien Mind*. (NB: See especially chapter 6, "The Impact of Weight.")

57. Bird and Emery 2009a, "Insightful Problem Solving and Creative Tool Modification by Captive Nontool-Using Rooks," in *Proceedings of the National Academy of Sciences*.

58. Houk and Geibel 1974, "Observation of Underwater Tool Use by the Sea Otter, *Enhydra lutris Linnaeus*," in *California Fish and Game*.

59. Toth et al. 1993, "Pan the Tool-Maker: Investigations into the Stone Tool-Making and Tool-Using Capabilities of a Bonobo (*Pan paniscus*)," in *Journal of Archaeological Science*.

60. Müller 2010, "Do Anvil-Using Banded Mongooses Understand Means-End Relationships? A Field Experiment," in *Animal Cognition*.

(FOJ/"Kachi Kachi Mountain"—Badger pretends to help old woman pound flour with mortar and pestle but then clubs and kills her with pestle.)
- B3c. Weaponized projectiles
    - B3c.1. The chimp who threw missiles[61]
        (see above, TMI/D2163.5.1.)
    - B3c.2. Chimps throw sticks at stuffed leopard[62]
        (TMI/D451.6.3.—Transformation: stick to weapon.)
    - B3c.3. Poop projectiles
        - B3c.3.a. Fieldfare thrush bird emits well-aimed poop projectiles[63]
            (IMF/103C*—Ass and lion each claims to be king of animals. Each shows the other how he fights. Lion uses claws to tear tree to shreds. Ass says that he shoots cannon balls, begins to bray, and defecates. Lion is frightened.) (SFLS/"The Little Bird"—Cow poops on cold and shivering little bird to help warm him.) (FOJ/"The Monkey and the Crab"—Monkey defecates into crab's burrow to try to flush him out.)
        - B3c.3.b. Accidental monkey poop dropping[64]
            (FOJ/"The Monkey and the Pheasant"—Dung spreads itself on steps. Monkey slips and hits his head.)
        - B3c.3.c. Chimpanzee poop throwing[65]
            (BAF/"The Two Friends"—Tortoise threatens to spoil leopard's basket with his poop.)
        - B3c.3.d. Elephants throw poop too[66]

---

61. Osvath 2009, "Spontaneous Planning for Future Stone Throwing by a Male Chimpanzee," in *Current Biology*.

62. Kortlandt 1975, "Wild Chimpanzees Using Clubs in Fighting an Animated Stuffed Leopard," in *War, Its Causes and Correlates*.

63. Löhrl 1983, "Zur Feindabwehr der Wacholderdrossel (*Turdus pilaris*) [Well-aimed defecation in the fieldfare (*Turdus pilaris*)]," in *Journal für Ornithologie*.

64. Souza-Alves and Ferrari 2010, "Responses of Wild Titi Monkeys, *Callicebus coimbrai* (Primates: Platyrrhini: Pitheciidae), to the Habituation Process," in *Zoologia*.

65. Personal communication with many zoo visitors; see also Hopkins et al. 2005, who, in their study, "Factors Influencing the Prevalence and Handedness for Throwing in Captive Chimpanzees (*Pan troglodytes*)," in *Journal of Comparative Psychology*, tiptoe around this delicate issue in their catalog of 2,455 instances of chimpanzees' throwing behavior in captivity. Although they do not mention what, exactly, the chimpanzees were tossing, we can infer from context that a substantial proportion of it was, indeed, feces.

66. Kühme 1963, "Ethology of the African Elephant (*Loxodonta africana* Blumenbach 1797) in Captivity," in *International Zoo Yearbook*.

(BAF/"The Hedgehog, the Camel and the Lion"—Hedgehog uses camel's excrement to scare away lion king.)

B3c.4. Crows throw rocks in political protest[67]

(TMI/J369.2.—Ape throws away nut because of its bitter rind.)

B3c.5. Ant-lions make sand projectiles[68]

(BAF/"The Frog and the Lion"—Hare throws sand in frog's eyes to blind him.)

B3c.6. Ants drop stone projectiles[69]

(CIP/*Malabar*—"Anger is a stone cast at a wasp's nest.")

B3c.7. Baboons throw stones as weapons[70]

---

67. Mohsin Raza (2012) reports for *RT News*:

In a scene reminiscent of Alfred Hitchcock's thriller *The Birds*, a murder of crows has stoned several expensive vehicles parked near a regional legislative body in the Russian Urals, prompting internet jokes about possible political motives. "When leaving the office, I saw a group of drivers of ministers' and deputies' cars who were moving chaotically and swinging their arms," local lawmaker Maksim Ryapasov wrote in his blog. The drivers told the MP that fuss was caused by crows that were grabbing rocks from the roof of the building and "bombarding" cars with them for several hours. The MP noted that there is a "stone garden" on the assembly's roof, which was set up under the initiative of the legislature's chairwoman Lyudmila Babushkina. Apparently, it was those stones the crows used as weapons. As a result of the "bird protest," the windshields of at least three cars were broken. "I really don't know whose cars were there. But I personally saw a crow that threw a stone and then flew to get another one from the terrace," Ryapasov, the head of Liberal-Democratic fraction in the regional parliament wrote. "I'm not kidding," he added. The news has become a hit in the Russian blogosphere. In a battle of wits, users are actively discussing the "protest action" of "politically-active birds." Experts though have their own explanation for birds' "extremism." Most likely, the crows were simply having fun, ornithologist Tatiana Surkova told "Aktualno" information agency. "Crows love collecting different items, including stones, and piling them somewhere or throwing them down," she said.

68. Pierce 1986, "A Review of Tool Use in Insects," in *Florida Entomologist*.

69. Möglich and Alpert 1979, "Stone Dropping by *Conomyrma bicolor* (Hymenoptera: Formicidae): A New Technique of Interference Competition," in *Behavioral Ecology and Sociobiology*.

70. Darwin (1871) states:

In the cases just mentioned stones and sticks were employed as implements; but they are likewise used as weapons. Brehm states, on the authority of the well-known traveller Schimper, that in Abyssinia when the baboons belonging to one species (*C. gelada*) descend in troops from the mountains to plunder the fields, they sometimes encounter troops of another species

(AGFT/"Hare in the Well in the Jungle"—Hare uses heavy stone to smash hyena on the head.) (IMF/74C*—Rabbit breaks jaguar's teeth with green pear, strikes him in eye with coconut. And badger throws green zapote to coyote, whose teeth are smashed.) (See also above, TMI/D2163.5.1.)

B3c.8. Elephants throw rocks at rhinos[71]
(BAF/"The Two Friends"—Dogs throw stones at leopards.)
(See also "E12. Animals and Warfare.")

(*C. hamadryas*), and then a fight ensues. The Geladas roll down great stones, which the Hamadryas try to avoid, and then both species, making a great uproar, rush furiously against each other. Brehm, when accompanying the Duke of Coburg-Gotha, aided in an attack with fire-arms on a troop of baboons in the pass of Mensa in Abyssinia. The baboons in return rolled so many stones down the mountain, some as large as a man's head, that the attackers had to beat a hasty retreat; and the pass was actually for a time closed against the caravan. It deserves notice that these baboons thus acted in concert. Mr. Wallace on three occasions saw female orangs, accompanied by their young, "breaking off branches and the great spiny fruit of the Durian tree, with every appearance of rage; causing such a shower of missiles as effectually kept us from approaching too near the tree." (50)

Hamilton, Buskirk, and Buskirk (1975) offered confirmatory (albeit less dramatic) evidence of Darwin's report:

Anecdotal reports of stone throwing by baboons have been dismissed on the basis of the unreliability of correspondents and the improbability of oriented throwing by a quadruped anatomically incapable of overhand throwing. In spite of several years of field study elsewhere in Africa, often in rocky terrain, there are no reports by professional field observers of deliberate stone throwing by baboons. Nevertheless, in the course of a one-year study of three chacma baboon (*Papio ursinus*) troops living on the desert floor of the Kuiseb Canyon in South West Africa we observed numerous instances of stone release directed toward us. Stoning by these baboons is done from the rocky walls of the canyon where they sleep and retreat when they are threatened by real or imagined predators. Stones are lifted with one hand and dropped over the side. The stone tumbles down the side of the cliff or falls directly to the canyon floor. We recorded the details of 23 such incidents involving the voluntary release of 124 stones towards us. . . . This frequently resulted in stones whizzing over our heads. Usually we could dodge; but occasionally two or more individuals release stones at approximately the same time, complicating evasion. (488)

71. Wickler and Seibt 1997, "Aimed Object-Throwing by a Wild African Elephant in an Interspecific Encounter," in *Ethology*.

B4. Animals Use Tools for Transporting Food
  B4a. Japanese ants make "jar" from sand to transport honey[72]
    (BAF/"How the Goat Outwitted the Hyena"—Goat collects wild honey in a jar.)
  B4b. Chimps use bowls to transport food/water[73]
    (AFS/22—Mantis uses a bucket as a bowl for meat and then uses a ladle to serve soup to All-Devourer.)
B5. Miscellaneous Animal Tool Tricks
  B5a. Elephants (sort of) learn stick trick to open lids[74]
    (AGFT/"Hare in the Well in the Jungle"—Hare fools hyena by using long straw to breathe underwater.)
  B5b. Digger wasps use stone hammers to pound nest soil[75]
    (FOJ/"The Monkey and the Pheasant"—Monkey and pheasant use mortar and pestle to grind rice.) (IMF/*22—Opossum tells tiger that he is pounding testicles. Tiger takes large stone, pounds his. Opossum flees.)
  B5c. Sponge tools
    B5c.1. Dolphins teach each other to use sponges[76]
      (See "C4. Animal Teachers.")
    B5c.2. Chimps use sponges to mop up water[77]
      (NFR/"The Tortoise and the Gourd of Wisdom"—Tortoise gathers all of earth's wisdom and contains it inside a gourd.) (ATU/211b—"The Two Birds and Their Loads." Two birds have a contest to see which can fly higher while carrying a load. One bird carries salt. The other carries cotton. It rains, soaking the cotton, so the bird carrying salt wins.)
    B5c.3. Ants use sponges too[78]
      (NFR/"The Tortoise and the Gourd of Wisdom"—After realizing that man has secrets not contained in his Gourd of Wisdom, tortoise cracks it open and the knowledge seeps out.) (ATU/211a—"The Two Donkeys

---

72. Tanaka and Ono 1978, "The Tool Use by Foragers of *Aphaenogaster famelica*," in *Japanese Journal of Ecology*.
73. Takeshita and van Hooff 1996, "Tool Use by Chimpanzees (*Pan troglodytes*) of the Arnhem Zoo Community," in *Japanese Psychological Research*.
74. Nissani 2006, "Do Asian Elephants (*Elephas maximus*) Apply Causal Reasoning to Tool-Use Tasks?," in *Journal of Experimental Psychology: Animal Behavior Processes*.
75. Brockmann 1985, "Tool Use in Digger Wasps (Hymenoptera: Sphecinae)," in *Psyche: A Journal of Entomology*.
76. Krützen et al. 2005, "Cultural Transmission of Tool Use in Bottlenose Dolphins," in *Proceedings of the National Academy of Sciences*.
77. Goodall 1964, "Tool-Using and Aimed Throwing in a Community of Free-Living Chimpanzees," in *Nature*.
78. Maák et al. 2017, "Tool Selection During Foraging in Two Species of Funnel Ants," in *Animal Behaviour*.

and Their Loads." A donkey loaded with salt falls into the river, and its load gets lighter. A second donkey carrying sponges tries to lighten its load by the same technique, but the sponges get heavier, and the donkey almost drowns.)

B5d. Apes do not know size of stick that will fit through hole, cannot get food[79]

(ATU/41—"The Wolf Overeats in the Cellar." The fox persuades the wolf to enter a cellar and steal food. The wolf eats so much that he cannot escape through the hole he entered. He is killed.)

B6. Animals Pulling Strings for Treats (variants: over 160 bird/mammals/insect species)[80]

B6a. [Random example #1] Vulture pulls string for pieces of chicken meat[81]

---

79. Visalberghi, Fragaszy, and Savage-Rumbaugh 1995, "Performance in a Tool-Using Task by Common Chimpanzees (*Pan troglodytes*), Bonobos (*Pan paniscus*), an Orangutan (*Pongo pygmaeus*), and Capuchin Monkeys (*Cebus apella*)," in *Journal of Comparative Psychology*; and Tebbich et al. 2007, "Performance in a Tool-Using Task by Common Chimpanzees (*Pan troglodytes*), Bonobos (*Pan paniscus*), an Orangutan (*Pongo pygmaeus*), and Capuchin Monkeys (*Cebus apella*)," in *Journal of Comparative Psychology*. See also Povinelli 2001, chapter 8 and note 31.

80. Jacobs and Osvath (2015) describe the ancient history of the string-pulling problem and its connection to modern studies of animal psychology:

The history of using this practice with animals is far older than comparative psychology itself. The first documented reference is from the Roman naturalist Pliny the Elder (23–79 AD), who describes goldfinches pulling up small buckets of water. . . . A source of entertainment, the practice became so common that, since the end of the Middle Ages, the goldfinch has been called *putter* in Dutch; meaning one who draws water from a well. Similar names were present in German, English, and French in the 19th century. . . . It spread to America . . . and may have originated independently in Japan, using varied tits. . . . The popularity of the practice is reflected in two 17th century paintings by Abraham Mignon; still-life pictures of fruit with goldfinches pulling water buckets. . . . Overall, the practice seems to have had a wider cultural and historical impact than any other tests of animal intelligence. Perhaps people found it appealing to watch birds pull strings because it appears unusually clever. That said, although previously regarded as an interesting feat . . . in the 19th century making captive birds work for their food and water was heavily criticized as unnatural and cruel and, therefore, not suitable for studies by naturalists. (89)

81. Ellison, Watson, and Demers 2015, "Testing Problem Solving in Turkey Vultures (*Cathartes aura*) Using the String-Pulling Test," in *Animal Cognition*.

(AFS/23—Fox uses rope to tie sheep to tree. 28—Tortoise hides mother in tree and then ties string to basket so his mother can pull up food.)

B6b. [Random example #2] Raven pulls string of least effort[82]
(BAF/"You Cannot Win against the Elephant"—Bush pig ties string to elephant's leg to try to pull him in as meat but cannot.) (PER/287—"The Arab and His Camel." A camel was asked if he preferred to go uphill or downhill. The camel asked if the flat way through the desert was closed. Wise camel.)

B6c. [Random example #3] Bees pull strings to get nectar[83]
(NFT/"The Wasp and the Bee"—Bee listens to God and therefore knows how to put together all the things God requires him to put together.)

B6d. [Random case study] Knots and strings

B6d.1. Apes understand knots[84]
(AFS/31—Hare flatters lion and then braids his mane into ropes and ties him to tree.) (FTM/"The Origin of the Tiger Clan"—Tiger ties rope to a pot and lowers it into a well.) (NFT/"The Tortoise and the Boar"—Tortoise ties rope to his tail.)

B6d.2. Apes do *not* understand knots[85]
(BAF/"The Hare, the Rat, the Lion and the Tortoise"— Tortoise not any good at tying strings.) (NFT/"The Tortoise and the Boar"—Tortoise ties rope to his tail to make himself look bigger; boar is fooled.)

B6d.3. Apes may or may not understand knots[86]
(SAI/"A 'monkey-fist' is an informal nautical term referring to a 'lumpy knot worked into the end of a long light line . . . to add weight to the end of this cord'" [Beck 1973, 193]) (TMI/J681.1.1.—Jackal and leopard tie tails together for mutual protection. Frightened, they run apart and injure each other.)

C. Animals and Communication

C1. Animals and Language Acquisition[87]

---

82. Pfuhl 2012, "Two Strings to Choose from: Do Ravens Pull the Easier One?," in *Animal Cognition*.
83. Alem et al. 2016, "Associative Mechanisms Allow for Social Learning and Cultural Transmission of String Pulling in an Insect," in *PLOS Biology*.
84. Mayer et al. 2014, "Abstract Knowledge in the Broken-String Problem: Evidence from Nonhuman Primates and Pre-Schoolers," in *PLOS One*.
85. Detailed in Povinelli 2001, chapter 9; see note 31.
86. Finch 1941, "The Solution of Patterned String Problems by Chimpanzees," In *Journal of Comparative Psychology*.
87. Anderson's (2004) *Doctor Dolittle's Delusion: Animals and the Uniqueness of Human Language* provides a lively introduction to the human ascription of language to animals.

C1a. Humans rear apes in their homes to teach them language[88] (AFS/25—Speaking frog leads girl on journey.) (ATU/517—"The Boy Who Understands the Language of Birds." A boy who understands bird language repeats a bird's prophecy to the boy's father.) (GGS/A man in a movie theater notices what looks like a chimpanzee sitting next to him. "Are you a chimpanzee?" asked the man, surprised. "Yes." "What are you doing at the movies?" The chimpanzee replies, "Well, I liked the book."[89]) (TC/"The Linguistic Cat [England]"—Cat overhears mice communicating in both cat and dog language. When cat hears mice say in dog language that dog has left, she pounces on them and says to herself that she always knew it would be useful to have a second language.)

---

88. As Franz Kafka's *Report to an Academy* amply testifies, humans have long believed in the alchemic possibilities of immersing chimpanzees (and other great apes) in human culture—including human language. In this case, the "gold" would be achieved by altering the natural mental trajectory of apes and turning them into humans; "silver" would be transforming these apes into almost-humans (early statements of these ideas can be found in the following: Witmer 1909; Furness 1916; Kellogg and Kellogg 1933; Hayes and Hayes 1951). Beginning with a project by Allen and Beatrice Gardner (and a chimpanzee named Washoe), a flurry of projects were unleashed in the 1960s and 1970s that attempted to bring this vision to life in earnest. The projects raised a number of great apes in human environments and used a diverse array of methodologies to try to teach them human language: gestural signs, plastic tokens, visual symbols, and even spoken English. For perspectives on the results of these ape language projects, I personally recommend Ristau and Robbins (1982) and the (quite frankly) devastating analysis by Rivas (2005). Other reviews and perspectives can be found in the following: Premack 1985; Hixson 1998; Lyn 2012; Tomasello 2017. (Though dated, I still find that one of the most readable [if overly romantic] explorations of this history can be found in Desmond [1979].) By the 1990s, the idea of so-called ape enculturation had become a lightning rod for explaining seemingly contradictory experimental results with apes on a variety of cognitive tasks. Numerous theorists proposed that the varying degrees of human enculturation could explain the (apparently) discrepant findings. The mere experience of spending time with loving human caregivers (language inputs aside) was seen as a powerful enough environmental input to massively reorganize the mind-brain of apes. Bering (2004) provides a thoughtful overview of the theoretical ideas at stake in this idea. (In due candor, I should mention that I spent five years of my life attempting to design and implement the "Early Experience and Enrichment Project"—an inclusive effort with teams of scientists from around the globe to test the idea once and for all. For a variety of reasons far too long and painful to detail here, the project never came to fruition [see CEG lab codebook, 8709-7 and associated file drawers; for some preliminary results, see Vonk and Povinelli 2011].) Curiously, the enculturation idea has largely fallen out of favor, despite the fact that there was no systematic attempt to test it. See also Anderson 2004. See note 86.

89. Jokes4us.com 2019b.

(NAAS/"Salmon Boy"—Drowned boy enculturated into the world of the Salmon People. "The Woman Who Married a Frog"—Frogs have learned human language by listening to them. "The Boy and the Rattlesnake"—Speaking rattlesnake.) (NFT/"Why Apes Look like People"—Tortoise proposes changing animals into humans.) (TMI/B210.1.—Person frightened by animals successfully replying to person's remarks. B210.3—Formerly, animals and man spoke the same language. K551.11.—Ten-year respite given to captive while he undertakes teaching elephant [ass] to speak.)
C1b. The chimp who invented words[90]
   (NAAS/"How Grandmother Spider Named the Clans"—Spider gives all animals their names.)
C1c. The chimp who asked a question[91]
   (NAAS/"How the Fawn Got Its Spots"—Deer asks the Great Mystery (Wakan Tanka) a rhetorical question. "Octopus and Raven"—Raven torments octopus by asking annoying question over and over again.)
C1d. Apes understand *no*
   C1d.1. Yes, they do[92]
      (AFS/23—Clever fox selectively repeats only last part of the wolf's plea to the lion ("Do not let him get away!") as "Let him get away!" Lion is fooled by the dropping of the negation and lets fox get away.)
   C1d.2. No they do not[93]
      (See previous—AFS/23.)
   C1d.3. Bonobos shake their heads no[94]
      (NAAS/"The Rabbit Dance"—Rabbit nods yes.)
C1e. The parrot Polly who asked for a cracker[95]

---

90. Fouts and Rigby (1977) reported that Washoe the chimp invented new "words" for things in his environment by combining signs he knew. For example, Washoe is reported to have created the novel utterances (gestures) *water-bird* for swans and *rock-berry* for Brazil nuts.
91. *NOVA* 1974, "The First Signs of Washoe," aired on PBS.
92. Premack 1976, *Intelligence in Ape and Man*.
93. Muncer and Ettlinger 1981, "Communication by a Chimpanzee: First-Trial Mastery of Word Order That Is Critical for Meaning, but Failure to Negate Conjunctions," in *Neuropsychologia*.
94. Schneider, Call, and Liebal 2010, "Do Bonobos Say No by Shaking Their Head?," in *Primates*.
95. Using the OED, I was able to trace the earliest use of *Poll* in reference to a parrot in Ben Jonson's *Every Man Out of His Humor* (first performed in 1599). Entries after that show an increasing use of the term *Poll* or *Pall*, as well as the closely allied *Polly*—most notably in Charles Dickens's *Dombey and Son*. I have also discovered an episode of a public radio show in the United States, *A Way with Words* (Barnette and Barrett 2009), that traced the origins of the specific phrase "Polly want a cracker" to a mock ad in a mock newspaper, *Bunkum Flag-Staff and Independent Echo*, published in 1849 in *The Knickerbocker* magazine. *A Way with Words* notes: "It starts, 'For sale, a Poll Parrot, cheap. He

(BAF/"The Girl and the Crocodile"—Speaking tree.) (NAAS/"The Alligator and the Hunter"—Speaking alligator.) (TMI/B211.3.—Speaking bird.)

C1f. The parrot who said she loved me[96]
(ATU/243—"The Tell-Tale Parrot." A parrot reports a woman's infidelity to her husband.) (IMF/237*D—Parrot's inappropriate remarks. A woman sends talking parrot to nuns in a convent. Its inappropriate remarks enrage a priest during religious service.) (TMI/B211.3.4.—Speaking parrot.)

C1g. Enculturated ape passes human language to her child[97]
(ATU/535—"The Boy Adopted by Tigers [Animals]." An abandoned boy is adopted by wild animals. The animals provide the boy with weapons and arrange a marriage for him.) (BAF/"The Friendship of the Wild Animals"—Lion enculturates boy who then returns to humans who raise him as a human.) (NFT/"Why Apes Look Like People"—Monkeys and apes find last dregs of tortoise secret medicine that changes animals into people.)

C1h. Humans and Horses invent common language[98]
(BAF/"The Language of the Animals"—King of the departed gives dead man gift of understanding all animal languages.) (FTM/"The Raja and the Cowherd"—Magic stone grants cowherd's wish to be able to understand the language of his cows.) (GGS/"All I pay my psychiatrist is the

---

says a remarkable variety of words and phrases, cries, "Fire! fire!" and "You rascal!" and "Polly want a cracker," and would not be parted with, but having been brought up with a sea-captain he is profane and swears too much.'" The episode also details an 1848 cartoon of a boy about to crack a parrot over the skull with a stick asking, "Polly want a cracker?" (I also discovered this bit of trivia: *Bits and Pieces* [2019], an online retailer, sells a motion-activated parrot statue that exclaims, "Polly want a cracker!" for [you guessed it] $19.99.)

96. Wikipedia (2019a) states: "Alex (May 1976-6 September 2007) was a grey parrot and the subject of a thirty-year (1977-2007) experiment by animal psychologist Irene Pepperberg, initially at the University of Arizona and later at Harvard University and Brandeis University. When Alex was about one year old, Pepperberg bought him at a pet shop. The name Alex was a backronym for avian language experiment, or avian learning experiment." Alex died unexpectedly but may have offered clues that he knew he was about to die. Carey (2007) explains in an obituary in *New York Times*: "Even up through last week, Alex was working with Pepperberg on compound words and hard-to-pronounce words. As she put him into his cage for the night last Thursday, she recalled, Alex looked at her and said: 'You be good, see you tomorrow. I love you.' He was found dead in his cage the next morning, Pepperberg said."

97. Fouts, Fouts, and Van Cantfort 1989, "The Infant Loulis Learns Signs from Cross-Fostered Chimpanzees," in *Teaching Sign Language to Chimpanzees*.

98. Brandt 2004, "A Language of Their Own: An Interactionist Approach to Human-Horse Communication," in *Society and Animals*.

cost of feed and hay, and he'll listen to me any day."—"A good rider can hear his horse speak to him. A great rider can hear his horse whisper"[99]—"He knows when you're happy. He knows when you're comfortable. He knows when you're confident. And he always knows when you have carrots."[100]) (CIP/*Louisianian Creole*—"Cutting off a mule's ears won't make him a horse.")

    C1i. Communication differences between dogs and wolves raised by humans[101]
        (BAF/"The Wolf"—Humans afraid of speaking wolf.)

C2. Animals and Language Dialects
    C2a. The dialects of whales[102]
        (TMI/B211.2.7.—Speaking sea-beast.)
    C2b. The dialects of birdsong[103]
        (TMI/B215.1.—Bird language.)
        (See also parrot dialect above, "C1e. The parrot Polly who asked for a cracker.")
    C2c. Chimpanzee dialects[104]
        (TMI/B211.2.10.—Speaking monkey.)
    C2d. All other mammal dialects[105]
        (AFS/38—Snake gives man magic charm that allows him to understand all animal languages.) (TMI/B212.0.1.—All kinds of animals understand the language of heaven. B215—Animal languages. The various animals have languages of their own. B217.6.—Animal languages learned by exchanging tongues with helpful dragon. N451.—Secrets overheard from animal conversation.)
    C2e. Lone chimp leader communicates via secret drumming code but then never does so again[106]

---

99. Williams 2009, "Notable Quotes," *Wildtree Farm*.
100. Young 2009, "Horse Quotes," *Learn about Horses*.
101. Virányi et al. 2008, "Comprehension of Human Pointing Gestures in Young Human-Reared Wolves (*Canis lupus*) and Dogs (*Canis familiaris*)," in *Animal Cognition*.
102. Deecke, Ford, and Spong 1999, "Quantifying Complex Patterns of Bioacoustic Variation: Use of a Neural Network to Compare Killer Whale (*Orcinus orca*) Dialects," in *The Journal of the Acoustical Society of America*.
103. Treisman 1978, "Bird Song Dialects, Repertoire Size, and Kin Association," in *Animal Behaviour*.
104. Mitani et al. 1992, "Dialects in Wild Chimpanzees?," in *American Journal of Primatology*.
105. Conner 1982, "Dialects versus Geographic Variation in Mammalian Vocalizations," in *Animal Behaviour*.
106. Boesch and Boesch-Acherman (2000) celebrate the astonishing intellectual feats of wild chimpanzees at their study site in the Tai forest. The height of their celebrations has distinctly musical overtones. They report that a chimpanzee named Brutus symbolically communicates to his fellow apes a proposal to change their travel direction "by drumming twice at two different trees." He proposes resting for an hour "by

(FTC/"Why Leopard Meets His Enemy Face-to-Face [Benin]"—Cat strikes a gong seven times as a coded message to let her kittens know it is safe to lower a rope.) (JSS/XXXVIII.—Monkey plays drum twice [*ribbim-bim-bim, ribbim-bim-bim*] to announce "spider not here" or once [*ribbim-bim-bim*] to announce "spider is here.") (TMI/B210.2.—Talking animal or object refuses to talk on demand.)

(See also "G1b.2.a. Chimpanzee drumming.")

C3. Animals and Discourse
    C3a. Animals tell stories
        C3a.1. Michael the gorilla recounts his mother's murder[107] (BAF/"The Fable of the Rat-King"—Rat king's counselor tells him a fable. "Do Not Be Fooled Twice"—Monkey tells fable to shark and then summarizes moral lesson.) (TMI/B122.6.—Bird summarizes history. B131.1.—Bird reveals murder. B134.2.—Dog betrays murder. B151.1.1.0.2.—Horse stops where murder has occurred. B159.4.—Vulture's chicks will not eat dead hero's leg, since they know he has been treacherously murdered.)
    C3b. Animals tell jokes
        C3b.1. Koko, the punning gorilla[108]

---

drumming twice at the same tree within two minutes," and he can even combine the two messages "and propose both a change in direction *and* an hours rest" by drumming "once at a first tree and then twice at another tree"—or, alternatively, "drum[ming] twice at a first tree . . . and then once further in the proposed direction" (236, emphasis added). Or at least Brutus used to do this. Alas, this noble chimpanzee leader "stopped using this code rather abruptly" in 1984. But this sudden cessation, combined with the fact that it has "only been observed in [the] Tai [forest] chimpanzees" (236), is all the more fascinating because it highlights the "arbitrariness" of the symbolic communication (237).

107. Michael was a companion gorilla to Koko, a gorilla raised by Dr. Penny Patterson and taught American Sign Language. Michael is reported to have learned about twenty words within his first year with The Gorilla Foundation (see Patterson and Linden 1981, *The Education of Koko*). Wikipedia (2018) provides an account of an oft-repeated story about Michael's retrieval of a traumatic childhood memory: "The following is an example of Michael's description of an event that is thought by humans at The Gorilla Foundation to be the death of his mother—killed by bushmeat poachers when he was quite young: 'Squash meat gorilla. Mouth tooth. Cry sharp-noise loud. Bad think-trouble look-face. Cut/neck lip (girl) hole.'"

A video of Michael allegedly signing about this event can be retrieved by visiting The Gorilla Foundation's 2010 post "Michael's Story."

108. Susan Armstrong-Buck (1989), professor of philosophy at Humboldt State University, has examined in detail the gorilla's sense of humor:

    Wit or humor has been expressed many times by Koko and Michael. Thus it may be their intelligence which has given gorillas the unfortunate reputation of stupidity or contrariness. For

(AFS/26—Hidden caterpillar fools hare and other animals into believing he is bigger than he is. After being fooled, all the animals laugh at the joke.) (TMI/A2851.—The four characteristics of wine: peacock: brilliant colors; ape: jokes; lion: boldness; hog: drunkenness.)

C4. Animal Teachers

    C4a. Chimp teaches infant how to crack a nut[109]

        (NAAS/"How the Spider Symbol Came to the People"—Spider teaches man how to be patient.)

    C4b. Ant teaches friend a new route[110]

        (BAF/"The Goat Becomes a Pilgrim"—Hyena poses as guide and tells goat he can show him the road to Mecca.)

    C4c. Unending tale types of animal teaching[111]

        (BAF/"The Goat Becomes a Pilgrim"—Goat as teacher.) (NAAS/"The Alligator and the Hunter"—Alligator teaches man to hunt.) (NFT/"The Lion and the Goat"—Lion instructs man how to lie down like a lion.)

D. Animals and Play

D1. Animals and Games

    D1a. Animals and games with objects

---

example, when asked to "smile" for the camera, Koko signed "sad frown" . . . Koko's laugh is a low chuckle, like a "suppressed, heaving human laugh" . . . Her humor seems to be incongruity based, like that of small children. Chuckles were evoked, for instance, by a research assistant accidentally sitting down on a sandwich and by another playfully pretending to feed M & M's to a toy alligator. In a striking example combining metaphor and humor, Koko made a joke about being a "sad elephant" because she was reduced to drinking water through a thick rubber straw as a solution to her constant nagging one morning for more drinks of juice.

See also Gamble 2001, "Humor in Apes," in *Humor*; and Patterson 1980, "Innovative Uses of Language by a Gorilla: A Case Study," in *Children's Language*, Vol. 2.

    109. Boesch 1991, "Teaching among Wild Chimpanzees," in *Animal Behaviour*; Musgrave et al. 2016, "Tool Transfers Are a Form of Teaching among Chimpanzees," in *Scientific Reports*.

    110. Leadbeater, Raine, and Chittka (2006) state: "Recent research on ants shows that running in tandem might serve the function of teaching naïve ants about the path to a target. Although these new experiments represent perhaps the most highly controlled study of teaching in animals to date, the findings prompt the question of how teaching formally differs from other forms of communication" (R232).

    111. Kline (2015) offers a great introduction into the spiraling controversy concerning whether animals teach each other, and if so, what is meant by "teaching."

D1a.1. The dog that fetched a stick, played tug-of-war, etc.[112]
(ATU/291—"Deceptive Tug of War." Small animal challenges two large animals to tug-of-war, arranges it so that they unwittingly pull against each other [or one end of rope is tied to a tree].) (IMF/280*F—Ant and fly engage in stone-throwing contest.)

D1a.2. Apes with pogo sticks[113]
(GGS/"Why did the farmer give his cow a pogo stick? *He wanted a milkshake!*"[114])

D1a.3. Chimps play blind man's bluff[115]
(BAF/"The Greedy Lion"—Lion drops pot on his head and can't get it off, stumbles around blindly.)

D1a.4. Animals play peekaboo
- D1a.4.a. Chimpanzees[116]
  (TMI/A179.8.—God hides from sun in shadow of a cloud. A734.1.—Sun hides in cave.)
- D1a.4.b. Pretty much any other animal you can think of[117]
  (GGS/What game do ghosts like to play? *Peek-a-BOO.*[118]) (TMI/F914.2.—Buffalo sucks [in] hero with drinking water and throws him up again in game of hide-and-seek.)

D1a.5. Apes invent game with piles of leaves[119]

---

112. Some writers have assumed that dogs play games (including tug-of-war) with each other in largely the same manner as they do with humans and that play with humans is actually just a poor substitute for their own games. For example, Rogerson (1992) states: "A dog that lives with another dog will usually play more games with that dog than with its owner" (55). Rooney, Bradshaw, and Robinson (2000), however, caution that the situation may be more complex than this.

113. Köhler (1917) 1925; see note 4.

114. Patrick C. 2019.

115. Takeshita and van Hooff (1996) describe how several members of a group of captive chimpanzees in the Netherlands played "blindman's bluff: walking with one's face covered by an object" (166).

116. Takeshita and van Hooff (1996) also describe several chimpanzees playing a "Peek-a-boo-like game: holding out one's hand to another individual while one's face is covered with a towel" (165).

117. A quick YouTube search will reveal hundreds of examples of the standard canon of animals playing peekaboo, including dogs, cats, turtles, rabbits, goats, birds, rats, hamsters, gorillas, zebras, bears, tigers, and so on.

118. SmileJokes.com 2013.

119. Nishida and Wallauer (2003) state:
Play in nonhuman animals has generally been viewed as being uniform among study sites. No studies have examined whether there are local variations in play. In this work we report an apparently locality-specific form of play that is basically solo locomotor play, but also has aspects of object play and social play. We describe this unusual "leaf-pile pulling" (LPL) pattern based on video footage of the chimpanzees of Mahale,

(TMI/B251.2.2.—Fish perform races as welcome to saint.)
        D1a.6. Vultures playing stick keep-away with alligators[120]
                (TMI/F267.—Fairies attend games.)
        D1a.7. The banana cannon[121]
                (TMI/B109.2.—Centipede plays at night with pearl. B765.12.—Venomous snakes play with precious stones.)
    D1b. Animals play chase
        D1b.1. The chimps play chase and tickle[122]
                (FTM/"The Fox and the Partridge"—Partridge plays chase with young girls.)
    D1c. Animal mind games
        D1c.1. Orangutan charades[123]
                (AGFT/"The Baboons and the Village Women"—Baboons resolve to learn acrobatic games to entertain villagers in order to gain food.)
        D1c.2. Experimenters teach chimps how to play rock paper scissors[124]
                (AGFT/"The Great Famine and the Law of the Jungle"—Hare convinces lion to play hide-and-seek among the rocks. Lion gets trapped. Hare eats him.)
        D1c.3. Chicken tic-tac-toe and the boy at the county fair[125]

Tanzania. Typically, when a party of chimpanzees moves in a procession down a slope in the dry season, a youngster will turn around and walk backward while raking many dry leaves with both hands. This activity accumulates many dry leaves while producing a lot of sound. After the player walks 1-15 m, he/she either turns around and walks forward or moves in a somersaulting fashion. The performer usually faces an individual that is immediately following him/her in the procession. The age of the performers ranges from 2 to 22 years, but 3-10 years are most typical" (167)

120. Davis Jr. 2013, "Play Behavior by Black Vultures?," in *Bird Observer*. See also Davis Jr. 2015, "Field Notes: Another Instance of Play Behavior in Black Vultures," in *Bird Observer*.

121. Mechling 1989, "'Banana Cannon' and Other Folk Traditions between Human and Nonhuman Animals," in *Western Folklore*.

122. Flack, Jeannotte, and de Waal 2004, "Play Signaling and the Perception of Social Rules by Juvenile Chimpanzees (*Pan troglodytes*)," in *Journal of Comparative Psychology*.

123. Cartmill and Byrne 2007, "Orangutans Modify Their Gestural Signaling According to Their Audience's Comprehension," in *Current Biology*.

124. Gao et al. 2018, "Learning the Rules of the Rock-Paper-Scissors Game: Chimpanzees versus Children," in *Primates*.

125. Chickens have been playing tic-tac-toe at county fairs for many years. Their behavior is controlled by training them (using basic Skinnerian operant conditioning) to peck at lights (invisible to their human competitor) that are projected onto the *X*s and *O*s. Sometime during the late 1990s, the attraction was integrated into modern casinos. Gregory (2012), writing for the *New York Times*, gives some context:

(FOJ/"The Rabbit and the Bear"—Rabbit proposes that he and bear play a game by tying their hands and feet together and rolling down mountain. Bear agrees it would be fun. They do it. Not fun at all.)

    D1c.4. Chimps beat humans at memory games[126]

(SFFT/"The Eagle and the Wren"—Eagle and wren hold competition to see who can fly highest. Wren beats eagle by riding on eagle's back.) (TMI/B565.—Parrot gives advice to queen playing chess, and she always wins.)

D1d. Strategy games
    D1d.1. Chimps play ultimatum and dictator games[127]

(TMI/B298.1.—Monkey plays chess.)

    D1d.2. Chimps are unaware of cheating during ultimatum games[128]

(ATU/217—"The Cat [Monkey] with the Candle." A man has a cat [monkey] trained to hold up lighted candles on its head. The king orders a mouse to be let loose. The cat drops the candle and chases the mouse. Often used as a method of cheating in a game.)

    D1d.3. Ravens do not understand tit for tat[129]

"People do love it," said Lisa Mizrachi, the advertising supervisor at the Mardi Gras Casino in Hallandale Beach, Fla., where people lined up in 2009 and 2010 for a chance to compete against Mardi G. the chicken and win $50. . . . "The tick-tack-toe chickens," Mr. Bailey said from his lakeside home in Hot Springs, Ark., are "not mental giants. But they are certainly a lot brighter than most people will give them credit for," he added. Mr. Boger, a former bullfighter and rodeo clown, said he and his wife, Connie, could make about $4,000 a week leasing tick-tack-toe-playing chickens to casinos. Each tick-tack-toe unit provided by Mr. Boger comes with 15 chickens. The chickens are rotated when one gets full, bored or tired, a nod to animal labor laws. A chicken wrangler serves as their caretaker. The game is now computerized, and building a new unit, Mr. Boger said, can cost up to $20,000. Mr. Boger's latest enterprise is a chicken that deals blackjack. "I haven't gotten that far with it," he said.

126. Humphrey 2012, "This Chimp Will Kick Your Ass at Memory Games—But How the Hell Does He Do It?," in *Trends in Cognitive Sciences*.

127. Proctor et al. 2013, "Chimpanzees Play the Ultimatum Game," in *Proceedings of the National Academy of Sciences*; Henrich and Silk 2013, "Interpretative Problems with Chimpanzee Ultimatum Game," in *Proceedings of the National Academy of Sciences*.

128. Kaiser et al. 2012, "Theft in an Ultimatum Game: Chimpanzees and Bonobos Are Insensitive to Unfairness," in *Biology Letters*.

129. Fraser and Bugnyar (2012) state: "We found support for long-term, but not short-term, reciprocation of agonistic support [in a group of thirteen captive ravens]. Ravens were more likely to support individuals who preened them, kin and dominant group members. These results suggest that ravens do not reciprocate on a calculated

(PER/323—"The Crow and Mercury." A crow was caught but released by Apollo on promise of an offering. The offering was never made, so when the crow is again captured, Mercury refused to help.)

D1e. Gambling animals
    D1e.1. Gambling monkeys like big bets[130]
        (ATU/7—"The Three Names." The bear and the fox wager as to which can name three trees first. The bear names different varieties of the same tree. The fox wins the wager.)
    D1e.2. Primate gambling task[131]
        (GGS/Why did the lion lose at poker? *Because he was playing with a bunch of cheetahs!*[132])
    D1e.3. Hot-hand bias in rhesus monkeys[133]
        (NFT/"The Hunter and the Deer"—Hunter finds deer-woman and brings her home as his second wife even though his first wife is wonderful. First wife discovers true origins of deer-woman and hunter loses both.)

D2. Animals and Alcohol and Drugs
  D2a. Animal intoxication
    D2a.1. The drunken elephants[134]
        (ATU/100—"The Wolf as the Dog's Guest Sings." The wolf drinks too much and sings in spite of the dog's objections. The wolf is killed.) (BAF/"The Animals at the Market Place"—Animals drink beer and smoke.) (GGS/"So drunk one is seeing pink elephants."[135])

---

tit-for-tat basis, but aid individuals from whom reciprocated support would be most useful and those with whom they share a good relationship" (171).

130. Chen and Stuphorn 2018, "Inactivation of Medial Frontal Cortex Changes Risk Preference," in *Current Biology*.

131. Proctor et al. 2014, "Gambling Primates: Reactions to a Modified Iowa Gambling Task in Humans, Chimpanzees and Capuchin Monkeys," in *Animal Cognition*.

132. Worstjokesever.com 2014.

133. Blanchard, Wilke, and Hayden 2014, "Hot-hand Bias in Rhesus Monkeys," in *Journal of Experimental Psychology: Animal Learning and Cognition*.

134. Siegel and Brodie 1984, "Alcohol Self-Administration by Elephants," in *Bulletin of the Psychonomic Society*. Note also the following pop cultural references: an alcoholic character in Jack London's (1913) *John Barleycorn* hallucinates "blue mice and pink elephants" (9); Dumbo, the adorable flying elephant in Disney's (1941) animated film, drinks water spiked with champagne and begins hallucinating in a singing and dancing musical episode, "Pink Elephants on Parade."

135. Brown 2014, "The Colorful History and Etymology of Pink Elephant," in *Early Sports and Pop Culture History Blog*.

D2a.2. Birds slur their songs on alcohol[136]
   (BAF/"The Animals at the Market Place"—Buffalo has hangover from drinking too much.) (GGS/"When the cock is drunk, he forgets about the hawk."[137])

D2a.3. Bats have high tolerance for alcoholic fruit[138]
   (JSS/XIX.—Spider gets cock drunk with rum-soaked corn.) (TMI/B299.3.—Animals discover liquor and get intoxicated.)

D2a.4. Vervet monkeys have been drinking for thirty-five years[139]
   (MRT/"The Grateful Minnow"—Fisherman spills some liquor in bucket of bait minnows. Drunk minnow is so grateful that when he is put on the line he swims straight to a big perch and bites him on the back, allowing fisherman to reel in perch.) (TMI/B294.2.2.—Monkey buys liquor. B182.1.1.—Magic dog vomits any liquor required of him.)

D2b. Animal drug use

D2b.1. Elephants on LSD[140]
   (BAF/"Who Will Bell the Leopard?"—Animal sorcerer pretends to prepare medicine that will incapacitate leopard.)

---

136. Birds are widely reported to eat fermented berries and become intoxicated. This may be the origin of the "birds of a feather" early American variant of "Where birds of every name and feather, Flock, and at times *get drunk* together" reported by Whiting (1977, 32). For a more recent confirmation that birds definitely slur their singing when drunk, see Olson et al. 2014, "Drinking Songs: Alcohol Effects on Learned Song of Zebra Finches," in *PLOS ONE*.

137. Ashanti Proverb 2015.

138. Orbach et al. 2010, "Drinking and Flying: Does Alcohol Consumption Affect the Flight and Echolocation Performance of Phyllostomid Bats?," in *PLOS ONE*.

139. Juarez et al. 1993, "Voluntary Alcohol Consumption in Vervet Monkeys: Individual, Sex, and Age Differences," in *Pharmacology Biochemistry and Behavior*.

140. In a textbook example of a mistake in allometry (the study of size and scaling), West, Pierce, and Thomas (1962) attempted to study the effects of LSD on elephant behavior. They calculated a dose of 287 milligrams by scaling up from the dosage known to send cats into a rage. However, they incorrectly used total body size as the scaling dimension. Within seconds, the elephant went into a rage and within five minutes it collapsed, defecated upon itself, and died. The proper scaling factor should have been *brain size*. The error was the equivalent of giving a human one thousand five hundred hits of acid at once. Fortunately, twenty years later, Siegel (1984) repeated the experiment on two Asian elephants using a proper dosage scaling. He discovered that the elephants "survived dosages of LSD (0.003–0.10 mg/kg) and exhibited changes in the frequency and/or duration of several behaviors as scored according to a quantitative observational system" (53).

D2b.2. Octopuses on ecstasy[141]
  (BAF/"The Well"—Jackal tricks rock rabbit into drinking fermented honey and steals water.)
D3. Animals and Playful Sexuality
 D3a. Chimps make sex toys[142]
  (TMI/B754.0.—Unusual sexual union of animals. B754.2—Elephants have sexual desire only after eating mandrakes.)
D4. Animals of Different Species Play Together (variants: dogs play with humans,[143] cats play with humans,[144] humans play with species {X},[145] colobus monkeys play with vervet monkeys,[146] chimps play with baboons,[147] rats play with mice,[148] spotted dolphins play with bottlenose dolphins.[149])

---

141. Edsinger and Dölen (2018) recently injected MDMA (also known as "ecstasy" or "Molly") into several octopuses to determine if it would affect their attraction to members of their species. They argue it did: "Here we provide evidence that, as in humans, the phenethylamine (+/-)-3,4-methylendioxymethamphetamine (MDMA) enhances acute prosocial behaviors in *Octopus bimaculoides*. . . . These data provide evidence that the neural mechanisms subserving social behaviors exist in *O. bimaculoides* and indicate that the role of serotonergic neurotransmission in regulating social behaviors is evolutionarily conserved" (3136). Despite the use of a toy octopus as a control, I remain dubious.

142. McGrew 2010, "Chimpanzee Technology," in *Science*; Tierney 2010, "When It Comes to Sex, Chimps Need Help, Too," in *New York Times*.

143. Rooney, Bradshaw, and Robinson 2001, "A Comparison of Dog-Dog and Dog-Human Play Behaviour," in *Applied Animal Behaviour Science*.

144. Mertens and Turner 1988, "Experimental Analysis of Human-Cat Interactions During First Encounters," in *Anthrozoös*.

145. Herzog 2010, *Some We Love, Some We Hate, Some We Eat: Why It's So Hard to Think Straight about Animals*.

146. Rose 1977, "Interspecific Play between Free Ranging Guerezas (*Colobus guereza*) and Vervet Monkeys (*Cercopithecus aethiops*)," in *Primates*.

147. Van Lawick-Goodall 1968, "The Behaviour of Free-Living Chimpanzees in the Gombe Stream Reserve," in *Animal Behaviour Monographs*.

148. Poole and Fish (1975) state:
> The playful behaviour of laboratory rats (*Rattus norvegicus*) was investigated in litters of five individuals with the mother present; parallel observations were made on mice (*Mus musculus*). Seven mixed litters containing four young rats and a young mouse fostered at birth were also observed. Solitary play was recorded in both species and took a similar form but social play was only observed in rats. In rats, solitary play frequently preceded social play. . . . Young mice did not respond playfully to social play from a rat litter mate; mice were less attractive to rats as playmates in comparison with fellow rats. (61)

149. Herzing and Johnson 1997, "Interspecific Interactions between Atlantic Spotted Dolphins (*Stenella frontalis*) and Bottlenose Dolphins (*Tursiops truncatus*) in the Bahamas, 1985-1995," in *Aquatic Mammals*.

(BAF/"The Snake and the Hog"—Snake and hog agree to be friends and play together.) (JSS/XXV.—Spider and monkey are drinking buddies.) (CIP/*Arabian*—"He who plays with a cat must bear its scratches.") (NFT/"The Tortoise and the Boar"—Tortoise and boar are bosom friends.)

(See also "E7. Animals of different species who befriend each other.")

D5. Pretend Play in Apes[150]

(BAF/"The Goat Becomes a Pilgrim"—Goat pretends to write with a pen. "Ingratitude, or the Hippopotamus, the Hare and the Hyena"—Hippopotamus pretends to be dead. "Whose Is the Child?"—King pretends to kill baby chick.) (FOJ/"The Hare, the Badger, Monkey and Otter"—Hare pretends to be lame to distract man while other animals steal his goods. "The Quail and the Badger"—Quail convinces badger to pretend to be a roadside stake. Badger does so. Quail perches on top of him.) (IMF/66B—Rabbit finds sham-dead coyote, says coyotes pass wind when dead. He does and rabbit knows that he is alive.)

E. Animals and Social Smarts

E1. Animals and Empathy

E1a. Empathic apes[151]

(IMF/207*D—Pig is sorry for the ass, who is sore and tired from work. Pig is well fed but ass reminds him that master's son is to be married within the year. Pig worries and becomes thin, but he is eaten at the wedding feast anyway.) (TMI/B292.5.—Bird sings to console man.)

E1b. Altruistic primates[152]

(NFT/"The Lion and the Goat"—Goat unlocks cage for trapped lion.) (NAAS/"Eagle Boy"—Eagle stays in captivity because he loves boy.)

E1c. Nonaltruistic primates[153]

(BAF/"The Girl and the Crocodile"—Ungrateful crocodile. "Ingratitude, or the Hippopotamus, the Hare and the Hyena"—Ungrateful hyena bites hippopotamus.)

---

150. Hayes 1951, *The Ape in Our House*; Gómez and Martín-Andrade 2005, "Fantasy Play in Apes," in *The Nature of Play: Great Apes and Humans*.

151. Palagi and Norscia 2013, "Bonobos Protect and Console Friends and Kin," In *PLOS ONE*; O'Connell 1995, "Empathy in Chimpanzees: Evidence for Theory of Mind?," in *Primates*.

152. Warneken and Tomasello 2006, "Altruistic Helping in Human Infants and Young Chimpanzees," in *Science*.

153. Silk et al. 2005, "Chimpanzees Are Indifferent to the Welfare of Unrelated Group Members," in *Nature*; Vonk et al. 2008, "Chimpanzees Do Not Take Advantage of Very Low Cost Opportunities to Deliver Food to Unrelated Group Members," in *Animal Behaviour*; Skerry, Sheskin, and Santos 2011, "Capuchin Monkeys Are Not Prosocial in an Instrumental Helping Task," in *Animal Cognition*.

E1d. Altruistic bees[154]

(AGFT/"The Woman and the Bird"—Bird takes pity on woman and returns her baby.)

E1e. River otter shows compassion[155]

(TMI/B299.5.2.—Animal fasts to express sympathy.)

E1f. Dog tries to save fish[156]

---

154. Rueppell, Hayworth, and Ross 2010, "Altruistic Self-Removal of Health-Compromised Honey Bee Workers from Their Hive," in *Journal of Evolutionary Biology*; Naeger et al. 2013, "Altruistic Behavior by Egg-Laying Worker Honeybees," in *Current Biology*.

155. Fashing and Nguyen 2011, "Behavior toward the Dying, Diseased, or Disabled among Animals and Its Relevance to Paleopathology," in *International Journal of Paleopathology*.

156. A YouTube video depicting a dog using vigorous wipes of its nose to splash water off a wet concrete deck onto several dead fish has been posted and reposted many times, stirring an equally vigorous debate about the dog's motives. One of these is entitled "Dog Tries to Save Fish Out of Water" (NoypiStuffVideos 2014) and received 443,345 views with 749 comments. Here is a sampling of some (unedited) recent comments: "I have more faith in this dog than humanity" (John Woo); "wow just sit back a laugh while the poor dog is scraping his nose raw to save this fishes life. people are really daft." (the woods); "Oh my god 00:27 it nudges it to see if it's alive yet, this is heartbreaking ;-;" (Daria); "god bless this dog" (•Fetch•); "What did humans do to deserve dogs?"; "Do all the people that THINK this dog is trying to bury or hide 'food,' ah no. This dog knows exactly what these fish need to survive and he's doing his best to help them. You can just see it in the way he looks at them and even noses one to see if it's OK. I just can't buy the bury or hide his food, not THIS dog and not this video! He may have been trained to do this, I don't know, but it's still amazing and very touching." (Rod Buchanan); "Dogs are angels while humans continue to exploit everything they can get their hands on :(" (rando); "this video proves dogs are better than cats" (GARTV101); "Wow . . . Most people here are so completley clueless. This dog isn't trying to save the fish, he's trying to bury them. 'Dogs are so thoughtful' and comments like that are so incredibly stupid. It's a common fact that dogs are caring, but they're also hunters, carnivores and gatherers. The dog has NO concern for the welfare of these fish, he's merely trying to bury them to be eaten later. Problem s becuase he's domesticated his instincts are intact, but his hunting skills arn't very acute. So he's using whatever he can to bur the fish" (Don't Watch This).

It should be noted that Elizabeth Price (2014) has posted a video entitled "Dog Tries to Save Fish—Proven Wrong" in which a dog eating from its bowl drops a piece of food on the floor. After smelling it intently, the dog repeatedly executes the same wiping motions against the floor toward the food as the dog "attempting to save" the fish. Although it has so far received only 14,963 views and a paltry fifty-four comments, the recent comments were intriguing: "So? People who pick up a wounded person use the same movements as someone who picks up a sack of cement. I guess paramedics are really only trying to pick up sacks of cement, then." (deneil topan); "There are hundreds of videos showing animals trying to save other animals lives from bears

(TMI/B299.5.1.—Animal mutilates self to express sympathy.)
- E1g. Dog rescues owner[157]
  (BAF/"Njo the Leopard and Mbomoka the Tortoise"—Baboon has sympathy for trapped tortoise; helps him.)
- E1h. Rats rescue friends[158]
  (ATU/75—"The Help of the Weak." A lion catches a rat. The lion lets the rat go free. Later, the rat helps the lion escape from a trap.) (BAF/"The Wild Dog and the Stork"—Stork helps wild dog remove bone from throat.)
- E1i. Rats are not really rescuing friends[159]
  (ATU/56b—"The Fox as Schoolmaster." A fox persuades a bird to let the fox educate the bird's children. The fox eats the children.)
- E1j. Ants bite string snare and liberate trapped friends[160]
  (ATU/233b.—"The Birds Fly Off with the Net." Birds who are caught in a net are freed when a mouse gnaws the net.) (See also "F8b. Noble ant faces death alone.")
- E1k. Animals helping members of other species[161]
  (ATU/239—"The Crow Helps the Deer Escape from the Snare." A deer helps a jackal, but when the deer is caught in a snare, the jackal refuses to help the deer. A crow

---

saving crows to cats savings puppies and on and on. Whomever posted this is dumb as hell and has no soul :/" (fuzzynubbins); "7 people got their delusions broken." (Militant Pacifist); "lmao my shiba always does this" (Parisa); "Does not prove anything" (TylerTheGamer); "Just goes to show that the dog in the 'Dog saves fish' video was actually just acting out of pure instinct to bury food with whatever is around—dirt, air, water, etc . . . The motions are the same, as are the reasons behind them. Heck, the dog in this video even seems to be the same breed (Shiba Inu?) There are many folks out there who try hard to hold onto the delusion that the dog in that viral video was trying to 'rescue' the fish" (vanizorc).

157. A quick Google search for "dog rescues owner" revealed 27,900 hits on September 21, 2018. A review revealed personal stories including (among others) dogs rescuing owners from innumerable situations: fires, lakes, rivers, being stuck without their phones, mud slicks, falling from cliffs, being stranded on toilet without toilet paper, and so on.

158. Bartal, Decety, and Mason 2011, "Empathy and Pro-Social Behavior in Rats," in *Science*.

159. Silberberg et al. 2014, "Desire for Social Contact, Not Empathy, May Explain 'Rescue' Behavior in Rats," in *Animal Cognition*.

160. Taylor et al. 2013, "Precision Rescue Behavior in North American Ants," in *Evolutionary Psychology*.

161. Consult YouTube for video evidence of members of one species helping members of another species. See, for example, ForfunTV (2017), with 1,404,118 current views. My personal favorite is at 1:09 of edogawa (2016), wherein the captive bear "helps" the wounded bird out of its moat to the bagpipes of "Amazing Grace." (NB: Ask Doctor Folklomindo about the history of the cultural appropriation of "Amazing Grace" as a device for stirring uplifting sentiments.)

convinces the deer to play dead to escape the snare.) (JSS/VI.—Blackbird leads army of animals to save spider from butchers.) (TMI/B540.1.—Birds throw some of their feathers to the endangered hero and he flies off. B381.1.—Wolf fetches a man to remove thorn from his pups' paws.)

E2. Mind-Reading Animals I. The Perceptions of Others

   E2a. Animals and the eyes of others[162]

      (BAF/"The Animals at the Market Place"—Lion claims to be able to command his wife simply by looking at her.) (FTM/"The King of the Birds"—Owl appointed king because his eyes look wise.) (TMI/1006.—Casting eyes.) (ATU/1006—"Casting Eyes." Ordered to cast eyes on this or that, ogre kills animals and throws their eyes at the object.)

   E2b. Animal follows human gaze (variants: apes, monkeys, horses, goats, dogs, tortoise)[163]

      (NFT/"The Lion, the Tortoise, and the Boar"—Lion warns tortoise and boar that he does not like to be looked in the face.)

   E2c. Animal knows what others can see (variants: monkeys, ravens, apes, cats, dogs, and all the other usual suspects)[164]

      (AFS/21—Young sun-god laments to spider that he wishes his father, the sky-god, had seen him catch a sheep so he would know how well or poorly he had performed.) (ATU/61—"The Fox Persuades the Cock to Crow with Closed Eyes." The

---

162. Biologists have long studied what happens to an animal when a pair of eyes appears in its visual field. For example, Gallup, Nash, and Ellison (1971) demonstrated that chickens stayed hypnotized longer when a pair of glass eyes mounted on sticks loomed over them. More recently, comparative psychologists have investigated whether animals know that the eyes are a portal to an unobservable world of the mind.

163. Since the first formal demonstration of gaze following by chimpanzees in the mid-1990s, the animal cognition literature in this area has exploded. A few illustrative references include the following: Povinelli and Eddy 1997, "Specificity of Gaze-Following in Young Chimpanzees," in *British Journal of Developmental Psychology*; Micheletta and Waller 2012, "Friendship Affects Gaze Following in a Tolerant Species of Macaque, *Macaca nigra*," in *Animal Behaviour*; Nawroth, von Borell, and Langbein 2015, "'Goats That Stare at Men': Dwarf Goats Alter Their Behaviour in Response to Human Head Orientation, but Do Not Spontaneously Use Head Direction as a Cue in a Food-Related Context," in *Animal Cognition*; Proops and McComb 2010, "Attributing Attention: The Use of Human-Given Cues by Domestic Horses (*Equus caballus*)," in *Animal Cognition*; and Wilkinson et al. 2010, "Gaze Following in the Red-Footed Tortoise (*Geochelone carbonaria*)," in *Animal Cognition*.

164. Again, voluminous literature has been created since the mid-1990s. For examples, see Bräuer, Call, and Tomasello 2007, "Chimpanzees Really Know What Others Can See in a Competitive Situation," in *Animal Cognition*; and Flombaum and Santos 2005, "Rhesus Monkeys Attribute Perceptions to Others," in *Current Biology*.

fox asks the cock to sing with closed eyes as the fox's father used to do. The fox captures the cock.) (BAF/"The Hare and the Lion"—Hare scratches out lion cubs' eyes so they will be unable to hunt when they're grown.) (JSS/IX.—Spider tricks death and blinds him with temper lime and escapes. XXXVII.—Cow keeps her newborn son out of sight in a stone hole because bull wants him killed.) (IMF/74*G—Coyote sees opossum pretend to rub prickly pear over his eyes. Coyote picks a prickly pear, rubs it over his eyes and cannot see. Buzzard helps him pull out spines, and his sight is restored. Coyote pursues opossum.) (NAAS/"How the Spider Symbol Came to the People"—Spider chastises man for running while looking at the ground as if he were blind.)

E2d. Chimpanzees and the evil eye[165]
(TMI/F989.2.—Bird's red eye cooks meat, looks intently.)

E2e. Animals know / do not know that others hear

    E2e.1. Chimpanzees know what others hear[166]
(NAAS/"Eagle Boy"—Eagle instructs boy to tie bells to the eagle's feet so that when the eagle and the boy fly away, the villagers will know.)

    E2e.2. Chimpanzees do *not* know what others hear[167]
(ADLG/"If the crow could have only fed in silence, he would have had more to eat, and much less contention and envy.")

    E2e.3. Dogs do know what others hear[168]
(BAF/"The Well"—Jackal tells hyena he will tell his story but *only* if the hyena *will listen*.)

    E2e.4. Scrub jays know when to be "quiet as a mouse"[169]
(JSS/VI.—Blackbird and spider in hiding. Blackbird tells spider to be quiet; otherwise, men will discover and shoot them.) (ATU/238—"The Keen Sight of the Dove and the Keen Hearing of the Frog." They boast to each other.)

---

165. Kaminski, Call, and Tomasello (2008) attempted to test something called the "evil-eye hypothesis" to explain why subordinate chimpanzees avoid food that a dominant animal has been looking at.

166. Melis, Call, and Tomasello 2006, "Chimpanzees (*Pan troglodytes*) Conceal Visual and Auditory Information from Others," in *Journal of Comparative Psychology*.

167. Bräuer, Call, and Tomasello 2008b, "Chimpanzees Do Not Take into Account What Others Can Hear in a Competitive Situation," in *Animal Cognition*.

168. Kundey et al. 2010, "Domesticated Dogs (*Canis familiaris*) React to What Others Can and Cannot Hear," in *Applied Animal Behaviour Science*.

169. Stulp et al. (2009) state: "[We conclude] that food-caching western scrub-jays conceal auditory information if—and only if—the competitors can hear, but cannot see the catchers. In short, western scrub-jays know when to be as quiet as a mouse."

E2e.5. And rhesus monkeys as well[170]
　　(FTM/"The Sparrow's Eggs"—Dying bull promises his ears will become a magic stone that boy can use to hear anything that happens anywhere in the world.)
E2f. Ravens specialize in eyeing spying ravens[171]
　　(BAF/"The Leopard and the Marten Kabundi"—Squirrel sees eyeball of leopard spying through hole in a sheet and flees before getting eaten. "The Owl"—Old lady changed into an owl because she spies on people.)
E2g. Dolphins are smart too[172]
　　(FTM/"The Magic Eyes"—Water maidens bring boy magic eyes so he can see, then take them away.)

[First Special Note to Doctor Folklomindo, or SNDF-1: *As per our preliminary discussions, I have elected not to build out the next section with the detail it so richly deserves. Frankly, there has been so much work on this topic over the past forty years—hundreds of studies crosscutting many of the other major sections of this index—that it may prove fruitful, at some point in the near future, to write a grant to hire ten postdocs to generate a separate FOMAN-COG limited to purported "mind-reading" capacities in animals.*]

E3. Mind-Reading Animals II. Thinking about Thinking (variants: apes, monkeys, dogs, elephants . . .)[173]
　　(AFS/21—"How Spider Read the Sky-God's Thoughts.") (BAF/"The Lion, the Hyena and the Jackal"—Lion ponders the source of jackal's knowledge.) (AGFT/"The Great Famine and the Law of the Jungle"—On a forced march from the jungle, exhausted vegetarian animals lie and say they are stopping to think. Lion asks what they are thinking about. Animals cannot give an answer, so lion knows they were not really thinking about anything. Predators eat them. Exhausted hare stops repeatedly to rest

---

170. Santos, Nissen, and Ferrugia 2006, "Rhesus Monkeys, *Macaca mulatta*, Know What Others Can and Cannot Hear," in *Animal Behaviour*.

171. Bugnyar, Reber, and Buckner 2016, "Ravens Attribute Visual Access to Unseen Competitors," in *Nature Communications*.

172. Xitco, Gory, and Kuczaj 2004, "Dolphin Pointing Is Linked to the Attentional Behavior of a Receiver," in *Animal Cognition*.

173. Since the late 1970s, the question of whether animals are "mind readers" has become an obsession of sorts in both comparative psychology and philosophy of mind (for the original statement of the problem, see Premack and Woodruff 1978). Routinely, the question is asked as to whether a particular species can "read the mind" of another conspecific. For an example that recently caught my attention, see Udell, Dorey, and Wynne 2011, "Can Your Dog Read Your Mind? Understanding the Causes of Canine Perspective Taking," in *Learning and Behavior*. Furthermore, the experimental literature on this topic crosses almost every other category in this catalog. Lurz (2011) provides one of many overviews of this topic.

but each time tricks lion into believing he is thinking deep thoughts. Lion believes him and spares his life.)

E4. Animals Distinguish between Accidental and Intentional Actions[174]

(BAF/"The Lizard and the Chain of Events"—Ant seeks cause of malady, but all animals explain away their roles as being caused by something else.) (NFT/"The Tortoise and the Forbidden Porridge"—Tortoise tells the diviner that he accidentally tripped over a stump and spilled the porridge on himself, when really, he ate it purposefully.)

E5. Animals and Pointing

E5a. Chimpanzees (learn to) point to deceive human dressed as a bandit[175]

(ATU/161—"The Farmer Betrays Fox by Pointing." The farmer has hidden the fox in a basket and promised not to tell. When the hunters come, he says, "The fox just went over the hill," but points to the basket.)

E5b. Animals understand (and don't understand) pointing (variants: apes, monkeys, dolphins, crows, ravens, dogs, horses, etc.)[176]

---

174. The old accidental-intentional distinction—a particularly thorny topic, even among humans. See Povinelli et al. 1998, "Young and Juvenile Chimpanzees' (*Pan troglodytes*) Reactions to Intentional versus Accidental and Inadvertent Actions," in *Behavioural Processes*; Call and Tomasello 1998, "Distinguishing Intentional from Accidental Actions in Orangutans (*Pongo pygmaeus*), Chimpanzees (*Pan proglodytes*) and Human Children (*Homo sapiens*)," in *Journal of Comparative Psychology*; and Call et al. 2004, "'Unwilling' versus 'Unable': Chimpanzees' Understanding of Human Intentional Action," in *Developmental Science*.

175. Woodruff and Premack 1979, "Intentional Communication in the Chimpanzee: The Development of Deception," in *Cognition*.

176. For an introduction to the topic of whether animals comprehend the meaning of the pointing gesture, I recommend the review by Miklósi and Soproni (2006). I feel badly for just gesturing at a review paper, but the research literature concerning whether (and which) animals can (and do) respond to (in various ways) the human (or humanlike) pointing gesture is so vast, so complicated, and oh so growing! But because that review is now more than a decade old, I point toward a slightly newer study, involving dolphins (Pack and Herman 2007). Additionally, Udell, Dorey, and Wynne (2008) show that (surprisingly?) wolves outperform dogs on comprehending the meaning of the pointing gesture, and Kirchhofer et al. (2012) show that dogs but not chimpanzees understand the pointing gesture.

A completely separate topic is whether animals produce the pointing gestures on their own. For claims that they do, I recommend Leavens, Hopkins, and Bard (1996); Veà and Sabater-Pi (1998); and Pika and Mitani (2006). Curiously, in his investigation of possible pointing by magpies, Kaplan (2011) argues that pointing does not require having hands and arms. In that there is some confusion here, a critical, theoretical paper by some dear colleagues of mine may be of help in insolating the underlying theoretical issues at stake: Povinelli, Bering, and

(AFS/40—Spider recognizes he has been pointed at while hiding in tree.) (BAF/"How Mboloko the Dwarf Deer Saved His Friend's Life"—Rat points at the cock. "The Lion, the Jackal and the Hyena"—Jackal points to hyena's distended stomach. "The Animals at the Market Place"—Elephant uses his trunk to point out things he wants his wife to do.) (FTC/"The Cat, the Dog, and Death [Haiti]"—Dog tries to get his nose to stop pointing at bone. His nose wins out.) (MRT/"The Pointer"—Hunter dog trained to point at birds points to man in city. Owner thinks he's mixed up until the man says his name is "Bob White.") (NAAS/"The Woman Who Married a Frog"—Frog points to lake.)

    E5c. Animals understand how to point with gaze[177]

(AGFT/"The Man and the Dove"—Dying dove uses her glances to communicate to man where snake is hiding.)

E6. Spiteful, Jealous, and Guilty Animals

    E6a. Chimps are vengeful but not spiteful[178]

(AFS/27—Gazelle makes drum to secretly summon the animals to exact revenge on the leopard for having killed the antelope.) (ATU/248—"The Dog and the Sparrow." A man runs over the dog, friend of the sparrow. The sparrow takes vengeance. The man loses his horse, his property, and finally his life.) (BAF/"Why the Heron Has a Bent Neck"—Jackal exacts revenge against heron. "The Elephant and the Hare"—Leopard attack of revenge against the lizards.) (PER/113—"A Thunny and a Dolphin." A thunny and dolphin wash ashore. The thunny was pleased to see the dolphin die first. 216—A wasp tormented a snake close to death. The snake decided to put his head under a wagon wheel in hopes to take the wasp with him in death. 494—A panther fell into a well. Some fed him and some pelted him. Overnight, he recovered strength and leaped out of the well. He killed those who abused him. 702—A dog sleeping on hay would not let other animals eat from the hay.) (RFT/"Prince Ivan, the Firebird and the Gray Wolf"—Gray wolf kills prince's horse just to fulfill prophecy.)

    E6b. The jealous animal

        E6b.1. Dog[179]

Giambrone 2003, "Chimpanzee 'Pointing': Another Error of the Argument by Analogy," in *Pointing: Where Language, Culture, and Cognition Meet*.

  177. Land's (1999) article "Motion and Vision: Why Animals Move Their Eyes," in *Journal of Comparative Physiology*, offers a little physiology to this debate.

  178. Jensen, Call, and Tomasello 2007, "Chimpanzees Are Vengeful but Not Spiteful," in *Proceedings of the National Academy of Sciences*; Jensen et al. 2006, "What's in It for Me? Self-Regard Precludes Altruism and Spite in Chimpanzees," in *Proceedings of the Royal Society of London B: Biological Sciences*.

  179. Harris and Prouvost 2014, "Jealousy in Dogs," in *PLOS ONE*.

(TMI/W181.1.—Sheep jealous of dog because he does nothing.) (ATU/200D*—"Why Cat Is Indoors and Dog Is Outside in Cold." A dog is jealous of a cat because the cat lives indoors.)

E6b.2. Cat[180]

(BAF/"Do Not Be Fooled Twice"—Shark's wife jealous of his friendship with monkey.)

E6b.3. Guinea pig[181]

(TMI/W181.4.—Jealous fox betrays wolf to peasant and then appropriates wolf's cave and food.)

E6b.4. Horse[182]

(TMI/L452.2.—Ass jealous of war horse until he sees him wounded.)

E6b.5. Bird[183]

(TMI/W181.5.—Raven jealous of partridge's way of flying.)

E6b.6. Rat[184]

(ATU/112—"Country Mouse Visits Town Mouse." Country mouse visits town mouse, who assumes country mouse is jealous of town mouse's homeplace. But country mouse prefers the country.) (BAF/"The Fable of the Frog and the Gazelle"—Gazelle jealous that frog has children.)

E6b.7. Rabbit[185]

(BAF/"The Elephant and the Hare"—Hare is jealous of elephant's garden.)

E6b.8. Just about all pets[186]

(JSS/XXIX.—Dog jealous because all the gals fawn over cat.)

E6c. That guilty look on your dog's face is (not) real[187]

---

180. Morris, Doe, and Godsell 2008, "Secondary Emotions in Non-Primate Species? Behavioural Reports and Subjective Claims by Animal Owners," in *Cognition and Emotion*.
181. Morris, Doe, and Godsell 2008.
182. Morris, Doe, and Godsell 2008.
183. Morris, Doe, and Godsell 2008.
184. Morris, Doe, and Godsell 2008.
185. Morris, Doe, and Godsell 2008.
186. Morris, Doe, and Godsell 2008.
187. Professor Alexandra Horowitz's (2009) article "Disambiguating the 'Guilty Look': Salient Prompts to a Familiar Dog Behaviour," in *Behavioural Processes*, pretty much sums up one of the major concerns of the FOMANCOG:

> Anthropomorphisms are regularly used by owners in describing their dogs. Of interest is whether attributions of understanding and emotions to dogs are sound, or are unwarranted applications of human psychological terms to non-humans. One attribution commonly made to dogs is that the "guilty look" shows that dogs feel guilt at doing a disallowed action. In the current study, this anthropomorphism is empirically tested.

(JSS/XVII.—Spider is ashamed of deceiving the king. Sulks away and hides.) (TMI/A737.8.1.—Sun hides face in shame: eclipse.)

E7. Fairness in Animals (a.k.a., "Inequity Aversion") and Other Morals[188]

E7a. Monkeys reject unequal pay for equal work[189]

(ATU/9—"The Unjust Partner." In the field and in the stable. The bear works; the idle monkey [fox] cheats the bear.)

E7b. Apes are okay with unequal pay[190]

(ATU/1030—"The Crop Division." In the division of the crop the monkey [fox] takes the corn. While sharing the corn they planted, the monkey [fox] takes the kernels and the bear takes the chaff. The monkey [fox] claims the difference in sound is because his share got wet.)

E7c. Dogs are not okay with unequal pay[191]

(AFS/23—Wolf upset at fox because fox's kill is always better. They agree to jointly kill animals so it will be

---

The behaviours of 14 domestic dogs (*Canis familiaris*) were videotaped over a series of trials and analyzed for elements that correspond to an owner-identified "guilty look." Trials varied the opportunity for dogs to disobey an owner's command not to eat a desirable treat while the owner was out of the room, and varied the owners' knowledge of what their dogs did in their absence. The results revealed no difference in behaviours associated with the guilty look. By contrast, more such behaviours were seen in trials when owners scolded their dogs. The effect of scolding was more pronounced when the dogs were obedient, not disobedient. These results indicate that a better description of the so-called guilty look is that it is a response to owner cues, rather than that it shows an appreciation of a misdeed. (447)

Ostojić, Tkalčić, and Clayton (2015) report that they replicated important aspects of those findings: "We manipulated whether or not dogs ate a 'forbidden' food item and whether or not the food was visible upon the owners' return. Based on their dogs' greeting behaviour, owners stated that their dog had eaten the food no more than expected by chance. In addition, dogs' greeting behaviours were not affected by their own action or the presence or absence of the food. Thus, our findings do not support the hypothesis that dogs show the 'guilty look' in the absence of a concurrent negative reaction by their owners" (97).

188. De Waal 2006, "Joint Ventures Require Joint Payoffs: Fairness among Primates," in *Social Research*.

189. Brosnan and de Waal 2003, "Monkeys Reject Unequal Pay," in *Nature*.

190. Bräuer, Call, and Tomasello 2008a, "Are Apes Inequity Averse? New Data on the Token-Exchange Paradigm," in *American Journal of Primatology*.

191. Horowitz 2012, "Fair Is Fine, but More Is Better: Limits to Inequity Aversion in the Domestic Dog," in *Social Justice Research*.

fair.) (PER/356—"The Sheep and the Dog." Sheep complained that they had to pay with wool for their good life, but the dog did not have to pay. Dog pointed out that without him, sheep would likely be dead.)

E7d. Long-tailed macaques are only not okay with unequal pay when workload is moderate[192]
(PER/092—"The Two Dogs." A hound berated a house dog for getting a larger share of the kill on the master's return. The house dog replied it was not his fault and said, "Talk to the master.")

E7e. Crows and raven do not like giving gifts to partners who are not working hard enough[193]
(PER/130—"The Belly and the Members." Belly had all the food; the rest of the body rebelled and refused to work. Parts soon relented as the whole body started to starve.)

E7f. Rats want fairness too[194]
(ATU/15—"The Theft of Butter by Playing Godfather." A fox and a mouse [wolf] live together. The fox pretends that he has been invited to be godfather and steals the butter stored by him and the mouse [wolf] for winter. He smears butter on the mouth [tail] of the sleeping mouse.)

E7g. Giving what you get and paying positive and negative events forward (variants: capuchin monkeys, rats . . .)[195]
(ATU/554—"The Grateful Animals." While traveling, a man helps three animals in trouble. Later in the journey, the grateful animals help the man win the princess.) (FOB/"The Traveller and the Goldsmith"—Man lowers rope into a pit. Monkey, snake, and tiger thank man for helping them escape and help him later.) (FTM/"Grateful Animals"—Man offers water to snake, monkey, and tiger and they later repay the kind deeds.) (TMI/J1612.—The lazy ass repaid in kind.) (NAAS/"The Rabbit Dance"—Rabbits teach humans a song and dance to show their gratitude for relying on them for food and clothing.)

(See also "E10i. Gratitude in animals.")

---

192. Massen et al. 2012, "Inequity Aversion in Relation to Effort and Relationship Quality in Long-Tailed Macaques (*Macaca fascicularis*)," in *American Journal of Primatology*.

193. Wascher and Bugnyar 2013, "Behavioral Responses to Inequity in Reward Distribution and Working Effort in Crows and Ravens," in *PLOS ONE*.

194. Oberliessen et al. 2016, "Inequity Aversion in Rats, *Rattus norvegicus*," in *Animal Behaviour*.

195. Leimgruber et al. 2014, "Give What You Get: Capuchin Monkeys (*Cebus apella*) and 4-Year-Old Children Pay Forward Positive and Negative Outcomes to Conspecifics," in *PLOS ONE*; Rutte and Taborsky 2008, "The Influence of Social Experience on Cooperative Behaviour of Rats (*Rattus norvegicus*): Direct vs. Generalised Reciprocity," in *Behavioral Ecology and Sociobiology*.

E7h. Bartering in animals (meat for sex, grooming for alliances, etc.) (variants: chimpanzees, ravens, penguins . . .)[196]
(BAF/"The Animals at the Market Place"—Animals set up a bartering market.) (FTM/"The Frog and the Jackal"—Jackal barters wood for bread from boy.)

E7i. General morality in animals[197]
(BAF/"The Elephant and the Hare"—Grand council of assembled animals rules that leopard's behavior has broken the moral code of the animals.)

E8. Selfish Apes[198]
(PER/149—"The Lion, the Fox, and the Ass." A lion hunted with others. When it came time to divide the spoils, the lion killed those who attempted to divide things evenly. The fox learned and lived. 348—"The Wolf and the Ass." A new wolf ruler was suggesting everyone share everything when an ass made it clear he should also share the sheep he had hid away. Oops!)

E9. When Animals Console Each Other

E9a. Raven bystanders console victims[199]
(BAF/"The Fly, or the Power of a Name"—With fly, tree mourns loss of fly's husband.)

E9b. Monkey consoles friends[200]
(BAF/"The Partridge"—Ants show sympathy for partridge whose eggs were eaten by snake.)

E9c. Chimpanzee consoles some friends more than others[201]
(BAF/"Lion and Man"—Lion consoles donkey, horse, camel, and mule who are overworked by man.)

E9d. Rat consoles stressed friend[202]
(BAF/"The Hedgehog, the Camel and the Lion"—Lion consoles sad hedgehog.) (FTM/"The Golden Peacock"—Antelope, tiger, and elephant console weeping boy.)

---

196. Gomes and Boesch 2009, "Wild Chimpanzees Exchange Meat for Sex on a Long-Term Basis," in *PLOS ONE*; Schino 2007, "Grooming and Agonistic Support: A Meta-Analysis of Primate Reciprocal Altruism," in *Behavioral Ecology*.

197. Flack and de Waal 2000, "'Any Animal Whatever': Darwinian Building Blocks of Morality in Monkeys and Apes," in *Journal of Consciousness Studies*; Sheskin and Santos 2012, "The Evolution of Morality: Which Aspects of Human Moral Concerns Are Shared with Nonhuman Primates," in *The Oxford Handbook of Comparative Evolutionary Psychology*.

198. Brosnan et al. 2009, "Chimpanzees (*Pan troglodytes*) Do Not Develop Contingent Reciprocity in an Experimental Task," in *Animal Cognition*.

199. Fraser and Bugnyar 2010, "Do Ravens Show Consolation? Responses to Distressed Others," in *PLOS ONE*.

200. Palagi et al. 2014, "Exploring the Evolutionary Foundations of Empathy: Consolation in Monkeys," in *Evolution and Human Behavior*.

201. Webb et al. 2017, "Long-Term Consistency in Chimpanzee Consolation Behaviour Reflects Empathetic Personalities," in *Nature Communications*.

202. Burkett et al. 2016, "Oxytocin-Dependent Consolation Behavior in Rodents," in *Science*.

E9e. Bystander Asian elephants reassure others in distress[203]
   (FOJ/"The Greedy Hawk"—Bear helps eagle in distress.)
E10. Animals and Cooperation
   E10a. Monkeys cooperate without knowing it[204]
      (TMI/B294.6.—Rabbit and elephant partners on trading expedition.)
   E10b. The bonobo who out-cooperated the chimpanzee[205]
      (BAF/"The Well"—During a severe drought many animals cooperate as never before and dig a well in record time. Only the jackal does not cooperate.)
   E10c. Chimp negotiators[206]
      (BAF/"The Drought"—Animals negotiate a truce. "The Lion and the Hyena"—Lion and hyena go to council for arbitration. "The Son of a Rat"—Rat negotiates with hunter.)
      (NFT/"The Lion, the Tortoise, and the Boar"—Lion, tortoise, and boar negotiate peace among their groups.)
   E10d. Chimps take turns[207]
      (AGFT/"The Story of Hyena and Squirrel"—Hyena and squirrel live together and take turns doing domestic chores.)
   E10e. Animals recognize competence
      E10e.1. Elephants lend a helping trunk[208]
         (TMI/B151.1.4.—Elephant determines road to be taken. B443.3.—Helpful elephant. J1024.1.—Captured elephants pull all at once and escape from net.)
      E10e.2. Chimpanzees recruit the best collaborators[209]
         (SFFT/"The Fox and the Wrens"—Fox cannot tell which wren is the father. Ultimately recognizes him because he is more competent than the other at threshing in a barn.)
   E10f. Chimps prefer to go it alone[210]

---

203. Plotnik and de Waal 2014. "Asian Elephants (*Elephas maximus*) Reassure Others in Distress," in *PeerJ*.

204. Visalberghi, Quarantotti, and Tranchida 2000, "Solving a Cooperation Task without Taking into Account the Partner's Behavior: The Case of Capuchin Monkeys (*Cebus apella*)," in *Journal of Comparative Psychology*.

205. Hare et al. 2007, "Tolerance Allows Bonobos to Outperform Chimpanzees on a Cooperative Task," in *Current Biology*.

206. Melis, Hare, and Tomasello 2009, "Chimpanzees Coordinate in a Negotiation Game," in *Evolution and Human Behavior*.

207. Yamamoto and Tanaka 2009, "Do Chimpanzees (*Pan troglodytes*) Spontaneously Take Turns in a Reciprocal Cooperation Task?," in *Journal of Comparative Psychology*.

208. Plotnik et al. 2011, "Elephants Know When They Need a Helping Trunk in a Cooperative Task," in *Proceedings of the National Academy of Sciences*.

209. Melis, Hare, and Tomasello 2006, "Chimpanzees Recruit the Best Collaborators," in *Science*.

210. Bullinger, Melis, and Tomasello 2011, "Chimpanzees, *Pan troglodytes*, Prefer Individual over Collaborative Strategies Towards Goals," in *Animal Behaviour*.

(NFT/"Why the Bat Only Comes Out at Night"—Bat shows different parts of body to warring factions to convince them he allied with each. No one trusts him. Now bat must be alone forever. "The Man, the Dove, and the Hawk"—Blind, lame man, choosing between promises made by dove and hawk, seeks advice from friend who tells him he must figure it out on his own.)

E10g. The chimp that refused to return the favor[211]

(ATU/155—"The Ungrateful Snake Returned to Captivity." A man rescues a serpent (or a bear), who in return seeks to kill the rescuer. Fox, as judge, advises the man to put the serpent back into captivity. 51a. "The Lion's Share." A lion asks a monkey if the lion's breath stinks. The monkey gives a flattering answer so the lion will not kill him. Later, the lion eats the monkey after all.)

E10h. Pigeons cooperate with computer[212]

(TMI/D1601.29. Self-playing gameboard.)

E10i. Gratitude in animals[213]

(ATU/156—"Androcles and the Lion." Man removes thorn from lion's foot. In gratitude, the lion later rewards the man.) (BAF/"The Goat Becomes a Pilgrim"—Hyena gives goat as gift to lion.) (FOB/"The Traveller and the Goldsmith"—Monkey washes traveler's feet in gratitude.) (FTC/"Why the Cat Falls on Her Feet [Native American]"—Cat rewarded for warning hero of dangerous snake.) (NAAS/"The Alligator and the Hunter"—Grateful alligator repays favor.)

E10j. Chimps share diminishing resources[214]

(BAF/"The Leopard's Share"—Tortoise shares elephant meat with leopard.)

---

211. Melis, Hare, and Tomasello 2008, "Do Chimpanzees Reciprocate Received Favours?," in *Animal Behaviour*.

212. Baker and Rachlin (2002) state:
Pigeons played a repeated prisoner's dilemma game against a computer that reflected their choices: If a pigeon cooperated on trial n, the computer cooperated on trial $n + 1$; if the pigeon defected on trial n, the computer defected on trial $n + 1$. Cooperation thus maximized reinforcement in the long term, but defection was worth more on the current trial. Under these circumstances, pigeons normally defect. However, when a signal correlated with the pigeon's previous choice immediately followed each current trial choice, some pigeons learned to cooperate. Furthermore, cooperation was higher when trials were close together in time than when they were separated by long intertrial intervals. (482)

213. Bonnie and de Waal 2004, "Primate Social Reciprocity and the Origin of Gratitude," in *The Psychology of Gratitude*.

214. Calcutt et al. 2014, "Captive Chimpanzees Share Diminishing Resources," in *Behaviour*.

E10k. Ants share their food[215]
   (IMF/100—In return for giving him better treatment, the dog invites the coyote (and his family) to a feast. 101—A farmer and his wife neglect an old dog who can no longer protect the farm animals. The coyote and the dog make an agreement. The dog will bark when the coyote attempts to steal an animal; then the two will share the food the farmer gives the old dog as reward.)
   (See also "E13c. Ant farming.")

[NOTE TO SELF: *I am learning that animals sharing hard-won food resources (or more often, pretending to share) is a common motif in folktales. Perhaps my colleagues in evolutionary psychology will be interested in building an index to create a detailed mapping of this motif onto their theories of how humans have evolved a cognitive module for thinking about food sharing.*]

E11. Deceptive Animals
   E11a. Trickster animals
      E11a.1. Primate tricksters
         E11a.1.a. Scientific motif-index of primates who deceive other primates in the wild (seriously)[216]
            (ATU/125—The Wolf Flees from the Wolf-head. The sheep have found a sack and wolf head. They make the wolf believe that they have killed a wolf. He flees in terror.)
            (For many more examples, see TMI/"K.—Deceptions" and numerous examples cited elsewhere in the FOMANCOG.)

[Second Special Note to Doctor Folklomindo, or SNDF-2: *Is it possible that the motif "animal [x] deceives animal [y]" is the most common construction of all animal tales worldwide for all eternity? Sure seems like it.*]

         E11a.1.b. Primate tricks human by hiding in the lab[217]
            (ATU/91—"Heart of Monkey as Medicine." When caught for his heart (as remedy), monkey makes his captor believe that he has

---

215. Wallis 1961, "Food-Sharing Behaviour of the Ants *Formica sanguinea* and *Formica fusca*," in *Behaviour*.
216. For a preliminary (albeit extensive) motif-index of tactical deception in primates, see Whiten and Byrne 1988, "Tactical Deception in Primates," in *Behavioral and Brain Sciences*.
217. Hare, Call, and Tomasello 2006, "Chimpanzees Deceive a Human Competitor by Hiding," in *Cognition*.

left his heart at home and is released.) (BAF/"The Elephant and the Hare"—Hare lies about stealing elephant's bananas.) (TMI/K874.1.—Ape pretends to delouse heron but plucks out his feathers.)

E11a.1.c. Ape tricks bird in captivity using bread crumbs[218]
(NFT/"The Tortoise and the Tug of War"— Using rope, tortoise tricks elephant and hippopotamus into playing tug-of-war against each other.)

E11a.1.d. Ape avoids ringing bell while stealing[219]
(ATU/110—"Belling the Cat." The mice buy a bell for the cat, but no one dares tie it on her.) (TMI/B81.13.10.—Mermaid prevents raising of sunken church bell. B271.3.— Animals ring bell and demand justice.)

E11a.2. Other animal tricksters

E11a.2.a. Bird mimics other species' calls, steals their food[220]
(ATU/57—"Raven with Cheese in His Mouth." A raven/crow has some cheese/meat in his mouth. The fox flatters the raven into singing. Raven drops his food and the fox gets it. 212—"The Lying Goat." Father sends his sons one after the other to pasture the goat. The goat always declares he has had nothing to eat. The father angrily sends his sons from home. When he tries to pasture the goat, he learns that he has been deceived. 292— "Ass Tries to Get a Cricket's Voice." Ass asks crickets what they eat to get such a voice. They answer, "Dew." He tries it and starves.)

E11a.2.b. Deceptive fish[221]
(SFLS/"[10]Simon and the Talking Fish"— Talking fish convinces man to bring him home, clean him, cook him, and eat him. Simon does, but then fish bursts out of his stomach.)

---

218. Köhler (1917) 1925; see note 4.
219. Melis, Call, and Tomasello 2006; see note 166.
220. Flower 2011, "Fork-Tailed Drongos Use Deceptive Mimicked Alarm Calls to Steal Food," in *Proceedings of the Royal Society of London B: Biological Sciences*.
221. Soares et al. 2014, "Cortisol Mediates Cleaner Wrasse Switch from Cooperation to Cheating and Tactical Deception," in *Hormones and Behavior*.

E11a.2.c. Dog steals food in the dark[222]
(BAF/"The Goat Becomes a Pilgrim"—Lion and hyena plot to eat goat in the dark.)

E11a.2.d. Cuttlefish cheaters always prosper[223]
(JSS/XII.—Spider wants to hire snake as his postman and offers snake bite of head and blood each night. Second night, spider realizes bites are too painful, decides to trick snake by inviting hare to be bit, but hare escapes. When snake comes, spider puts black pot over his own head and snake bites pot, breaks teeth; spider is safe. XIX.—Spider invites screech owl to play music at a dance but tricks owl. Eats him for breakfast. Becomes leader of owl's band and becomes greatest player and biggest "raskil" in the world.) (K896.1.—Beaver and porcupine trick each other. Beaver carries porcupine and abandons him in the center of a lake. Porcupine causes the lake to freeze and escapes. He then carries beaver and abandons him in the top of a tree. K15.1.—Climbing match won by deception: squirrel as "child." The ogre agrees to contest against the man's young one [i.e., a squirrel]. K17.4.—Jumping frog contest. Frog filled with shot. K41.2.—Pig and dog as plowmen. Pig plows while dog sleeps. Then dog runs back and forth in furrow to claim victory. K18.3.—Throwing contest: bird substituted for stone. The ogre throws a stone; the hero is a bird that flies out of sight. K25.2.—Contest

---

222. Kaminski, Pitsch, and Tomasello 2013, "Dogs Steal in the Dark," in *Animal Cognition*.

223. Brown, Garwood, and Williamson (2012) state:
Here, we show that this ability is tactically employed by male mourning cuttlefish (*Sepia plangon*) to mislead conspecifics during courtship in a specific social context amenable to cheating 39 per cent of the time, while it was never employed in other social contexts. Males deceive rival males by displaying male courtship patterns to receptive females on one side of the body, and simultaneously displaying female patterns to a single rival male on the other, thus preventing the rival from disrupting courtship. The use of tactical deception in such a complex communication network indicates that sociality has played a key role in the cognitive evolution of cephalopods. . . . The old adage that cheaters never prosper is far from applicable in the animal kingdom. (729)

in flying with load. One animal chooses cotton; the other, seeing that rain is coming, chooses salt and wins. K171.0.2.—Jackal cheats other animals of elephant they have killed together. K171.9.—Monkey cheats fox of his share of bananas. Climbs on a tree and tosses peelings down upon fox. K233.5.—Jackal refuses payment for being carried. K11.9.—Obstacle race between deer and hare. Hare accused of removing obstacles from his course.)

   E11a.2.e. Animal sneaks around barrier[224]
    (CIP/*Chinese*— "A mole can undermine the strongest rampart.")
   E11a.2.f. Snake deception[225]
    (TMI/B176.1.1.—Serpent as deceiver in paradise.)
   E11a.2.g. Elephants engage in large-scale deception[226]
    (NFT/"The Elephant and the Tortoise"— Singing bird warns elephant that tortoise is deceiving him.)
  E11b. Animals tricked by disguised humans
   E11b.1. Chimps and the "bad guy" who beats the haystack[227]
    (ATU/206—"Straw Threshed a Second Time." Animals eating at night say they have good food because the straw has not been well threshed. The master hears and threshes it a second time. They grow hungry. 210—"The Traveling Animals and the Wicked Man." The animals and objects hide themselves in various parts of a house. With their characteristic powers, they punish the cruel owner of the house and kill him. 570—"The Rat-Catcher." The colorfully dressed Pied Piper lures vermin into the streets and into the river, where they are drowned.)

---

224. Schiller 1949, "Analysis of Detour Behavior. I. Learning of Roundabout Pathways in Fish," in *Journal of Comparative and Physiological Psychology*; see note 4.

225. Shine 2012, "Sex at the Snake Den: Lust, Deception, and Conflict in the Mating System of Red-Sided Gartersnakes," in *Advances in the Study of Behavior*. [Personal note to Doctor Folklomindo: If people don't believe me after this one, I give up!]

226. Morris 1986, "Large Scale Deception: Deceit by Captive Elephants," in *Deception: Perspectives on Human and Nonhuman Deceit*.

227. The experimenters trained apes to suck juice through straws as they watched videos of (for example) humans (some of whom were, curiously, dressed as apes) running and hiding in one of two haystacks; another human appeared and beat the haystacks with (you guessed it) a stick. The apes' eye movements were analyzed to determine if they have a theory of mind (Krupenye et al. 2016).

E11b.2. Chimps learn to distrust human dressed as bandit[228]
(ATU/102—"The Dog as Wolf's Shoemaker." The dog says that he will make shoes for the wolf, but he tricks the wolf. The dog demands material for the shoes and then successively eats the cow, hog, and so on furnished to him. The wolf recognizes that he is being tricked by the dog.)

E11c. Animals using decoys/blinds

E11c.1. Alligators use sticks as decoy to fool birds[229]
(AFS/20—Lioness creates decoy by putting out pieces of bark to resemble meat. Hyena is fooled and captured.) (ATU/175—The "Tarbaby and the Rabbit." Rabbit, who has been stealing fruit from a garden, is captured by means of a tarbaby, a decoy covered with tar. Rabbit tries to make the tarbaby talk and finally becomes so angry that he strikes it. He sticks to the tarbaby and is captured.)

E11c.2. Lions sneak up on prey using cover[230]
(IMF/74*F—Rabbit covers himself with honey and rolls in dry leaves, which stick to him. He is completely covered and disguised.) (SFFT/"The Fox's Stratagem"—Fox uses clump of heather to hide himself as he swims up to ducks. He succeeds and eats two of them.)

E12. Animals and Warfare

E12a. Animals wield weapons

E12a.1. Apes use spears to hunt bush babies[231]

---

228. In a landmark study by Woodruff and Premack (1979), a human "bad guy" was dressed up as a bandit and solicited advice from young chimps about the location of hidden food. If the bandit could figure out which box the food was hidden inside, he nastily ate the food in front on them. Another experimenter was dressed as a "good guy" and shared the food with the chimps.

229. Dinets, Brueggen, and Brueggen (2015) state: "We report the use of twigs and sticks as bird lures by two crocodilian species. At least one of them uses this method predominantly during the nest-building season of its prey. This is the first known case of a predator not just using objects as lures, but also taking into account the seasonality of prey behavior. It provides a surprising insight into previously unrecognized complexity of archosaurian behavior" (74).

230. Hopcraft, Sinclair, and Packer (2005) have studied the issue using long-term radiotelemetry: "As expected for a sit-and-wait predator, resting lions spent more time in areas with good cover. On a broad-scale, lions shifted their ranges according to the seasonal movement of prey, but at a finer scale (< 100 m) lions fed in areas with high prey 'catchability' rather than high prey density. Plains lions selected erosion embankments, view-sheds from rocky outcrops, and access to free water. Woodland lions tended to use erosion embankments, and woody vegetation" (559).

231. Pruetz and Bertolani 2007, "Savanna Chimpanzees, *Pan troglodytes verus*, Hunt with Tools," in *Current Biology*. As no hunting was

(AFS/22—Porcupine heats spear to defeat All-Devourer. 23—Wolf kills fox's mother with spear.) (BAF/"Njo the Leopard and Mbomoka the Tortoise"—Tortoise uses spear to kill leopard.)

E12a.2. Chimps take down drone with sticks[232]

(AFS/23—Wolf breaks off stick from bush to thrash fox. Fox then uses stick to beat wolf.) (FTM/"The Sparrow's Eggs"—Dying bull promises that his tail will become magic stick that boy can use to kill enemies.)

(See also "B1a. Sticks for reaching.")

---

observed, this one is a real head-scratcher—especially because at last count it's been cited 532 times. Which raises another question: Why *don't* chimpanzees hunt with tools?

232. In the peer-reviewed journal *Primates*, van Hooff and Lukkenaar (2015) report an attack by chimps against a drone:

> On 10 April 2015, a Dutch TV crew was filming at the Royal Burgers Zoo in Arnhem, The Netherlands. It was the intention to film the chimpanzees in the enclosure from close-by and from above with the means of a drone. When the drone came a bit closer to the chimpanzees, a female individual made two sweeps with a branch that she held in one hand. The second one was successful and downed the drone. The use of the stick in this context was a unique action. It seemed deliberate given the decision to collect it and carry it to a place where the drone might be attacked. This episode adds to the indications that chimpanzees engage in forward planning of tool-use acts. (289)

To celebrate the popularity of this paper, *Primates* created a special new "Social Media Impact Award." The editor-in-chief, Tetsuro Matsuzawa, explains:

> To celebrate the 60th anniversary of the Japan Monkey Centre (JMC) in 2016, we decided to establish a new annual prize for the paper with the highest social impact published in the journal *Primates*. The high social impact paper is selected by the Editor-in-Chief, Vice Editor-in-Chief, and Associate Editor in charge of Public Relations, based on data sources such as the Altmetric score (mentions in the media and social networking sites) and full-text downloads. The winner of the *Primates* Social Impact Award 2016 is Jan A. R. A. M. van Hooff. His paper with Bas Lukkenaar, titled "Captive chimpanzee takes down a drone: tool use toward a flying object" . . . got a lot of media attention, was frequently mentioned in social networks, and was highly downloaded. Their work thus contributed greatly to enhancing the reputation of our journal. For this achievement, the lead author will receive a gift from the Japan Monkey Centre and Springer. The co-author will receive a declaration attesting to his contributions. . . . After the paper was published, Prof. van Hooff kindly provided original video material with subtitles explaining the displayed behaviors, so that interested readers can view them and judge for themselves. . . . Please join us in congratulating them and enjoy watching the video. (2017, 5)

E12a.3. Beavers use tools in aggressive display[233]
(TMI/B264.3.—Duel of buffalo and tiger. Buffalo arms self.)

E12a.4. Ants use stones to block entrances to other ants' colonies[234]
(AFS/31—Animal villagers block burrow entrance to trap trickster hare inside.)

E12a.5. Saber rattling by chimpanzees[235]
(ATU/104—"The Cowardly Duelers." War between the domestic and wild animals. The cat raises her tail; the wild animals think it is a gun and flee.) (TMI/B260.—Animal warfare.)

E12a.6. Monkeys club poisonous snake[236]
(AFS/29—Lioness ties hyena to tree, fetches sticks to club him.) (IMF/176—Rabbit knocks at the cave door, beats the lion with a club, then hides. 225—Buzzard invites monkey to fiesta in the clouds. With guitar, rabbit climbs on back of buzzard, who flies. Buzzard tries to make the rabbit fall, but later hits him over the head with the guitar, helps buzzard fly back to earth.) (MRT/"Battling Bow Weevil"—Big bow weevil beats small bow weevil with ax handle for being lazy.)

E12b. Animal warfare

E12b.1. Chimps patrol territory boundaries in silence[237]
(AFS/39—Elephant's wife gathers brothers at night and makes them swear to be silent as they steal

---

233. Thomsen, Campbell, and Rosell 2007, "Tool-Use in a Display Behaviour by Eurasian Beavers (Castor fiber)," in *Animal Cognition*.

234. Möglich and Alpert 1979, "Stone Dropping by *Conomyrma bicolor* (Hymenoptera: Formicidae): A New Technique of Interference Competition," in *Behavioral Ecology and Sociobiology*.

235. Kortlandt (1962) states: "I have mentioned the brandishing and throwing of clubs [by the chimpanzees] during intimidation displays, but this is apparently a kind of saber rattling rather than real fighting. I never saw one animal actually hit another with a club, nor did I see any wounds or scars. As a matter of fact, in most cases the intimidation display did not seem to be aimed at any individual; my impression is that it served mainly as an outlet that enabled the adult males to live together in peace" (134).

236. Boinski 1988, "Use of a Club by a Wild White-Faced Capuchin (*Cebus capucinus*) to Attack a Venomous Snake (*Bothrops asper*)," in *American Journal of Primatology*.

237. Watts and Mitani 2001, "Boundary Patrols and Intergroup Encounters in Wild Chimpanzees," in *Behaviour*. See also Mitani and Watts 2005, "Correlates of Territorial Boundary Patrol Behaviour in Wild Chimpanzees," in *Animal Behaviour*.

Question: Stealth hunters (e.g., lions and pythons) are quiet when they hunt, no? What is the difference? Worth asking, I think. See also FOMANCOG: "E2e. Animals know/do not know that others hear."

everything except a cow, a sheep, and a goat.) (FTX/"Why the Leopard Can Only Catch Prey on Its Left Side" [Ghana]—"Cat teaches leopard how to be silent while hunting.")

(See also "E2e. Animals know / do not know that others hear" and "C4. Animal Teachers.")

E12b.2. Ground squirrels post sentinels[238]

(BAF/"The Drought"—Animals take turns standing guard.)

E12b.3. Chimp war against the stuffed leopards[239]

(TMI/B262.—War between domestic and wild animals. B263.—War between other groups of animals. B263.2.—War between elephants and ants. B263.4—War between birds and reptiles.)

E12b.4. War among the chimps[240]

(TMI/B263.6.—War of monkeys and grasshoppers. B268.1—Army of apes.)

---

238. Blumstein 1999, "Selfish Sentinels," in *Science*; van Der Merwe and Brown 2008, "Mapping the Landscape of Fear of the Cape Ground Squirrel (*Xerus inauris*)," in *Journal of Mammalogy*.

239. Kortlandt (1962) states:

In my opinion chimpanzees do use weapons against leopards. Although I did not find any evidence for this in my field studies, I have observed it in apes in captivity. At the Pasteur Institute in Guinea I put a tame leopard on the wall of a large compound in which an adult male chimpanzee, three mothers and five juveniles were living under semiwild conditions. As soon as they caught sight of the cat, the adults ran toward it, screaming loudly and rising to their hind legs. Soon thereafter they grabbed the sticks I had previously scattered in their enclosure and threatened the leopard with them. Two of the apes, after finding the largest of the sticks, charged furiously at their enemy. The leopard was, however, just beyond their reach. Since these apes were near maturity when they were captured, they undoubtedly had had experience with leopards in the wild. In another experiment I brought a caged tiger near a half-grown male chimpanzee that had been born in the zoo and had never before seen a large beast of prey. Within a few seconds the chimpanzee picked up some wooden cubes I had put in his cage and began to bombard the tiger with them. (134-38)

Kortlandt later conducted experiments in Africa in which stuffed leopards were projected, rolled, and otherwise thrust unawares upon chimpanzees. He filmed the chimps' reactions—which include throwing sticks and clubbing the leopard, eventually decapitating it. For a readily accessible clip of one of Kortlandt's famous stuffed leopard experiments, see the YouTube video "Chimps Attacking Leopard" (everythingispointless 2007).

240. Feldblum et al. 2018, "The Timing and Causes of a Unique Chimpanzee Community Fission Preceding Gombe's 'Four-Year War,'" in *American Journal of Physical Anthropology*.

- E12b.5. War among the lions[241]
  - (TMI/B263.8.—War between lion and other animals.)
- E12b.6. War among the hyenas[242]
  - (TMI/B263.5.1.—War between birds and eagle.)
- E12b.7. War among the cheetahs[243]
  - (TMI/B263.3.—War between crows and owls.)
- E12b.8. War among the wolves[244]
  - (TMI/B263.1.—War between toads and frogs. B263.7.—War between serpents and storks.)

E13. Animals and Domestication
- E13a. Chimps on the brink of controlling fire[245]
  - (BAF/"The Goat Becomes a Pilgrim"—Hyena orders hare to gather firewood.) (FOB/"The Traveller and the Goldsmith"—Cold monkeys try to use glowworm to start a fire. Bird admonishes them for being foolish.) (FOJ/"The Rabbit and the Bear"—Rabbit uses fire-starting stone to light bear on fire.) (JSS/IX.—Spider sends his gal to Death to beg for fire. XXVIII.—Spider goes to candle fly to ask for fire.)
- E13b. Chimpanzees who (would) cook sweet potatoes (if they could)[246]
  - (AFS/22—Mantis instructs porcupine to cook sheep meat for him so he can dine with humans. Porcupine complies. 23—Wolf and fox cook their kill in a pot. 31—Hare and tortoise start a fire to cook their stolen sweet potatoes. 39—Elephant husband sent to fetch wood for fire.) (FOJ/"Kachi Kachi Mountain"—Badger cooks soup using old woman he has killed.) (GGS/What do monkeys wear when they are cooking? *Ape-rons!*[247]) (TMI/D1601.—Magic calabash cooks and cares for child. A1420.2.—Gods teach how to seek and prepare food.)
- E13c. Ant farming[248]

---

241. Heinsohn and Packer 1995, "Complex Cooperative Strategies in Group-Territorial African Lions," in *Science*.

242. Kruuk and Kruuk 1972, *The Spotted Hyena: A Study of Predation and Social Behavior*.

243. Caro and Collins 1986, "Male Cheetahs of the Serengeti," in *National Geographic Research*.

244. Mech et al. 1998, *The Wolves of Denali*.

245. Pruetz and LaDuke 2010, "Brief Communication: Reaction to Fire by Savanna Chimpanzees (*Pan troglodytes verus*) at Fongoli, Senegal: Conceptualization of 'Fire Behavior' and the Case for a Chimpanzee Model," in *American Journal of Physical Anthropology*; see also note 5 and Edwards 2010.

246. Warneken and Rosati 2015, "Cognitive Capacities for Cooking in Chimpanzees," in *Proceedings of the Royal Society B*.

247. Hanson 2015.

248. Sosa-Calvo et al. 2017, "Rediscovery of the Enigmatic Fungus-Farming Ant '*Mycetosoritis*' asper Mayr (Hymenoptera: Formicidae): Implications for Taxonomy, Phylogeny, and the Evolution of Agriculture in Ants," in *PLOS ONE*.

(AFS/31—The hare convinces the antelope to cultivate a field and grow beans.) (BAF/"The Eyes of Justice"—Jackal and sheep start a farm.)

E13d. Animals and their homes

E13d.1. Chimps adapt to living in caves[249]

(AFS/25—Frog builds great city.) (ATU/112—"Town Mouse and Country Mouse." Country mouse visits town mouse. Former prefers poverty with safety.) (BAF/"The Goat Becomes a Pilgrim"—Hyena takes goat to cave for night.) (TMI/A151.1.2.—Home of gods in cave. A1232.3.—Mankind emerges from caves. A1414.7.3.—Cave as repository of fire. R45.3.1.—Bear keeps human wife captive in cave with stone at entrance.)

E13d.2. The bowerbird home decorator[250]

(BAF/"The Weaver Bird and the Hummingbird"—Weaverbird weaves a beautiful, comfortable nest.)

E13d.3. Chimps build comfortable nest[251]

(ATU/43—"The Bear Builds a House of Wood; the Fox, of Ice." In summer the fox wants to drive the bear out of his house. 241—"The Officious Bird and the Monkey." Bird, sitting in its nest during a cold rain, asks shivering monkey why it doesn't build a house since it has hands like a man. The enraged monkey destroys the bird's nest.) (TMI/B572.—Animals build palace home for hero.)

E13e. Gibbon monogamy (variants: thousands of passerine and nonpasserine birds)[252]

(ATU/96—"When the Hare Was Married." 224—"Wedding of the Turkey and the Peacock." All birds are invited to the wedding except the eagle. This omission starts a great conflict.) (TMI/K579.4.—Monkey saved from trap by feigning marriage.)

E13f. Animals understanding of roles

---

249. Pruetz and Bertolani 2009, "Chimpanzee (*Pan troglodytes verus*) Behavioral Responses to Stresses Associated with Living in a Savanna-Mosaic Environment: Implications for Hominin Adaptations to Open Habitats," in *PaleoAnthropology*.

250. Diamond 1986, "Animal Art: Variation in Bower Decorating Style among Male Bowerbirds *Amblyornis Inornatus*," in *Proceedings of the National Academy of Sciences*; Diamond 1987, "Bower Building and Decoration by the Bowerbird *Amblyornis inornatus*," in *Ethology*; Diamond 1988, "Experimental Study of Bower Decoration by the Bowerbird Amblyornis inornatus, Using Colored Poker Chips," in *American Naturalist*.

251. Stewart, Pruetz, and Hansell 2007, "Do Chimpanzees Build Comfortable Nests?," in *American Journal of Primatology*.

252. Reichard 1995, "Extra-Pair Copulations in a Monogamous Gibbon (*Hylobates lar*)," in *Ethology*.

E13f.1. Role taking (variants: chimps, monkeys, crows . . .)[253] (ATU/85—"The Mouse, the Bird, and the Sausage." The mouse, the bird, and the sausage keep house together, each with appropriate duties. When they exchange roles, all goes ill.)

E13f.2. Division of labor in animal societies

    E13f.2.a. Insect societies[254] (PER/504—"The Bees, the Drones, and the Wasp." Drones took over a hive. The bees objected and asked the wasp to judge the issue. The wasp asked each side to build a comb. Bees did; drones did not. Bees won.)

    E13f.2.b. Wolf society[255] (BAF/"The Jackal's Greed"—Lion, jackal, crow, hog, gazelle, and hare form a cooperative living arrangement where everyone has specific duties.) (TMI/J512.7.1.—Elephant, giraffe, snake, and ant try keeping house together: requirements different.)

    E13f.2.c. Animal division of labor in the popular imagination[256]

---

253. Bullinger et al. (2011) state:

We assessed chimpanzees' ability to coordinate in a Stag Hunt game. Dyads were confronted with a situation in which each individual was already foraging on a low-value food (hare) when a high-value food (stag) appeared that required collaboration for retrieval, with a solo attempt to get the stag resulting in a loss of both options. In one condition visibility between partners was open whereas in the other it was blocked by a barrier. Regardless of condition, dyads almost always (91%) coordinated to choose the higher valued collaborative option. Intentional communication or monitoring of the partner's behavior before decision making—characteristic of much human coordination—were limited. Instead, all dyads adopted a leader-follower strategy in which one partner took the risk of going first, presumably predicting that this would induce the other to join in (sometimes communicating if she was slow to do so). These results show that humans' closest primate relatives do not use complex communication to coordinate but most often use a less cognitively complex strategy that achieves the same end. (1296)

See also Povinelli, Nelson, and Boysen 1992, "Comprehension of Role Reversal in Chimpanzees: Evidence of Empathy?," in *Animal Behaviour*; and Povinelli, Parks, and Novak 1992, "Role Reversal by Rhesus Monkeys, but No Evidence of Empathy," in *Animal Behaviour*.

254. Robinson 1992, "Regulation of Division of Labor in Insect Societies," in *Annual Review of Entomology*.

255. Mech 1999, "Alpha Status, Dominance, and Division of Labor in Wolf Packs," in *Canadian Journal of Zoology*.

256. Though not strictly copacetic with the scope of other works cited herein, I do believe Doctor Folklomindo will take particular

(TMI/B238.—Animal council assigns place and work to all. A1472.—Beginning of division of labor.) (cf. basically all known animal tales.)
- E13g. Animals lounging at jungle pools
  - E13g.1. Chimpanzees relaxing in pool[257]
    (AFS/31—Hare lounges and swims in pool with tortoise.) (NAAS/"Turtle Races with Beaver"—Turtle creates a comfortable home in a small pond where he can sun himself.)
- E13h. Animals who love their pets
  - E13h.1. Koko's kitten[258]
    (TMI/A2513.2.—How cat was domesticated.)
- E14. Animals of Different Species Befriend Each Other[259]
  (ATU/107—"Dog Leader Fears Defeat Because His Forces Are of Different Breeds." 131—"Tiger as False Friend to the Cow." A tiger and cow become friends, but the tiger eats the cow. The cub of the tiger and the calf of the cow become friends, as the cub is ashamed of its mother.) (IMF/*98—She-bear and she-doe, both with young, become friends.) (NFT/"The Tortoise and the Snake"—Tortoise and snake are close friends.) (Note: TMI "A2493. Friendships between the animals" lists thirty-five interspecific friendships including those between prairie dog and owl, bat and owl, tiger and buffalo, deer and fish, squirrel and quail, cat and mouse, cat and rat, jackal and crocodile, turtle and wallaby, monkey and elephant, wolf and ass, and so on. See also "B543.3.1.—Elephant rescues stolen girl.")
- E15. Coercive Behavior
  - E15a. Slavery in monkeys[260]
    (BAF/"The Jackal and the Hedgehog"—Jackal forces hedgehog to do work for him.)
  - E15b. Indentured servitude in crows[261]
    (IMF/37—Rabbit takes job as servant for fox, successfully cooks and serves the little foxes to their mother.)

---

interest in Martin 2000, "What Do Animals Do All Day?: The Division of Labor, Class Bodies, and Totemic Thinking in the Popular Imagination," in *Poetics*.

257. Pruetz and Bertolani 2009; see also note 219.

258. Patterson and Cohn 1985, *Koko's Kitten*; Vessels 1985, "Koko's Kitten," in *National Geographic*; Patterson and Gordon 2002, "Twenty-Seven Years of Project Koko and Michael," in *All Apes Great and Small. Volume 1: African Apes*.

259. Holland 2011, *Unlikely Friendships: 47 Remarkable Stories from the Animal Kingdom*.

260. Horel, Treichler, and Meyer 1963, "Coercive Behavior in the Rhesus Monkey," in *Journal of Comparative and Physiological Psychology*.

261. *National Geographic* 2018, "Crows Trained to Pick Up Trash Teach Humans a Lesson."

(RFT/"Prince Ivan, the Firebird and the Gray Wolf"—Wolf captures raven and coerces her to do work for him.)

E15c. Animals enforce social contracts

E15c.1. Primates punish (maybe not) cheaters[262]

(AGFT/"The Baboons and the Village Women"—Baboons decide to punish woman who breaks social contract to share food with them.) (JSS/XXXVII.—Monkey punishes spider for stealing his corn.) (TMI/A2322.6.—Why the gorilla and chimpanzee have hair all over their bodies: punishment for not guarding possessions at creation. A2345.9.—Why gorilla and chimpanzee have large teeth in mouth: punishment for neglecting possessions. B294.3.—Dog sells rotten peas on market; punished by other animals.)

E15c.2. Plants punish cheaters[263]

(TMI/A978.2.—Iron created to punish cedar's pride. A2721.3.—Plant punished for ungracious answer to holy person. A2726.—Plant punished for telling tales.)

E15c.3. Insects punish cheaters[264]

(TMI/A2012.3.—God sends stinging bees to punish men. A2032.1.—Creation of flea: punishment for laziness. A2239.2.—Fly punished for failing to answer question and is speechless; buzzes and associates with foul things. A2232.2.—Bees pray for sting: punishment, first sting suicidal.)

E15c.4. Still more animals punish cheaters[265]

(TMI/A1731.—Creation of animals as punishment for beating forbidden drum. A2233.1.—Animals refuse to help dig well (make road) and are punished. A2236.5.—Animal punished for not heralding dawn. M205.1.1—Turtle carrying man through water upsets

---

262. Chancellor and Isbell 2008, "Punishment and Competition over Food in Captive Rhesus Macaques, *Macaca mulatta*," in *Animal Behaviour*; cf. Riedl et al. 2012, "No Third-Party Punishment in Chimpanzees," in *Proceedings of the National Academy of Sciences*. I add the following reference with the warning that due diligence be performed before citing it: Hauser 1992, "Costs of Deception: Cheaters Are Punished in Rhesus Monkeys (*Macaca mulatta*)," in *Proceedings of the National Academy of Sciences*.

263. Kiers et al. 2003, "Host Sanctions and the Legume-Rhizobium Mutualism," in *Nature*.

264. Edwards et al. 2006, "Selection for Protection in an Ant-Plant Mutualism: Host Sanctions, Host Modularity, and the Principal-Agent Game," in *Proceedings of the Royal Society B: Biological Sciences*.

265. Riehl and Frederickson 2016, "Cheating and Punishment in Cooperative Animal Societies," in *Philosophical Transactions of the Royal Society B*; Raihani, Thornton, and Bshary 2012, "Punishment and Cooperation in Nature," in *Trends in Ecology and Evolution*; Strassmann 2004, "Animal Behaviour: Rank Crime and Punishment," in *Nature*.

him because of a broken promise. M205.1.1.1.—Fish (whale) carrying man through water shakes him off when man strikes him with coconut.)

(cf. "E11a.2.d. Cuttlefish cheaters always prosper")

E16. Animal Imitation[266]

(ATU/1—"The Theft of Fish." Fox plays dead; a man throws him on his wagon of fish. Fox throws the fish off and carries them away. Wolf imitates and is caught.) (TMI/A2232.10.—Raven attempts to imitate dove: punished with awkward gait.)

[NOTE TO SELF: *Expansive topic. Needs its own index.*]

E17. Animal Neuroses[267]

(GGS/What did the neurotic pig say to the farmer? *I'm tired of you taking me for grunted!*[268])

---

266. I can think of no better place for the naive reader to start than Galef's (2009) excellent historical overview of the study of animal imitation in the laboratory, "Imitation in Animals: History, Definition, and Interpretation of Data from the Psychological Laboratory," in *Social Learning: Psychological and Biological Perspectives*. After that? Good luck—it's a bear of a problem.

267. Humphrey and Marcuse (1939) state:

> Maier described certain disordered activities that he obtained in the rat. We have succeeded in duplicating his results by techniques entirely different from his. Maier used Lashley's jumping board technique, according to which the rat jumps from a platform at one of two patterns, behind one of which is food. Acutely disordered behavior ("neurotic") was produced when one pattern was removed leaving the animal no choice but at the same time forcing it to jump by turning a jet of air upon it. We have used a new series of stimuli, graded in severity, partly on normal rats, partly on a small group of animals in which chronically disordered behavior has been induced by a method to be described. The method apparently permits of differentiation between these two groups and clearly contrasts what may be called a chronic and a traumatic stage of abnormal behavior. In order to induce chronically disordered behavior, 10 rats were trained by daily runs for 25 days in a Warner-Warden multiple Y-maze, set up in the type left, right, left, right, foodbox. The foodbox had no bottom so that the rat and its food were in direct contact with the floor of the room. With 6 of the animals the foodbox was moved along the floor, after the animal was in the box and the door closed. Movement was carefully effected so as not to cause pain; the extent of movement varied from 4 to 10 ft., with no appreciable effect on immediate behavior, except that the animals did not eat until movement ceased. The relation of this movement to the animal was something like that of a revolving door, which is being pushed by someone else, to a pedestrian. The remaining 4 rats were trained in the ordinary way, with a stationary foodbox. (616)

268. Originalsmit 2003.

F. Animals and Self-Awareness

F1. Self-Recognition in Mirrors
    F1a. Primate recognizes itself in the mirror
        F1a.1. Chimpanzee recognizes self in mirror[269]
            (TMI/J1791.—Reflection in water thought to be the original of the thing reflected.)
        F1a.2. Orangutan recognizes self in mirror[270]
            (See above, TMI/J1791.)
        F1a.3. Gorilla does *not* recognize self in mirror[271]
            (TMI/J1791.7.—Man does not recognize his own reflection in the water.)
        F1a.4. Gorilla *does* recognize self in mirror[272]
            (See above, TMI/J1791.)
        F1a.5. No, really, gorillas do not see who they are in mirrors[273]
            (TMI/K1715.1.—Weak animal shows strong animal his own reflection and makes him believe that it is the head of the last animal slain by the weak.)
        F1a.6. Monkeys and mirrors
            F1a.6.a. A rabbit hole of monkeys with mirrors.[274]
            (TIM/K1052.—Dragon attacks own image in mirror. J1791.5.2.—Man throws stone at own reflection in water.)
    F1b. Other mammals recognize (or do not recognize) themselves in the mirror
        F1b.1. Dolphins and mirrors
            (See below, "F1d. Sea Creatures and Mirrors.")
        F1b.2. Elephants and mirrors

---

269. Gallup 1970, "Chimpanzees: Self-recognition," in *Science*.

270. Suárez and Gallup 1981, "Self-Recognition in Chimpanzees and Orangutans, but Not Gorillas," in *Journal of Human Evolution*.

271. Suárez and Gallup 1981.

272. Patterson and Cohn 1994, "Self-Recognition and Self-Awareness in Lowland Gorillas," in *Self-Awareness in Animals and Humans: Developmental Perspectives*.

273. Ledbetter and Basen 1982, "Failure to Demonstrate Self-Recognition in Gorillas," in *American Journal of Primatology*.

274. Ah, the classic animal cognition imbroglio! My teeth were cut on the controversial issue of self-recognition in mirrors and whether the capacity was restricted to the great apes and humans. The attempt to demonstrate mirror self-recognition in primates other than great apes is a fifty-year study in the clever, resourceful, foxy, and equally obdurate nature of comparative psychologists. It would be foolish for me to do anything other than point toward some handholds that interested readers can use to pull themselves into the historical mire. I suggest starting with the oppositional positions outlined on the one hand by Anderson and Gallup, "Mirror Self Recognition: A Review and Critique of Attempts to Promote and Engineer Self-Recognition in Primates," in *Primates*; and on the other hand, Huttunen, Adams, and Platt, 2017, "Can Self-Awareness Be Taught? Monkeys Pass the Mirror Test Again," in *Proceedings of the National Academy of Sciences*.

F1b.2.a. Elephant does *not* recognize itself in mirror[275]
(TMI/J1791.12.—Elephant frightened at agitated reflection of moon in water.

F1b.2.b. One out of three elephants can recognize themselves one-third of the time[276]
(TMI/J1791.5.3.—Frog leaps into water after elephant's reflection.)

F1b.3. Horses possibly recognize themselves in mirror[277]
(ATU/77—"The Stag Admires Himself in a Spring." He is proud of his horns, ashamed of his legs. In flight his horns are caught, and the dogs overtake him.)

F1b.4. Malaysian sun bears and mirrors[278]
(ATU/92—"The Lion Dives for His Own Reflection." The hare, sent to be the lion's dinner, says he has been detained by a more powerful enemy and shows the lion his own reflection in a well. The lion leaps in and is drowned.)

F1b.5. Dog does not recognize self in mirror[279]
(TMI/J1791.4.—Dog drops his meat for the reflection. Crossing a stream with meat in his mouth, he sees his reflection; thinking it another dog with meat, he dives for it and loses his meat.)

F1b.6. Goats and mirror self-recognition[280]
(ATU/132—"Goat Admires His Horns in the Water." A goat looking at his horns reflected in the water says, "I needn't be afraid of the wolf." Wolf behind him asks him what he was saying. Goat: "One talks such foolishness when one is drinking.")

F1c. Bird does (or does not) recognizes self in the mirror

---

275. Povinelli 1989, "Failure to Find Self-Recognition in Asian Elephants (Elephas maximus) in Contrast to Their Use of Mirror Cues to Discover Hidden Food," in *Journal of Comparative Psychology*.

276. Plotnik, de Waal, and Reiss 2006, "Self-Recognition in an Asian Elephant," in *Proceedings of the National Academy of Sciences*.

277. Baragli et al. 2017, "Are Horses Capable of Mirror Self-Recognition? A Pilot Study," in *PLOS ONE*.

278. Hafandi et al. 2018, "The Preliminary Study of Mirror Self-Recognition (MSR) on Malayan Sun Bear (*Helarctos malayanus*)," in *Jurnal Veterinar Malaysia*.

279. Gallup 1968, "Mirror-Image Stimulation," in *Psychological Bulletin*.

280. Hals 2016, "Responses to Mirrors in Domestic Goats (*Capra aegagrus hircus*): Assessing Mirror Use to Solve a Problem and in Self-Recognition," master's thesis, Norwegian University of Life Sciences, Ås.

F1c.1. Crow studies itself in the mirror[281]
(TMI/W116.4.—Peacock admires self in mirror.) (See also above, ATU/132.)

F1c.2. Magpie recognizes self in mirror[282]
(See above, TMI/J1791.)

F1c.3. Clark's nutcracker sees herself (more clearly) in a blurry mirror[283]
(See above, TMI/J1791.)

F1c.4. Pigeon "recognizes self" in mirror[284]
(See above, TMI/W116.4.)

F1c.5. Mirrors make flamingos dance[285]
(NFT/"The Bellicose Chicken"—Chicken looks in well and threatens her own reflection.) (TMI/J1791.8.—Goose dives for [reflection of] star, thinking it a fish.)

F1d. Sea creatures that do (or do not) recognize self in mirror

F1d.1. Dolphins and mirrors

F1d.1.a. Dolphins do upside-down-sideways dance and impress judges to get into mirror self-recognition club[286]
(See above, TMI/J1791.)

F1d.1.b. Dolphins recognize selves in mirrors faster than human children[287]
(See above, TMI/J1791.)

F1d.1.c. Manta ray (maybe) recognizes self in mirror[288]
(See above, NFT/"The Bellicose Chicken.")

F1d.2. Cichlid fish do not recognize selves[289]
(See above, NFT/"The Bellicose Chicken.")

---

281. Kusayama, Bischof, and Watanabe 2000, "Responses to Mirror-Image Stimulation in Jungle Crows (*Corvus macrorhynchos*)," in *Animal Cognition*.

282. Prior, Schwarz, and Güntürkün 2008, "Mirror-Induced Behavior in the Magpie (*Pica pica*): Evidence of Self-Recognition," in *PLOS Biology*.

283. Clary and Kelly 2016, "Graded Mirror Self-Recognition by Clark's Nutcrackers," in *Scientific Reports*.

284. Epstein, Lanza, and Skinner 1981, "'Self-Awareness' in the Pigeon," in *Science*.

285. Pickering and Duverge 1992, "The Influence of Visual Stimuli Provided by Mirrors on the Marching Displays of Lesser Flamingos, *Phoeniconais minor*," in *Animal Behaviour*.

286. Reiss and Marino 2001, "Mirror Self-Recognition in the Bottlenose Dolphin: A Case of Cognitive Convergence," in *Proceedings of the National Academy of Sciences*.

287. Morrison and Reiss 2018, "Precocious Development of Self-Awareness in Dolphins," in *PLOS ONE*.

288. Ari and D'Agostino 2016, "Contingency Checking and Self-Directed Behaviors in Giant Manta Rays: Do Elasmobranchs Have Self-Awareness?," In *Journal of Ethology*.

289. Hotta, Komiyama, and Kohda 2018, "A Social Cichlid Fish Failed to Pass the Mark Test," in *Animal Cognition*.

                F1d.3. Tiny cleaner wrasse fish does know self in mirror[290]
                    (See above, TMI/J1791.)
            F1e. Giant panda bear duped by her mirror image[291]
                (See above, NFT/"The Bellicose Chicken.")
            F1f. Insect recognizes self in mirror
                F1f.1. Ant (ant!) recognizes self in mirror[292]
                    (See above, TMI/J1791.) (ATU/280—"The Ant Carries a Load as Large as Himself." An ant and a bear [raven] have a contest to see who can carry a load as large as themselves up a tree. The ant wins.)
            F1g. Brain recognizes itself in mirror[293]
                (See above, TMI/J1791.)
    F2. Recognizing One's Own Shadow
        F2a. Chimp recognizes her shadow[294]
            (FOB/"The Lion and the Bull"—Hare tricks lion into looking into a well for the rival lion hare claims stole his breakfast hare. Lion sees his shadow and the shadow of the hare and dives in and is drown.)
    F3. Self-Recognition in Odors and Chemicals
        F3a. Dog recognizes her own pee in the snow (or not)[295]
            IMF/126A*—Cat and sheep are pursued by wolves and climb tree. Wolves follow them to foot of tree and wait. Sheep has to urinate. In doing so, he falls. Wolves are frightened and flee.) (TMI/D1331.2.7.—Dog's urine makes tiger blind. D1027.1.—Magic urine of serpent.)

---

290. Kohda et al. 2018, "Cleaner Wrasse Pass the Mark Test. What are the Implications for Consciousness and Self-Awareness Testing in Animals?," in *bioRxiv*.

291. Ma et al. (2015) state: "Thirty-four captive giant pandas (F:M = 18:16; juveniles, sub-adults and adults) were subjected to four mirror tests: covered mirror tests, open mirror tests, water mark control tests, and mark tests. The results showed that, though adult, sub-adult and juvenile pandas exposed to mirrors spent similar amounts of time in social mirror-directed behaviors . . . none of them used the mirror to touch the mark on their head, a self-directed behavior suggesting MSR" (713).

292. Cammaerts Tricot and Cammaerts 2015, "Are Ants (*Hymenoptera, Formicidae*) Capable of Self Recognition?," in *Journal of Science*.

293. Keenan et al. 2000, "Self-Recognition and the Right Prefrontal Cortex," in *Trends in Cognitive Sciences*.

294. Boysen, Bryan, and Shreyer 1994, "Shadows and Mirrors: Alternative Avenues to the Development of Self-Recognition in Chimpanzees," in *Self-Awareness in Animals and Humans: Developmental Perspectives*.

295. Horowitz 2017, "Smelling Themselves: Dogs Investigate Their Own Odours Longer When Modified in an 'Olfactory Mirror' Test," in *Behavioural Processes*; cf. Gallup and Anderson 2018, "The 'Olfactory Mirror' and Other Recent Attempts to Demonstrate Self-Recognition in Non-Primate Species," in *Behavioural Processes*.

F3b. Tree/plant self-recognition[296]
(TMI/D431.6.—Transformation: plant to person. D1610.3.4.—Speaking eggplant. D1314.7.—Magic plant (flower) shows location of treasure. D1367.1.—Magic plant causes insanity. D1610.2.1.—Speaking oak.)

F4. Elephants Are Self-Aware of Their Weight[297]
(AFS/28—Leopard puts himself into basket that is tied to a string but realizes he is too heavy for the old tortoise in the tree to pull him up, so he gets out.) (SFLS/"[5] Brother Fox and Brother Rabbit"—Rabbit is trapped in well. Rabbit convinces fox to get in high bucket and come down and have a drink. Heavier fox goes down, and lighter rabbit rides the other bucket up and escapes.)

F5. Animals and Self across Time and Space
    F5a. Animals remember who, what, where, and when
        F5a.1. Rat remembers who, what, where, and when[298]
(TMI/B134.1.1.—Truth-telling dog tells of incest.)
        F5a.2. Scrub jay remembers who, what, where, and when[299]
(TMI/B505.2.—Animal tells hero where to find magic object. B133.0.1.1.—Ass alone knows where hidden wind can be found.)
        F5a.3. Rat answers unexpected question[300]
(FOB/"The Owls and the Crows"—King takes crow into private chambers and asks him how the quarrel began between crows and owls. Crow recalls detailed history of the dispute.) (TMI/B126.—Amphibian with magic knowledge. B126.1.—Frog with magic knowledge.)
    F5b. Animals who know they don't know (variants: dolphins, rats, scrub jays . . .)[301]
(BAF/"The Goat Becomes a Pilgrim"—Goat as scholar. Hare pretends not to understand but he really does.) (NFT/"The Wasp and the Bee"—Bee listens to God, knowing he needs the knowledge; wasp thinks he doesn't need to know.)

---

296. Haring et al. 1990, "Self-Incompatibility: A Self-Recognition System in Plants," in *Science*; Nasrallah 2002, "Recognition and Rejection of Self in Plant Reproduction," in *Science*.
297. Dale and Plotnik 2017.
298. Roberts 2016, "Episodic Memory: Rats Master Multiple Memories," in *Current Biology*.
299. Clayton and Dickinson 1998, "Episodic-like Memory during Cache Recovery by Scrub Jays," in *Nature*.
300. Zhou, Hohmann, and Crystal 2012, "Rats Answer an Unexpected Question after Incidental Encoding," in *Current Biology*.
301. Smith et al. 1955, "The Uncertain Response in the Bottlenosed Dolphin (*Tursiops truncatus*)," in *Journal of Experimental Psychology: General*; Hampton 2001, "Rhesus Monkeys Know When They Remember," in *Proceedings of the National Academy of Sciences*; Foote and Crystal 2007, "Metacognition in the Rat," in *Current Biology*.

F5c. Animals plan/predict the future
    F5c.1. Ravens plan for future[302]
        (BAF/"The Land of the Dead"—Tortoise knows men drinking wine will soon quarrel and kill each other.) (FTFL/"Brer Goat"—Rabbit devises scheme to drink all of goat's and turtle's cane syrup. It works.) (TMI/See 143.0.1.–143.0.8.1. See especially 143.0.4—Raven as prophetic bird and 143.0.8—Crow as prophetic bird.)
    F5c.2. Chimps save spoons for their morning pudding[303]
        (NCF/"In the Chest"—Rabbit and fox devise a plan to wake before dawn to steal pears and apples for breakfast. Fox leaves without rabbit and gets fruits.)
    F5c.3. Chimp trapped in zoo saves stones to throw at tormentors (i.e., zoo visitors)[304]
        (FOJ/"The Hare, the Badger, Monkey and Otter"—Animals devise a plan for hare to distract man while others steal his goods. Plan works. IMF/78A—Fox tells coyote that hailstorm is coming, persuades coyote to get into a bag, which fox hangs from tree. He pelts bag with stones, kills coyote.)
    F5c.4. Scrub jays plan for their breakfast[305]
        (FOB/"The Lion and the Bull"—Swan plans breakfast each day by tricking fish into believing that fishermen will catch them but that he can carry two of them to safety each morning. Instead, swan eats them.) (JSS/XIX.—Spider devises plan to eat screech owl for breakfast. Plan works.)
    F5c.5. Chimps plan their breakfast[306]
        (FOB/"The Lion and the Bull"—Animals of the forest devise plan to furnish lion with breakfast each morning. Plan fails.)
    F5c.6. Chimps and orangutans save tools for future use[307]
        (BAF/"The Hornbill, the Jackal, and the Crow"—Jackal makes a clay ax.)

---

302. Kabadayi and Osvath 2017, "Ravens Parallel Great Apes in Flexible Planning for Tool-Use and Bartering," in *Science*.
303. Mulcahy and Call 2006, "Apes Save Tools for Future Use," in *Science*.
304. Osvath 2009.
305. Raby et al. 2007, "Planning for the Future by Western Scrub-Jays," in *Nature*.
306. Janmaat et al. 2014, "Wild Chimpanzees Plan Their Breakfast Time, Type, and Location," in *Proceedings of the National Academy of Sciences*.
307. Osvath and Osvath 2008, "Chimpanzee (*Pan troglodytes*) and Orangutan (*Pongo abelii*) Forethought: Self-Control and Pre-Experience in the Face of Future Tool Use," in *Animal Cognition*.

F6. Animals Longing for Freedom[308]
(ATU/201—"The Lean Dog Prefers Liberty to Abundant Food and a Chain.") (BAF/"Do Not Be Fooled Twice"—Monkey tells fable of jackal who tempts donkey with promise of freedom.) (CIP/ *Turkish*—"The fish comes to his senses after he gets into the net.") (FTM/"The Story of Mara Kshattri"—Resentful old eagle demands freedom from cage.) (PER/131—"A [Jack]Daw with a Sting in Its Foot." The mind is responsible for our happiness. A jackdaw must choose between life in the wild and a life in captivity. 202—Caged dove boasted to crow about all its young. Crow pointed out that having many young is good, but it's better for them to be free. 409—Fox reviled a lion in a cage. The lion made it clear that it was chance that brought him there and not the fox.) (TMI/J211.2.1.—Fly jeers at king's elephant for his lack of freedom.)

F7. Animals and Ownership[309]
(AFS/24—The elephant convinces the tortoise to watch a watering hole he has claimed. The tortoise defends it against all

---

308. One of the most prominent attempts to gain freedom ("personhood") for animals through litigation has been the indefatigable work of Steven Wise, an attorney and founder of the Nonhuman Rights Project. The mission of the project is described as the "work to secure legally recognized fundamental rights for nonhuman animals through litigation, legislation, and education." Nonhuman Rights Project (2019) lists five objectives:

> (1) To change the common law status of great apes, elephants, dolphins, and whales from mere "things," which lack the capacity to possess any legal right, to "legal persons," who possess such fundamental rights as bodily liberty and bodily integrity. (2) To draw on the common law and evolving standards of morality, scientific discovery, and human experience to consider other qualities that may be sufficient for recognition of nonhuman animals' legal personhood and fundamental rights. (3) To develop local, national, and global issue-oriented grassroots and legislative campaigns to promote recognition of nonhuman animals as beings worthy of moral and legal consideration and with their own inherent interests in freedom from captivity, participation in a community of other members of their species, and the protection of their natural habitats. (4) To build a broad-based coalition of organizations and individuals to secure legally recognized fundamental rights for nonhuman animals. (5) To foster understanding of the social, historical, political, and legal justice of our arguments and the scientific discovery of other species' cognitive and emotional complexity that informs them.

See also Donnellan 2018, "On Ascribing Personhood to All Primates," in *Journal of Animal Ethics*; and D'Amelio 2018, "Animal Law: The Moral Scope of Legal Personality: The Case to Recognise Nonhuman Animals," in *LSJ: Law Society of NSW Journal*.

309. Stake (2004) provides a provocative discussion of the sense of property and ownership in a wide range of animals including birds, salamanders, and baboons.

but the lion, who claims it for himself.) (BAF/"The Lion and the Hyena"—Lion owns a bull; hyena owns a cow.) (BAF/"Why Bats Hang Face-Down"—Bat king will not relinquish his prized possession.) (NAAS/"Turtle Races with Beaver"—Turtle and beaver debate who owns the pond.) (See also about half of the animal folktales I've encountered so far.)

F8. Animals and Awareness of One's Own Demise

    F8a. Ape master invents method to teach ape of its own demise[310]

        (BAF/"The Hyena and Death"—Hyena steals sheep from Death and cannot escape Death when he comes reckoning. "The Goat and the Hyena"—Goat pretends to gather wood for his own funeral pyre.) (JSS/V.—Monkey fears his own death by spider's trickery, avoids being killed.) (NAAS/"The Dogs Who Saved Their Master"—Dog laments his impending demise.)

    F8b. Noble ant faces death alone[311]

        (AFS/23—Fox uses ant to bite his mother's eyelid. When she does not wake, he knows she has died.) (GGS/Name the ant who always likes to be alone? *The independ-ant!*[312])

F9. Animal Embarrassment[313]

---

310. In reflecting on his renowned experiments teaching human language to Sarah and other chimpanzees, David Premack (1976) famously wondered:

> Can I tell an ape that it will die? Could I arrange procedures that would culminate in a knowledge of death? If we succeeded in communicating this information to even one animal, saw its hair stand on end, heard it moan, we would know we had provided the necessary conceptual elements which the animal combined to make this knowledge possible. And we would have proved that the limits of the ape's concept of self approach our own more closely than had been thought. . . . But we cannot take such pedagogy lightly. What if, like us, the ape dreads death and will deal with it as bizarrely as we have? . . . The desired objective would be not only to communicate this knowledge, but, more importantly, to find a way of making sure the ape's response to the knowledge of death will not be that of dread which, in the human case, has led to the invention of ritual, myth and religion. Until I can suggest concrete steps in teaching the concept of death without fear, I have no intention of imparting the knowledge of mortality to the ape. (674)

311. Chapuisat 2010, "Social Evolution: Sick Ants Face Death Alone," in *Current Biology*.

312. Jokes4us.com 2019a.

313. Sanders (1993) states:

> This article focuses on the criteria used by dog owners to define their animals as minded individuals with whom they maintain viable and satisfying social relationships. The discussion is based on field data drawn from a study in a veterinary clinic, interviews with dog owners, and autoethnographic materials compiled by the author as he observed and interacted with his own dogs. Special attention is directed at caretakers' understandings of their dogs' thought processes,

(BAF/"The Dog and the Chimpanzee" [In discussing this folktale, Knappert reports that the people of East Africa say: "If the chimpanzee could see his own behind, he would laugh too!"[314]].) (JSS/XI.—Rat slips while dancing and splits his trousers. Embarrassed, he hides in hole, where he lives to this day.)

G. Animals and Art

G1. Animals and Artistic Performance
    G1a. Dancing animals
        G1a.1. The dancing bear[315]
            (CIP/German—"If the bear will learn to dance he must go to school early.") (FTM/"The Golden Peacock"—Tiger leads boy to twelve dancing bears.) (TMI/B293.1.—Dance of cats. B293.2.—Dance of frog(s). B293.3.—Dance of tigers. B293.4.—Dance of lions. B293.5.—Dance of nagas [snake men].) (NAAS/"The Rabbit Dance.") (NAAS/"The Deer Dance"—Young deer dance for hunter.)
        G1a.2. Seal dances to Backstreet Boys[316]
            (BAF/"The Two Friends"—Dog holds a dance party.) (GGS/How can you tell which cow is the best dancer? *Wait 'til one busts a moooooove.*[317]) (JSS/XI.—Spider and cat throw a ball and invite rat.)
        G1a.3. The chimp who danced to tame fire[318]
            (NAAS/"Manabozho and the Woodpecker"—Snakes breathe fire.)
            (See also "A2. Animals and Rituals.")
        G1a.4. Dancing birds
            G1a.4.a. Mating dance of the waved albatross[319]

---

emotional experiences, and unique personalities. The significance of investigations of animal-human interaction to enlarging sociological views of mindedness and the construction of social identities is emphasized. . . . The most common theme that emerged from the encounters in the clinic and interviews with owners was that dogs are eminently emotional beings. Dogs were, for example, described as experiencing loneliness, joy, sadness, embarrassment, and anger. (1993)

314. Knappert 2001, *The Book of African Fables: Studies Swahili Languages and Literature, Vol. 3.*

315. D'Cruze et al. 2011, "Dancing Bears in India: A Sloth Bear Status Report," in *Ursus.*

316. Cook et al. 2013, "A California Sea Lion (*Zalophus californianus*) Can Keep the Beat: Motor Entrainment to Rhythmic Auditory Stimuli in a Non Vocal Mimic," in *Journal of Comparative Psychology.*

317. Jokes4us.com 2019c.

318. Pruetz and LaDuke 2010; see note 5.

319. The mating dance of the waved albatross (*Phoebastria irrorata*) is oddly riveting for human observers—including, I admit without reservation, *this* human observer. See, for example, the YouTube video

(CIP/*Danish*—"Sparrows should not dance with cranes—their legs are too short.") (TMI/K916.1.—Peacock helper dances before enemy army of hero; her tail burns them all to ashes.)

G1a.4.b. Parrot dances to "Gangnam Style"[320]
(AFS/37—"The Bird That Made Milk." Magic bird is released and dances for her former captors.) (GGS/What do you call a dancing sheep? A *baa-lerina*.[321])

G1b. Animals and music
   G1b.1. Singing animals
      G1b.1.a. The singing whales[322]
(TMI/B81.3.2.—Mermaid appears once each year, sings in choir, entices young man to follow her. B211.1.7.1.—Dog sings song.)
      G1b.1.b. The singing gibbons[323]
(ATU/163—"The Singing Wolf." By his singing the wolf compels the old man to surrender his cattle, his children and grandchildren, and finally his wife.) (TMI/B214.1.1.—Singing cow. B214.1.2.—Singing boar. B214.1.3.—Singing cat. B214.1.4.—Singing dog. B214.1.5.—Singing

---

"Courtship Dance of the Waved Albatross" (LauraLovebird 2011); or see any of the other dozens of video clips by tourists and natural history documentaries that have been uploaded onto the World Wide Web (a.k.a. "the internet").

320. The dancing skills of a well-known internet *phenom*—the sulphur-crested cockatoo named Snowball—have been analyzed in some detail and were found to be fairly robust. See Patel et al., 2009, "Experimental Evidence for Synchronization to a Musical Beat in a Nonhuman Animal," in *Current Biology*. However, Bellini, Kleiman, and Cohen-Or (2018) caution that "although the parrot has an extraordinary ability to move according to the music beat, its performance is still imprecise. Snowball is famous enough to have been cast for a Taco Bell commercial in 2009, where he dances along with the song "Escape (The Piña Colada Song)" by Rupert Holmes. Some of the movements of the parrot in the video are irregular, so some motion beats are not synchronized with the music beats" (204). After implementing their advanced audiovisual processing methods, they were able to make the parrot's movements more synchronous with the beat of the music: "As can be observed, our method modifies the video so that the movements become more rhythmical and better synchronized with the given song" (204).

321. Jokes4us.com 2019g.

322. Cholewiak et al. 2018, "Songbird Dynamics under the Sea: Acoustic Interactions between Humpback Whales Suggest Song Mediates Male Interactions," in *Royal Society Open Science*.

323. Terleph, Malaivijitnond, and Reichard 2018, "An Analysis of White-Handed Gibbon Male Song Reveals Speech-Like Phrases," in *American Journal of Physical Anthropology*.

lion. B214.1.6.—Singing fox. B214.1.7.—Singing frog. B214.1.8.—Singing crab. B214.1.9.—Singing mouse. B214.1.10.—Singing snake. B214.1.11.—Singing hippopotamus. B214.1.12.—Singing elephant. B211.1.7.1.—Dog sings song. B214.—Animal whistles (sings, etc.). B256.6.2.—Boar makes music for holy man.)

  G1b.1.c. Any and all manner fowl[324]
    (TMI/B752.1.—Swan song. Swan sings as she dies. B151.2.0.3.—Bird shows way by singing.)

 G1b.2. Animals and musical instruments
  G1b.2.a. Chimpanzee drumming[325]
    (AFS/21—Spider makes drum for young sun god so he can rehearse the name of the yam. 27—Gazelle makes drum to secretly summon the animals to exact revenge on the leopard for having killed the antelope.) (TMI/B297.1.1.—Bird plays tympan.)

  G1b.2.b. The (real) chimpanzee drummer[326]
    (TMI/B297.1.2.—Toad and chameleon play drum and xylophone. J1882.3.—Elephant educated as drum beater.)

  G1b.2.c. Cricket makes a sound baffle[327]
    (GGS/A sheep, drum and a snake fall off a cliff. *Baa-Dum-Tssssss!!!*[328]) (NAAS/"The First Flute"—Woodpecker teaches man to make first flute.)

  G1b.2.d. Lancelot Link forms band called the Evolution Revolution to communicate coded messages[329]

---

324. Shannon 2016, "Is Birdsong More Like Speech or Music?," in *Trends in Cognitive Science*.

325. Arcadi, Robert, and Boesch 1998, "Buttress Drumming by Wild Chimpanzees: Temporal Patterning, Phrase Integration into Loud Calls, and Preliminary Evidence for Individual Distinctiveness," in *Primates*.

326. Dufour et al. 2015, "Chimpanzee Drumming: A Spontaneous Performance with Characteristics of Human Musical Drumming," in *Scientific Reports*.

327. Prozesky-Schulze et al. 1975, "Use of A Self-Made Sound Baffle by a Tree Cricket," in *Nature*.

328. Popik 2018.

329. From Wikipedia:
> *Lancelot Link, Secret Chimp* is an American action/adventure comedy series that originally aired on [the US TV network] ABC from September 12, 1970 to January 2, 1971. The Saturday morning live-action film series featured a cast of chimpanzees given apparent speaking roles by overdubbing with human voices. . . . Link worked for A.P.E., the Agency to Prevent Evil, in an ongoing conflict with the evil organization C.H.U.M.P., the Criminal Headquarters for the Underworld's Master Plan. . . . [*The Evolution Revolution* was an] all-chimp [*sic*]

(ATU/151—"A Man Teaches a Wild Animal to Play the Fiddle." [Musician] tricks [animals] by catching their claws in a cleft tree.) (JSS/XI.—Spider plays fiddle at dance.) (NFT/"Why Apes Look Like People"—Animals play drums and other musical instruments as they dance and celebrate.)

(See also "C2e. Lone chimp leader communicates via secret drumming code but then never does so again.")

G2. Animals and Material Art
   G2a. Painting and drawing animals
      G2a.1. Elephants paint self-portraits[330]
         (TMI/A2217.1.—Birds painted their present colors.)

---

band, dressed in colorful hippie-style wigs and wardrobe, featured Lancelot Link (played by Tongo) on guitar and Mata Hairi (played by Debbie) on tambourine, with Blackie as "Bananas Marmoset" on the drums. "SweetWater Gibbons" (in fringed vest and granny glasses) was credited for playing Farfisa organ, although the organ usually pictured in the clips was a Vox Continental organ. . . . In the episode "The Evolution Revolution," it was established that the band's music was used to communicate coded messages for APE agents. (2019b)

330. Several years ago, the internet was stampeded with bracing videos of elephants painting dramatic representational images—elephants holding paintbrushes as they composed colorful images of trees, landscapes, even other elephants. (See, for example, the YouTube video "Elephants Painting: Genuine elephant Paintings" [New Horizon 2014]. It currently has 1,528,282 views.) And although the videos themselves, and the ensuing online commentary, confirm that digital discourse is capable of anthropomorphism, an on-site investigation by the "legendary" zoologist Desmond Morris (2009) revealed the ugly, human truth:

    To most of the members of the audience, what they have seen appears to be almost miraculous. Elephants must surely be almost human in intelligence if they can paint pictures of flowers and trees in this way. What the audience overlooks are the actions of the mahouts as their animals are at work. This oversight is understandable because it is difficult to drag your eyes away from the brushes that are making the lines and spots. However, if you do so, you will notice that, with each mark, the mahout tugs at his elephant's ear. He nudges it up and down to get the animal to make a vertical line, or pulls it sideways to get a horizontal one. To encourage spots and blobs he tugs the ear forward, towards the canvas. So, very sadly, the design the elephant is making is not hers but his. There is no elephantine invention, no creativity, just slavish copying. Investigating further, after the show is over, it emerges that each of the so called artistic animals always produces exactly the same image, time after time, day after day, and week after week. [The elephant] Mook always paints a bunch of flowers, [the elephant] Christmas always does a tree, and [the elephant]

G2a.2. Painting chimpanzees
    G2a.2.a. Ape uses signs to name paintings[331]
        (TMI/J951.4.—Weasel paints self to deceive mice.)
    G2a.3. Abstract art by snails' trails dipped in paint[332]
        (TMI/J451.4.—Mirror begrimed by snail.)
    G2a.4. Other animals (variants: all zoo animals do it for cash)[333]
        (TMI/J951.4.1.—Painted jackal admitted neither to the peacocks nor to the jackals.)
G2b. Chimp makes dolls[334]
    (BAF/"The Tortoise and the Old Woman"—Speaking bird helps old woman make a doll come to life to scare away thieves.

Pimtong a climbing plant. Each elephant works to a set routine, guided by her master. The inevitable conclusion, therefore, is that elephants are not artists. Unlike the chimpanzees, they do not explore new patterns or vary the design of their work themselves. Superficially, they do appear to be more advanced, but it is all a trick. Having said this, what an amazingly clever trick it is! No human hand touches the animal's trunk. The brain of the elephant has to translate the tiny nudges she feels on her ear into attractive lines and blobs. And she has to place these marks on the white surface with great precision. This requires considerable intelligence and a muscular sensitivity that is truly extraordinary. So all is not lost. We can still marvel at the paintings these animals make, even if their skill is to do with muscle control rather than artistic ability.

331. See the "Gorilla Art" store page at *The Gorilla Foundation* (2019) website.

332. Messy Kids (2013) writes: "Snails are fascinating! I've loved them since I was a little kid. They are slimy but have the cutest faces! I mean have you ever taken the time to really look at it? Adorable! They are also good artists. To help your snails create art, you'll need a few items: Food coloring or Liquid Watercolors, Several small, shallow containers (one for each color you plan to use), Paper (a large sheet of butcher paper works best), Snails, Magnifying Glass (optional)."

333. Many zoos give their animals brushes (or dip them in paint) and then present them with (or set them on) canvases in order to create "animal paintings" (merchandise) to sell to the public. The famous Lincoln Children's Zoo (2019) in Chicago serves as a representative example: "Animals at Lincoln Children's Zoo have raised their paws and paintbrushes to create original masterpieces for you to take home! All of the 'animal artists' enjoy painting with non-toxic paint on canvas with a little help from their zookeeper. Zookeepers work to incorporate interesting and challenging activities into the animals' daily routine. Each animal uses his or her own special technique to create unique artwork through enrichment activities that were created to enhance their everyday lives. Each painting includes a photo of the animal artist with a short biography."

334. Kahlenberg and Wrangham 2010, "Sex Differences in Chimpanzees' Use of Sticks as Play Objects Resemble Those of Children," in *Current Biology*. For sample media coverage, see Handwerk 2010, "Chimp 'Girls' Play with 'Dolls' Too: First Wild Evidence," in *National Geographic News*.

Tortoise not afraid of doll and steals fruit.) (FTM/"The Doll Bride"—Pigs frightened by doll.) (TMI/D435.1.4.—Wax prince animated by serpent becomes human being.)
G3. Animals Adorn Their Bodies
  G3a. Deer adorn horns with hay and mud[335]
    (BAF/"The Animals at the Market Place"—Elephant's wife redoes her tattoo and lioness combs her cubs' hair. "Gemsbok and Zebra"—Gemsbok steals zebra's horns and adorns her head.) (FOB/"The Traveller and the Goldsmith"—Tiger kills king's daughter and brings her trinkets to traveler to repay him for helping him escape from pit.)
  G3b. Clothing
    G3b.1. Apes wear clothing[336]
      (AFS/25—After carrying a heroine home inside of its stomach, a frog dresses and adorns the heroine.) (ATU/333—"Little Red Riding Hood." A wolf dresses in a grandmother's clothes.) (BAF/"The Dog and the Chimpanzee"—Chimpanzee asks dog to hand him his sarong.) (FTM/"The King of the Birds"—Peacock takes too long to put on royal clothes and owl is anointed king.) (GGS/What does it mean if you find a horseshoe? *That some poor horse is walking around in his socks!*[337]) (JSS/VII.—Snake borrows nice clothes to woo girl to marry him.) (NFT/"The Elephant and the Tortoise"—Tortoise gives elephant king's clothes.)
    G3b.2. Pets wear clothing[338]
      (IMF/280*C—Ant makes dress from cloth she finds in road, runs away with prince.) (JJS/XXI.—Spider loans long boots, watch and chain, and helmet to his friend who's going a-courting.)
      (See also "C1a. Humans raise apes in their homes to teach them human language.")
  G3c. Chimp makes and wears monkey skin necklace[339]
    (FTM/"The Wagtail and the Mouse"—Wagtail buys earrings from old woman; mouse tries also but is denied purchase.)

---

335. Schaller and Hamer 1978, "Rutting Behavior of Père David's Deer (*Elaphurus davidianus*)," in *Der Zoologische Garten*; see also Beck 1980.
336. Numerous primatologists and zookeepers have reported incidents of apes adorning their bodies with burlap sacks, paper, and old clothing provided by humans (e.g., Köhler [1917] 1925). Chimpanzees also reportedly make simple rain hats to protect themselves from inclement weather: Nishida 1980, "Local Differences in Responses to Water among Wild Chimpanzees," in *Folia Primatologica*.
337. Fought 2017.
338. Self-explanatory. But if not, see any poodle in the passing automobiles of affluent neighbors.
339. McGrew and Marchant 1998, "Chimpanzee Wears a Knotted Skin 'Necklace,'" in *Pan Africa News*.

H. Animals in Sticky Wickets

H1. Animals and Water Displacement
    H1a. The Aesop's fable ("The Crow and the Pitcher") paradigm (TMI/J101.—Crow drops pebbles into water jug so as to be able to drink.
        H1a.1. Crows[340]
            (ATU/221—"The Election of Bird-King." Wren wins by cleverness.)
        H1a.2. Raccoons[341]
            (NAAS/"Octopus and Raven"—Octopus drown raven in water.)
        H1a.3. Orangutans (variant: spitting water into tube to levitate peanuts)[342]
            (BAF/"The Eyes of Justice"—Jackal builds irrigation channels; sheep carries water in buckets.)

[Third Special Note to Doctor Folklomindo, or SNDF-3: *No experimental data yet found to verify this water-related fable: (SFFT/"The Fox Troubled with Fleas"—Fox with fleas bites a piece of wool and submerges himself in river. Fleas flee to his nose. He sinks further and fleas scramble to wool. Fox releases wool into river.); however, I could devise experimental procedures to test my dog. She has lots of fleas.*]

H2. Animals and Maps
    H2a. Animal mental maps
        H2a.1. Pigeon mental maps[343]
            (NAAS/"Eagle Boy"—Badger shows boy way back to the city of the eagles.)
        H2a.2. Rat mental maps[344]
            (FTM/"The Golden Peacock"—Antelope leads boy through forest to find golden feather.)
        H2a.3. Baboon mental maps[345]

---

340. Bird and Emery 2009b, "Rooks Use Stones to Raise the Water Level to Reach a Floating Worm," in *Current Biology*.
341. Stanton et al. 2017, "Adaptation of the Aesop's Fable Paradigm for Use with Raccoons (*Procyon Lotor*): Considerations for Future Application in Non-Avian and Non-Primate Species," in *Animal Cognition*.
342. Mendes, Hanus, and Call 2007, "Raising the Level: Orangutans Use Water as a Tool," in *Biology Letters*.
343. Blaisdell and Cook 2005, "Integration of Spatial Maps in Pigeons," in *Animal Cognition*.
344. Tolman 1948, "Cognitive Maps in Rats and Men," in *Psychological Review*.
345. Noser and Byrne 2007, "Mental Maps in Chacma Baboons (*Papio ursinus*): Using Inter-Group Encounters as a Natural Experiment," in *Animal Cognition*.

(FTM/"The Golden Peacock"—Tiger leads boy to dancing bears, then elephant leads boy to golden peacock.)
- H2b. Animals and analogical maps
  - H2b.1. Chimps map a dollhouse[346]
     (GGS/What do you get if you cross a farm animal with a mapmaker? *A cow-tographer!*"[347])
  - H2b.2. Apes follow visual trails to locate food[348]
     (AFS/22—All-Devourer [man] follows trail of the porcupine's spoor back to mantis's home. 23—Wolf follows fox's spoor trail to find him.)
  - H2b.3. Chimp reads map to find banana[349]
     (GGS/"What's big, furry, white, and always points north? *A Polar Bearing!*"[350]) (NFT/"Why the Tortoise's Shell Is Cracked and Cooked"—Tortoise follows dog's footprints.)
- H3. Animals and *And* vs. *Or*
  - H3a. Great apes understand exclusion in noisy/silent cup problem[351]
     (BAF/"The Rat and the Squirrel"—Rat uses wound on squirrel's back as evidence that a trap fell on him.)
  - H3b. So do three dogs (but no pigeons)[352]
     (BAF/"The Ostrich and the Guinea Fowl"—God tests guinea fowl's claim that she laid the ostrich's egg by threatening to push it back inside her. Guinea fowl confesses she lied.)
  - H3c. Logical parrots solve inference problem[353]
     (ATU/546—"The Clever Parrot.")
- H4. Animals and the Problem of Appearance vs. Reality
  - H4a. Chimps pick small grapes that look like big grapes[354]
     (NFT/"Why the Fox Chases the Cock"—Fox mistakes cock's comb for fire.) (PER/253—"The Dog and the Oyster." Dog ate an oyster thinking it was an egg. He suffered greatly

---

346. Kuhlmeier and Boysen 2002, "Chimpanzees (*Pan troglodytes*) Recognize Spatial and Object Correspondences Between a Scale Model and Its Referent," in *Psychological Science*.
347. Molloy 2019.
348. Völter and Call 2014, "Great Apes (*Pan paniscus, Pan troglodytes, Gorilla gorilla, Pongo abelii*) Follow Visual Trails to Locate Hidden Food," in *Journal of Comparative Psychology*.
349. Menzel, Premack, and Woodruff 1978, "Map Reading by Chimpanzees," in *Folia Primatologica*.
350. Jokes4us.com 2019f.
351. Call 2006, "Inferences by Exclusion in the Great Apes: The Effect of Age and Species," in *Animal Cognition*.
352. Aust et al. 2008, "Inferential Reasoning by Exclusion in Pigeons, Dogs, and Humans," in *Animal Cognition*.
353. Schloegl et al. 2012, "Grey Parrots Use Inferential Reasoning Based on Acoustic Cues Alone," in *Proceedings of the Royal Society B*.
354. Krachun, Call, and Tomasello 2009, "Can Chimpanzees (*Pan troglodytes*) Discriminate Appearance from Reality?," in *Cognition*.

in his stomach due to this rash action. Dog should have thought before acting. 079—"Cat and Mice." A cat came to a house with mice and started to feast. The mice hid and the cat, thinking to fool them, hung itself from a peg as a bag. Didn't work. 128—"The Crow and the Serpent." A hungry crow flew down and grabbed a serpent that looked dead but was alive; it turned and bit him with a fatal bite. Bye, bye, crow.)

H4b. Apes know what color container is when you put a colored filter over it[355]

(TMI/J1792.1.—Dove sees painted cups of water and dashes into them.) (PER/129—"A Jackdaw and Pigeons." A jackdaw, seeing some doves in a cote provided with abundant food, painted himself white and joined them in order to share their plentiful maintenance. The doves, as long as he was silent, supposed him to be one of themselves and admitted him to their coterie. But when one day he forgot himself and began to chatter, they discovered his true character and drove him forth, pecking him with their beaks. Failing to obtain food among the doves, he returned to the jackdaws. They too, not recognizing him on account of his color, expelled him from living with them. So, desiring two ends, he obtained neither. 511—"The Weasel and the Mice." An infirm weasel tried to trick mice by rolling in flour as a disguise. An older mouse saw through the trick.)

H4c. Apes understand (after training) the workings of mirrors and shadows[356]

(AFS/22—Porcupine instructs mantis how a large shadow will signal the appearance of the All-Devourer [the man].) (CFT/"M'su Carencro and Mangeur de Poulet"—Rabbit sees chicken hawk's shadow and knows what it means. Rabbit escapes.) (TMI/J953.13.—Fox thinks his elongated shadow at sunrise makes him as large as elephant.)

(For animals understanding reflective properties of mirrors, see above, ATU/92—"The Lion Dives for His Own Reflection," and below, FOB/"The Owls and the Crows.")

H5. Animal Great Escapes

H5a. Inky the octopus escapes down the drain[357]

---

355. Krachun et al. 2016, "Smoke and Mirrors: Testing the Scope of Chimpanzees' Appearance-Reality Understanding," in *Cognition*.

356. Völter and Call 2018, "Intuitive Optics: What Great Apes Infer from Mirrors and Shadows," in *Animal Cognition*.

357. Brulliard (2016) states:
Inky the octopus didn't even try to cover his tracks. By the time the staff at New Zealand's National Aquarium noticed that he was missing, telltale suction cup prints were the main clue to an easily solved mystery. Inky had said see ya to his tankmate, slipped through a gap left by maintenance workers at the

(ATU/73—"Blinding the Guard." The rabbit, imprisoned in a hollow tree, induces his guard to look up at him. He spits tobacco juice into the guard's eyes and blinds the guard, thus effecting his escape.)

(See also "J. Animals and Magic [Sleight of Hand].")

H5b. Chimps escape from compound to freedom using fallen tree (variant: monkeys)[358]

(CIP/*Louisianian Creole*—"When the tree falls the kid can climb it.") (IMF/2030*K—Old woman finds coin, buys broom, and makes ladder to climb to heaven. Various animals pass

---

top of his enclosure and, as evidenced by the tracks, made his way across the floor to a six-inch-wide drain. He squeezed his football-sized body in—octopuses are very malleable, aquarium manager Rob Yarrall told the New Zealand website Stuff—and made a break for the Pacific. "He managed to make his way to one of the drain holes that go back to the ocean. And off he went," Yarrall told Radio New Zealand. "And he didn't even leave us a message." The cephalopod version of "Shawshank Redemption" took place three months ago, but it only became public Tuesday. Inky, who already had some local renown in the coastal city of Napier, quickly became a global celebrity cheered on by strangers.

358. Primatologists have long reported on the ability of monkeys and apes to use fallen branches, trees, or similar implements to escape from outdoor zoos or research compounds (see photos of one such chimp escape in Yerkes 1943, plate 49). Case studies can be found in Menzel (1973); McGrew, Tutin, and Midgett (1975); and de Waal (1982). I was curious if any recent incidents had captured the popular imagination, so I conducted a quick Google News search. Several recent episodes appeared, including "Seven Chimps Make Epic Escape from Kansas City Zoo Enclosure," "Chimp Sends Tourists Screaming in Terror as It Escapes Zoo Enclosure—Only to Peer Back in through the Glass," and "Monkeys Use Trees to Catapult Themselves Out of Japanese Laboratory." The latter was especially intriguing, as Demetriou (2010) reports:

Monkeys at a research institute in Japan have used the branches of trees to catapult themselves over an electric fence in order to escape. A group of 15 monkeys at Kyoto University's primate research institute . . . which are the focus of a string of high-profile scientific studies, escaped from their forest home which is encased by a 17ft high electric fence. The monkeys made their bid for freedom by using tree branches to fling themselves one by one over the high voltage electric fence located nearly three metres away. However, despite the intelligence shown in their great escape, the primates appeared unsure as to what to do with their newfound freedom: the monkeys remained by the gates of the research centre and were lured back into captivity by scientists armed with peanuts. "It was an incredible escape and the first time something like this has ever happened," Hirohisa Hirai, the deputy head of the Primate Research Institute told the Daily Telegraph. "We think that maybe there was some kind of dispute among the monkeys in the forest and so this group decided to leave."

by, are given permission to climb with her: cat, dog, cow, ass, horse, lion, tiger, and elephant. Finally, ladder breaks; old lady and animals fall.)

H6. Mediations on Animals Meditating on Gravitation (experimental paradigm variants: traps, tubes; animal variants: apes, monkeys, dogs defy gravity)[359]

(BAF/"The Fox and the Crow"—Fox throws crow into the air thinking she will return. She does not.)

H7. Animal Curiosity

H7a. Rat curiosity[360]

(CIP/*Arabian*—"If the camel gets his nose in the tent his body will soon follow.")

H7b. All manner of zoo animals[361]

(ADLG/"The camel begging for horn lost its ears as well.")

H8. Animals and Ambiguity

H8a. Bears vs. gorillas[362]

(ADLG/"A precipice before, a wolf behind.")

H9. Causal Reasoning

H9a. Rats do causal inference[363]

(AFS/23—Fox sees mother's wound and infers that wolf has killed her. 31—Trickster hare leads lion to supposed footprints of thieves so lion can know true thieves. 36—Caterpillar enters home of hare but hides when hare returns. Hare notices caterpillar's tracks and infers that someone is hiding.)

H9b. Animals understand the difference between correlation and causation[364]

---

359. Cacchione, Call, and Zingg 2009, "Gravity and Solidity in Four Great Ape Species (*Gorilla gorilla, Pongo pygmaeus, Pan troglodytes, Pan paniscus*): Vertical and Horizontal Variations of the Table Task," in *Journal of Comparative Psychology*; Hood et al. 1999, "Gravity Biases in a Non-Human Primate?," in *Developmental Science*; Osthaus, Slater, and Lea 2003, "Can Dogs Defy Gravity? A Comparison with the Human Infant and a Non-Human Primate," in *Developmental Science*.

360. Berlyne 1955, "The Arousal and Satiation of Perceptual Curiosity in the Rat," in *Journal of Comparative and Physiological Psychology*; Billingslea 1940, "The Relationship between Emotionality, Activity, Curiosity, Persistence and Weight in the Male Rat," in *Journal of Comparative Psychology*.

361. Glickman and Sroges 1966, "Curiosity in Zoo Animals," in *Behaviour*.

362. McGuire, Vonk, and Johnson-Ulrich 2017, "Ambiguous Results When Using the Ambiguous-Cue Paradigm to Assess Learning and Cognitive Bias in Gorillas and a Black Bear," in *Behavioral Sciences*.

363. Beckers et al. 2006, "Reasoning Rats: Forward Blocking in Pavlovian Animal Conditioning is Sensitive to Constraints of Causal Inference," in *Journal of Experimental Psychology: General*; Blaisdell et al. 2006, "Causal Reasoning in Rats," in *Science*.

364. Curious, given that most humans do not. But seriously, Doctor Folklomindo, the reference here is a paper involving chimpanzees that

(ATU/114—"[Rooster] Believes That His Crowing Makes the Sun Rise." The rooster is disappointed when the sun rises without his aid.)

H9c. Crows understand unseen causal mechanisms[365]
(AFS/27—Leopard makes a trap to ensnare antelope.) (BAF/"The Lion and the Hare"—Hare notices deep footprints and understands lion is nearby. "Hawk, Heron, Tortoise and Lion"—Lion deduces heron is guilty of plucking out hawk's eyes based on heron's beak and movements.) (NAAS/"Manabozho and the Woodpecker"—Woodpecker explains that the hidden power of Manabozho's enemy is in the knot of his hair.)

H9d. Crows do *not* understand unseen causal mechanisms[366]
(FOB/"The Owls and the Crows"—Crow recounts story of how the hare fooled the king elephant into believing the moon god was angry by having elephant wash in fountain at night. The reflected moon wavers, and because elephant does not understand reflecting surfaces, he thinks the moon god is upset.) (IMF*138—Coyote sees the cock seize his hen wife, squeeze her, cause egg to come out. Coyote goes home, squeezes his own wife, but cock tells him to stop, that he will hurt her. Coyote visits his friend the bean, who beats his beanstalk and beans come down. Coyote goes home, takes a stick, and beats his house. Bean tells him that he will not get beans from the house but from bean plant. Coyote goes home and sees his friend the bee. Latter strikes self with ax; honey comes out. When bee visits coyote, latter cuts himself with ax but only blood comes out. Bee tells him: You are not a bee.)

H10. Animal Essentialists (or, Animals Believe in the Essences of Things)

H10a. Monkeys are not fooled when apple is covered by coconut shell[367]

I am currently reviewing for the journal *Animal Cognition*. It is possibly the worst paper I have ever read. But my tolerance has become quite low, so perhaps it is not, in fact, the worst paper I have ever read. I cannot reveal the citation due to appropriate confidentiality agreements, but I can cite the work with human children it was attempting to (loosely) emulate: Meltzoff, Waismeyer, and Gopnik (2012).

365. Taylor et al. 2009, "Do New Caledonian Crows Solve Physical Problems through Causal Reasoning?," in *Proceedings of the Royal Society B*; Edwards et al. 2014, "Do Capuchin Monkeys (*Cebus apella*) Diagnose Causal Relations in the Absence of a Direct Reward?," In *PLOS ONE*.

366. Taylor et al. 2014, "Of Babies and Birds: Complex Tool Behaviours Are Not Sufficient for the Evolution of the Ability to Create a Novel Causal Intervention," in *Proceeding of the Royal Society B*.

367. Phillips and Santos 2007, "Evidence for Kind Representations in the Absence of Language: Experiments with Rhesus Monkeys (*Macaca mulatta*)," in *Cognition*.

(ADLG/"An ape is ape still, though it wear jewels of gold.") (PER/050—In a test a cat was turned into a young maiden. She found a young man and they were to be wed. At the wedding, Venus released a mouse and the maiden chased it. 176—A farmer takes pity on a frozen snake and brings it home. Thawed, the snake reverts to character and bites all.)

- H10b. Monkeys *still* not fooled when apple covered by coconut shell[368]

    (ADLG/"Bad crow, bad egg.") (PER/351—"The Fawn and His Mother." A fawn questions deer about why they flee a dog when they are so much bigger. Nobody could answer; it is just in their nature, they tell the fawn.) (NAAS/"The Boy and the Rattlesnake"—Snake bites boy who helps him and then mocks boy for thinking that a snake could be anything other than a snake.)

- H10c. Limits to the belief in essences in apes[369]

    (ADLG/"Many a good cow hath but a bad calf.") (AFS/23—Fox plucks out his hair to deceive wolf who wants to eat him. Wolf is fooled.) (BAF/"The Fable of the Rat-king"—Rat king asks wise men if innate fear of cats can be eradicated.

[Fourth Special Note to Doctor Folklomindo, or SNDK-4: *I feel myself growing weary, eyes glazing over, pushing on with nothing but my deepest belief that this will all prove worth it one day. So please (please!) know that for many of the topics that follow, my scant consideration of vast experimental literature, with roots dating back well over a hundred years, says nothing about the nuances of human thinking about the animals buried therein. Until now, I was making bold gestures toward the troves of scientific investigations that we must master; from here forward, I am reduced to the merest flick of my wrist or thumbing of my nose, this way or that . . .*]

H11. Animals and Money[370]

(AFS/31—Hare hoards lion's money to use later.) (FTM/"The Mongoose and the Donkey"—Mongoose demands to know where girl's

---

368. Phillips, Shankar, and Santos 2010, "Essentialism in the Absence of Language? Evidence from Rhesus Monkeys (*Macaca mulatta*)," in *Developmental Science*.

369. Cacchione et al. 2016, "Are Apes Essentialists? Scope and Limits of Psychological Essentialism in Great Apes," in *Animal Cognition*.

370. Wolfe 1936, "Effectiveness of Token Rewards for Chimpanzees," in *Comparative Psychology Monographs*; Brosnan and de Waal 2004, "Socially Learned Preferences for Differentially Rewarded Tokens in the Brown Capuchin Monkey (*Cebus apella*)," in *Journal of Comparative Psychology*; Evans et al. 2012, "Delaying Gratification for Food and Tokens in Capuchin Monkeys (*Cebus apella*) and Chimpanzees (*Pan troglodytes*): When Quantity is Salient, Symbolic Stimuli Do Not Improve Performance," in *Animal Cognition*.

father keeps his money. "The Tiger's Vow"—Tiger has cave filled with gold and silver that he has hoarded. "The King of the Sparrows"—Cow produces golden dung that man steals. "The Snake and the Cock"—Snake hoards money in anthill. "The Lucky Buffaloes"—Buffaloes produce earthen pots of money on their horns.) (GGS/Where do fish keep their money? *In a river-bank!*[371]—How do you stop an angry tiger from charging? *Take away his credit cards!*[372]) (JSS/III.—Pig refuses to be bribed with promise of a silver door and a golden cage. XLIX.—Hog negotiates pay from rat for being a lookout.) (TMI/B294.2.1.—Monkey's money stolen. B294.2.2.—Monkey buys liquor. B294.3.—Dog sells rotten peas at market, is punished by other animals.)

H12. Animals Do Math (variants: chimpanzees, monkeys, salamanders, frogs . . .)[373]

(AFS/29—Hyena is forced to count lioness's footsteps to calculate when she has crossed four rivers.) (BAF/"The Eyes of Justice"—Jackal intentionally miscounts in order to cheat sheep.) (FTC/"Why Leopard Meets His Enemy Face-to-Face [Benin]"—Leopard spies on cat getting into tree. Cat strikes a gong to let her kittens know it is safe to lower a rope. Leopard cannot count, so she uses claws to put tally marks on tree to keep track of the number of times mother cat strikes the gong.) (GGS/What is the owl's favorite kind of math? *Owlgebra!*[374]—How do you count cows? *With a cowculator!*[375]) (TMI/B184.3.0.5.—Herd of magic swine that cannot be counted twice with the same result. J1851.1.1.—Numskull in a boat throws his money to the frogs in the water so that the frogs can count it.)

---

371. Bestfishingjokes.com 2002.
372. Whitlock 2015.
373. For parrots, see Pepperberg 2006, "Grey Parrot (*Psittacus erithacus*) Numerical Abilities: Addition and Further Experiments on a Zero-Like Concept," in *Journal of Comparative Psychology*; for chimpanzees, Biro and Matsuzawa 2001, "Use of Numerical Symbols by the Chimpanzee (*Pan troglodytes*): Cardinals, Ordinals, and the Introduction of Zero," in *Animal Cognition*; for mockingbirds, Farnsworth and Smolinski 2006, "Numerical Discrimination by Wild Northern Mockingbirds," in *The Condor: Ornithological Applications*; for insects, Dacke and Srinivasan 2008, "Evidence for Counting in Insects," in *Animal Cognition*; for salamanders, Krusche, Uller, and Dicke 2010, "Quantity Discrimination in Salamanders," in *Journal of Experimental Biology*; for monkeys, Beran, Perdue, and Evans 2015, "Monkey Mathematical Abilities," in *The Oxford Handbook of Numerical Cognition*; for frogs, Stancher et al. 2015, "Numerical Discrimination by Frogs (*Bombina orientalis*)," in *Animal Cognition*; and for other species . . . no, I choose to stop here.
374. Shou 2018.
375. Worstjokesever.com 2017.

H13. Inhibitory Control (variants: dogs, rhesus monkeys, rats, etc.)[376] (FTC/"The Cat, the Dog, and Death [Haiti]"—Cat and dog on way to plead with God. Dog wants immortality; cat does not. Both try to delay the other by placing food along the path. Cat avoids temptation of butter. Dog knows he should not stop to gnaw on bone, but he cannot control himself. Cat gets to God first and wins the petition.) (NFT/"The Tortoise and the Forbidden Porridge"—Tortoise struggles against looking in secret delicious-smelling calabash . . . until he cannot!)
(See also "F5c. Animals plan/predict the future.")

H14. Animal Memory (variants: all animals)
   H14a. Elephants never forget
      H14a.1. Elephants have the memory of an elephant[377]

---

376. Diamond 1990, "Developmental Time Course in Human Infants and Infant Monkeys, and the Neural Bases of, Inhibitory Control in Reaching," in *Annals of the New York Academy of Sciences*; Vlamings, Hare, and Call 2010, "Reaching around Barriers: The Performance of the Great Apes and 3-5-Year-Old Children," in *Animal Cognition*; Homberg et al. 2007, "Serotonin Transporter Deficiency in Rats Improves Inhibitory Control but Not Behavioural Flexibility," in *European Journal of Neuroscience*.

377. In an essay discussing his landmark studies of the memory and intelligence of a female Asian elephant, Bernhard Rensch (1957) mentions an effort to compare her performance to other animals that sounds like something straight out of animal fable:

> Recently one of our collaborators attempted to teach the patterns that had been learned by [our] elephant to a horse, an ass and a zebra in the Münster Zoo. Some minor alterations had to be made in the experiments, of course, to suit them to the new animals. As we had more or less expected, the ass and the zebra could not compete with the elephant in the number of stimulus pairs learned. The ass could master only 13, the zebra only 10. But the horse, surprisingly enough, learned all the 20 pairs that the elephant had mastered. This seems to indicate that the horse possesses a very efficient visual learning capacity. We have not yet had time to compare its memory span with that of the elephant, but in a retest after three months it performed well. (49)

Rensch also mentions the "fantastic stories about the feats and 'cleverness' of elephants":

> Even so experienced an observer as J. H. Williams, who worked and lived with elephants in the forests of Burma for twenty-five years, says in his excellent book *Elephant Bill* that the elephant 'never stops learning because he is always thinking.' Williams reports quite seriously that domesticated elephants have been known to stuff mud into the bells round their necks to muffle them before going forth to steal bananas at night. Most of these tales credit elephants with far too much insight into the future to be believable. (44)

Were Rensch still alive, he might find interest in the FOMANCOG entry "E2e. Animals know/do not know that others hear." For further discussion of elephant intelligence, see Bates et al. 2008, "African

(GGS/An elephant was drinking out of the river one day when he spotted a turtle lying fast asleep on a log. The elephant walked over and kicked the unsuspecting turtle clear across the river. A passing giraffe who happened to see this asked the elephant, "Why did you do that?" The elephant replied, "Because I recognized it as the same turtle that bit my trunk thirty-eight years ago." The giraffe said, "Wow, what a memory you've got!" "Yes," said the elephant, proudly. "Turtle recall."[378])

H14a.2. Elephants do *not* have the memory of an elephant[379]
(GGS/Why do elephants have short tails? *Because they can't remember long stories!*[380])

H14a.3. Humans have the memory of an elephant for folktales about elephants[381]
(GGS/A man saw a baby elephant limping in the woods. Getting him to raise his leg, the man pulled a large thorn out of the baby's foot. Years later, the man was at a circus and one of the elephants kept looking at him and getting all excited. *Could it be him?* the man wondered. So the man went up to the elephant gate and the elephant reached over with his trunk. He grabbed the man with his trunk *and slammed him against the wall*, killing him instantly. I guess it was not the same elephant.[382])

H14b. Dolphin smarts
H14b.1. Dolphins are super smart[383]

Elephants Have Expectations about the Locations of Out-Of-Sight Family Members," in *Biology Letters*.

378. Laffgaff.com 2019.

379. Nissani 2008, "Elephant Cognition: A Review of Recent Experiments," in *Gajah: Journal of the IUCN/SSC Asian Elephant Specialist Group*; Perdue et al. 2012, "Putting the Elephant Back in the Herd: Elephant Relative Quantity Judgments Match Those of Other Species," in *Animal Cognition*.

380. Jokes4us.com 2019e.

381. Chen, Mo, and Honomichl (2004) state: "Substantial culture-specific analogical transfer was found when American and Chinese participants' performance was compared on isomorphs of problems solved in European versus Chinese folk tales. There was evidence of transfer even among participants who did not report being reminded of the source tale while solving the target problem. Comparisons of different versions of a target problem indicated that similarity of solution tool affected accessing, mapping, and executing components of problem solving, whereas similarity of goal object had only a moderate effect on accessing" (415).

382. Al N. 2016, "Elephant's Memory," *The Spoof!*

383. For the argument in favor of the idea that dolphins are incredibly smart and different from most other animal species, see

(GGS/Did the dolphin accidentally break the vase? *No, dolphins do everything on porpoise!*[384])

H14b.2. No they are not[385]
(GGS/Why don't dolphins pass their exams? *Because they work below C-Level!*[386])

H14c. Honeybees with good and bad memories[387]
(GGS/What are the cleverest bees? *Spelling bees!*—Why do bees hum? *Because they've forgotten the words!*[388])

H15. Animals Do/Do Not Do Analogies
(FTFL/"The Hungry Bear"—Fox uses his tail to communicate symbolically with other animals: "up" means fight; "down" means retreat.) (MRT/"The Hunting Dog of Tomigbee Bottoms"—Dog learns analogy between train signal flag and waving of his tail. Uses his tail to stop train so he can get on and go hunting far away. Returns using same method.)

H16. Animals in Sticky Wickets Involving Weight[389]
(BAF/"The Tortoise and the Sparrowhawk"—Tortoise complains that parcel of meat is too heavy to carry. "Lion and Man"—Donkey complains of the weight of the packs that man puts on his back. "The Fly and the Buffalo"—Fly worries he is too heavy for buffalo's head.) (FOJ/"The Fish Thief"—Fox on sled steals fish and replaces it with a stone so fisherman will notice his load is lighter.) (IMF/122*Q—Fox enters house of hen, a seamstress. He puts her in bag and starts to take her home. On the way, she cuts a hole with scissors, escapes from bag, and fills it with stones. Fox arrives home and empties bag into kettle of boiling water. He and his family are scalded, killed.)

Marino et al. 2007, "Cetaceans Have Complex Brains for Complex Cognition," in *PLOS Biology*. See also Bruck 2013.

384. Jokesbykids.com 2021.

385. For the argument that dolphins are *not* incredibly smart and different from most other animal species, see Manger 2013, "Questioning the Interpretations of Behavioral Observations of Cetaceans: Is There Really Support for a Special Intellectual Status for this Mammalian Order?," in *Neuroscience*—but cf. Güntürkün's (2014) obligatory hedging reply, "Is Dolphin Cognition Special?," in *Brain, Behavior and Evolution*.

386. Jokes4us.com 2019d.

387. Brandes, Frisch, and Menzel 1988, "Time-Course of Memory Formation Differs in Honey Bee Lines Selected for Good and Poor Learning," in *Animal Behaviour*.

388. Jokester 2011.

389. Visalberghi and Néel 2003, "Tufted Capuchins (*Cebus apella*) Use Weight and Sound to Choose between Full and Empty Nuts," in *Ecological Psychology*; Schrauf and Call 2009, "Great Apes' Performance in Discriminating Weight and Achromatic Color," in *Animal Cognition*; Schrauf et al. 2012, "Do Chimpanzees Use Weight to Select Hammer Tools?," in *PLOS ONE*; see also, and in my opinion, especially, Povinelli 2012; see note 55.

I. **Animals and Medicine**[390]

I1. Animals and Resuscitation
    I1a. Cat tries CPR to revive her dead friend[391]
        (TMI/E79.1.—Resuscitation by passing helpful animal over corpse. E79.1.1.—Resuscitation by bird flying over dead. B172.2.—Magic bird's song. Wakes the dead.)
    I1b. Dog tries to resuscitate fish[392]
        (TMI/B301.5.—Faithful animals resuscitate master. E53.1.—Mummified dog is kept in box. Revives and resuscitates dead hero.)
        (See also "E1f. Dog tries to save fish.")
I2. Animals and Medication
    I2a. Animals cure stomach aches, parasites, toxins, mites, poison, etc.
        I2a.1. Monkeys and birds eating dirt[393]
            (TMI/B512.—Medicine shown by animal.)

---

390. This is a burgeoning area of research. For orientation, I recommend the following: de Roode, Lefèvre, and Hunter 2013, "Self-Medication in Animals," in *Science*; Huffman 1997, "Current Evidence for Self-Medication in Primates: A Multidisciplinary Perspective," in *American Journal of Physical Anthropology*; and Huffman 2003, "Animal Self-Medication and Ethno-Medicine: Exploration and Exploitation of the Medicinal Properties of Plants," in *Proceedings of the Nutrition Society*.

391. More evidence of the anthropomorphic projective space created by online videos of animals comes from a popular YouTube video (viraldcom 2010)—with 1,212,484 views and counting—in which a cat interacts with another (dead) cat that has been accidentally killed by an automobile. A sampling of viewer comments follows: "honestly im normaly that rock that never gets emotional or cryies but god i burst into tears thinking about this and the poeple that disliked this have no soul!" (applejuice); "That moment he stops reviving, accepts the truth and simply lays down and weeps, that was gut wrenching to watch. :(" (Victor B); "Cat: Hey buddy. . . . you hear me? Wake up . . . why won't you wake up? Buddy. . . . please. . . . wake up. . . . don't leave me . . ." (Konata Izumi); "What a hero. That poor cat didn't quit on his partner until those people came and took her." (Isaac Hoffer); "that really is one of the saddest things I have ever seen. A cat . . . crying. when his eyes were closed that had to have been what he/she was feeling or doing. Just like 'come on buddy, come on, why aren't you moving, what has happened to you?' Just WOW." (john doe); "to all the people who don't treat animals as equally as humans.. . . . here's what makes them better than humans." (Yashwanth Vinod); "I am gonna find the driver and stab him to death and cut his head off and show it to the poor cat"; "PLLEEEEEEAAAASSSEEEE tell me this isn't real please tell me this isn't real!!! I'm already crying my eyes out don't make it harder!!!" (Morgan Green); "cats can't talk but they have soul :)" (Hưng Nguyễn); "Animals have feeling just [like] we do. there is no difference" (Tony Illustrations).

392. See note 156. Really, do see it, because it's pretty amazing.

393. Krishnamani and Mahaney 2000, "Geophagy among Primates: Adaptive Significance and Ecological Consequences," in *Animal Behaviour*;

I2a.2. Tigers cure their parasites (variants: wild dogs, civets, jackals, tigers)[394]
(BAF/"Do Not Be Fooled Twice"—Shark needs monkey's heart as medicine for wife.)

I2a.3. Wolves cure their stomachaches[395]
(BAF/"The Goat Becomes a Pilgrim"—Goat makes amulet to cure lion's stomachache.)

I2a.4. Bison eat bark to cure the runs[396]
(IMF/122—Coyote meets opossum, who is stirring a kettle. Opossum says that he is making candles but actually he has only excrement in water. While coyote stirs kettle, opossum escapes.) (TMI/B535.0.1.1.—Bison as nurse for child.)

I2a.5. Fruit flies drink alcohol to kill parasites[397]
(TMI/B511.5.1.—Vulture cures blindness.)

I2a.6. The sparrow who built her nest with high-nicotine cigarette butts to reduce mite infestations[398]
(TMI/B511.4.—Rat cures man of wound.)

I2a.7. The elephants who ingest painkillers after a long march[399]
(NFT/"The Elephant and the Tortoise"—Tortoise as physician.)

I2a.8. The red-fronted lemur eats plants for antiparasitic properties[400]
(TMI/B191.4.—Rat gives magic medicine.)

I2a.9. The golden bamboo lemur takes cyanide for liver detox[401]
(NAAS/"Why Possum Has a Naked Tail"—Rabbit tricks possum with bad medicine.)

Brightsmith, Taylor, and Phillips 2008, "The Roles of Soil Characteristics and Toxin Adsorption in Avian Geophagy," in *Biotropica*.

394. Consult table 1 in Huffman 2003. See note 390.
395. Consult table 1 in Huffman 2003. See note 390.
396. Consult table 1 in Huffman 2003. See note 390.
397. Milan, Kacsoh, and Schlenke 2012, "Alcohol Consumption as Self-Medication against Blood-Borne Parasites in the Fruit Fly," in *Current Biology*.
398. Suárez-Rodríguez, López-Rull, and Garcia 2013, "Incorporation of Cigarette Butts into Nests Reduces Nest Ectoparasite Load in Urban Birds: New Ingredients for an Old Recipe?," in *Biology Letters*.
399. Huffman and Vitazkova 2007, "Primates, Plants, and Parasites: The Evolution of Animal Self-Medication and Ethnomedicine," in *Ethnopharmacology: Volume II*.
400. Peckre et al. 2018, "Potential Self-Medication Using Millipede Secretions in Red-Fronted Lemurs: Combining Anointment and Ingestion for a Joint Action against Gastrointestinal Parasites?," in *Primates*.
401. Yamashita et al. 2010, "Semi-Quantitative Tests of Cyanide in Foods and Excreta of Three Hapalemur Species in Madagascar," in *American Journal of Primatology*.

I2a.10. Lizards eat plant root to counter venomous snakebite[402]
(FTM/"How the Snake-Clan Began"—Crab makes snake suck venom out of dead boy so he can return to life.)

I2b. Animals and prenatal care
I2b.1. Pregnant lemurs nibble tamarin fig leaves to aid in milk production[403]
(BAF/"The Goat and the Hyena"—Goat professes to be an expert in lactation medicine.)
I2b.2. Fruit flies lay eggs in plants containing high ethanol levels to protect babies from being killed by wasps[404]
(RFT/"Prince Ivan, the Firebird and the Gray Wolf"—Raven brings vials of death-water and life-water to wolf. Wolf sprinkles water of life on prince to bring him back to life.)

I2c. Self-anointing monkeys
I2c.1. Titi monkey self-anoints with orchid flower[405]
(IMF/123—Rabbit mother leaves children while she goes to get yucca flowers.)
I2c.2. Capuchin monkey self-anoints with millipedes[406]
(NFT/"Why Apes Look Like People"—Monkeys and apes find tortoise's secret medicine that changes animals into people and rub it on their bodies.)
I2c.3. Owl monkey self-anoints with millipedes[407]
(FOB/"The Traveller and the Goldsmith"—Snake brings man leaves that cure snakebite.)
I2c.4. Spider monkey self-anoints with millipedes[408]
(FOJ/"The Rabbit and the Bear"—Rabbit rubs miso soup on bear's wounds claiming it is medicine. Ouch!)

---

402. Shurkin 2014, "News Feature: Animals That Self-Medicate," in *Proceedings of the National Academy of Sciences*.

403. Sauther 1994, "Wild Plant Use by Pregnant and Lactating Ring-tailed Lemurs, with Implications for Early Hominid Foraging," in *Eating on The Wild Side: The Pharmacologic, Ecologic and Social Implications of Using Noncultigens*.

404. Kacsoh et al. 2013, "Fruit Flies Medicate Offspring after Seeing Parasites," in *Science*.

405. Souza-Alves et al. 2018, "Self-Anointing Behaviour in Captive Titi Monkeys (*Callicebus spp.*)," in *Primate Biology*.

406. Weldon et al. 2003, "Benzoquinones from Millipedes Deter Mosquitoes and Elicit Self-Anointing in Capuchin Monkeys (*Cebus spp.*)," in *Naturwissenschaften*.

407. Zito, Evans, and Weldon 2003, "Owl Monkeys (*Aotus spp.*) Self-Anoint with Plants and Millipedes," in *Folia Primatologica*.

408. Laska, Bauer, and Hernandez Salazar 2007, "Self-Anointing Behavior in Free-Ranging Spider Monkeys (*Ateles geoffroyi*) in Mexico," in *Primates*.

I3. Animals and Medical Treatment
    I3a. Ants treat injuries of wounded nest mates[409]
        (NFT/"Why the Tortoise's Shell Is Cracked and Crooked"—Ants help tortoise glue his shell back together. Tortoise complains that ants smell bad. Ants leave him to mend himself.)

J. Animals and Magic (Sleight of Hand)

J1. Animals Do Magic
    J1a. Orangutan uses magic wand to make card vanish[410]
        (BAF/"The Lizard and the Chain of Events"—Tortoise as magician.) (JSS/XXXVIII.—Monkey consults dark-art cards to determine whether spider is lying about stealing his crops.) (TMI/B191.—Animal as magician. B191.1—Weasel as conjurer.)
J2. Animals and Appearing/Disappearing Objects[411]
    J2a. Disappearing coin trick
        J2a.1. Dog duped by disappearing coin[412]
            (BAF/"The Girl and the Lion"—Lion has great knowledge of magic.)
        J2a.2. Chimp duped by disappearing coin[413]
            (FTM/"The Snake's Ring"—Snake gives boy magic ring and palace appears.)

---

409. Frank, Wehrhahn, and Linsenmair 2018, "Wound Treatment and Selective Help in a Termite-Hunting Ant," in *Proceedings of the Royal Society B*.

410. The video "Guy Performs Magic Trick for Orangutan" (DailyPicksandFlicks 2016a) is a must-see—indeed, it has been seen 7,589,071 times. Do not be misled by the title. The orangutan uses a magic wand at the end to perform its own magic trick. Sample comments follow: "Naww cute, how he put the card back on the glass" (CoRa Youngmin); "0:57 Orangutan: hm. Okay seems easy enough. pulls out magic wand just a few taps and it should do the job-card falls Orangutan: ._ . . . " (• Sauce •); "Human resorts to silly card tricks. ORANGUTAN HAS A WAND!! :o" (EnigmaDrath); "OMG! That orangutan used that stick like a wizarding wand! He should definitely be named 'Hairy Potter.'" (Painindeass1million); "Orangutan-I was told you would be coming. Grabs Staff I've much to teach you beyond silly illusions my son." (Doomreb); "The orangutan is not impressed. He is surrounded by things he can't explain. This is just one more." (Pat Downs); "How the hell did he get [the card] on the other side to begin with?" (MojoMaelstrom).

411. For scientists' takes on the proliferation of magical, sleight-of-hand performances by animals, see the following: Coren 2014, "Magic Tricks, Consciousness, and Mental Imagery in Dogs," in *Psychology Today*; Martinez-Conde 2016, "Did the Baboon Feel the Magic?," in *Scientific American: Illusion Chasers*; and Garcia-Pelegrin et al. 2020, "An Unexpected Audience: Experiments with Magic Effects Might be Informative about Cognition in Animals," in *Science Magazine*.

412. Ahonen 2014, "Taikuutta Koirille—Magic for Dogs"—18,461,033 views.

413. Techy 2017, "Monkeys React to Magic"—20,149,716 views.

J2a.3. Cat duped by disappearing coin[414]
  (BAF/"The Lizard and the Chain of Events"—Tortoise as magician.)
J2a.4. Monkey threatens zoo visitor after card disappears[415]
  (FTM/"The Story of Mara Kshattri"—Quail magician.)
J2b. Disappearing ball routine
 J2b.1. Orangutan duped by disappearing cup-in-ball routine[416]
  (BAF/"The Girl and the Lion"—Bird puts curse on woman.)
 J2b.2. Dog tricked by fake ball toss[417]
  (BAF/"The Elephant and the Hare"—Lizard magician.)
J2c. Zoo animals and the disappearing carrot
  (variants: cow, horse, goat, llama, fish, tortoise, geese . . .)[418]
  (FTM/"The Story of Mara Kshattri"—Quail magician.)

---

414. The video "Cat Mind Blown!" (Cole and Marmalade 2016) depicts a pet cat watching its owner set a coin on a wooden box, followed by a mechanical paw emerging from the box and stealing the coin. The video then zooms in on the pet cat's face. The video has been watched 1,088,432 times. Here are a few sample comments: "So cute he was like: Wtf was that? 0 _ 0 'realizes camera pointing at him' uuuhhh hi?" (I); "That was the cutest 24 seconds of my entire life." (.); "Did you see that?! There is a tiny cat trapped in that box!!" (ermub); "Vietnam Flashback" (Zea); "wow, I'm a grown man, who is a contractor in afghanistan on my 4th deployment, this is the highlight of my day" (Brian K).

415. The YouTube video "Baboon Is Amazed by Man's Magic Trick" (*America's Funniest Home Videos* 2016) has received 4,383,399 views. Here are some sample comments: "You could make a religion out of this" (CJusticeHappen21); "he probably faked the reaction just so he didnt hurt the mans feelings" (Bob The Peach); "Amazing how intelligent they are. They understand object permanence." (Mark M); "I love how you can literally tell his train of thought. 'oh yes, another human. Yeah you've got a paper in your hand, yes I can see it you can stop waving it arou-SHUT UP!!!!! WHAT?!!! oh my g-AND THERE IT IS AGAIN!!! Okay, okay, that was pretty cool, and—YOU DID IT AGAIN!!!!!'" (Annette maple); "00:01 'What do you want.' 00:02 'Go away.' 00:05 'YOOOOOOOOO!!!!!!!'" (NumPad).

416. To understand what is at stake with anthropomorphism, Simply Fit 2015,"Orangutan Finds Magic Trick Hilarious"—with 2,345,583 views—is an absolute must-see.

417. 5loaves2fish1962 2011, "Funny Fake Throwing Ball on the Swimming Pool with the Funny Dog"—2,577 views.

418. Ahonen 2015, "How Different Animals React to Magic?"—742,354 views. Sample comments follow: "The goats were like: 'we don't need yo magic!'" (Lunar Aurora); "do it with a shark" (Craig K); "Thee Alpacas are quite the intelligent looking creatures" (Randy); "the alcapas went on a nope train." (The Humble Geometric Figure of Doom); "good way to lose a finger :p" (Jackie Johnson); "I felt so sorry for the horses and the cows. They were nibbling his fingers xD" (Rhiannn :3); "Oh this is too great! I like the one alpaca who was like 'It's a trap! RUN!'" (HijackedGiraffe); "Didn't really expect much reaction from animals

J2d. Objects that suddenly appear
  J2d.1. Ape startled by robot making banana magically appear[419]
    (FTM/"The Bear and the Guitar"—Bear plays magic guitar; boy kills bear and steals guitar.)
  J2d.2. Cat stares at appearance of magic stick[420]
    (GGS/What do you call a cat who does tricks? A *magic kit!*[421])

[NOTE TO FUTURE SELF:
  Woe, woe, O future me;
  Don't judge your past self too harshly.
  Gone is my beginner's steam—
  Folklore research needs a bigger team!
  Hear my plaintive, lonely moan;
  I've not the chops to go it alone!
  cf. "E10f. Chimps prefer to go it alone."]

J2e. Dogs baffled by disappearing-owner trick (a.k.a. blanket trick)[422]
  J2e.1. German shepherd baffled

---

that rely more on smell and touch to find food rather than sight. Predators, primates, birds of prey and parrots would likely have much better reactions." (Elizabeth Ludwig); "It was a Pony not a Donkey maybe a Mule but no donkey" (Diestro Energy); "They're pretty much all just going 'The food is gone? Alright.'" (Monody); "Omg the goats XDDD My stomach hurts!" (SUY Inès); "can you try it with dolphins or elephants ?" (Kytetiger).

419. Doctor Folklomindo and I were correct about robots becoming folkloric performers (see preface)! In a YouTube video (Simon Pierro 2020) titled "Chimp vs. Robot Magic," a robot performs traditional magic for a chimpanzee by pulling a literal banana out of the robot's digital sleeve (i.e., screen).

420. 1Voice1life 2016, "Cat Confused by Its Owner's Magic Trick."

421. Pug 2017.

422. I have launched an informal investigation into the internet-based #WhatTheFluffChallenge. If you do not know of it, I recommend you pour yourself a glass of whiskey and spend the next several hours (at least) watching as many of the hundreds (thousands?) of videos that have been posted in response to this viral internet challenge. For now, let me simply say that it is described as a "game" in which human pet owners film themselves getting their animals' attention (frequently dogs and cats, but other species as well) as they hold sheets in front of their bodies. The pet owners then quickly drop the sheets as they duck behind a doorway or couch. The performance creates the illusion (folk illusion?) that the person has vanished. Based on the multitude (and I do mean multitude) of videos created and posted, and the millions of views they have received, I conclude my investigation with the interim conclusion that humans find this "game" very amusing. For one of many compilation videos, see Dogs Are Awesome 2018, "Best 'What

  J2e.2. Huskie baffled
  J2e.3. Poodle baffled
  J2e.4. Pitbull baffled
  J2e.5. Pug baffled
  J2e.6. Dalmatian baffled
  J2e.7. Cocker spaniel baffled
  J2e.8. Labrador baffled
  J2e.9. Beagle baffled
  J2e.10. Retriever baffled
  J2e.11. Terrier baffled
  J2e.12. Chow chow baffled
  J2e.13. Bulldog baffled
  J2e.14. Heeler baffled
    J2e.14.a. Heeler humps blanket
  J2e.15. Cat (not dog) baffled
[*Et cetera*]

K. Aesop's Fables

K1. Crow and Pitcher[423]
K2. Hare and Tortoise[424]
K3. Grasshopper and the Ant[425]
K4. Lion and the Donkey[426]
K5. [X] and the [Y][. . .]

[Note to Self: *Check with Doctor Folklomindo as to the canonical number of Aesop's fables and all known variants and how they are indexed in ATU and TMI . . .*]

L. Culture and Traditions in Animals

L1. Great Ape Traditions[427]

---

the Fluff' Challenge Videos Ever | What the Fluff Challenge Compilation! Part 18," with 574,456 views.
 423. Hennefield et al. 2018, "Meta-Analytic Techniques Reveal That Corvid Causal Reasoning in the Aesop's Fable Paradigm Is Driven by Trial-and-Error Learning," in *Animal Cognition*. See also H1a.1. above.
 424. "The story of 'The Tortoise and the Hare' came to life when the two animals were placed side by side to race each [other]. As expected, the rabbit started off strong but laid back towards the middle of the event and watched as the tortoise slowly, but surely, win the race" (DailyPicksandFlicks 2016b). See also *USA Today* 2017, "Tortoise Races Hare, Guess What Happens," with 81,321 views.
 425. Smith 2015, "Debunking the 'Ant vs. Grasshopper' Myth," in *JSTOR Daily*.
 426. Future scientific study to be included in forthcoming updates of the FOMANCOG.
 427. Biro, Sousa, and Matsuzawa 2006, "Ontogeny and Cultural Propagation of Tool Use by Wild Chimpanzees at Bossou, Guinea: Case

L2. Norway Rat Traditions for Food Choice
  L2a. Cayenne pepper food traditions[428]
  L2b. Cinnamon-flavored food traditions[429]
L3. Brown-Headed Cowbird Courtship Traditions[430]
L4. Guppy Traditions[431]
L5. Fruit Fly Traditions for Egg-Laying Sites[432] (and et cetera)

[Fifth and Final Special Note to Doctor Folklomindo, or SNDF-5: *The following are some miscellaneous groups of motifs running through the study of animal cognition that frequently animate the discussion. Perhaps they should be considered for inclusion in future revisions of the FOMANCOG.*]

M. Animals and the Quest to Know Who Is the Smartest

(BAF/"The Jackal and the Cat"—Jackal boasts he is the most intelligent animal. "The Tortoise and the Elephant"—Elephant flattered as most intelligent animal; winds up as king's dinner meat. "The Drought"—Elephant is wisest; knows where water is closest to surface.) (TMI/J1662.—[Cat] saves herself on a tree. The fox, who knows a hundred tricks, is captured. J461.8.—Elephant and ape debate about superiority. Owl gives them task neither can perform and ends futile debate.)

N. Animals Who Train Other Animals

(BAF/"Do Not Be Fooled Twice"—Monkey trains shark with fruit.) (IMF/113*C—Cat invites hungry mouse to eat cheese that his master left on table. Mouse goes back to his hole and tells other mice, who go next day and eat more cheese. Cat tells other cats. When mice come again, cats lie in wait and eat mice.)

Studies in Nut Cracking and Leaf Folding," in *Cognitive Development in Chimpanzees*.

428. Galef and Aleen 1995, "A New Model System for Studying Behavioural Traditions in Animals," in *Animal Behaviour*.

429. Galef and Aleen 1995.

430. Freeberg 2004, "Social Transmission of Courtship Behavior and Mating Preferences in Brown-Headed Cowbirds, *Molothrus ater*," in *Animal Learning and Behavior*.

431. Reader, Kendal, and Laland 2003, "Social Learning of Foraging Sites and Escape Routes in Wild Trinidian Guppies," in *Animal Behaviour*.

432. Battesti et al. 2012, "Spread of Social Information and Dynamics of Social Transmission within Drosophila Groups," in *Current Biology*.

References

1Voice1life. 2016. "Cat Confused by Its Owner's Magic Trick." May 1, 2016. Accessed March 1, 2019. reddit.com/r/aww/comments/4he2n7/cat_is_confused_by_its_owners_magic_trick/.

5loaves2fish1962. 2011. "*Funny Fake Throwing Ball on the Swimming Pool with the Funny Dog.*" May 12, 2011. YouTube video, 5:52. https://www.youtube.com/watch?v=ug9jm6udiZY.

Adu, Omotayo, Olawale Idewu, Barbara K. Walker, and Warren S. Walker. 1961. *Nigerian Folk Tales*. New Brunswick, NJ: Rutgers University Press.

Ahonen, Jose. 2014. "Taikuutta Koirille—Magic for Dogs." March 21, 2014. YouTube video, 1:48. https://www.youtube.com/watch?time_continue=15&v=VEQXeLjY9ak.

———. 2015. "How Different Animals React to Magic?" August 13, 2015. YouTube video, 1:57. https://www.youtube.com/watch?v=bTXcFE7SKNw.

Alem, Sylvain, Clint J. Perry, Xingfu Zhu, Olli J. Loukola, Thomas Ingraham, Eirik Søvik, and Lars Chittka. 2016. "Associative Mechanisms Allow for Social Learning and Cultural Transmission of String Pulling in an Insect." *PLOS Biology* 14 (10): e1002564. https://doi.org/10.1371/journal.pbio.1002564.

America's Funniest Home Videos. 2016. "Baboon Is Amazed by Man's Magic Trick." March 15, 2016. YouTube video, 0:16. https://www.youtube.com/watch?v=dm8Q4fgv8Qo.

Anderson, James R. 1990. "Use of Objects as Hammers to Open Nuts by Capuchin Monkeys (*Cebus apella*)." *Folia Primatologica* 54 (34): 138–45.

Anderson, James R., and Gordon G. Gallup Jr. 2015. "Mirror Self-Recognition: A Review and Critique of Attempts to Promote and Engineer Self-Recognition in Primates." *Primates* 56 (4): 317–26.

Anderson, Stephen R. 2004. *Doctor Dolittle's Delusion: Animals and the Uniqueness of Human Language*. New Haven, CT: Yale University Press.

Arcadi, Adam Clark, Daniel Robert, and Christophe Boesch. 1998. "Buttress Drumming by Wild Chimpanzees: Temporal Patterning, Phrase Integration into Loud Calls, and Preliminary Evidence for Individual Distinctiveness." *Primates* 39 (4): 505–18.

Ari, Csilla, and Dominic P. D'Agostino. 2016. "Contingency Checking and Self-Directed Behaviors in Giant Manta Rays: Do Elasmobranchs Have Self-Awareness?" *Journal of Ethology* 34 (2): 167–74.

Armstrong-Buck, Susan. 1989. "Nonhuman Experience: A Whiteheadian Analysis." *Process Studies* 18 (1): 11–18.

Ashanti Proverb. 2015. "Alcohol." *Forbes Quotes*. Accessed June 1, 2019. https://www.forbes.com/quotes/author/ashanti-proverb/.

Aust, Ulrike, Friederike Range, Michael Steurer, and Ludwig Huber. 2008. "Inferential Reasoning by Exclusion in Pigeons, Dogs, and Humans." *Animal Cognition* 11 (4): 587–97.

Baker, Forest, and Howard Rachlin. 2002. "Self-Control by Pigeons in the Prisoner's Dilemma." *Psychonomic Bulletin and Review* 9 (3): 482–88.

Baragli, Paolo, Elisa Demuru, Chiara Scopa, and Elisabetta Palagi. 2017. "Are Horses Capable of Mirror Self-Recognition? A Pilot Study." *PLOS ONE* 12 (5): e0176717. https://doi.org/10.1371/journal.pone.0176717.

Barash, David P., Patrick Donovan, and Rinda Myrick. 1975. "Clam Dropping Behavior of the Glaucous-Winged Gull (*Larus glaucescens*)." *Wilson Bulletin* 87 (1): 60–64.

Barnes, Simon. 2016. "Is This Proof Chimps Believe in God? Scientists Baffled by Footage of Primates Throwing Rocks and 'Building Shrines at Sacred Tree' for No Reason." *DailyMail*. March 3, 2016. https://www.dailymail.co.uk/sciencetech/article-3475816/Is-proof-chimps-believe-God-Scientists-baffled-footage-primates-throwing-rocks-building-shrines-sacred-tree-no-reason.html.

Barnette, Martha, and Grant Barrett. 2009. "Tweet! Tweet! Polly Wanna Cracker!" February 28, 2009, in *A Way with Words*, produced by Stefanie Levine, podcast, MP3 audio, 51:00. https://www.waywordradio.org/tweet-tweet-polly-wanna-cracker/.

Bartal, Inbal Ben-Ami, Jean Decety, and Peggy Mason. 2011. "Empathy and Pro-Social Behavior in Rats." *Science* 334 (6061): 1427–30.

Bates, Lucy A., Katito N. Sayialel, Norah W. Njiraini, Joyce H. Poole, Cynthia J. Moss, and Richard W. Byrne. 2008. "African Elephants Have Expectations about the Locations of Out-of-Sight Family Members." *Biology Letters* 4 (1): 34–36.

Battesti, Marine, Celine Moreno, Dominique Joly, and Frederic Mery. 2012. "Spread of Social Information and Dynamics of Social Transmission within Drosophila Groups." *Current Biology* 22 (4): 309–13.

BBC Studios. 2007. "Wild crows inhabiting the city use it to their advantage—David Attenborough—BBC Wildlife." February 12, 2007. YouTube video, 2:15. https://www.youtube.com/watch?v=BGPGknpq3e0.

Beck, Benjamin B. 1980. *Animal Tool Behavior: The Use and Manufacture of Tools*. New York: Garland STPM.

Beck, Horace. 1973. *Folklore and the Sea*. Middleton, CT: Wesleyan University Press.

Beckers, Tom, Ralph R. Miller, Jan De Houwer, and Kouji Urushihara. 2006. "Reasoning Rats: Forward Blocking in Pavlovian Animal Conditioning Is Sensitive to Constraints of Causal Inference." *Journal of Experimental Psychology: General* 135 (1): 92–102.

Bekoff, Marc. 2009. "Animal Emotions, Wild Justice and Why They Matter: Grieving Magpies, a Pissy Baboon, and Empathic Elephants." *Emotion, Space and Society* 2 (2): 82–85.

Bellini, Rachele, Yanir Kleiman, and Daniel Cohen-Or. 2018. "Dance to the Beat: Synchronizing Motion to Audio." *Computational Visual Media* 4 (3): 197–208.

Bentley-Condit, Vicki K., and E. O. Smith. 2010. "Animal Tool Use: Current Definitions and an Updated Comprehensive Catalog." *Behaviour* 147 (2): 185–221.

Beran, Michael J., Bonnie M. Perdue, and Theodore A. Evans. 2015. "Monkey Mathematical Abilities." In *The Oxford Handbook of Numerical Cognition*, edited by Roi Cohen Kadosh and Ann Dowker, 237–57. Oxford: Oxford University Press.

Bercovitch, Fred B. 2013. "Giraffe Cow Reaction to the Death of Her Newborn Calf." *African Journal of Ecology* 51 (2): 376–79.

Bering, Jesse M. 2001. "Theistic Percepts in Other Species: Can Chimpanzees Represent the Minds of Non-Natural Agents?" *Journal of Cognition and Culture* 1 (2): 107–37.

———. 2004. "A Critical Review of the "Enculturation Hypothesis": The Effects of Human Rearing on Great Ape Social Cognition." *Animal Cognition* 7 (4): 201–12.

Berlyne, Daniel E. 1955. "The Arousal and Satiation of Perceptual Curiosity in the Rat." *Journal of Comparative and Physiological Psychology* 48 (4): 238–46.

Bestfishingjokes.com. 2002. "Where Do Fish Keep Their Money?" December 16, 2002. Accessed June 1, 2019. http://www.bestfishingjokes.com/ratejokes.php?jokeid=8.

Billingslea, F. 1940. "The Relationship between Emotionality, Activity, Curiosity, Persistence and Weight in the Male Rat." *Journal of Comparative Psychology* 29 (3): 315–25.

Bird, Christopher D., and Nathan J. Emery. 2009a. "Insightful Problem Solving and Creative Tool Modification by Captive Nontool-Using Rooks." *Proceedings of the National Academy of Sciences* 106 (25): 10370–75.

———. 2009b. "Rooks Use Stones to Raise the Water Level to Reach a Floating Worm." *Current Biology* 19 (16): 4101–14.

Biro, Dora, Tatyana Humle, Kathelijne Koops, Claudia Sousa, Misato Hayashi, and Tetsuro Matsuzawa. 2010. "Chimpanzee Mothers at Bossou, Guinea Carry the Mummified Remains of Their Dead Infants." *Current Biology* 20 (8): R351–52.

Biro, Dora, and Tetsuro Matsuzawa. 2001. "Use of Numerical Symbols by the Chimpanzee (*Pan troglodytes*): Cardinals, Ordinals, and the Introduction of Zero." *Animal Cognition* 4 (3–4): 193–99.

Biro, Dora, Claudia Sousa, and Tetsuro Matsuzawa. 2006. "Ontogeny and Cultural Propagation of Tool Use by Wild Chimpanzees at Bossou, Guinea: Case Studies in Nut Cracking and Leaf Folding." In *Cognitive Development in Chimpanzees*, edited by Tetsuro Matsuzawa, M. Tomonaga, and M. M. Tanaka, 476–508. Tokyo: Springer.

Bits and Pieces. n.d. "Motion Sensor Parrot Garden Sculpture." Accessed February 23, 2019. https://www.bitsandpieces.com/product/motion-sensor-parrot-garden-sculpture.

Blaisdell, Aaron P., and Robert G. Cook. 2005. "Integration of Spatial Maps in Pigeons." *Animal Cognition* 8 (1): 7–16.

Blaisdell, Aaron P., Kosuke Sawa, Kenneth J. Leising, and Michael R. Waldmann. 2006. "Causal Reasoning in Rats." *Science* 311 (5763): 1020–22.

Blanchard, Tommy C., Andreas Wilke, and Benjamin Y. Hayden. 2014. "Hot-hand Bias in Rhesus Monkeys." *Journal of Experimental Psychology: Animal Learning and Cognition* 40 (3): 280–86.

Blumstein, Daniel T. 1999. "Selfish Sentinels." *Science* 284 (5420): 1633–34.

Boesch, Christophe. 1991. "Teaching among Wild Chimpanzees." *Animal Behaviour* 41 (3): 530–32.

Boesch, Christophe, and Hedwige Boesch-Achermann. 2000. *The Chimpanzees of the Taï Forest: Behavioural Ecology and Evolution.* Oxford: Oxford University Press.

Boesch, Christophe, and Hedwige Boesch. 1984. "Mental Map in Wild Chimpanzees: An Analysis of Hammer Transports for Nut Cracking." *Primates* 25 (2): 160–70.

Boinski, Sue. 1988. "Use of a Club by a Wild White-Faced Capuchin (*Cebus capucinus*) to Attack a Venomous Snake (*Bothrops asper*)." *American Journal of Primatology* 14 (2): 177–79.

Bonnie, Kristin E., and Frans B. M. de Waal. 2004. "Primate Social Reciprocity and the Origin of Gratitude." In *The Psychology of Gratitude*, edited by Robert A. Emmons and Michael E. McCullough, 213–29. Oxford: Oxford University Press.

Botkin, Benjamin, ed. 1978. *A Treasury of Mississippi River Tales.* New York: Bonanza Books.

Boysen, Sarah T., Kirstin M. Bryan, and Traci A. Shreyer. 1994. "Shadows and Mirrors: Alternative Avenues to the Development of Self-Recognition in Chimpanzees." In *Self-Awareness in Animals and Humans: Developmental Perspectives,* edited by S. T. Parker, R. W. Mitchell, and M. L. Boccia, 227–40. New York: Cambridge University Press.

Brandes, Ch., B. Frisch, and R. Menzel. 1988. "Time-Course of Memory Formation Differs in Honey Bee Lines Selected for Good and Poor Learning." *Animal Behaviour* 36 (4): 981–85.

Brandt, Keri. 2004. "A Language of Their Own: An Interactionist Approach to Human-Horse Communication." *Society and Animals* 12 (4): 299–316.

Brant, George. 2010. *Elephant's Graveyard.* New York: Samuel French.

Bräuer, Juliane, Josep Call, and Michael Tomasello. 2007. "Chimpanzees Really Know What Others Can See in a Competitive Situation." *Animal Cognition* 10 (4): 439–48.

———. 2008a. "Are Apes Inequity Averse? New Data on the Token-Exchange Paradigm." *American Journal of Primatology* 71 (2): 175–81.

———. 2008b. "Chimpanzees Do Not Take into Account What Others Can Hear in a Competitive Situation." *Animal Cognition* 11 (1): 175–78.

Brightsmith, Donald J., John Taylor, and Timothy D. Phillips. 2008. "The Roles of Soil Characteristics and Toxin Adsorption in Avian Geophagy." *Biotropica* 40 (6): 766–74.

Brockmann, H. Jane. 1985. "Tool Use in Digger Wasps (Hymenoptera: Sphecinae)." *Psyche: A Journal of Entomology* 92 (23): 309–29.

Brosnan, Sarah F., and Frans B. M. de Waal. 2003. "Monkeys Reject Unequal Pay." *Nature* 425 (6955): 297–99.

———. 2004. "Socially Learned Preferences for Differentially Rewarded Tokens in the Brown Capuchin Monkey (*Cebus apella*)." *Journal of Comparative Psychology* 118 (2): 133–39.

Brosnan, Sarah Frances, Joan B. Silk, Joseph Henrich, Mary Catherine Mareno, Susan P. Lambeth, and Steven J. Schapiro. 2009. "Chimpanzees (*Pan troglodytes*) Do Not Develop Contingent Reciprocity in an Experimental Task." *Animal Cognition* 12 (4): 587–97.

Brown, Arthur E. 1879. "Grief in the Chimpanzee." *American Naturalist* 13 (3): 173–75.

Brown, Culum, Martin P. Garwood, and Jane E. Williamson. 2012. "It Pays to Cheat: Tactical Deception in a Cephalopod Social Signalling System." *Biology Letters*: rsbl2012.0435.

Brown, Frank C., and Newman Ivy White, eds. 1952. *The Frank C. Brown Collection of North Carolina Folklore, Vol. One*. Durham, NC: Duke University Press.

Brown, Peter Jensen. 2014. "The Colorful History and Etymology of Pink Elephant." *Early Sports and Pop Culture History Blog*. August 20, 2014. Accessed June 1, 2019. https://esnpc.blogspot.com/2014/08/the-colorful-history-and-etymology-of.html.

Brown, Susan G., William P. Dunlap, and Terry L. Maple. 1982. "Notes on Water-Contact by a Captive Male Lowland Gorilla." *Zoo Biology* 1 (3): 243–49.

Bruchac, Joseph. 1992. *Native American Animal Stories*. Golden, CO: Fulcrum.

Bruck, Jason N. 2013. "Decades-Long Social Memory in Bottlenose Dolphins." *Proceedings of the Royal Society of London B* 280 (1768): 20131726. https://royalsocietypublishing.org/doi/10.1098/rspb.2013.1726.

Brulliard, Karin. 2016. "Octopus Slips Out of Aquarium Tank, Crawls across Floor, Escapes down Pipe to Ocean." *Washington Post*, April 13, 2016. https://www.washingtonpost.com/news/animalia/wp/2016/04/13/octopus-slips-out-of-aquarium-tank-crawls-across-floor-escapes-down-pipe-to-ocean/?noredirect=on&utm_term=.a9cb88c5cc26.

Bugnyar, Thomas, Stephan A. Reber, and Cameron Buckner. 2016. "Ravens Attribute Visual Access to Unseen Competitors." *Nature Communications* 7: 10506. https://www.ncbi.nlm.nih.gov/pmc/articles/PMC4740864/pdf/ncomms10506.pdf.

Bullinger, Anke F., Alicia P. Melis, and Michael Tomasello. 2011. "Chimpanzees, *Pan troglodytes*, Prefer Individual Over Collaborative Strategies towards Goals." *Animal Behaviour* (5): 1135–41.

Bullinger, Anke F., Emily Wyman, Alicia P. Melis, and Michael Tomasello. 2011. "Coordination of Chimpanzees (*Pan troglodytes*) in a Stag Hunt Game." *International Journal of Primatology* 32 (6): 1296–310.

Burkett, James P., Elissar Andari, Zachary V. Johnson, Daniel C. Curry, Frans B. M. de Waal, and Larry J. Young. 2016. "Oxytocin-Dependent Consolation Behavior in Rodents." *Science* 351 (6271): 375–78.

Burrison, John A., ed. 1989. *Athens Storytellers: Folktales and Legends from the South*. Athens: University of Georgia Press.

Cacchione, Trix, Josep Call, and Robert Zingg. 2009. "Gravity and Solidity in Four Great Ape Species (*Gorilla gorilla, Pongo pygmaeus, Pan troglodytes, Pan paniscus*): Vertical and Horizontal Variations of the Table Task." *Journal of Comparative Psychology* 123 (2): 168–80.

Cacchione, Trix, Christine Hrubesch, Josep Call, and Hannes Rakoczy. 2016. "Are Apes Essentialists? Scope and Limits of Psychological Essentialism in Great Apes." *Animal Cognition* 19 (5): 921–37.

Calcutt, Sarah E., Elizabeth V. Lonsdorf, Kristin. E. Bonnie, Marissa. S. Milstein, and Stephen R. Ross. 2014. "Captive Chimpanzees Share Diminishing Resources." *Behaviour* 151: 1967–82.

Call, Josep. 2006. "Inferences by Exclusion in the Great Apes: The Effect of Age and Species." *Animal Cognition* 9 (4): 393–403.

Call, Josep, Brian Hare, Malinda Carpenter, and Michael Tomasello. 2004. "'Unwilling' versus 'Unable': Chimpanzees' Understanding of Human Intentional Action." *Developmental Science* 7 (4): 488–98.

Call, Josep, and Michael Tomasello. 1998. "Distinguishing Intentional from Accidental Actions in Orangutans (*Pongo pygmaeus*), Chimpanzees (*Pan proglodytes*) and Human Children (*Homo sapiens*)." *Journal of Comparative Psychology* 112 (2): 192–206.

Cammaerts Tricot, Marie-Claire, and Roger Cammaerts. 2015. "Are Ants (*Hymenoptera, Formicidae*) Capable of Self Recognition?" *Journal of Science* 5 (7): 521–32.

Canale, Gustavo Rodrigues, Carlos Eduardo Guidorizzi, Maria Cecília Martins Kierulff, and Cassiano Augusto Ferreira Rodrigues Gatto. 2009. "First Record of Tool Use by Wild Populations of the Yellow-Breasted Capuchin Monkey (*Cebus xanthosternos*) and New Records for the Bearded Capuchin (*Cebus libidinosus*)." *American Journal of Primatology* 71 (5): 366–72.

Carey, Benedict. 2007. "A Thinking Parrot's Loving Good-Bye." *New York Times*, September 11, 2007. https://www.nytimes.com/2007/09/11/world/americas/11iht-parrot.1.7459250.html.

Caro, Timothy M., and D. Anthony Collins. 1986. "Male Cheetahs of the Serengeti." *National Geographic Research* 2 (1): 75–86.

Carr, W. J., Michael R. Landauer, and Renee Sonsino. 1981. "Responses by Rats to Odors from Living versus Dead Conspecifics." *Behavioral and Neural Biology* 31 (1): 67–72.

Cartmill, Erica A., and Richard W. Byrne. 2007. "Orangutans Modify Their Gestural Signaling According to Their Audience's Comprehension." *Current Biology* 17 (15): 1345–48.

Chancellor, Rebecca L., and Lynne A. Isbell. 2008. "Punishment and Competition over Food in Captive Rhesus Macaques, *Macaca mulatta*." *Animal Behaviour* 75 (6): 1939–47.

Chapuisat, Michel. 2010. "Social Evolution: Sick Ants Face Death Alone." *Current Biology* 20 (3): R104–5.

Chen, Xiaomo, and Veit Stuphorn. 2018. "Inactivation of Medial Frontal Cortex Changes Risk Preference." *Current Biology* 28 (19): 3114–22.e4.

Chen, Zhe, Lei Mo, and Ryan Honomichl. 2004. "Having the Memory of an Elephant: Long-Term Retrieval and the Use of Analogues in Problem Solving." *Journal of Experimental Psychology: General* 133 (3): 415–33.

Cholewiak, Danielle M., Salvatore Cerchio, Jeff K. Jacobsen, Jorge Urbán-R, and Christopher W. Clark. 2018. "Songbird Dynamics under the Sea: Acoustic Interactions between Humpback Whales Suggest Song Mediates Male Interactions." *Royal Society Open Science* 5 (2): 171298. https://royalsocietypublishing.org/doi/10.1098/rsos.171298.

Clary, Dawson, and Debbie M. Kelly. 2016. "Graded Mirror Self-Recognition by Clark's Nutcrackers." *Scientific Reports* 6 (36459): 1–11.

Clayton, Nicola S. 2007. "Animal Cognition: Crows Spontaneously Solve a Metatool Task." *Current Biology* 17 (20): R894–95.

Clayton, Nicola S., and Anthony Dickinson. 1998. "Episodic-like Memory during Cache Recovery by Scrub Jays." *Nature* 395 (6699): 272–74.

Cole and Marmalade. 2016. "Cat Mind Blown!" April 4, 2016. YouTube video, 0:23. https://www.youtube.com/watch?v=yzP3kyAukHw.

Conner, Douglas A. 1982. "Dialects versus Geographic Variation in Mammalian Vocalizations." *Animal Behaviour* 30 (1): 297–98.

Cook, Peter, Andrew Rouse, Margaret Wilson, and Colleen Reichmuth. 2013. "A California Sea Lion (*Zalophus californianus*) Can Keep the Beat: Motor Entrainment to Rhythmic Auditory Stimuli in a Non Vocal Mimic." *Journal of Comparative Psychology* 127 (4): 412–27.

Coren, Stanley. 2014. "Magic Tricks, Consciousness, and Mental Imagery in Dogs." *Psychology Today*, January 15, 2019. https://www.psychologytoday.com/us/blog/canine-corner/201403/magic-tricks-consciousness-and-mental-imagery-in-dogs.

Cristol, Daniel A., and Paul V. Switzer. 1999. "Avian Prey-Dropping Behavior. II. American Crows and Walnuts." *Behavioral Ecology* 10 (3): 220–26.

Cronin, Katherine A., Edwin J. C. van Leeuwen, Innocent Chitalu Mulenga, and Mark D. Bodamer. 2011. "Behavioral Response of a Chimpanzee Mother toward Her Dead Infant." *American Journal of Primatology* 73 (5): 415–21.

Cuthbert, Lori, and Douglas Main. 2018. "Orca Mother Drops Calf, After Unprecedented 17 Days of Mourning." *National Geographic*, August 13, 2018. https://www.nationalgeographic.com/animals/2018/08/orca-mourning-calf-killer-whale-northwest-news/.

Dacke, Marie, and Mandyam V. Srinivasan. 2008. "Evidence for Counting in Insects." *Animal Cognition* 11 (4): 683–89.

DailyPicksandFlicks. 2016a. "Guy Performs Magic Trick for Orangutan." October 11, 2016. YouTube video, 1:10. https://www.youtube.com/watch?v=onoLAlHrAfY.

———. 2016b. "Tortoise vs. Hare." October 10, 2016. YouTube video, 0:39. https://www.youtube.com/watch?v=m7NuVjpi72c.

Dale, Rachel, and Joshua M. Plotnik. 2017. "Elephants Know When Their Bodies Are Obstacles to Success in a Novel Transfer Task." *Scientific Reports* 7: 46309. https://www.nature.com/articles/srep46309.

D'Amelio, Stephanie. 2018. "Animal Law: The Moral Scope of Legal Personality: The Case to Recognise Nonhuman Animals." *LSJ: Law Society of NSW Journal* 43: 74–75.

Darwin, Charles. 1871. *The Descent of Man and Selection in Relation to Sex*. London: John Murray.

Davis, William E., Jr. 2013. "Play Behavior by Black Vultures?" *Bird Observer* 41 (5): 290–92.

———. 2015. "Field Notes: Another Instance of Play Behavior in Black Vultures." *Bird Observer* 43 (4): 242. https://www.birdobserver.org/Issues/2015/August-2015/field-notes-another-instance-of-play-behavior-in-black-vultures.

D'Cruze, Neil, Ujjal Kumar Sarma, Aniruddha Mookerjee, Bhagat Singh, Jose Louis, Rudra Prasanna Mahapatra, Vishnu Prasad Jaiswal, Tarun Kumar Roy, Indu Kumari, and Vivek Menon. 2011. "Dancing Bears in India: A Sloth Bear Status Report." *Ursus* 22 (2): 99–106.

De Caro, Frank, ed. 1992. *The Folktale Cat*. Little Rock: August House.

Deecke, Volker B., John K. B. Ford, and Paul Spong. 1999. "Quantifying Complex Patterns of Bioacoustic Variation: Use of a Neural Network to Compare Killer Whale (*Orcinus orca*) Dialects." *Journal of the Acoustical Society of America* 105 (4): 2499–507.

Demetriou, Danielle. 2010. "Monkeys Use Trees to Catapult Themselves Out of Japanese Laboratory." *Telegraph*, July 7, 2010. https://www.telegraph.co.uk/news/worldnews/asia/japan/7876267/Monkeys-use-trees-to-catapult-themselves-out-of-Japanese-laboratory.html.

De Roode, Jacobus C., Thierry Lefèvre, and Mark D. Hunter. 2013. "Self-Medication in Animals." *Science* 340 (6129): 150–51.

Desmond, Adrian J. 1979. *The Ape's Reflexion*. London: Blond and Briggs.

De Waal, Frans B. M. 1982. *Chimpanzee Politics: Power and Sex among Apes*. New York: Harper and Row.

———. 2006. "Joint Ventures Require Joint Payoffs: Fairness among Primates." *Social Research* 73 (2): 349–64.

Diamond, Adele. 1990. "Developmental Time Course in Human Infants and Infant Monkeys, and the Neural Bases of, Inhibitory Control in Reaching." *Annals of the New York Academy of Sciences* 608 (1): 637–76.

Diamond, Jared. 1986. "Animal Art: Variation in Bower Decorating Style among Male Bowerbirds *Amblyornis Inornatus*." *Proceedings of the National Academy of Sciences* 83 (9): 3042–46.

———. 1987. "Bower Building and Decoration by the Bowerbird *Amblyornis inornatus*." *Ethology* 74 (3): 177–204.

———. 1988. "Experimental Study of Bower Decoration by the Bowerbird *Amblyornis inornatus*, using colored poker chips." *American Naturalist* 131 (5): 631–53.

Dinets, V., J. C. Brueggen, and J. D. Brueggen. 2015. "Crocodilians Use Tools for Hunting." *Ethology Ecology and Evolution* 27 (1): 74–78.

Dogs Are Awesome. 2018. "Best 'What the Fluff' Challenge Videos Ever | What the Fluff Challenge Compilation! Part 18." June 30, 2018. YouTube video, 6:10. https://www.youtube.com/watch?v=umFoo96P0h4.

Donnellan, Laura. 2018. "On Ascribing Personhood to All Primates." *Journal of Animal Ethics* 8 (1): 103–8.

Douglas, George. 1977. *Scottish Fairy and Folk Tales*. New York: Arno.

Douglas-Hamilton, Iain, Shivani Bhalla, George Wittemyer, and Fritz Vollrath. 2006. "Behavioural Reactions of Elephants towards a Dying and Deceased Matriarch." *Applied Animal Behaviour Science* 100 (1–2): 87–102.

Douglas-Hamilton, Iain, and Oria Douglas-Hamilton. 1975. *Among the Elephants*. London: Collins.

Dufour, Valérie, Nicolas Poulin, Charlotte Curé, and Elisabeth H. M. Sterck. 2015. "Chimpanzee Drumming: A Spontaneous Performance with Characteristics of Human Musical Drumming." *Scientific Reports* 5: 11320.

Dumbo. 1941. Directed by Ben Sharpsteen, written by Joe Grant and Dick Huemer. 64 min. Disney.

edogawa, konan. 2016. "Amazing . . . When Animals Help Each Other." July 21, 2016. YouTube video, 3:44. https://www.youtube.com/watch?v=XsrN7RHzDcc.

Edsinger, Eric, and Gül Dölen. 2018. "A Conserved Role for Serotonergic Neurotransmission in Mediating Social Behavior in Octopus." *Current Biology* 28 (19): 3136–42.E4. https://doi.org/10.1016/j.cub.2018.07.061.

Edwards, Brian J., Benjamin M. Rottman, Maya Shankar, Riana Betzler, Vladimir Chituc, Ricardo Rodriguez, Liara Silva, Leah Wibecan, Jane Widness, and Laurie R. Santos. 2014. "Do Capuchin Monkeys (*Cebus apella*) Diagnose Causal Relations in the Absence of a Direct Reward?" *PLOS ONE* 9 (2): e88595. https://doi.org/10.1371/journal.pone.0088595.

Edwards, David P., Mark Hassall, William J. Sutherland, and W. Yu Douglas. 2006. "Selection for Protection in an Ant-Plant Mutualism: Host Sanctions, Host Modularity, and the Principal-Agent Game." *Proceedings of the Royal Society B: Biological Sciences* 273 (1586): 595–602.

Edwards, Lin. 2010. "Chimps Dance in the Face of Fire." *Phys.org*. January 19, 2010. https://phys.org/news/2010-01-chimps.html.

Ellison, Anne Margaret, Jane Watson, and Eric Demers. 2015. "Testing Problem Solving in Turkey Vultures (*Cathartes aura*) Using the String-Pulling Test." *Animal Cognition* 18 (1): 111–18.

Elwin, Verrier. 1944. *Folk-Tales of Mahakoshal*. London: Oxford University Press.

Epstein, Robert, Robert P. Lanza, and Burrhus Frederic Skinner. 1981. "'Self-Awareness' in the Pigeon." *Science* 212 (4495): 695–96.

Erwin, J. 1974. "Laboratory-Reared Rhesus Monkeys Can Use Their Tails as Tools." *Perceptual and Motor Skills* 39 (1): 129–30.

Escape from the Planet of the Apes. 1971. Directed by Don Taylor, written by Paul Dehn and Pierre Boulle. Twentieth Century Fox.

Evans, T. A., M. J. Beran, F. Paglieri, and E. Addessi. 2012. "Delaying Gratification for Food and Tokens in Capuchin Monkeys (*Cebus apella*) and Chimpanzees (*Pan troglodytes*): When Quantity Is Salient, Symbolic Stimuli Do Not Improve Performance." *Animal Cognition* 15 (4): 539–48.

everythingispointless. 2007. "Chimps Attacking Leopard." July 22, 2007. YouTube video, 1:31. https://www.youtube.com/watch?reload=9&v=bKpZUsRJWBg.

Farnsworth, George L., and Jennifer L. Smolinski. 2006. "Numerical Discrimination by Wild Northern Mockingbirds." *Condor: Ornithological Applications* 108 (4): 953–57.

Fashing, Peter J., and Nga Nguyen. 2011. "Behavior toward the Dying, Diseased, or Disabled among Animals and Its Relevance to Paleopathology." *International Journal of Paleopathology* 1 (3–4): 128–29.

Fashing, Peter J., Nga Nguyen, Tyler S. Barry, C. Barret Goodale, Ryan J. Burke, Sorrel C. Z. Jones, Jeffrey T. Kerby, Laura M. Lee, Niina O. Nurmi, and Vivek V. Venkataraman. 2010. "Death among Geladas (*Theropithecus gelada*): A Broader Perspective on Mummified Infants and Primate Thanatology." *American Journal of Primatology* 73 (5): 405–9.

Feldblum, Joseph T., Sofia Manfredi, Ian C. Gilby, and Anne E. Pusey. 2018. "The Timing and Causes of a Unique Chimpanzee Community Fission Preceding Gombe's 'Four-Year War.'" *American Journal of Physical Anthropology* 166 (3): 730–44.

Finch, G. 1941. "The Solution of Patterned String Problems by Chimpanzees." *Journal of Comparative Psychology* 32 (1): 83–90.

Flack, Jessica C., and Frans B. M. de Waal. 2000. "'Any Animal Whatever': Darwinian Building Blocks of Morality in Monkeys and Apes." *Journal of Consciousness Studies* 7 (1–2): 1–29.

Flack, Jessica C., Lisa A. Jeannotte, and Frans B. M. de Waal. 2004. "Play Signaling and the Perception of Social Rules by Juvenile Chimpanzees (*Pan troglodytes*)." *Journal of Comparative Psychology* 118 (2): 149–59.

Flombaum, Jonathan I., and Laurie R. Santos. 2005. "Rhesus Monkeys Attribute Perceptions to Others." *Current Biology* 15 (5): 447–52.

Flower, Tom. 2011. "Fork-Tailed Drongos Use Deceptive Mimicked Alarm Calls to Steal Food." *Proceedings of the Royal Society B: Biological Sciences* 278 (1711): 1548–55.

Foote, Allison L., and Jonathon D. Crystal. 2007. "Metacognition in the Rat." *Current Biology* 17 (6): 551–55.

ForfunTV. 2017. "Animal Heroes 2017—Amazing Animals Helping and Rescuing Other Animals—Compilation 2017." October 14, 2017. YouTube video, 13:58. https://www.youtube.com/watch?v=axDkW51K5sc.

Fought, Emily. 2017. "15 Horse Jokes to Share with Your Friends." *Cowgirl Magazine*. June 27, 2017. Accessed June 11, 2019. https://cowgirlmagazine.com/horse-jokes/.

Fouts, Roger S., Deborah H. Fouts, and Thomas E. Van Cantfort. 1989. "The Infant Loulis Learns Signs from Cross-Fostered Chimpanzees." In *Teaching Sign Language to Chimpanzees*, edited by R. Allen Gardner, Beatrix T. Gardner, and Thomas E. Van Cantfort, 280–92. Albany: State University of New York Press.

Fouts, Roger S., and Randall L. Rigby. 1977. "Man-Chimpanzee Communication." In *How Animals Communicate*, edited by Thomas Sebeok, 1034–54. Bloomington: Indiana University Press.

Frank, Erik T., Marten Wehrhahn, and K. Eduard Linsenmair. 2018. "Wound Treatment and Selective Help in a Termite-Hunting Ant." *Proceedings of the Royal Society B* 285 (1872): 20172457.

Fraser, Orlaith N., and Thomas Bugnyar. 2010. "Do Ravens Show Consolation? Responses to Distressed Others." *PLOS ONE* 5 (5): e10605.

———. 2012. "Reciprocity of Agonistic Support in Ravens." *Animal Behaviour* 83 (1): 171–77.

Freeberg, Todd M. 2004. "Social Transmission of Courtship Behavior and Mating Preferences in Brown-Headed Cowbirds, *Molothrus ater*." *Animal Learning and Behavior* 32 (1): 122–30.

Furness, William H. 1916. "Observations on the Mentality of Chimpanzees and Orang-utans." *Proceedings of the American Philosophical Society* 55 (3): 281–90.

Galef, Bennett G., Jr. 2009. "Imitation in Animals: History, Definition, and Interpretation of Data from the Psychological Laboratory." In *Social Learning: Psychological and Biological Perspectives*, edited by Thomas R. Zentall and Bennet G. Galef Jr., 2–28. Mahwah, NJ: Lawrence Erlbaum.

Galef, Bennett G., Jr., and Craig Aleen. 1995. "A New Model System for Studying Behavioural Traditions in Animals." *Animal Behaviour* 50 (3): 705–17.

Gallup, Gordon G., Jr. 1968. "Mirror-Image Stimulation." *Psychological Bulletin* 70 (6 pt. 1): 782–93.

———. 1970. "Chimpanzees: Self-Recognition." *Science* 167 (3914): 86–87.

Gallup, Gordon G., Jr., and James R. Anderson. 2018. "The 'Olfactory Mirror' and Other Recent Attempts to Demonstrate Self-Recognition in Non-Primate Species." *Behavioural Processes* 148: 16–19.

Gallup, Gordon G., Jr., Richard F. Nash, and Alton L. Ellison Jr. 1971. "Tonic Immobility as a Reaction to Predation: Artificial Eyes as a Fear Stimulus for Chickens." *Psychonomic Science* 23 (1): 79–80.

Gamble, Jennifer. 2001. "Humor in Apes." *Humor* 14 (2): 163–79.

Gao, Jie, Yanjie Su, Masaki Tomonaga, and Tetsuro Matsuzawa. 2018. "Learning the Rules of the Rock-Paper-Scissors Game: Chimpanzees versus Children." *Primates* 59 (1): 7–17.

Garcia-Pelegrin, Elias, Alexandra K. Schnell, Clive Wilkins, and Nicola S. Clayton. 2020. "An Unexpected Audience: Experiments with Magic Effects Might be Informative about Cognition in Animals." *Science* 369 (6510): 1424–26.

Glickman, Stephen E., and Richard W. Sroges. 1966. "Curiosity in Zoo Animals." *Behaviour* 26 (1–2): 151–87.

Gomes, Cristina M., and Christophe Boesch. 2009. "Wild Chimpanzees Exchange Meat for Sex on a Long-Term Basis." *PLOS ONE* 4 (4): e5116. https://doi.org/10.1371/journal.pone.0005116.

Gómez, Juan-Carlos, and Beatriz Martín-Andrade. 2005. "Fantasy Play in Apes." In *The Nature of Play: Great Apes and Humans*, edited by Anthony D. Pellegrini and Peter K. Smith, 139–72. New York: Guilford.

Goodall, Jane. 1964. "Tool-Using and Aimed Throwing in a Community of Free-Living Chimpanzees." *Nature* 201 (4926): 1264–66.

———. 1971. *In the Shadow of Man*. Boston: Houghton-Mifflin.

———. 1977. "Infant Killing and Cannibalism in Free-Living Chimpanzees." *Folia Primatologica* 28 (4): 259–82.

———. 1999. *Reason for Hope: A Spiritual Journey*. New York: Warner Books.

The Gorilla Foundation. 2010. "Michael's Story." February 26, 2010. https://www.koko.org/node/276.

———. 2014. "PRESS RELEASE: Koko Remembers Robin Williams." August 11, 2014. https://www.koko.org/koko-tribute-robin-williams.

———. 2019. "Gorilla Art." Accessed February 22, 2019. http://www.koko.org/gorilla-art-0.

Gregory, Kia. 2012. "Chinatown Fair Is Back, without Chickens Playing Tick-Tack-Toe." *New York Times*, June 10, 2012. https://www.nytimes.com/2012/06/11/nyregion/chinatown-fair-returns-but-without-chicken-playing-tick-tack-toe.html.

Grobecker, David B. 1978. "Crows Use Automobiles as Nutcrackers." *Auk* 95: 760–61.

Güntürkün, Onur. 2014. "Is Dolphin Cognition Special?" *Brain, Behavior and Evolution* 83 (3): 177–80.

Hafandi, A., R. Hanafi, H. Azwan, M. N. Mohd Hezmee, H. A. Hassim, Z. I. Zeid, K. Jayaseelan, and T. A. Tengku Rinalfi Putra. 2018. "The Preliminary Study of Mirror Self-Recognition (MSR) on Malayan Sun Bear (*Helarctos malayanus*)." *Jurnal Veterinar Malaysia* 30 (1): 23–25.

Hals, Silje Kristine. 2016. "Responses to Mirrors in Domestic Goats (*Capra aegagrus hircus*): Assessing Mirror Use to Solve a Problem and in Self-Recognition." Master's thesis, Norwegian University of Life Sciences, Ås.

Hamilton, William J., Ruth E. Buskirk, and William H. Buskirk. 1975. "Defensive Stoning by Baboons." *Nature* 256: 488–89.

Hampton, Robert R. 2001. "Rhesus Monkeys Know When They Remember." *Proceedings of the National Academy of Sciences* 98 (9): 5359–62.

Handwerk, Brian. 2010. "Chimp 'Girls' Play With 'Dolls' Too: First Wild Evidence." *National Geographic News*, December 22,

2010. https://news.nationalgeographic.com/news/2010/09/101220-chimpanzees-play-nature-nurture-science-animals-evolution/.

Hanson, Steve. 2015. "Monkey Jokes for Kids." *Glow Word Books*. Accessed June 1, 2019. https://www.glowwordbooks.com/blog/2015/08/29/monkey-jokes-for-kids/.

Hare, Brian, Josep Call, and Michael Tomasello. 2006. "Chimpanzees Deceive a Human Competitor by Hiding." *Cognition* 101 (3): 495–514.

Hare, Brian, Alicia P. Melis, Vanessa Woods, Sara Hastings, and Richard Wrangham. 2007. "Tolerance Allows Bonobos to Outperform Chimpanzees on a Cooperative Task." *Current Biology* 17 (7): 619–23.

Haring, Volker, Julie E. Gray, Bruce A. McClure, Marilyn A. Anderson, and Adrienne E. Clarke. 1990. "Self-Incompatibility: A Self-Recognition System in Plants." *Science* 250 (4983): 937–41.

Harris, Christine R., and Caroline Prouvost. 2014. "Jealousy in Dogs." *PLOS ONE* 9 (7): e94597.

Harrod, James B. 2014. "The Case for Chimpanzee Religion." *Journal for the Study of Religion, Nature and Culture* 8 (1): 8–45.

Hart, Benjamin L., Lynette A. Hart, Michael McCoy, and C. R. Sarath. 2001. "Cognitive Behaviour in Asian Elephants: Use and Modification of Branches for Fly Switching." *Animal Behaviour* 62 (5): 839–47.

Hauser, Marc D. 1992. "Costs of Deception: Cheaters Are Punished in Rhesus Monkeys (*Macaca mulatta*)." *Proceedings of the National Academy of Sciences* 89 (24): 12137–39.

Hayes, Catherine. 1951. *The Ape in Our House*. New York: Harper and Brothers.

Hayes, Keith J., and Catherine Hayes. 1951. "The Intellectual Development of a Home-Raised Chimpanzee." *Proceedings of the American Philosophical Society* 95 (2): 105–9.

Heinsohn, Robert, and Craig Packer. 1995. "Complex Cooperative Strategies in Group-Territorial African Lions." *Science* 269 (5228): 1260–62.

Hennefield, Laura, Hyesung G. Hwang, Sara J. Weston, and Daniel J. Povinelli. 2018. "Meta-Analytic Techniques Reveal That Corvid Causal Reasoning in the Aesop's Fable Paradigm Is Driven by Trial-and-Error Learning." *Animal Cognition* 21 (6): 735–48.

Henrich, Joseph, and Joan B. Silk. 2013. "Interpretative Problems with Chimpanzee Ultimatum Game." *Proceedings of the National Academy of Sciences* 110 (33): E3049. https://www.pnas.org/content/110/33/E3049.

Hernandez-Aguilar, R. Adriana, Jim Moore, and Travis Rayne Pickering. 2007. "Savanna Chimpanzees Use Tools to Harvest the Underground Storage Organs of Plants." *Proceedings of the National Academy of Sciences* 104 (49): 19210–213.

Herzing, D. L., and C. M. Johnson. 1997. "Interspecific Interactions between Atlantic Spotted Dolphins (*Stenella frontalis*) and Bottlenose Dolphins (*Tursiops truncatus*) in the Bahamas, 1985–1995." *Aquatic Mammals* 23 (2): 85–99.

Herzog, Hal. 2010. *Some We Love, Some We Hate, Some We Eat: Why It's So Hard to Think Straight about Animals*. New York: Harper.
Hixson, Michael D. 1998. "Ape Language Research: A Review and Behavioral Perspective." *Analysis of Verbal Behavior* 15 (1): 17–39.
Holland, Jennifer S. 2011. *Unlikely Friendships: 47 Remarkable Stories from the Animal Kingdom*. New York: Workman.
Homberg, Judith R., Tommy Pattij, Mieke C. W. Janssen, Eric Ronken, Sietse F. de Boer, Anton N. M. Schoffelmeer, and Edwin Cuppen. 2007. "Serotonin Transporter Deficiency in Rats Improves Inhibitory Control but Not Behavioural Flexibility." *European Journal of Neuroscience* 26 (7): 2066–73.
Hood, Bruce M., Marc D. Hauser, Linda Anderson, and Laurie Santos. 1999. "Gravity Biases in a Non-Human Primate?" *Developmental Science* 2 (1): 35–41.
Hooper, Rowan. 2016. "What Do Chimp 'Temples' Tell Us about the Evolution of Religion?" *NewScientist*. May 4, 2016. https://www.newscientist.com/article/2079630-what-do-chimp-temples-tell-us-about-the-evolution-of-religion/.
Hopcraft, J. Grant C., A. R. E. Sinclair, and Craig Packer. 2005. "Planning for Success: Serengeti Lions Seek Prey Accessibility Rather Than Abundance." *Journal of Animal Ecology* 74 (3): 559–66.
Hopkins, William D., Jamie L. Russell, Claudio Cantalupo, Hani Freeman, and Steven J. Schapiro. 2005. "Factors Influencing the Prevalence and Handedness for Throwing in Captive Chimpanzees (*Pan troglodytes*)." *Journal of Comparative Psychology* 119 (4): 363–70.
Horel, James A., F. Robert Treichler, and Donald R. Meyer. 1963. "Coercive Behavior in the Rhesus Monkey." *Journal of Comparative and Physiological Psychology* 56 (1): 208–10.
Horowitz, Alexandra. 2009. "Disambiguating the 'Guilty Look': Salient Prompts to a Familiar Dog Behaviour." *Behavioural Processes* 81 (3): 447–52.
———. 2012. "Fair Is Fine, but More Is Better: Limits to Inequity Aversion in the Domestic Dog." *Social Justice Research* 25 (2): 195–212.
———. 2017. "Smelling Themselves: Dogs Investigate Their Own Odours Longer When Modified in an 'Olfactory Mirror' Test." *Behavioural Processes* 143: 17–24.
Hotta, Takashi, Shiho Komiyama, and Masanori Kohda. 2018. "A Social Cichlid Fish Failed to Pass the Mark Test." *Animal Cognition* 21 (1): 127–36.
Houk, J. L., and J. J. Geibel. 1974. "Observation of Underwater Tool Use by the Sea Otter, *Enhydra lutris* Linnaeus." *California Fish and Game* 60 (4): 207–8.
Hubbs, Carl L. 1953. "Dolphin Protecting Dead Young." *Journal of Mammalogy* 34 (4): 498.
Huffman, Michael A. 1997. "Current Evidence for Self-Medication in Primates: A Multidisciplinary Perspective." *American Journal of Physical Anthropology* 104 (S25): 171–200.

———. 2003. "Animal Self-Medication and Ethno-Medicine: Exploration and Exploitation of the Medicinal Properties of Plants." *Proceedings of the Nutrition Society* 62 (2): 371–81.
Huffman, Michael A., and Sylvia K. Vitazkova. 2007. "Primates, Plants, and Parasites: The Evolution of Animal Self-Medication and Ethnomedicine." *Ethnopharmacology: Volume II*: 183–201.
Humphrey, George, and Fred Marcuse. 1939. "New Methods of Obtaining Neurotic Behavior in Rats." *American Journal of Psychology* 52 (4): 616–19.
Humphrey, Nicholas. 2012. "This Chimp Will Kick Your Ass at Memory Games—But How the Hell Does He Do It?" *Trends in Cognitive Sciences* 16 (7): 353–55.
Huttunen, Annamarie W., Geoffrey K. Adams, and Michael L. Platt. 2017. "Can Self-Awareness Be Taught? Monkeys Pass the Mirror Test—Again." *Proceedings of the National Academy of Sciences* 114 (13): 3281–83.
Iglesias, Teresa L., Richard McElreath, and Gail L. Patricelli. 2012. "Western Scrub-Jay Funerals: Cacophonous Aggregations in Response to Dead Conspecifics." *Animal Behaviour* 84 (5): 1103–11.
Jacobs, Ivo F., and Mathias Osvath. 2015. "The String-Pulling Paradigm in Comparative Psychology." *Journal of Comparative Psychology* 129 (2): 89–120.
Janmaat, Karline R. L., Leo Polansky, Simone Dagui Ban, and Christophe Boesch. 2014. "Wild Chimpanzees Plan Their Breakfast Time, Type, and Location." *Proceedings of the National Academy of Sciences* 111 (46): 16343–48.
Jekyll, Walter, ed. (1907) 1966. *Jamaican Song and Story*. New York: Dover.
Jensen, Keith, Josep Call, and Michael Tomasello. 2007. "Chimpanzees Are Vengeful but Not Spiteful." *Proceedings of the National Academy of Sciences* 104 (32): 13046–50.
Jensen, Keith, Brian Hare, Josep Call, and Michael Tomasello. 2006. "What's in It for Me? Self-Regard Precludes Altruism and Spite in Chimpanzees." *Proceedings of the Royal Society B: Biological Sciences* 273 (1589): 1013–21.
Jokesbykids.com. 2021. "Dolphin Jokes." Accessed January 5, 2021. https://www.jokesbykids.com/dolphin/.
Jokes4us.com. 2019a. "Ant Jokes." Accessed June 1, 2019. http://www.jokes4us.com/animaljokes/antjokes.html.
———. 2019b. "Chimp Jokes." Accessed June 1, 2019. http://www.jokes4us.com/animaljokes/chimpjokes.html.
———. 2019c. "Cow Jokes." Accessed June 1, 2019. http://www.jokes4us.com/animaljokes/cowjokes.html.
———. 2019d. "Dolphin Jokes." Accessed June 1, 2019. http://www.jokes4us.com/animaljokes/dolphinjokes.html.
———. 2019e. "Elephant Jokes." Accessed June 1, 2019. http://www.jokes4us.com/animaljokes/elephantjokes.html.

———. 2019f. "Geography Jokes." Accessed June 1, 2019. http://www.jokes4us.com/miscellaneousjokes/schooljokes/geographyjokes.html.

———. 2019g. "Sheep Jokes." Accessed June 1, 2019. http://www.jokes4us.com/animaljokes/sheepjokes.html.

Jokester. 2011. "Funny Questions and Answers about Bees." *Funny Grins*. June 5, 2011. Accessed June 1, 2019. https://www.funnygrins.com/2011/funny-stuff/jokes/animals-and-wildlife/funny-questions-and-answers-about-bees.

Juarez, Jorge, Carlos Guzman-Flores, Frank R. Ervin, and Roberta M. Palmour. 1993. "Voluntary Alcohol Consumption in Vervet Monkeys: Individual, Sex, and Age Differences." *Pharmacology Biochemistry and Behavior* 46 (4): 985–88.

Kabadayi, Can, and Mathias Osvath. 2017. "Ravens Parallel Great Apes in Flexible Planning for Tool-Use and Bartering." *Science* 357 (6347): 202–4.

Kacsoh, Balint Z., Zachary R. Lynch, Nathan T. Mortimer, and Todd A. Schlenke. 2013. "Fruit Flies Medicate Offspring after Seeing Parasites." *Science* 339 (6122): 947–50.

Kafka, Franz. 1992. "A Report for an Academy." In *The Transformation (Metamorphosis) and Other Stories: Works Published during Kafka's Lifetime*, translated and edited by Malcom Pasley, 187–95. New York: Penguin.

Kahlenberg, Sonya M., and Richard W. Wrangham. 2010. "Sex Differences in Chimpanzees' Use of Sticks as Play Objects Resemble Those of Children." *Current Biology* 20 (24): R1067–68. https://doi.org/10.1016/j.cub.2010.11.024.

Kaiser, Ingrid, Keith Jensen, Josep Call, and Michael Tomasello. 2012. "Theft in an Ultimatum Game: Chimpanzees and Bonobos are Insensitive to Unfairness." *Biology Letters* 8 (6): 942–45.

Kaminski, Juliane, Josep Call, and Michael Tomasello. 2008. "Chimpanzees Know What Others Know, but Not What They Believe." *Cognition* 109 (2): 224–34.

Kaminski, Juliane, Andrea Pitsch, and Michael Tomasello. 2013. "Dogs Steal in the Dark." *Animal Cognition* 16 (3): 385–94.

Kaplan, Gisela. 2011. "Pointing Gesture in a Bird—Merely Instrumental or a Cognitively Complex Behavior?" *Current Zoology* 57 (4): 453–67.

Keenan, Julian Paul, Mark A. Wheeler, Gordon G. Gallup Jr., and Alvaro Pascual-Leone. 2000. "Self-Recognition and the Right Prefrontal Cortex." *Trends in Cognitive Sciences* 4 (9): 338–44.

Kehoe, Laura. 2016. "Mysterious New Behaviour Found in Our Closest Living Relatives." *The Conversation*. February 29, 2016. http://theconversation.com/mysterious-new-behaviour-found-in-our-closest-living-relatives-55512.

Kellogg, W. N., and L. A. Kellogg. 1933. *The Ape and the Child*. New York: Whittlesey House.

Kiers, E. Toby, Robert A. Rousseau, Stuart A. West, and R. Ford Denison. 2003. "Host Sanctions and the Legume-Rhizobium Mutualism." *Nature* 425: 78–81.

King, Barbara. 2013. *How Animals Grieve*. Chicago: University of Chicago Press.

Kirchhofer, Katharina C., Felizitas Zimmermann, Juliane Kaminski, and Michael Tomasello. 2012. "Dogs (*Canis familiaris*), but Not Chimpanzees (*Pan troglodytes*), Understand Imperative Pointing." *PLOS ONE* 7 (2): e30913. https://doi.org/10.1371/journal.pone.0030913.

Kline, Michelle Ann. 2015. "How to Learn about Teaching: An Evolutionary Framework for the Study of Teaching Behavior in Humans and Other Animals." *Behavioral and Brain Sciences* 38 (31): 1-71.

Knappert, Jan. 2001. *The Book of African Fables: Studies Swahili Languages and Literature, Vol. 3*. Lewiston, NY: Edwin Mellen.

Knatchbull, Wyndham, trans. 1819. *Kalila and Dimna, or the Fables of Bidpai*. Oxford: W. Baxter for J. Parker.

Kohda, Masanori, Hatta Takashi, Tmohiro Takeyama, Satoshi Awata, Hirokazu Tanaka, Jun-ya Asai, and Alex Jordan. 2018. "Cleaner Wrasse Pass the Mark Test. What Are the Implications for Consciousness and Self-Awareness Testing in Animals?" *bioRxiv*: 397067. https://doi.org/10.1101/397067.

Köhler, Wolfgang. (1917) 1925. *The Mentality of Apes*. Translated from the second revised edition by Ella Winter. New York: Harcourt, Brace & World.

Kooriyama, Takanori. 2009. "<Note> The Death of a Newborn Chimpanzee at Mahale: Reactions of Its Mother and Other Individuals to the Body." *Pan Africa News* 16 (2): 19-21.

Kortlandt, Adriaan. 1962. "Chimpanzees in the Wild." *Scientific American* 206 (5): 128-40.

———. 1975. "Wild Chimpanzees Using Clubs in Fighting an Animated Stuffed Leopard." In *War, Its Causes and Correlates*, edited by Martin A. Nettleship, R. Dalegivens, and Anderson Nettleship, 297-98. Chicago: Aldine.

Krachun, Carla, Josep Call, and Michael Tomasello. 2009. "Can Chimpanzees (*Pan troglodytes*) Discriminate Appearance from Reality?" *Cognition* 112 (3): 435-50.

Krachun, Carla, Robert Lurz, Jamie L. Russell, and William D. Hopkins. 2016. "Smoke and Mirrors: Testing the Scope of Chimpanzees' Appearance-Reality Understanding." *Cognition* 150: 53-67.

Krishnamani, R., and William C. Mahaney. 2000. "Geophagy among Primates: Adaptive Significance and Ecological Consequences." *Animal Behaviour* 59 (5): 899-915.

Krupenye, Christopher, Fumihiro Kano, Satoshi Hirata, Josep Call, and Michael Tomasello. 2016. "Great Apes Anticipate That Other Individuals Will Act According to False Beliefs." *Science* 354 (6308): 110-14.

Krusche, Paul, Claudia Uller, and Ursula Dicke. 2010. "Quantity Discrimination in Salamanders." *Journal of Experimental Biology* 213 (11): 1822-28.

Krützen, Michael, Janet Mann, Michael R. Heithaus, Richard C. Connor, Lars Bejder, and William B. Sherwin. 2005. "Cultural

Transmission of Tool Use in Bottlenose Dolphins." *Proceedings of the National Academy of Sciences* 102 (25): 8939–43.

Kruuk, Hans, and H. Kruuk. 1972. *The Spotted Hyena: A Study of Predation and Social Behavior*. Chicago: University of Chicago Press.

Kühl, Hjalmar S., Ammie K. Kalan, Mimi Arandjelovic, Floris Aubert, Lucy D'Auvergne, Annemarie Goedmakers, Sorrel Jones, et al. 2016. "Chimpanzee Accumulative Stone Throwing." *Nature Scientific Reports* 6 (22219). https://doi-org.proxyiub.uits.iu.edu/10.1038/srep22219.

Kuhlmeier, Valerie A., and Sarah T. Boysen. 2002. "Chimpanzees (*Pan troglodytes*) Recognize Spatial and Object Correspondences between a Scale Model and Its Referent." *Psychological Science* 13 (1): 60–63.

Kühme, Wolfdietrich. 1963. "Ethology of the African Elephant (*Loxodonta africana* Blumenbach 1797) in Captivity." *International Zoo Yearbook* 14 (1): 113–21.

Kumazawa-Manita, Noriko, Hiroshi Hama, Atsushi Miyawaki, and Atsushi Iriki. 2013. "Tool Use Specific Adult Neurogenesis and Synaptogenesis in Rodent (*Octodon degus*) Hippocampus." *PLOS ONE* 8 (3). https://doi.org/10.1371/journal.pone.0058649.

Kundey, Shannon M. A., Andres De Los Reyes, Chelsea Taglang, Rebecca Allen, Sabrina Molina, Erica Royer, and Rebecca German. 2010. "Domesticated Dogs (*Canis familiaris*) React to What Others Can and Cannot Hear." *Applied Animal Behaviour Science* 126 (1–2): 45–50.

Kusayama, Taichi, Hans-Joachim Bischof, and Shigeru Watanabe. 2000. "Responses to Mirror-Image Stimulation in Jungle Crows (*Corvus macrorhynchos*)." *Animal Cognition* 3 (1): 61–64.

Laffgaff.com. 2019. "Funny Elephant Puns." Accessed June 1, 2019. http://laffgaff.com/funny-elephant-puns/.

Lambert, Megan L., Martina Schiestl, Raoul Schwing, Alex H. Taylor, Gyula K. Gajdon, Katie E. Slocombe, and Amanda M. Seed. 2017. "Function and Flexibility of Object Exploration in Kea and New Caledonian Crows." *Royal Society Open Science* 4 (9): 170652. https://doi-org.proxyiub.uits.iu.edu/10.1098/rsos.170652.

Land, Michael F. 1999. "Motion and Vision: Why Animals Move Their Eyes." *Journal of Comparative Physiology* A 185 (4): 341–52.

Laska, Matthias, Verena Bauer, and Laura Teresa Hernandez Salazar. 2007. "Self-Anointing Behavior in Free-Ranging Spider Monkeys (*Ateles geoffroyi*) in Mexico." *Primates* 48 (2): 160–63.

LauraLovebird. 2011. "Courtship Dance of the Waved Albatross." December 6, 2011. YouTube video, 0:47. https://www.youtube.com/watch?v=LqgTekYbZKg.

Leadbeater, Elouise, Nigel E. Raine, and Lars Chittka. 2006. "Social Learning: Ants and the Meaning of Teaching." *Current Biology* 16 (9): R323–25.

Leavens, David A., William D. Hopkins, and Kim A. Bard. 1996. "Indexical and Referential Pointing in Chimpanzees (*Pan troglodytes*)." *Journal of Comparative Psychology* 110 (4): 346–53.

Ledbetter, David H., and Jeffry A. Basen. 1982. "Failure to Demonstrate Self-Recognition in Gorillas." *American Journal of Primatology* 2 (3): 307-10.
Leimgruber, Kristin L., Adrian F. Ward, Jane Widness, Michael I. Norton, Kristina R. Olson, Kurt Gray, and Laurie R. Santos. 2014. "Give What You Get: Capuchin Monkeys (*Cebus apella*) and 4-Year-Old Children Pay Forward Positive and Negative Outcomes to Conspecifics." *PLOS ONE* 9 (1): e87035. https://doi.org/10.1371/journal.pone.0087035.
Ley, Ronald. 1990. *A Whisper of Espionage*. Garden City Park, NY: Avery.
Lincoln Children's Zoo. 2019. "Animal Art." Accessed February 22, 2019. https://www.lincolnzoo.org/animals/animal-art/.
The Lion King. 1994. Directed by Roger Allers and Rob Minkoff, written by Irene Mecchi, Jonathan Roberts, and Linda Woolverton. 88 min. Disney.
Löhrl, Hans. 1983. "Zur Feindabwehr der Wacholderdrossel (*Turdus pilaris*) [Well-aimed defecation in the fieldfare (*Turdus pilaris*)]." *Journal für Ornithologie* 124 (3): 271-79.
London, Jack. 1913. *John Barleycorn*. London: Mills and Boon, Limited.
Lord, Albert B., ed. 1970. *Russian Folk Tales*. Avon, CT: Heritage.
Lurz, Robert W. 2011. *Mindreading Animals: The Debate over What Animals Know about Other Minds*. Cambridge, MA: MIT Press.
Lyn, Heidi. 2012. "Apes and the Evolution of Language: Taking Stock of 40 Years of Research." In *The Oxford Handbook of Comparative Evolutionary Psychology*, edited by Jennifer Vonk and Todd K. Shackelford, 356-78. Oxford: Oxford University Press.
Ma, Xiaozan, Yuan Jin, Bo Luo, Guiquan Zhang, Rongping Wei, and Dingzhen Liu. 2015. "Giant Pandas Failed to Show Mirror Self-Recognition." *Animal Cognition* 18 (3): 713-21.
Maák, István, Gábor Lőrinczi, Pauline Le Quinquis, Gábor Módra, Dalila Bovet, Josep Call, and Patrizia d'Ettorre. 2017. "Tool Selection during Foraging in Two Species of Funnel Ants." *Animal Behaviour* 123: 207-16.
Manger, P. R. 2013. "Questioning the Interpretations of Behavioral Observations of Cetaceans: Is There Really Support for a Special Intellectual Status for This Mammalian Order?" *Neuroscience* 250: 664-96.
Maple, T. 1974. "Do Crows Use Automobiles as Nutcrackers?" *Western Birds* 5: 97-98.
Marino, Lori, Richard C. Connor, R. Ewan Fordyce, Louis M. Herman, Patrick R. Hof, Louis Lefebvre, David Lusseau, Brenda McCowan, Esther A. Nimchinsky, Adam A. Pack, Luke Rendell, Joy S. Reidenberg, and Diana Reiss. 2007. "Cetaceans Have Complex Brains for Complex Cognition." *PLOS Biology* 5 (5): e139. https://doi.org/10.1371/journal.pbio.0050139.
Martin, John Levi. 2000. "What Do Animals Do All Day? The Division of Labor, Class Bodies, and Totemic Thinking in the Popular Imagination." *Poetics* 27: 195-231.

Martinez-Conde, Susana. 2016. "Did the Baboon Feel the Magic?" *Scientific American: Illusion Chasers*. March 27, 2016. Accessed January 15, 2019. https://blogs.scientificamerican.com/illusion-chasers/did-the-baboon-feel-the-magic/.

Marvin, Dwight Edwards. 1916. *Curiosities in Proverbs: A Collection of Unusual Adages, Maxims, Aphorisms, Phrases and Other Popular Dicta from Many Lands*. New York and London: G. P. Putnam's Sons.

Massen, Jorg J. M., Lisette M. van den Berg, Berry M. Spruijt, and Elisabeth H. M. Sterck. 2012. "Inequity Aversion in Relation to Effort and Relationship Quality in Long-Tailed Macaques (*Macaca fascicularis*)." *American Journal of Primatology* 74 (2): 145–56.

Matsuzawa, Tetsuro. 2017. "Primates Social Impact Award 2016." *Primates* 58 (1): 5.

Mayer, Carolina, Josep Call, Anna Albiach-Serrano, Elisabetta Visalberghi, Gloria Sabbatini, and Amanda Seed. 2014. "Abstract Knowledge in the Broken-String Problem: Evidence from Nonhuman Primates and Pre-Schoolers." *PLOS ONE* 9 (10): e108597. https://doi.org/10.1371/journal.pone.0108597.

McComb, Karen, Lucy Baker, and Cynthia Moss. 2006. "African Elephants Show High Levels of Interest in the Skulls and Ivory of Their Own Species." *Biology Letters* 2 (1): 26–28.

McGrew, William C. 2010. "Chimpanzee Technology." *Science* 328 (5978): 579–80.

McGrew, William C., and Linda F. Marchant. 1998. "Chimpanzee Wears a Knotted Skin 'Necklace.'" *Pan Africa News* 5 (1): 8–9.

McGrew, William C., Caroline E. G. Tutin, and Palmer S. Midgett Jr. 1975. "Tool Use in a Group of Captive Chimpanzees I. Escape." *Zeitschrift fuer Tierpsychologie* 37 (2): 145–62.

McGuire, Molly C., Jennifer Vonk, and Zoe Johnson-Ulrich. 2017. "Ambiguous Results When Using the Ambiguous-Cue Paradigm to Assess Learning and Cognitive Bias in Gorillas and a Black Bear." *Behavioral Sciences* 7 (3): 51.

Mech, L. David. 1999. "Alpha Status, Dominance, and Division of Labor in Wolf Packs." *Canadian Journal of Zoology* 77 (8): 1196–203.

Mech, L. David, Layne G. Adams, Thomas J. Meier, John W. Burch, and Bruce W. Dale. 1998. *The Wolves of Denali*. Minneapolis: University of Minnesota Press.

Mechling, Jay. 1989. "'Banana Cannon' and Other Folk Traditions between Human and Nonhuman Animals." *Western Folklore* 48 (4): 312–23.

Melis, Alicia P., Josep Call, and Michael Tomasello. 2006. "Chimpanzees (*Pan troglodytes*) Conceal Visual and Auditory Information from Others." *Journal of Comparative Psychology* 120 (2): 154–62.

Melis, Alicia P., Brian Hare, and Michael Tomasello. 2006. "Chimpanzees Recruit the Best Collaborators." *Science* 311 (5765): 1297–300.

———. 2008. "Do Chimpanzees Reciprocate Received Favours?" *Animal Behaviour* 76 (3): 951–62.

———. 2009. "Chimpanzees Coordinate in a Negotiation Game." *Evolution and Human Behavior* 30 (6): 381–92.
Meltzoff, Andrew N., Anna Waismeyer, and Alison Gopnik. 2012. "Learning about Causes from People: Observational Causal Learning in 24-Month-Old Infants." *Developmental Psychology*, 48 (5): 1215–28.
Mendes, Natacha, Daniel Hanus, and Josep Call. 2007. "Raising the Level: Orangutans Use Water as a Tool." *Biology Letters* 3: 453–55.
Menzel, Emil W., Jr. 1973. "Further Observations on the Use of Ladders in a Group of Young Chimpanzees." *Folia Primatologica* 19 (6): 450–57.
Menzel, Emil W., Jr., David Premack, and Guy Woodruff. 1978. "Map Reading by Chimpanzees." *Folia Primatologica* 29 (4): 241–49.
Mertens, Claudia, and Dennis C. Turner. 1988. "Experimental Analysis of Human-Cat Interactions during First Encounters." *Anthrozoös* 2 (2): 839–37.
Messy Kids. 2013. "Snail Painting." Accessed February 22, 2019. http://messypreschoolers.blogspot.com/2013/05/snail-painting.html.
Micheletta, Jérôme, and Bridget M. Waller. 2012. "Friendship Affects Gaze Following in a Tolerant Species of Macaque, *Macaca nigra*." *Animal Behaviour* 83 (2): 459–67.
Miklósi, Ádam, and Krisztina Soproni. 2006. "A Comparative Analysis of Animals' Understanding of the Human Pointing Gesture." *Animal Cognition* 9 (2): 81–93.
Milan, Neil F., Balint Z. Kacsoh, and Todd A. Schlenke. 2012. "Alcohol Consumption as Self-Medication against Blood-Borne Parasites in the Fruit Fly." *Current Biology* 22 (6): 488–93.
Miller, W. R., and R. M. Brigham. 1988. "'Ceremonial' Gathering of Black-Billed Magpies (*Pica pica*) after the Sudden Death of a Conspecific." *Murrelet*: 78–79.
Mitani, John C., Toshikazu Hasegawa, Julie Gros-Louis, Peter Marler, and Richard Byrne. 1992. "Dialects in Wild Chimpanzees?" *American Journal of Primatology* 27 (4): 233–43.
Mitani, John C., and David P. Watts. 2005. "Correlates of Territorial Boundary Patrol Behaviour in Wild Chimpanzees." *Animal Behaviour* 70 (5): 1079–86.
Möglich, Michael H. J., and Gary D. Alpert. 1979. "Stone Dropping by *Conomyrma bicolor* (Hymenoptera: Formicidae): A New Technique of Interference Competition." *Behavioral Ecology and Sociobiology* 6 (2): 105–13.
Molloy, Mark. 2019. "World Environment Day Jokes." *My Town Tutors*. June 12, 2019. Accessed June 21, 2019. http://www.mytowntutors.com/world-environment-day-jokes/.
Morris, Desmond. 2009. "Can Jumbo Elephants Really Paint? Intrigued by Stories Naturalist Desmond Morris Sets Out to Find the Truth." *Daily Mail*, February 21, 2009. https://www.dailymail.co.uk/sciencetech/article-1151283/Can-jumbo-elephants-really

-paint--Intrigued-stories-naturalist-Desmond-Morris-set-truth.html.

Morris, Maxinne D. 1986. "Large Scale Deception: Deceit by Captive Elephants." In *Deception: Perspectives on Human and Nonhuman Deceit*, edited by Robert W. Mitchell and Nicholas S. Thompson, 183-91. Albany: State University of New York Press.

Morris, Paul H., Christine Doe, and Emma Godsell. 2008. "Secondary Emotions in Non-Primate Species? Behavioural Reports and Subjective Claims by Animal Owners." *Cognition and Emotion* 22 (1): 3-20.

Morrison, Rachel, and Diana Reiss. 2018. "Precocious Development of Self-Awareness in Dolphins." *PLOS ONE* 13 (1): e0189813. https://doi.org/10.1371/journal.pone.0189813.

Moss, Cynthia J. 1988. *Elephant Memories: Thirteen Years in the Life of an Elephant Family*. New York: William Morrow.

Mulcahy, Nicholas J., and Josep Call. 2006. "Apes Save Tools for Future Use." *Science* 312 (5776): 1038-40.

Müller, Corsin A. 2010. "Do Anvil-Using Banded Mongooses Understand Means-End Relationships? A Field Experiment." *Animal Cognition* 13 (2): 325-30.

Muncer, Steven J., and George Ettlinger. 1981. "Communication by a Chimpanzee: First-Trial Mastery of Word Order That Is Critical for Meaning, But Failure to Negate Conjunctions." *Neuropsychologia* 19 (1): 73-78.

Musgrave, Stephanie, David Morgan, Elizabeth Lonsdorf, Roger Mundry, and Crickette Sanz. 2016. "Tool Transfers Are a Form of Teaching among Chimpanzees." *Scientific Reports* 6: 34783. https://doi-org.proxyiub.uits.iu.edu/10.1038/srep34783.

N., Al. 2016. "Elephant's Memory." *The Spoof!* June 30, 2016. Accessed June 10, 2019. https://www.thespoof.com/jokes/15263/elephants-memory.

Naeger, Nicholas L., Marianne Peso, Naïla Even, Andrew B. Barron, and Gene E. Robinson. 2013. "Altruistic Behavior by Egg-Laying Worker Honeybees." *Current Biology* 23 (16): 1574-78.

Nasrallah, June B. 2002. "Recognition and Rejection of Self in Plant Reproduction." *Science* 296 (5566): 305-8.

National Geographic. 2018. "Crows Trained to Pick Up Trash Teach Humans a Lesson." August 24, 2018. Video, 1:16. https://video.nationalgeographic.com/video/news/00000165-68a0-df80-affd-f9a53be80000.

Nawroth, Christian, Eberhard von Borell, and Jan Langbein. 2015. "'Goats That Stare at Men': Dwarf Goats Alter Their Behaviour in Response to Human Head Orientation, but Do Not Spontaneously Use Head Direction as a Cue in a Food-Related Context." *Animal Cognition* 18 (1): 65-73.

New Horizon. 2014. "Elephants Painting: Genuine Elephant Paintings." February 26, 2014. https://www.youtube.com/watch?v=uypIj_BYzAw.

Nishida, Toshisada. 1980. "Local Differences in Responses to Water among Wild Chimpanzees." *Folia Primatologica* 33 (3): 189-209.

Nishida, Toshisada, and William Wallauer. 2003. "Leaf-Pile Pulling: An Unusual Play Pattern in Wild Chimpanzees." *American Journal of Primatology* 60 (4): 167–73.

Nissani, Moti. 2006. "Do Asian Elephants (*Elephas maximus*) Apply Causal Reasoning to Tool-Use Tasks?" *Journal of Experimental Psychology: Animal Behavior Processes* 32 (1): 91–96.

Njururi, Ngumbu. 1966. *Agikuyu Folk Tales*. London: Oxford University Press.

Nonhuman Rights Project. 2019. Accessed February 16, 2019. https://www.nonhumanrights.org/.

Noser, Rahel, and Richard W. Byrne. 2007. "Mental Maps in Chacma Baboons (*Papio ursinus*): Using Inter-Group Encounters as a Natural Experiment." *Animal Cognition* 10 (3): 331–40.

NOVA. 1974. "The First Signs of Washoe," season 1, episode 10. Aired May 5, 1974. PBS.

NoypiStuffVideos. 2014. "Dog Tries to Save Fish Out of Water." August 12, 2014. YouTube video, 0:44. https://www.youtube.com/watch?v=gBx1bi9BHDg.

Oberliessen, Lina, Julen Hernandez-Lallement, Sandra Schäble, Marijn van Wingerden, Maayke Seinstra, and Tobias Kalenscher. 2016. "Inequity Aversion in Rats, *Rattus norvegicus*." *Animal Behaviour* 115: 157–66.

O'Connell, Sanjida M. 1995. "Empathy in Chimpanzees: Evidence for Theory of Mind?" *Primates* 36 (3): 397–410.

Oldham, Charles. 1930. "On the Shell-Smashing Habit of Gulls." *Ibis* 72 (2): 239–43.

Olson, Christopher R., Devin C. Owen, Andrey E. Ryabinin, and Claudio V. Mello. 2014. "Drinking Songs: Alcohol Effects on Learned Song of Zebra Finches." *PLOS ONE* 9 (12): e115427. https://doi.org/10.1371/journal.pone.0115427.

Orbach, Dara N., Nina Veselka, Yvonne Dzal, Louis Lazure, and M. Brock Fenton. 2010. "Drinking and Flying: Does Alcohol Consumption Affect the Flight and Echolocation Performance of Phyllostomid Bats?" *PLOS ONE* 5 (2): e8993. https://doi.org/10.1371/journal.pone.0008993.

Originalsmit. 2003. "I Got a New Joke." *Home of Poi*. Accessed June 1, 2019. https://www.homeofpoi.com/en/community/forums/topics/242198/2/I-got-a-new-joke-Page-2.

Osterath, Brigitte. 2016. "Do Animals Mourn Their Dead?" *DW*. September 21, 2016. https://www.dw.com/en/do-animals-mourn-their-dead/a-19564029.

Osthaus, Britta, Alan M. Slater, and Stephen E. G. Lea. 2003. "Can Dogs Defy Gravity? A Comparison with the Human Infant and a Non-Human Primate." *Developmental Science* 6 (5): 489–97.

Ostojić, Ljerka, Mladenka Tkalčić, and Nicola S. Clayton. 2015. "Are Owners' Reports of Their Dogs' 'Guilty Look' Influenced by the Dogs' Action and Evidence of the Misdeed?" *Behavioural Processes* 111: 97–100.

Osvath, Mathias. 2009. "Spontaneous Planning for Future Stone Throwing by a Male Chimpanzee." *Current Biology* 19 (5): R190-91. https://doi.org/10.1016/j.cub.2009.01.010.

Osvath, Mathias, and Helena Osvath. 2008. "Chimpanzee (*Pan troglodytes*) and Orangutan (*Pongo abelii*) Forethought: Self-Control and Pre-Experience in the Face of Future Tool Use." *Animal Cognition* 11 (4): 661-74.

Pack, Adam A., and Louis M. Herman. 2007. "The Dolphin's (*Tursiops truncatus*) Understanding of Human Gazing and Pointing: Knowing What and Where." *Journal of Comparative Psychology* 121 (1): 34-45.

Palagi, Elisabetta, Stefania Dall'Olio, Elisa Demuru, and Roscoe Stanyon. 2014. "Exploring the Evolutionary Foundations of Empathy: Consolation in Monkeys." *Evolution and Human Behavior* 35 (4): 341-49.

Palagi, Elisabetta, and Ivan Norscia. 2013. "Bonobos Protect and Console Friends and Kin." *PLOS ONE* 8 (11): e79290. https://doi.org/10.1371/journal.pone.0079290.

Patel, Aniruddh D., John R. Iversen, Micah R. Bregman, and Irena Schulz. 2009. "Experimental Evidence for Synchronization to a Musical Beat in a Nonhuman Animal." *Current Biology* 19 (10): 827-30.

Patrick C. 2019. "A Cow and a Pogo Stick." *Boy's Life: Think and Grin*. Accessed June 1, 2019. https://jokes.boyslife.org/jokes/cow-pogo-stick/.

Patterson, Francine. 1980. "Innovative Uses of Language by a Gorilla: A Case Study." In *Children's Language, Vol. 2*, edited by Keith Nelson, 497-561. New York: Gardner.

Patterson, Francine, and Ronald H. Cohn. 1985. *Koko's Kitten*. New York: Scholastic Books.

———. 1994. "Self-Recognition and Self-Awareness in Lowland Gorillas." In *Self-Awareness in Animals and Humans: Developmental Perspectives*, edited by S. T. Parker, R. W. Mitchell, and M. L. Boccia, 273-90. Cambridge: Cambridge University Press.

Patterson, Francine, and Wendy Gordon. 2002. "Twenty-Seven Years of Project Koko and Michael." In *All Apes Great and Small. Volume 1: African Apes*, edited by Biruté M. F. Galdikas, Nancy Erickson Briggs, Lori K. Sheeran, Gary L. Shapiro, and Jane Goodall, 165-76. Boston: Springer.

Patterson, Francine, and Eugene Linden. 1981. *The Education of Koko*. New York: Holt, Rinehart and Winston.

Peckre, Louise R., Charlotte Defolie, Peter M. Kappeler, and Claudia Fichtel. 2018. "Potential Self-Medication Using Millipede Secretions in Red-Fronted Lemurs: Combining Anointment and Ingestion for a Joint Action against Gastrointestinal Parasites?" *Primates* 59 (5): 483-94.

Pepperberg, Irene M. 2006. "Grey Parrot (*Psittacus erithacus*) Numerical Abilities: Addition and Further Experiments on a Zero-Like Concept." *Journal of Comparative Psychology* 120 (1): 1-11.

Perdue, Bonnie M., Catherine F. Talbot, Adam M. Stone, and Michael J. Beran. 2012. "Putting the Elephant Back in the Herd: Elephant Relative Quantity Judgments Match Those of Other Species." *Animal Cognition* 15 (5): 955-61.

Pfuhl, Gerit. 2012. "Two Strings to Choose From: Do Ravens Pull the Easier One?" *Animal Cognition* 15 (4): 549-57.

Phillips, Webb, and Laurie R. Santos. 2007. "Evidence for Kind Representations in the Absence of Language: Experiments with Rhesus Monkeys (*Macaca mulatta*)." *Cognition* 102 (3): 455-63.

Phillips, Webb, Maya Shankar, and Laurie R. Santos. 2010. "Essentialism in the Absence of Language? Evidence from Rhesus Monkeys (*Macaca mulatta*)." *Developmental Science* 13 (4): F1-F7.

Pickering, Simon P. C., and Laurent Duverge. 1992. "The Influence of Visual Stimuli Provided by Mirrors on the Marching Displays of Lesser Flamingos, *Phoeniconais minor*." *Animal Behaviour* 43 (6): 1048-50.

Pierce, John D., Jr. 1986. "A Review of Tool Use in Insects." *Florida Entomologist* 69 (1): 95-104.

Pierro, Simon. 2020. "Chimp vs. Robot Magic." February 10, 2020. YouTube video, 2:32. https://www.youtube.com/watch?v=OmpE81nv0II.

Pika, Simone, and John Mitani. 2006. "Referential Gestural Communication in Wild Chimpanzees (*Pan troglodytes*)." *Current Biology* 16 (6): R191-92.

Plotnik, Joshua M., and Frans B. M. de Waal. 2014. "Asian Elephants (*Elephas maximus*) Reassure Others in Distress." *PeerJ* 2:e278. https://doi.org/10.7717/peerj.278.

Plotnik, Joshua M., Frans B. M. de Waal, and Diana Reiss. 2006. "Self-Recognition in an Asian Elephant." *Proceedings of the National Academy of Sciences* 103 (45): 17053-57.

Plotnik, Joshua M., Richard Lair, Wirot Suphachoksahakun, and Frans B. M. de Waal. 2011. "Elephants Know When They Need a Helping Trunk in a Cooperative Task." *Proceedings of the National Academy of Sciences* 108 (12): 5116-21.

Poole, Trevor B., and Jane Fish. 1975. "An Investigation of Playful Behaviour in *Rattus norvegicus* and *Mus musculus* (Mammalia)." *Journal of Zoology* 175 (1): 61-71.

Popik, Barry. 2018. "A Lamb, a Drum, and a Snake." *Big Apple*. Accessed June 10, 2019. https://www.barrypopik.com/index.php/new _ york _ city/entry/a _ lamb _ a _ drum _ and _ a _ snake _ fall.

Povinelli, Daniel J. 1989. "Failure to Find Self-Recognition in Asian Elephants (*Elephas maximus*) in Contrast to Their Use of Mirror Cues to Discover Hidden Food." *Journal of Comparative Psychology* 103 (2): 122-31.

———. 2001. *Folk Physics for Apes*. Oxford: Oxford University Press.

———. 2012. *World Without Weight: Perspectives on an Alien Mind*. Oxford: Oxford University Press.

Povinelli, Daniel J., Jesse M. Bering, and Steve Giambrone. 2003. "Chimpanzee 'Pointing': Another Error of the Argument by Analogy." In *Pointing: Where Language, Culture, and Cognition Meet*, edited by Sotaro Kita, 35–68. Mahwah, NJ: Lawrence Erlbaum Associates.

Povinelli, Daniel J., and Timothy J. Eddy. 1997. "Specificity of Gaze-Following in Young Chimpanzees." *British Journal of Developmental Psychology* 15 (2): 213–22.

Povinelli, Daniel J., Kurt E. Nelson, and Sarah T. Boysen. 1992. "Comprehension of Role Reversal in Chimpanzees: Evidence of Empathy?" *Animal Behaviour* 43 (4): 633–40.

Povinelli, Daniel J., Kathleen A. Parks, and Melinda A. Novak. 1992. "Role Reversal by Rhesus Monkeys, but No Evidence of Empathy." *Animal Behaviour* 44 (1): 269–81.

Povinelli, Daniel J., Helen K. Perilloux, James E. Reaux, and Donna T. Bierschwale. 1998. "Young and Juvenile Chimpanzees' (*Pan troglodytes*) Reactions to Intentional versus Accidental and Inadvertent Actions." *Behavioural Processes* 42 (2–3): 205–18.

Premack, David. 1976. *Intelligence in Ape and Man*. Hillsdale, NJ: Erlbaum.

———. 1985. "'Gavagai!' or the Future History of the Animal Language Controversy." *Cognition* 19 (3): 207–96.

Premack, David, and Guy Woodruff. 1978. "Does the Chimpanzee Have a Theory of Mind?" *Behavioral and Brain Sciences* 1 (4): 515–26.

Price, Elizabeth. 2014. "Dog Tries to Save Fish—Proven Wrong." August 15, 2014. YouTube video, 0:54. https://www.youtube.com/watch?v=WlItCRZtMXE.

Prior, Helmut, Ariane Schwarz, and Onur Güntürkün. 2008. "Mirror-Induced Behavior in the Magpie (*Pica pica*): Evidence of Self-Recognition." *PLOS Biology* 6 (8): e202. https://doi.org/10.1371/journal.pbio.0060202.

Proctor, Darby, Rebecca A. Williamson, Frans B. M. de Waal, and Sarah F. Brosnan. 2013. "Chimpanzees Play the Ultimatum Game." *Proceedings of the National Academy of Sciences* 110 (6): 2070–75.

———. 2014. "Gambling Primates: Reactions to a Modified Iowa Gambling Task in Humans, Chimpanzees and Capuchin Monkeys." *Animal Cognition* 17 (4): 983–95.

Proops, Leanne, and Karen McComb. 2010. "Attributing Attention: The Use of Human-Given Cues by Domestic Horses (*Equus caballus*)." *Animal Cognition* 13 (2): 197–205.

Prozesky-Schulze, L., O. P. M. Prozesky, F. Anderson, and G. J. J. Van Der Merwe. 1975. "Use of a Self-Made Sound Baffle by a Tree Cricket." *Nature* 255: 142–43.

Pruetz, Jill D., and Paco Bertolani. 2007. "Savanna Chimpanzees, *Pan troglodytes verus*, Hunt with Tools." *Current Biology* 17 (5): 412–17.

———. 2009. "Chimpanzee (*Pan troglodytes verus*) Behavioral Responses to Stresses Associated with Living in a Savanna-Mosaic Environment: Implications for Hominin Adaptations to Open Habitats." *PaleoAnthropology*: 252–62.

Pruetz, Jill D., and Thomas. C. LaDuke. 2010. "Brief Communication: Reaction to Fire by Savanna Chimpanzees (*Pan troglodytes verus*) at Fongoli, Senegal: Conceptualization of 'Fire Behavior' and the Case for a Chimpanzee Model." *American Journal of Physical Anthropology*, 141 (4): 646-50.

Pug, Momo J. 2017. "LOL Clean Cat Jokes." *Pug City*. October 28, 2017. Accessed June 1, 2019. https://pugcity.org/bonusstuff/clean-cat-jokes-for-kids.

Raby, Caroline R., Dean M. Alexis, Anthony Dickinson, and Nicola S. Clayton. 2007. "Planning for the Future by Western Scrub-Jays." *Nature* 445 (7130): 919-21.

Radin, Paul, and Einore Marvel, eds. 1952. *African Folktales and Sculpture*. Bollingen Foundation, Series XXII. New York: Pantheon.

Raihani, Nichola J., Alex Thornton, and Redouan Bshary. 2012. "Punishment and Cooperation in Nature." *Trends in Ecology and Evolution* 27 (5): 288-95.

Raza, Mohsin. 2012. "Russian Angry Birds: Crows 'Attack' MPs Cars with Stones." *RT News*, October 22, 2012. https://www.rt.com/news/crows-stone-cars-sverdlovsk-962/.

Reader, Simon M., Jeremy R. Kendal, and Kevin N. Laland. 2003. "Social Learning of Foraging Sites and Escape Routes in Wild Trinidian Guppies." *Animal Behaviour* 66: 729-39.

Reichard, Ulrich. 1995. "Extra-Pair Copulations in a Monogamous Gibbon (*Hylobates lar*)." *Ethology* 100 (2): 99-112.

Reiss, Diana, and Lori Marino. 2001. "Mirror Self-Recognition in the Bottlenose Dolphin: A Case of Cognitive Convergence." *Proceedings of the National Academy of Sciences* 98 (10): 5937-42.

Reneaux, J. J. 1992. *Cajun Folktales*. Little Rock: August House.

Rensch, Bernhard. 1957. "The Intelligence of Elephants." *Scientific American* 196 (2): 44-49.

Riedl, Katrin, Keith Jensen, Josep Call, and Michael Tomasello. 2012. "No Third-Party Punishment in Chimpanzees." *Proceedings of the National Academy of Sciences* 109 (37): 14824-29.

Riehl, Christina, and Megan E. Frederickson. 2016. "Cheating and Punishment in Cooperative Animal Societies." *Philosophical Transactions of the Royal Society B* 371: 20150090. https://doi.org/10.1098/rstb.2015.0090.

Riley, Henry Thomas, ed. 1909. *A Dictionary of Latin and Greek Quotations, Proverbs, Maxims and Mottos*. London: George Bell and Sons.

Ristau, Carolyn A., and Donald Robbins. 1982. "Language in the Great Apes: A Critical Review." In *Advances in the Study of Behavior vol. 12*, edited by J. F. Rosenblatt, R. B. Hinde, C. Beer, and M. C. Busnel, 141-255. New York: Academic.

Rivas, Esteban. 2005. "Recent Use of Signs by Chimpanzees (*Pan troglodytes*) in Interactions with Humans." *Journal of Comparative Psychology* 119 (4): 404-17.

Robe, Stanley L. 1973. *Index of Mexican Folktales, Including Narrative Texts from Mexico, Central America, and the Hispanic United States*. Berkeley: University of California Press.

Roberts, William A. 2016. "Episodic Memory: Rats Master Multiple Memories." *Current Biology* 26 (20): 2821-26.

Robinson, Gene E. 1992. "Regulation of Division of Labor in Insect Societies." *Annual Review of Entomology* 37 (1): 637-65.

Rogerson, J. 1992. *Training Your Dog*. London: Popular Dogs.

Rooney, Nicola J., John W. S. Bradshaw, and Ian H. Robinson. 2000. "A Comparison of Dog-Dog and Dog-Human Play Behaviour." *Applied Animal Behaviour Science* 66 (3): 235-48.

———. 2001. "Do Dogs Respond to Play Signals Given by Humans?" *Animal Behaviour* 61 (4): 715-22.

Rose, M. D. 1977. "Interspecific Play between Free Ranging Guerezas (*Colobus guereza*) and Vervet Monkeys (*Cercopithecus aethiops*)." *Primates* 18 (4): 957-64.

Rueppell, Olav, Miranda K. Hayworth, and N. P. Ross. 2010. "Altruistic Self-Removal of Health-Compromised Honey Bee Workers from Their Hive." *Journal of Evolutionary Biology* 23 (7): 1538-46.

Rutte, Claudia, and Michael Taborsky. 2008. "The Influence of Social Experience on Cooperative Behaviour of Rats (*Rattus norvegicus*): Direct vs. Generalised Reciprocity." *Behavioral Ecology and Sociobiology* 62 (4): 499-505.

Samuel French. 2019. "Elephant's Graveyard (Full Length Version)." Accessed March 1, 2019. https://www.samuelfrench.com/p/1939/elephants-graveyard-full-length-version/.

Sanders, Clinton R. 1993. "Understanding Dogs: Caretakers' Attributions of Mindedness in Canine-Human Relationships." *Journal of Contemporary Ethnography* 22 (2): 205-26.

Santos, Laurie R., Aaron G. Nissen, and Jonathan A. Ferrugia. 2006. "Rhesus Monkeys, *Macaca mulatta*, Know What Others Can and Cannot Hear." *Animal Behaviour* 71 (5): 1175-81.

Saucier, Corinne L. 1972. *Folk Tales from French Louisiana*. Baton Rouge: Claitor's.

Sauther, Michelle L. 1994. "Wild Plant Use by Pregnant and Lactating Ringtailed Lemurs, with Implications for Early Hominid Foraging." In *Eating on The Wild Side: The Pharmacologic, Ecologic and Social Implications of Using Noncultigens* edited by Nina L. Etkin, 240-56. Tucson: University of Arizona Press.

Schaller, G. B., and A. Hamer. 1978. "Rutting Behavior of Père David's Deer (*Elaphurus davidianus*)." *Der Zoologische Garten* 48: 1-15.

Schiller, Paul H. 1949. "Analysis of Detour Behavior. I. Learning of Roundabout Pathways in Fish." *Journal of Comparative and Physiological Psychology* 42 (6): 463-75.

Schino, Gabriele. 2007. "Grooming and Agonistic Support: A Meta-Analysis of Primate Reciprocal Altruism." *Behavioral Ecology* 18 (1): 115-20.

Schloegl, Christian, Judith Schmidt, Markus Boeckle, Brigitte M. Weiß, and Kurt Kotrschal. 2012. "Grey Parrots Use Inferential Reasoning Based on Acoustic Cues Alone." *Proceedings of the Royal Society B* 279: 4135-42.

Schneider, Christel, Josep Call, and Katja Liebal. 2010. "Do Bonobos Say NO by Shaking Their Head?" *Primates* 51 (3): 199-202.

Schrauf, Cornelia, and Josep Call. 2009. "Great Apes' Performance in Discriminating Weight and Achromatic Color." *Animal Cognition* 12 (4): 567–74.

Schrauf, Cornelia, Josep Call, Koki Fuwa, and Satoshi Hirata. 2012. "Do Chimpanzees Use Weight to Select Hammer Tools?" *PLOS ONE* 7 (7): e41044. https://doi.org/10.1371/journal.pone.0041044.

Seed, Amanda, and Richard Byrne. 2010. "Animal Tool-Use." *Current Biology* 20 (23): R1032–39.

Seed, Amanda, Eleanor Seddon, Bláthnaid Greene, and Josep Call. 2012. "Chimpanzee 'Folk Physics': Bringing Failures into Focus." *Philosophical Transactions of the Royal Society of London B: Biological Sciences* 367 (1603): 2743–52.

Shannon, Robert V. 2016. "Is Birdsong More Like Speech or Music?" *Trends in Cognitive Science* 20 (4): 245–47.

Sheskin, Mark, and Laurie Santos. 2012. "The Evolution of Morality: Which Aspects of Human Moral Concerns Are Shared with Nonhuman Primates." In *The Oxford Handbook of Comparative Evolutionary Psychology*, edited by Jennifer Vonk and Todd K. Shackelford, 434–49. Oxford: Oxford University Press.

Shine, Richard. 2012. "Sex at the Snake Den: Lust, Deception, and Conflict in the Mating System of Red-Sided Gartersnakes." *Advances in the Study of Behavior* 44: 1–51.

Shou, Laura. 2018. "List of Math Jokes." *Math.Princeton*. Accessed June 15, 2019. https://web.math.princeton.edu/~lshou/mathjokes.html.

Shumaker, Robert W., Kristina R. Walkup, and Benjamin B. Beck. 2001. *Animal Tool Behavior: The Use and Manufacture of Tools by Animals*. Baltimore: Johns Hopkins University Press.

Shurkin, Joel. 2014. "News Feature: Animals That Self-Medicate." *Proceedings of the National Academy of Sciences* 111 (49): 17339–41.

Siegel, Ronald K. 1984. "LSD-Induced Effects in Elephants: Comparisons with Musth Behavior." *Bulletin of the Psychonomic Society* 22 (1): 53–56.

Siegel, Ronald K., and Mark Brodie. 1984. "Alcohol Self-Administration by Elephants." *Bulletin of the Psychonomic Society* 22 (1): 49–52.

Silberberg, Alan, Candice Allouch, Samantha Sandfort, David Kearns, Heather Karpel, and Burton Slotnick. 2014. "Desire for Social Contact, Not Empathy, May Explain 'Rescue' Behavior in Rats." *Animal Cognition* 17 (3): 609–18.

Silk, Joan B., Sarah F. Brosnan, Jennifer Vonk, Joseph Henrich, Daniel J. Povinelli, Amanda S. Richardson, Susan P. Lambeth, Jenny Mascaro, and Steven J. Schapiro. 2005. "Chimpanzees Are Indifferent to the Welfare of Unrelated Group Members." *Nature* 437 (7063): 1357–59.

Simply Fit. 2015. "Orangutan Finds Magic Trick Hilarious." December 9, 2015. YouTube video, 0:38. https://www.youtube.com/watch?v=OLrYzY3jVPY.

Skerry, A. E., M. Sheskin, and L. R. Santos. 2011. "Capuchin Monkeys Are Not Prosocial in an Instrumental Helping Task." *Animal Cognition* 14 (5): 647–54.

Small, Maureen P., and Robert W. Thacker. 1994. "Land Hermit Crabs Use Odors of Dead Conspecifics to Locate Shells." *Journal of Experimental Marine Biology and Ecology* 182 (2): 169–82.

SmileJokes.com. 2013. "Peek a Boo." Accessed June 1, 2019. http://smilejokes.com/jokes/halloween-jokes/peek-a-boo/.

Smith, J. David, Jonathan Schull, Jared Strote, Kelli McGee, Roian Egnor, and Linda Erb. 1955. "The Uncertain Response in the Bottlenosed Dolphin (*Tursiops truncatus*)." *Journal of Experimental Psychology: General* 124 (4): 391–408.

Smith, Margaret. 2015. "Debunking the 'Ant vs. Grasshopper' Myth." *JSTOR Daily*. June 1, 2019. https://daily.jstor.org/debunking-ant-vs-grasshopper-myth/.

Soares, Marta C., Sónia C. Cardoso, Alexandra S. Grutter, Rui F. Oliveira, and Redouan Bshary. 2014. "Cortisol Mediates Cleaner Wrasse Switch from Cooperation to Cheating and Tactical Deception." *Hormones and Behavior* 66 (2): 346–50.

Sosa-Calvo, Jeffrey, Ana Ješovnik, Heraldo L. Vasconcelos, Mauricio Bacci Jr., and Ted R. Schultz. 2017. "Rediscovery of the Enigmatic Fungus-Farming Ant '*Mycetosoritis*' asper Mayr (Hymenoptera: Formicidae): Implications for Taxonomy, Phylogeny, and the Evolution of Agriculture in Ants." *PLOS ONE* 12 (5): e0176498. https://doi.org/10.1371/journal.pone.0176498.

Souza-Alves, João Pedro, Natasha M. Albuquerque, Luana Vinhas, Thayane S. Cardoso, Raone Beltrão-Mendes, and Leandro Jerusalinsky. 2018. "Self-Anointing Behaviour in Captive Titi Monkeys (*Callicebus* spp.)." *Primate Biology* 5 (1): 1–5.

Souza-Alves, João Pedro, and Stephen F. Ferrari. 2010. "Responses of Wild Titi Monkeys, *Callicebus coimbrai* (Primates: Platyrrhini: Pitheciidae), to the Habituation Process." *Zoologia* 27 (6): 861–66.

Spinage, Clive A. 1994. *Elephants*. London: T & A D Poyser Natural History.

Stake, Jeffrey Evans. 2004. "The Property 'Instinct.'" *Philosophical Transactions of the Royal Society* 359: 1763–74.

Stancher, G., R. Rugani, L. Regolin, and G. Vallortigara. 2015. "Numerical Discrimination by Frogs (*Bombina orientalis*)." *Animal Cognition* 18 (1): 219–29.

Stanton, Lauren, Emily Davis, Shylo Johnson, Amy Gilbert, and Sarah Benson-Amram. 2017. "Adaptation of the Aesop's Fable Paradigm for Use with Raccoons (*Procyon Lotor*): Considerations for Future Application in Non-Avian and Non-Primate Species." *Animal Cognition* 20 (6): 1147–52.

Stewart, Fiona A., Jill D. Pruetz, and Mike H. Hansell. 2007. "Do Chimpanzees Build Comfortable Nests?" *American Journal of Primatology* 69 (8): 930–39.

Strassmann, Joan E. 2004. "Animal Behaviour: Rank Crime and Punishment." *Nature* 432: 160–62.

Stulp, Gert, Nathan J. Emery, Simon Verhulst, and Nicola S. Clayton. 2009. "Western Scrub-Jays Conceal Auditory Information

When Competitors Can Hear but Cannot See." *Biology Letters* 5: 583–85.

Suárez, Susan D., and Gordon G. Gallup Jr. 1981. "Self-Recognition in Chimpanzees and Orangutans, but Not Gorillas." *Journal of Human Evolution* 10 (2): 175–88.

Suárez-Rodríguez, Monserrat, Isabel López-Rull, and Constantino Macías Garcia. 2013. "Incorporation of Cigarette Butts into Nests Reduces Nest Ectoparasite Load in Urban Birds: New Ingredients for an Old Recipe?" *Biology Letters* 9 (1): 20120931.

Sugiyama, Yukimaru, Hiroyuki Kurita, Takeshi Matsui, Satoshi Kimoto, and Tadatoshi Shimomura. 2009. "Carrying of Dead Infants by Japanese Macaque (*Macaca fuscata*) Mothers." *Anthropological Science* 117 (2): 113–19.

Synge, J. M. (1907) 1992. *The Aran Islands*. New York: Penguin.

Takeshita, Hideko, and Jan A. R. A. M. van Hooff. 1996. "Tool Use by Chimpanzees (*Pan troglodytes*) of the Arnhem Zoo Community." *Japanese Psychological Research* 38 (3): 163–73.

Tanaka, T., and Y. Ono. 1978. "The Tool Use by Foragers of *Aphaenogaster famelica*." *Japanese Journal of Ecology* 28 (1): 495–98.

Taylor, Alex H., Lucy G. Cheke, Anna Waismeyer, Andrew N. Meltzoff, Rachael Miller, Alison Gopnik, Nicola S. Clayton, and Russell D. Gray. 2014. "Of Babies and Birds: Complex Tool Behaviours Are Not Sufficient for the Evolution of the Ability to Create a Novel Causal Intervention." *Proceeding of the Royal Society B* 281 (1787): 20140837. https://www.ncbi.nlm.nih.gov/pmc/articles/PMC4071556/.

Taylor, Alex H., Gavin R. Hunt, Felipe S. Medina, and Russell D. Gray. 2009. "Do New Caledonian Crows Solve Physical Problems through Causal Reasoning?" *Proceedings of the Royal Society B* 276 (1655): 247–54.

Taylor, Katherine, Allison Visvader, Elise Nowbahari, and Karen L. Hollis. 2013. "Precision Rescue Behavior in North American Ants." *Evolutionary Psychology* 11 (3): 665–77.

Tebbich, Sabine, Amanda M. Seed, Nathan J. Emery, and Nicola S. Clayton. 2007. "Non-Tool-Using Rooks, *Corvus frugilegus*, Solve the Trap-Tube Problem." *Animal Cognition* 10 (2): 225–31.

Techy, Devin. 2017. "Monkeys React to Magic." September 25, 2017. YouTube video, 3:42. https://www.youtube.com/watch?v=spMkaJp975s&t=6s%5D.

Teleki, Geza. 1973. "Group Response to the Accidental Death of a Chimpanzee in Gombe National Park, Tanzania." *Folia Primatologica* 20: 81–94.

Terleph, Thomas A., S. Malaivijitnond, and Ulrich H. Reichard. 2018. "An Analysis of White-Handed Gibbon Male Song Reveals Speech-Like Phrases." *American Journal of Physical Anthropology* 166 (3): 649–60.

Thomsen, Liat R., Ruairidh D. Campbell, and Frank Rosell. 2007. "Tool-Use in a Display Behaviour by Eurasian Beavers (*Castor fiber*)." *Animal Cognition* 10 (4): 477–82.

Tierney, John. 2010. "When It Comes to Sex, Chimps Need Help, Too," *New York Times*, May 3, 2010. https://www.nytimes.com/2010/05/04/science/04tier.html?mtrref=www.google.com.

Tolman, Edward C. 1948. "Cognitive Maps in Rats and Men." *Psychological Review* 55 (4): 189–208.

Tomasello, Michael. 2017. "What Did We Learn from the Ape Language Studies?" In *Bonobos: Unique in Mind, Brain, and Behavior*, edited by Brian Hare and Shinya Yamamoto, 95–104. Oxford: Oxford University Press.

Toth, Nicholas, Kathy D. Schick, E. Sue Savage-Rumbaugh, Rose A. Sevcik, and Duane M. Rumbaugh. 1993. "Pan the Tool-Maker: Investigations into the Stone Tool-Making and Tool-Using Capabilities of a Bonobo (*Pan paniscus*)." *Journal of Archaeological Science* 20 (1): 81–91.

Treisman, Michel. 1978. "Bird Song Dialects, Repertoire Size, and Kin Association." *Animal Behaviour* 26: 814–17.

Udell, Monique A. R., Nicole R. Dorey, and Clive D. L. Wynne. 2008. "Wolves Outperform Dogs in Following Human Social Cues." *Animal Behaviour* 76 (6): 1767–73.

———. 2011. "Can Your Dog Read Your Mind? Understanding the Causes of Canine Perspective Taking." *Learning and Behavior* 39 (4): 289–302.

USA Today. 2017. "Tortoise Races Hare, Guess What Happens." March 13, 2017. YouTube video, 0:43. https://www.youtube.com/watch?v=FrL9iYXGSX4.

Van der Merwe, Marius, and Joel S. Brown. 2008. "Mapping the Landscape of Fear of the Cape Ground Squirrel (*Xerus inauris*)." *Journal of Mammalogy* 89 (5): 1162–69.

Van Hooff, Jan A. R. A. M., and Bas Lukkenaar. 2015. "Captive Chimpanzee Takes Down a Drone: Tool Use toward a Flying Object." *Primates* 56 (4): 289–92.

Van Lawick-Goodall, Jane. 1968. "The Behaviour of Free-Living Chimpanzees in the Gombe Stream Reserve." *Animal Behaviour Monographs* 1 (3): 161–311.

Van Lawick-Goodall, Jane, and Hugo van Lawick-Goodall. 1966. "Use of Tools by the Egyptian Vulture, *Neophron percnopterus*." *Nature* 212: 1468–69.

Veà, Joaquim, and Jordi Sabater-Pi. 1998. "Spontaneous Pointing Behaviour in the Wild Pygmy Chimpanzee (*Pan paniscus*)." *Folia Primatologica* 69 (5): 289–90.

Vessels, Jane. 1985. "Koko's Kitten." *National Geographic* 167 (1): 110–13.

Viraldcom. 2010. "Cat Tries to Revive Dead Friend." May 2, 2010. YouTube video, 4:10. https://www.youtube.com/watch?v=zaP7STV1aFs.

Virányi, Zsófia, Márta Gácsi, Enikő Kubinyi, József Topál, Beatrix Belényi, Dorottya Ujfalussy, and Ádám Miklósi. 2008. "Comprehension of Human Pointing Gestures in Young Human-Reared Wolves (*Canis lupus*) and Dogs (*Canis familiaris*)." *Animal Cognition* 11 (3): 373–87.

Visalberghi, Elisabetta, Dorothy M. Fragaszy, E. Ottoni, P. Izar, M. Gomes de Oliveira, and F. R. D. Andrade. 2007. "Characteristics of Hammer Stones and Anvils Used by Wild Bearded Capuchin Monkeys (*Cebus libidinosus*) to Crack Open Palm Nuts." *American Journal of Physical Anthropology* 132 (3): 426–44.

Visalberghi, Elisabetta, Dorothy M. Fragaszy, and Sue Savage-Rumbaugh. 1995. "Performance in a Tool-Using Task by Common Chimpanzees (*Pan troglodytes*), Bonobos (*Pan paniscus*), an Orangutan (*Pongo pygmaeus*), and Capuchin Monkeys (*Cebus apella*)." *Journal of Comparative Psychology* 109 (1): 52–60.

Visalberghi, Elisabetta, and Cecile Néel. 2003. "Tufted Capuchins (*Cebus apella*) Use Weight and Sound to Choose between Full and Empty Nuts." *Ecological Psychology* 15 (3): 215–28.

Visalberghi, Elisabetta, Benedetta Pellegrini Quarantotti, and Flaminia Tranchida. 2000. "Solving a Cooperation Task without Taking into Account the Partner's Behavior: The Case of Capuchin Monkeys (*Cebus apella*)." *Journal of Comparative Psychology* 114 (3): 297–301.

Vlamings, Petra H. J. M., Brian Hare, and Josep Call. 2010. "Reaching around Barriers: The Performance of the Great Apes and 3–5-Year-Old Children." *Animal Cognition* 13 (2): 273–85.

Völter, Christoph J., and Josep Call. 2014. "Great Apes (*Pan paniscus, Pan troglodytes, Gorilla gorilla, Pongo abelii*) Follow Visual Trails to Locate Hidden Food." *Journal of Comparative Psychology* 128 (2): 199–208.

———. 2018. "Intuitive Optics: What Great Apes Infer from Mirrors and Shadows." *Animal Cognition* 21 (4): 493–512.

Vonk, Jennifer, Sarah F. Brosnan, Joan B. Silk, Joseph Henrich, Amanda S. Richardson, Susan P. Lambeth, Steven J. Schapiro, and Daniel J. Povinelli. 2008. "Chimpanzees Do Not Take Advantage of Very Low Cost Opportunities to Deliver Food to Unrelated Group Members." *Animal Behaviour* 75 (5): 1757–70.

Vonk, Jennifer, and Daniel J. Povinelli. 2011. "Social and Physical Reasoning in Human-Reared Chimpanzees: New Data from a Set of Preliminary Studies." In *Perception, Causation, and Objectivity: Issues in Philosophy and Psychology*, edited by Johannes Roessler, Hemdat Lerman, and Naomi Eilan, 342–52. Oxford: Oxford University Press.

Wagner, C. Michael, Eric M. Stroud, and Trevor D. Meckley. 2011. "A Deathly Odor Suggests a New Sustainable Tool for Controlling a Costly Invasive Species." *Canadian Journal of Fisheries and Aquatic Sciences* 68 (7): 1157–60.

Wallis, D. I. 1961. "Food-Sharing Behaviour of the Ants *Formica sanguinea* and *Formica fusca*." *Behaviour* 17 (1): 17–47.

Warneken, Felix, and Alexandra G. Rosati. 2015. "Cognitive Capacities for Cooking in Chimpanzees." *Proceedings of the Royal Society B* 282 (1809). https://doi-org /10.1098/rspb.2015.0229.

Warneken, Felix, and Michael Tomasello. 2006. "Altruistic Helping in Human Infants and Young Chimpanzees." *Science* 311 (5765): 1301–3.

Warren, Ymke, and Elizabeth A. Williamson. 2004. "Transport of Dead Infant Mountain Gorillas by Mothers and Unrelated Females." *Zoo Biology* 23 (4): 375–78.

Wascher, Claudia A. F., and Thomas Bugnyar. 2013. "Behavioral Responses to Inequity in Reward Distribution and Working Effort in Crows and Ravens." *PLOS ONE* 8 (2): e56885. https://doi.org/10.1371/journal.pone.0056885.

Watts, David P., and John C. Mitani. 2001. "Boundary Patrols and Intergroup Encounters in Wild Chimpanzees." *Behaviour* 138 (3): 299–327.

Webb, Christine E., Teresa Romero, Becca Franks, and Frans B. M. de Waal. 2017. "Long-Term Consistency in Chimpanzee Consolation Behaviour Reflects Empathetic Personalities." *Nature Communications* 8 (1): 292.

Weldon, Paul J., Jeffrey R. Aldrich, Jerome A. Klun, James E. Oliver, and Mustapha Debboun. 2003. "Benzoquinones from Millipedes Deter Mosquitoes and Elicit Self-Anointing in Capuchin Monkeys (*Cebus spp.*)." *Naturwissenschaften* 90 (7): 301–4.

West, Louis Jolyon, Chester M. Pierce, and Warren D. Thomas. 1962. "Lysergic Acid Diethylamide: Its Effects on a Male Asiatic Elephant." *Science* 138 (3545): 1100–3.

Whiteley, J. D., J. S. Pritchard, and P. J. B. Slater. 1990. "Strategies of Mussel Dropping by Carrion Crows *Corvus c. corone*." *Bird Study* 37 (1): 12–17.

Whiten, Andrew, and Richard W. Byrne. 1988. "Tactical Deception in Primates." *Behavioral and Brain Sciences* 11 (2): 233–44.

Whiten, Andrew, Jane Goodall, William C. McGrew, Toshisada Nishida, Vernon Reynolds, Yukimaru Sugiyama, Caroline E. G. Tutin, Richard W. Wrangham, and Christophe Boesch. 2001. "Charting Cultural Variation in Chimpanzees." *Behaviour* 138 (11–12): 1481–516.

Whiting, Bartlett Jere. 1977. *Early American Proverbs and Proverbial Phrases*. Cambridge, MA: Harvard University Press.

Whitlock, Jeff. 2015. "Animal Jokes." *The Online Zoo*. Accessed June 1, 2019. http://www.theonlinezoo.com/jokes.html.

Wickler, Wolfgang, and Uta Seibt. 1997. "Aimed Object-Throwing by a Wild African Elephant in an Interspecific Encounter." *Ethology* 103 (5): 365–68.

Wikipedia. 2018. "Michael (gorilla)," last modified December 9, 2018. Accessed January 19, 2019. https://en.wikipedia.org/wiki/Michael_(gorilla).

———. 2019a. "Alex (parrot)," last modified January 14, 2019. Accessed January 19, 2019. https://en.wikipedia.org/wiki/Alex_(parrot).

———. 2019b. "*Lancelot Link, Secret Chimp*." Last modified January 24, 2019. Accessed February 22, 2019. https://en.wikipedia.org/wiki/Lancelot_Link,_Secret_Chimp.

Wilkinson, Anna, Isabella Mandl, Thomas Bugnyar, and Ludwig Huber. 2010. "Gaze Following in the Red-Footed Tortoise (*Geochelone carbonaria*)." *Animal Cognition* 13 (5): 765–69.

Williams, Jimmy. 2009. "Notable Quotes." *Wildtree Farm*. Accessed June 1, 2019. http://wildtreefarm.com/quotes.htm.

Witmer, Lightner. 1909. "A Monkey with a Mind." *Psychological Clinic* 3 (7): 179–205.

Wolfe, John B. 1936. "Effectiveness of Token Rewards for Chimpanzees." *Comparative Psychology Monographs* 12: 1–72.
Woodruff, Guy, and David Premack. 1979. "Intentional Communication in the Chimpanzee: The Development of Deception." *Cognition* 7 (4): 333–62.
Worstjokesever.com. 2014. "Cheetah Jokes." Accessed June 1, 2019. https://worstjokesever.com/cheetah.
———. 2017. "Cow." Accessed June 1, 2019. https://worstjokesever.com/cow.
Xitco, Mark J., John D. Gory, and Stan A. Kuczaj. 2004. "Dolphin Pointing Is Linked to the Attentional Behavior of a Receiver." *Animal Cognition* 7 (4): 231–38.
Yamagiwa, Juichi, Takakazu Yumoto, Mwanza Ndunda, and Tamaki Maruhashi. 1988. "Evidence of Tool-Use by Chimpanzees (*Pan troglodytes schweinfurthii*) for Digging Out a Bee-Nest in the Kahuzi-Biega National Park, Zaire." *Primates* 29 (3): 405–11.
Yamamoto, Shinya, and Masayuki Tanaka. 2009. "Do Chimpanzees (*Pan troglodytes*) Spontaneously Take Turns in a Reciprocal Cooperation Task?" *Journal of Comparative Psychology* 123 (3): 242–49.
Yamashita, Nayuta, Chia L. Tan, Christopher J. Vinyard, and Cathy Williams. 2010. "Semi-Quantitative Tests of Cyanide in Foods and Excreta of Three Hapalemur Species in Madagascar." *American Journal of Primatology* 72 (1): 56–61.
Yerkes, Robert M. 1916. "The Mental Life of Monkeys and Apes: A Study of Ideational Behavior." *Behavior Monographs* 3 (Serial number 12): 11–45.
———. 1943. *Chimpanzees: A Laboratory Colony*. New Haven, CT: Yale University Press.
Young, Jessica. 2009. "Horse Quotes." *Learn about Horses*. Accessed June 1, 2019. https://www.learn-about-horses.com/horse-quotes.html/.
Zhou, Wenyi, Andrea G. Hohmann, and Jonathon D. Crystal. 2012. "Rats Answer an Unexpected Question after Incidental Encoding." *Current Biology* 22 (12): 1149–53.
Zimmerman, Klaus. 1952. "Werkzeug-Benutzung durch eine Zwergmaus." *Zeitschrift für Tierpsychologie* 9 (1): 121–22.
Zito, Michael, Sian Evans, and Paul J. Weldon. 2003. "Owl Monkeys (*Aotus spp.*) Self-Anoint with Plants and Millipedes." *Folia Primatologica* 74 (3): 159–61.

DANIEL J. POVINELLI and K. BRANDON BARKER contributed equally to the creation of this index.

INDEX

Italicized page numbers refer to illustrations.

Aelian, 26, 28
Aesop, 16, 86
Aesop's Fable Paradigm: anthropomorphism and, 9; apparatus and, 66; causal relationships and, 17, 19, 38, 56nn5–6; child psychology and, 38–39; criteria for inclusion in meta-analysis, 45–46, 56n9; crows' tool use in nature and, 41, 119–120; crows' training and, 41–42, 56n8; cultural background and, 14; depiction of, *40*; as experimental method, 38; in FOMANCOG, 184; genre theory and, 100–101; moral of folktale and, 15–16, 19; perceptual contact and, 67; purpose of tale and, 73; questions for meta-analysis of, 45; results of meta-analysis and, 47–48, *48*; Richards's analysis and, 13–14; role of human-like reasoning, 18; statistical approach of meta-analysis, 46–47; treatment of experimental data in, 42–43, *44*, 45, 57nn10–11; trial-and-error hypothesis and, 18–19, 38, 42–43, 49; volume of research on, 41
alcohol/drugs, 139–141
alligators, 9, 132, 135, 137, 155, 160
altruistic behaviors, 142–145
ambiguity, 188
American Folklore Society, 2, 8
animal cognition: altruistic behaviors and, 142–145; anthropomorphism and, 9, 62, 95; awe and, 110–112; bartering and, 153; bees and, 92–93; causal reasoning and, 17, 19, 38, 56nn5–6, 69–70, 72, 188–189; children and, 38–39, 50, 55n1; claims of human-like cognition and, 39; communication and, 39; complex cognition and, 41, 49; difficulty of understanding, 98–99; Doctor Fomomindo and, 8–9; end-point training effect and, 63; fable about challenges of studying, 107–108; folklore and, 6–7; generalization and, 71; higher-order abstractions and, 61–64, 106–107; language and, 129–135; mental continuity with humans and, 61; methodological shortcoming of research in, 53; perceptual contact and, 66–67; perceptual-motor feedback hypothesis and, 18–19; popular press and, 40; recognition of zero concept and, 92; scrub-jay imperative, 68–69; self-awareness and, 60, 63; spatial/temporal planning behaviors, 175; subjectivity and research on, 50, 106; teaching and, 135; three-trial role and, 65; tools and, 39; trial-and-error learning and, 63–64; *what*-systems and, 72; wire-bending task and crows and, 65
animal question, 12–14; difficulty in solving and, 19; historical view of, 96–99, 102n1; humanness and, 61; popular press and, 41; Richards on, 19n5
animals: adornment and, 183; alcohol/drugs and, 139–141; ambiguity and, 188; analogies and, 194; *and* vs. *or* problems and, 185; appearance vs. reality problems, 185–186; art and, 101, 178–183; awareness of own demise, 177; awe and, 110–112; bartering and, 153; causal reasoning and, 188–189; coercive behavior, 167–169; consolation behaviors and, 153–154; consoling behavior, 153–154; cooperation of, 154–156; curiosity of, 188; current literature about, 13; dangers of objective description of, 4; deception and, 156–160; desire for freedom and, 176; domestication, 164–167; embarrassment and, 177–178; escape behaviors, 186–188; essentialism and, 189–190; fairness concept and, 151–153; funeral rituals and, 113–114; gambling and, 139; game playing and, 39, 135–139; gravity and, 188; grief and, 114–116; historical trends in ideas about cognition and, 96–99, 102n1; human interest in, 95;

animals (*Cont.*)
  imitation and, 169; inhibitory control, 192; interspecies friendship, 167; intoxication and drugs and, 139–141; knots and strings and, 128–129; ladders and, 121; language and, 96–98, 129–135; magic and, 198–200; maps and, 184–185; math and, 191; medicine and, 195–198; memory and, 192–194; mind-reading in, 147–149; mirror self-recognition and, 60, 73n1, 170–173, 170n274; money and, 190–191; negative emotions and, 149–151; neurotic behavior, 169; ownership and, 176–177; perceptions of others and, 145–147; play behaviors, 141–142; projectiles and, 121–126; projection onto, 91, 100–101; questions about differences between humans and, 12–13; reactions to death and, 114–118; ritualized patterns of behavior and, 112–118; self-awareness and, 170–174; selfishness and, 153; spatial/temporal memory and, 174; as stand-ins for humans in fables, 82, 86; sticks as tools and, 118–121; tools for transporting food and, 126–128; traditions and, 202–203; uses of by psychologists, 13–14; warfare activity, 160–164; weight and, 194. See also individual types
Animals, Animals, Animals (television show), 10n2
anthropomorphism, 101; Aesop's Fable Paradigm and, 9, 68; animal cognition and, 9, 62, 95; bees and, 92; Gould and, 81; guilt in pets and, 150n187; philosophy and, 86; trends in scientific research and, 101
ant-lions, 125
ants, 125, 127, 128, 135, 144, 156, 162, 164, 173, 177, 198
apes: altruistic behaviors and, 142; *and* vs. *or* problems and, 185; appearance vs. reality problems and, 185; awareness of own demise, 177, 177n310; awe and, 110–111; clothing and, 183; deception and, 157, 159; fairness concept and, 151; game-playing behavior and, 136; gravity and, 188; knots and, 129; language and, 130–132; magic tricks and, 200; maps and, 185; mind-reading and, 147; perception of others and, 145; play behavior and, 142; pointing and, 148; theory of mind and, 159n227; tools and, 121, 129; warfare activity and, 160
Aphrodite and the Weasel, 85
Archilochus, 82
Archimedes, 87

Aristotle, 82
Armstrong-Buck, Susan, 134n108
art, material, 7, 101, 181–183
associative (trial-and-error) learning, 18–19, 38, 42, 42–43, 49
Avianus, 27, 28–29, 31, 34
awe, 110–112

baboons, 115, 125, 125n70, 184
Babrius, 31, 34, 36n14
bacteria, 81–82
Barker, K. Brandon, 3, 4–8
Barnes, Simon, 112n6
bartering, 153
bats, 140, 155, 177
bears, 99, 116, 121, 138, 139, 151, 154, 165, 178, 188
beavers, 30, 162
Beck, Benjamin B., 118n27
bees, 92–93, 129, 143, 194
Bekoff, Marc, 113n7
Berlin, Isaiah, 82–83
Bianor, 23–24, 28
Bird, Christopher, 2, 10, 16
Bird Brain: An Exploration of Avian Intelligence (Emery), 20n9
birds: dancing and, 178–179; deception and, 157; intoxication and, 140; jealousy and, 150; language and, 133; medicine and, 195; mirror self-recognition and, 171–172; monogamy and, 165; other types of, 46; ritual behaviors and, 113; singing and, 180; tools and, 123. See also individual types
bison, 196
blinds. See decoys
bonobos, 98, 123, 131, 154
bowerbirds, 165
Boy Who Cried "Wolf!," 33
Bugnyar, Thomas, 138n129

calculus, 80, 83, 87
capuchin monkeys, 152
Cashman, Ray, 74n6
cats, 145, 150, 195, 199–201
causal reasoning, 17, 19, 38, 56nn5–6, 69–70, 72, 188–189
cemeteries, 24–25, 35
cheetahs, 164
Chen, Zhe, 193n381
chickens, 137, 137n125, 145n162
children: Aesop's Fable Paradigm and, 13; answers to the animal question and, 15; as audience for fables, 33, 35; comparisons of

240 Index

crows to, 16, 19, 41, 56n5; *The Emperor's New Mind* and, 89; field of animal cognition and, 38–39, 50, 55n1; folklorizing of, 89–90; mirror self-recognition and, 172

chimpanzees: adornment and, 183; appearance vs. reality problems, 185; awe and, 111nn3–5; causal relationships and, 72; comparisons to humans and, 97; consolation behaviors and, 153; cooperation and, 154–155; dancing and, 178; deception and, 159, 160n228; domestication and, 164–167, 166n253; drumming and, 133, 133n106, 180–181; escape behavior and, 187; game playing behavior and, 136–138, 136n119; gaze following and, 145n163; grief and, 115n13, 116; language and, 130n88, 131, 131n90, 133, 133n106; magic tricks and, 198; maps and, 185; material art and, 182; math and, 191; mirror self-recognition and, 60, 170; music and, 180; negative emotions and, 149; perceptions of others and, 145–146; perceptual contact and, 66–67; pointing and, 148; poop throwing and, 124, 124n65; reactions to death, 115, 117; ritualized patterns of behavior and, 110n1, 112n6; sexual play and, 141; spatial/temporal planning behaviors, 175; teaching and, 135; tools for transporting food and, 128; tool use and, 118n25, 119, 121, 123–125, 128; warfare activity and, 161–163

cichlid fish, 172
civets, 196
Clark's nutcrackers, 172
Clayton, Nicola, 150n187
cleaner wrasse fish, 172
cognitive folklore, 8, 9, 70–71
Collectio Augustana, 30, 32–33
comparative cognition: causal effects and, 17, 19, 38, 56n5–6, 69–70, 72, 188–189; human tendency for narrative and, 70–71; methodological shortcoming of research in, 53; what- vs. why-systems, 72
Compleat Academic, The, 51
complex cognition, 41, 49
Consilience (Wilson), 83
cooperation, 154–156
corvids *See* crows; ravens; rooks; scrub jays
cows, 10n2, 77, 99, 124, 136, 146, 160, 163, 167,178, 179, 199
coyotes, 112, 126, 142, 146, 156, 175, 189, 196
crabs, 118, 124, 180
crickets, 157, 180
"Crow and the Pitcher, The": ancient appearances of story of, 23–27, 35; anthropocentrism and, 86; breaking up a task and, 87; familiarity of, 23; first appearances of story as fable, 26–29; in folklorist-scientist narrative, 5–6, 15; genre theory and, 16; illustrations of, 28, 32, 34, 35; moral and, 3, 15–16; as motivation for scientific research of crows, 2; narrative forms of, 28–29, 35; purpose of folklore and, 15–16; structural type of, 84; varying morals of, 31–32; volume of research inspired by, 41

crows: Aesop's Fable Paradigm and, 46, 95–96, 100, 184; causal relationships and, 17, 38, 56nn5–6, 189; coercive behavior and, 167; comparison with children and, 16, 19, 41; domestication and, 166; fairness concept and, 152; mirror self-recognition and, 172; perceptual contact and, 67; pointing and, 148; projectiles and, 121–122, 121n50, 124–125, 125n67; rain and, 111; tool use in nature and, 41, 119–120; wire-bending task and, 65

Cuthbert, Lori, 114n12
cuttlefish, 158, 158n223, 169

dancing, 178–179
Darwin, Charles, 9, 61, 96, 118n25, 125n70
David and Goliath (Gladwell), 88
David and Goliath story, 88
death, reactions to, 114–118, 177
deception, 156–160
decoys, 101, 160
deer, 111, 115, 120, 131, 139, 144, 167, 178, 183
Demetriou, Danielle, 187n358
Descent of Man, The (Darwin), 61, 96, 103
De Waal, Frans, 98, 116n19
digger wasps, 128
Doctor Fomomindo, 8–9
dogs: altruism and, 143–144, 143n156; *and* vs. *or* problems and, 185; awareness of own odor and, 173; deception and, 158; emotions and, 96; fairness concept and, 151; gravity and, 188; guilt and, 150; inhibitory control and, 192; jealousy and, 149; language and, 133; magic tricks and, 198–201; medicine and, 195–196; mindedness and, 177n313; mind-reading and, 147, 147n173; mirror self-recognition and, 171; perceptions of others and, 145–146; play behavior and, 136, 136n112; pointing and, 148
dolphins, 115, 128, 147, 148, 170, 172, 193–194
domestication, 164–167
drugs, 139–141
ducks, 97, 101

Dumont, Louis, 84, 93
Dundes, Alan, 12, 14–15
Durkheim, Emile, 91–92

Edison, Thomas, 2
Edwards, Lin, 111n5
"Einfache Formen" (Ranke), 91
Elementary Forms of Religious Life, The (Durkheim), 91
elephants: consolation behaviors and, 154; cooperation and, 154; deception and, 159; drugs and, 140n140; intoxication and, 139; material art and, 181, 181n330; medicine and, 196; memory and, 192–193, 192n377; mind-reading and, 147; mirror self-recognition and, 170–171; poop throwing and, 124; ritual behaviors and, 113–114, 113–114nn9–10; self-awareness and, 174; tools and, 119, 128; weaponized projectiles and, 126
Emery, Nathan, 2, 10, 16
empathy, 39, 63, 90, 142–145
"Emperor's New Clothes, The," 88–89
Emperor's New Mind, The (Penrose), 88–89
end-point training effect, 63
epimythium, 27, 29–30. *See also* morals
essentialism, 189–190
Eurasian jays, 46
experimental paradigm, 19n4

"Fable, A" (Twain), 3, 99–100
fables: animal cognition, 107–108; animals as stand-ins for humans and, 82, 86; anthropocentrism and, 86; audience for, 33–35; bees and, 92–93; book illustration and, 35; epimythia/morals as written feature of, 27; hierarchy and, 83–84, 93; human cultural practice and, 4; myth scholarship vs., 87; other types of narrative vs., 29–31; popular science and, 87–88; purpose of, 33–35; science's interaction with, 3; structural types of, 84–85; with human characters, 88
fabling gestures, 76–77
fairness concept, 151–153
"fakles," 76–79
fire, 111, 144n157, 164, 178
fish, 157, 172–173, 199
flamingos, 172
folk ideas, 15–16, 54. *See also* fabling gestures; folklore
folklore: animal cognition and, 6–7; animal question and, 13–15; catalogs of structural types and, 106; children and, 89–90;

Durkheim and, 91–92; motifs and, 15, 18; problems solving and, 193n381
Folk Physics, 67, 70–71
Folk Stories of Children, The (Sutton-Smith), 16–17
Fossey, Diane, 97
"Fox and the Ape, The" (Fomomindo), 107–108
"Fox and the Grapes, The," 85
Fraser, Orlaith, 138n129
Frazer, James G., 96
frogs, 191
From Mandeville to Marx (Dumont), 93
fruit flies, 196–197
Full House (Gould), 81
funeral rituals, 113–114

Gallup, Gordon G., Jr., 60, 73n1
gambling, 139
game playing, 39, 135–139
Gardner, Allen, 130n88
Gardner, Beatrice, 130n88
geese, 101, 172, 199
generalization, 71
genre theory, 15, 91, 100–101
gibbons, 165, 179
giraffes, 115, 166, 193
Gladwell, Malcolm, 88
goats, 112, 145, 171, 199
goldfinches, 128n80
Goodall, Jane, 97, 110–111nn2–3
gorillas, 97, 115, 120, 134, 167, 170, 188
Gould, Stephen Jay, 81–84
grackles, 46
gratitude, 120, 155
gravity, 65, 71, 107, 188
Gray, Russel, 18
Greek miracle, 87
grief, 114–116
guinea pigs, 150
gulls, 122

Hansen, William, 3, 8, 15, 85
Harrod, James, 110n1
"Hedgehog and the Fox, The" (Berlin), 82–83, 86
Hedgehog, the Fox, and the Magister's Pox, The (Gould), 83
Hennefield, Laura, 3, 8
Hermeneumata (Pseudo-Dositheus), 26–27, 32–33
hierarchy, 83–84, 93
Hooper, Rowan, 112n6

Horowitz, Alexandra, 150n187
horses, 132, 145, 148, 150, 171, 199
humor, 134nn107–108
Humphrey, George, 169n267
hyenas, 113, 164
Hywang, Hyesung G., 3, 8

insects, 166, 168
insight (Köhler), 65–66

jackals, 196
Jacobs, Joseph, 31, 34
Jelbert, Sarah, 17–18
jokes, 134–135, 134nn107–108
Jolles, André, 91–92

Kafka, Franz, 9
Kehoe, Laura, 112n6
Köhler, Wolfgang, 65–66, 112n4
Koko (gorilla), 115n17, 134nn107–108
Kortlandt, Adriaan, 162, 163n239
Kuhn, Thomas, 14, 19n7

Lancelot Link, Secret Chimp, 180n329
language: acquisition of, 129–133; animals and, 96–98; dialects and, 133–134; discourse and, 134–135; human narrative tendency and, 70–71; *why*-systems and, 72
larks, 114
lemurs, 196–197
Lévi-Strauss, Claude, 100, 103n4
Liberate the Chimps Society, 60
Life on the Mississippi (Twain), 1–2
Linden, Eugene, 98–99
"Lion and the Man Disputing, The," 86
"Lion and the Mouse, The," 77, 81, 84, 86
lions, 160, 160n230, 164
literary criticism, 100
lizards, 197
llamas, 199
local character anecdotes, 74n6
Long, William J., 96–97
Lukkenaar, Bas, 161n232

macaques, 115, 152
magic, ix, 198–200
Magliocco, Sabina, 102n1
magpies, 113, 113n7, 117, 148n176, 172
Main, Douglas, 114n12
Malaysian sun bears, 171
Mandeville, Bernard de, 93
manta rays, 172

maps, 184–185
Marcuse, Fred, 169n267
math, 191. *See also* calculus; numerical reasoning
McKendry, John, 35
Mechling, Jay, 19n7, 95
medicine, 195–198
memory, 192–194
Mentality of Apes, The (Köhler), 112n4
mice, 12, 130, 141, 157, 182, 186, 2021
Michael (gorilla), 134nn107–108
mirrors, 60, 170–173. *See also* "Fable, A" (Twain)
mirror self-recognition (MSR), 60, 73n1, 170–173, 170n274
Mississippi River, 1–3, 99
Missouri River, 1
Mojo, 8
money, 2, 16, 51, 54, 190–191
monkeys: affection and, 96; alcohol and, 145; coercive behavior in, 167; consolation behaviors and, 153; cooperation and, 154; domestication and, 166; essentialism and, 189–190; fairness concept and, 151; gravity and, 188; inhibitory control and, 192; magic tricks and, 199; math and, 191; medicine and, 195, 197; mind-reading and, 147; mirror self-recognition and, 170; play behavior and, 139–140; pointing and, 148; tools and, 119–120, 123–124; warfare activity and, 162
morals: of ancient Crow and Pitcher stories, 27, 31–32; "The Crow and the Pitcher" and, 15–16; as feature of written fables, 27; other narrative forms and, 29–30; purpose of folklore and, 15; varying for a single tale, 31–32
Morris, Desmond, 181n330
Motif-Index of Folk-Literature (Thompson), 15, 31
mules, 96, 133, 153, 200
Mullen, Patrick B., 74n6
music, 133–134, 180–181. *See also* singing animals
Mythiamboi Aisopeioi (Babrius), 31
myth scholarship, 87

Natural History (Pliny), 24–25
neuroses, 169
New Caledonian crows, 17, 119
Nishida, Toshisada, 136n119
Nonhuman Rights Project, 176n308
numerical reasoning, 39. *See also* math; calculus

octopuses, 120, 131, 141n141, 186
Old Man and His Sons, 86–87
On the Characteristics of Animals (Aelian), 26
opossums, 111
orangutans, 137, 170, 175, 184, 198–199
orcas, 114, 114n12
Ostojić, Ljerka, 150n187
Osvath, Mathias, 128n80

Palatine Anthology (Bianor), 23–24
pandas, 173
parrots, 120, 131–132, 131–132nn95–96, 179, 185
peer review, 45
Penrose, Roger, 88–90
Pepperberg, Irene, 132n96
perceptual contact, 66–67
Phaedrus, 29, 32, 34
Philosophical Investigations (Wittgenstein), 84, 85
philosophy, 82–85, 86
pigeons, 155, 155n212, 172, 184–185
pigs, 113, 129, 142, 158, 169
Pinker, Steven, 97–98
piranhas, 116
plants, 96, 168, 174
Pliny the Elder, 24–25, 28, 128
Plutarch, 25, 28
pointing, 148–149, 148n176
poop (as projectile), 124
Popper, Carl, 80, 87
popular press, 40, 50–51
popular science writers, 73, 76, 87–88
porcupines, 96–97, 117, 158, 161, 164, 185, 186
Povinelli, Daniel J., 4–8, 39–40, 60
pregnancy, 197
Premack, David, 177n310
Preuss, Todd, 63
primates, 156, 168, 170. *See also individual species*
Primates (journal), 161n232
Pseudo-Dositheus, 26–29, 31–32
psychological research: directionality and, 51; as part of larger career, 53–54; proof of theory bias and, 51–52; replication crisis and, 50, 57n15; storytelling and, 51, 53–54
"Psychological Uses of Animals" (Richards), 13
psychologists, 2, 50–52
psychology: bias toward "good stories" of, 38; directionality and, 51; as inseparable from behavior of psychologists, 15; press and, 73; replication crisis and, 50; subjectivity and, 50

rabbits, 16, 100, 112, 119, 126, 131, 138, 150
racoons, 2, 100, 184
rain, 24, 28, 110–111, 112, 159, 165,
"Raising the Level: Orangutans Use Water as a Tool" (Mendes et al.), viii, 19n1, 184n342
Ranke, Kurt, 91
rats, 117, 141n148, 144, 150, 152–153, 174, 184, 188, 192
ravens: Aelian on, 26; Bird and Emery research of problem-solving abilities of, 2, 10; confusions with crows and, 27; consolation behaviors and, 153; fairness concept and, 152; funeral ritual tales and, 113; game-playing behavior and, 138; perceptions of others and, 145, 147; perceptual-motor feedback hypothesis and, 18–19; Pliny's accounts of abilities of, 24–25; Plutarch on, 25; pointing and, 148; scientific explanations for fabled behavior and, 3–4; spatial/temporal planning behaviors, 175; strings and, 129; tool use and, 3–4, 119
religion, 61, 92, 100, 103n3, 106, 110n1, 112n6, 113
Rensch, Bernhard, 192n377
replication, 50, 57n15
rhesus monkeys, 147, 192
Richards, Graham, 13–14
ritual, viii, 110n1, 112–118
river otters, 142, 143
rodents, 119, 153n202
Romanes, Georges, 96
rooks, 12, 18, 38, 41, 46
Roosevelt, Theodore, 97

salamanders, 191
salmon, 114, 131
Schrempp, Gregory, 4, 8, 19
science: animal question and, 13–14; Dundes's definition of folk beliefs and, 15–16; folkloric forms and, 92, 101–102. *See also* animal cognition; psychology
Scrub-jay imperative, 68–69
scrub jays, 46, 68, 113, 113n8, 146, 174–175
sea lampreys, 117
seals, 100, 178
sea otters, 123
selfishness, 153
Simple Forms (Jolles), 91–92
singing animals, 179–180
Skinner, B. F., 42
Skinner boxes, 42
slavery, 167
Smith, Adam, 93

snakes, 112–113, 122, 131, 133, 137, 142, 149, 152, 155, 158, 159, 166, 167, 178
sparrows, 196
spirituality, awe, 110–112
sponge tools, 127–128
squirrels, 147, 154, 158, 163, 167, 185
stories, 134
Sutton-Smith, Brian, 16–17
Synge, John Millington, 122

Taylor, Alex, 18
teaching, 135
Tesla, Nikola, 2
theory of mind, 7, 20n6, 61, 63, 66, 69–72, 142n151
tigers, 99, 121, 127, 129, 132, 136, 152, 162, 167, 173, 178, 196
Tkalčić, Mladenka, 150n187
Tolstoy, Leo, 82–84
tools: animal cognition and, 39; knots and strings, 128–129; ladders, 121; projectiles, 121–126; sticks, 118–121; for transport of food, 126–128
"Tortoise and the Gourd of Wisdom, The," 108
"Tortoise and the Hare, The," 16–17, 33, 80, 83–84
tortoises, 117, 120, 121, 122, 124, 127, 129, 132, 142, 144, 145, 148, 154, 157, 159, 164, 199
totemism, 91, 103n4
"Town Mouse and the Country Mouse, The," 29, 150, 165
Tractatus (Wittgenstein), 85
trial-and-error (associative) learning, 38, 42, 56n5

Turner, Pamela, 31
Twain, Mark, 1–4, 99–100
Tylor, E. B., 83

"Using the Aesop's Fable Paradigm to Investigate Causal Understanding of Water Displacement by New Caledonian Crows," 17

van Hooff, Jan A. R. A. M., 161n232
vervet monkeys, 140
vultures, 123, 128, 134, 137, 196

Wallauer, William, 136n119
warfare activity, 160–164
waterfalls, 111
Wealth of Nations, The (Smith), 93
weight, 26, 61–62, 67, 69, 106, 123, 174, 194
whales, 114, 133, 169, 176n308, 179
Which are More Intelligent, Land Animals or Sea Animals? (Plutarch), 25
Wilson, E. O., 83–84
Wise, Steven, 176n308
Wittgenstein, Ludwig, 84–86, 88
Wolfe, Cary, 19n20
wolves, 113, 133, 148n176, 164, 166, 196
World without Weight (Povinelli), 62, 68

Xenophanes, 77, 80, 86

Zeno of Elea, 80, 83, 87
zero concept, 92, 191n373
Zumwalt, Rosemary, 19

www.ingramcontent.com/pod-product-compliance
Lightning Source LLC
Chambersburg PA
CBHW021351300426
44114CB00012B/1179